This book contains over fifty funny poems with colour illustrations created by Colin West. There are poems about crazy creatures such as the Snoope and Lolloping Lollop, eccentric characters such as Miss Flibberty-Gibbet, and rather silly folk such as Fritz, who frolicked in the foothills, and had his dreams somewhat crushed. With lashings of good humour, clever rhymes and hilarious drawings, this pick of Colin West's most amusing work is truly his funniest stuff yet!

THE FUNNIEST STUFF

Pictures and Poems by Colin West

Matador
9 Priory Business Park,
Wistow Road, Kibworth Beauchamp,
Leicestershire. LE8 0RX
Tel: 0116 279 2299
Email: books@troubador.co.uk
Web: www.troubador.co.uk/matador
Twitter: @matadorbooks

ISBN 978 1785893 391

British Library Cataloguing in Publication Data.
A catalogue record for this book is available from the British Library.

Typeset in 11pt Baskerville by Troubador Publishing Ltd, Leicester, UK

Matador is an imprint of Troubador Publishing Ltd

Contents

She Put her Hair in Curlers

She put her hair in curlers
And tied it up in bows,
And rode a horse on rollerskates,
A ball upon her nose!

The Wizard and the Lizard

Once a wizard in a blizzard
Caught a lizard down a well.
First he took it, then he shook it,
Did he cook it? Time will tell.

How he stuttered as he muttered,
Till he spluttered out a spell.
Then, hey presto! Full of zest-o!
Have you guessed? O do not yell!

It was tragic that his magic
Word *Kadajic* wasn't right,
For the lizard in the blizzard
Gave the wizard such a fright.

It grew larger than a Rajah,
With a barge, a butt, a bite,
First it wobbled till it hobbled,
Then it gobbled him up quite!

Aunt Priscilla

Frail and fragile Aunt Priscilla
Wrestled with a wild gorilla–
Seldom has there been such fighting–
Scratching, punching, kicking, biting!
Boy! You should have seen Priscilla
Bash to bits that bad gorilla!

Inquisitiveness

Please, how does one spell *definite*?
Has it a double *f* in it?
Please, how old was Euripides?
And where are the Antipodes?
Please, where does one find phosphorous?
And how big is the Bosporus?
Please, why are you so furious?
Do tell me, I'm so curious.

Avoiding a Disturbance

The hooting of klaxons
Annoys Anglo Saxons
In Darlington, Durham and Dover.
So when on their scooters,
They don't honk their hooters,
But nonchalantly run you over.

Christine Crump

Christine Crump
is crunching crisps:

Cheese and onion,
Cheese and onion.

Christine Crump
has crunched them.

Christine Crump
is crunching crisps:

Smoky bacon, smoky bacon.
Cheese and onion,
Cheese and onion.

Christine Crump
has crunched them.

Christine Crump
is crunching crisps:

Ready salted, ready salted,
Smoky bacon, smoky bacon,
Cheese and onion
cheese and onion.

Christine Crump
has crunched them.

Christine Crump
is crunching crisps:
Curry flavour, curry flavour,
Ready salted, ready salted
Smoky bacon, smoky bacon,
Cheese and onion,
cheese and onion.

Christine Crump
has crunched them.

Christine Crump
is crunching crisps:

Salt and vinegar,
salt and vinegar,
Curry flavour, curry flavour,
Ready salted, ready salted,
Smoky bacon, smoky bacon,
Cheese and onion,
cheese and onion.

Christine Crump
has crunched them.

Christine Crump
is feeling sick…

Poor old Christine,
poor old Christine.

She has indigestion.

Michael

Michael likes 'Michael',
He doesn't like 'Mike',
He rides on a 'cycle',
And not on a 'bike'.
He doesn't like 'Mickey',
He doesn't like 'Mick',
Don't offer a 'bikky'–
It might make him sick.

Knock, Knock

No, I do not wish to hear
Another knock knock joke.
I've heard your knock knock
Jokes before,
So please don't knock knock
On my door.
I'll sure knock knock
Your block off
If you knock knock
Any more.

The Persian Cat

My pet aversion is the Persian
Of all breeds of cat,
To me this pussy seems so fussy
Over this and that.

He never stays in Homes for Strays in
Which his cousins dwell,
Instead this feline makes a beeline
For the Grand Hotel.

For there he'd sooner dine on tuna
Served from tiny tins
Than go pickin' bits of chicken
Out of people's bins.

The Sloojee

The Sloojee strikes on nights like this,
When everything is still,
It strikes you if you snore too much,
And makes you feel quite ill.

It makes you wail, it makes you weep,
It makes you mutter in your sleep,
It makes you frown, it makes you fidget,
It makes you dislocate a digit.

It makes you wince, it makes you twice,
It makes your kneecaps turn to ice,
It makes you mope, it makes you moan,
It makes you scratch your funny bone.

It makes you scream, it makes you shriek,
It makes your blood run rather weak,
It makes you shake, it makes you shiver,
It makes you grateful for your liver.

It makes you spit, it makes you spout,
It makes your goosebumps all come out,
It makes you twitch, it makes you tremble,
It makes your toe joint reassemble.

The Sloojee strikes, and having struck,
The Sloojee slobbers on,
For when you cease to snore out loud,
It knows its job is done.

Parsons, Priests and Country Vicars

Parsons, priests and country vicars
Love the food of city slickers,
They go to cafés with their vergers
For crinkle chips and cheesyburgers,
They shake on ketchup, spread on mustard,
And wash it down with prunes and custard!

Eat Your Food Up, Artie

Artie, Artie, eat your food up,
Eat your food up, Artie,
You look the sort that never has
A meal that's good and hearty.
Artie, Artie, eat your food up,
Eat your tripe and onions,
For if you don't, your feet will have
A nasty bout of bunions.
Artie, Artie, eat your food up,
Eat your beef and carrots,
Unless you want to grow a beak
And feathers like a parrot's.
Artie, Artie, eat your food up,
Artie, I'm not joking.
(So Artie ate an artichoke,
Now look at Artie choking.)
Artie, Artie, cough your food up,
Cough your food up, Artie.
I'll eat my words and we shall have
Just jelly at your party!

The Retired Sergeant Major

His final round has long been fired,
And Sgt-Major Green (retired)
Within his garden may be found,
For this is now his stamping ground.

He's up each day at crack of dawn
To give a haircut to his lawn,
And then at 0600 hours,
He's off inspecting troops of flowers.

They hold their heads erect as if
Their very stems are frightened stiff,
And woe betide should one be bent,
Disgracing the whole regiment.

At noon, ex-Sgt-Major Green
In vegetable plot is seen,
Where in a bucket he will shove
Potatoes, for the peeling of.

Observe him stride about the place,
(No weed dare ever show its face)
And all the time he's on parade
He bears a highly-polished spade,

Until we see at eventide
Him armed with an insecticide,
For as the sun sinks in the west,
He wages war on Garden Pest.

Veronica

Whenever Veronica
Plays her harmonica,
She makes such a hideous row
That, seeking a proper tune,
The moment seems opportune
To visit a faraway cow.

A Wisp of a Wasp

I'm a wisp of a wasp with a worry,
I'm hiding somewhere in Surrey,
I've just bit upon
The fat sit upon
Of the King–so I left in a hurry!

Rhubarb, Rhubarb

Rhubarb, rhubarb, what a lot
Of lovely rhubarb you have got
Growing in your rhubarb plot.
Rhubarb, rhubarb, rhubarb.

"Rhubarb, rhubarb, thank you so!
Rhubarb's all I ever grow,
And I *talk* it too, you know,
Rhubarb, rhubarb, rhubarb!"

The Snoope

Upon the beauty of the Snoope
I must recite a sonnet,
As earthworms slither through the soil,
And poets prance upon it,
I've never seen another beast
That wears a bright blue bonnet.

Upon his head and hands and feet
He grows the finest bristles,
And as he goes upon his way,
He warbles and he whistles.
It's such a joy to watch him waltz
Between the thorns and thistles.

So to the beauty of the Snoope
I dedicate this ditty,
I hope I'll see another soon
In countryside or city.
Alas, till then, I can but wish
That I were *half* as pretty.

The Woebegone and Woebetide

O woe betide you if upon
Your bed you find a Woebegone,
And woebegone you if beside
That beast there sits a Woebetide.

These beasts are often found in pairs,
There is no friendship quite like theirs,
They love each other, but it's true
They do not care for me or you.

So if by chance you come upon
The beast they call the Woebegone,
Be off! Or you'll end up inside
His only friend the Woebetide.

(And likewise, you should run and hide
If you should see a Woebetide–
Or else you might end up upon
The menu of the Woebegone.)

Belated Bertie

As Maud and Mary walked to school,
Maud said unto the other,
"I fear we must the title 'fool'
Bestow upon my brother.

For Bertie is an idle boy
Whose mischief drives me frantic,
His time he seems but to employ
In planning some new antic.

Just yesterday he 'cut his thumb'
Whilst carving up the mutton,
The sight of blood quite struck him dumb,
I summoned Doctor Dutton.

Then Bertie, full of mirth, did bawl
(I wish they'd lock the wretch up),
You see, it wasn't blood at all,
But just tomato ketchup."

"Your brother is a fool indeed,"
Reciprocated Mary,
"In future, of his tricks take heed,
Of false alarms be wary."

Then as upon their way they went,
Their homework to deliver,
The air by frightful screams was rent,
And racing to the river,

Maud found beyond the river bank
Her brother who was drowning,
But sighed, "Aha, another prank!
No more I'll take your clowning."

And thus they left him to his fate,
To reach school by eight thirty.
They both arrived a little late,
But not as late as Bertie!

Rosemary's Friends

O, Rosemary's friends are her mantleshelf folk:
A shepherd, two sweethearts, a milkmaid with yoke,
And grandest of all is a cricketer chap
Who stands at the wicket in flannels and cap,
Awaiting a ball that's about to be bowled,
For years he's been batting–no wonder he's old,
But happy is Rosie to have such a man,
And yesterday morning she told me her plan:
"I'm off to have tea with W.G. Grace
And polish the porcelain beard on his face!"

Don't Ask Me About Myself

Don't ask me about myself,
Or why I talk in stanzas,
For all the questions that you ask,
I haven't got the answers.

I may know why the world is flat,
Or why the sea is sand,
But elbow grease and trouser crease,
I cannot understand.

I'll tell you why the Moon is cheese,
Or why bananas bend,
But one odd sock or writer's block,
I cannot comprehend.

So ask me of freshwater fish,
And famous ballet dancers,
But don't ask me about myself,
I haven't got the answers.

O How I hate the Poet!

The purpose of a porpoise,
Or a turtle or a tortoise,
Or a salamander well I understand.
The reason for a rumpus
Or a camel or a compass,
Or a saxophone is plain to any man.

The meaning of a mangle,
Or a spangle on a bangle,
Or a hemisphere is very clear to see,
But one thing I must mention,
Quite beyond my comprehension,
Is the problem that the poet poses me.

For a poet's life is Heaven,
He'll arise around eleven,
And have an avocado for his lunch,
Then he'll maybe write a sonnet
All about an Easter bonnet–
His words come like bananas in a bunch!

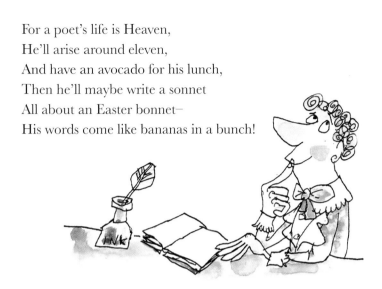

Then he spends the twilight hours
Sat in sofas sniffing flowers,
And sipping lots and lots of lemon tea,
With his fancy cuffs and collars,
I would give a hundred dollars
To someone who could explain his use to me!

Whatnot

There's a shop in the High Street that deals in antiques,
And I've looked in the window for weeks and for weeks,
But I've not yet been able to understand why
The price of a Whatnot should be quite so high.

A Thingamabob wouldn't be such a price,
A What-you-may-call-it would look just as nice,
But neither of these things would cost half as much,
And you buy them in shops where you're welcome to touch.

An Oojamaflip is as rare and as big,
And so for that matter's a Thingamajig,
But neither of these is expensive to buy,
So why is the price of a Whatnot so high?

The Birthday Cake

O why did Mavis have to make
Me such a soppy birthday cake,
With icing pink and ribbon red?
Why couldn't she have made instead
A cake of which I could be proud—
Aren't F.A. Cup-shaped ones allowed?

Mabel

I wonder what the matter is with Mabel?
She never seems to want to come indoors.
Is it because we're rude as we are able,
And push her underneath the kitchen table
And make her stay down there upon all fours?

Let Basil go to Basildon

Let Basil go to Basildon,
Let Lester go to Leicester,
Let Steven go to Stevenage
With raincoat and sou'wester.

Let Peter go to Peterhead,
Let Dudley go to Dudley,
Let Milton go to Milton Keynes–
The pavements there are puddly.

Let Felix go to Felixstowe,
Let Barry go to Barry,
Let Mabel go to Mablethorpe,
But I at home shall tarry.

Let Alice go to Alice Springs,
Let Florence go to Florence,
Let Benny go to Benidorm,
Where rain comes down in torrents.

Let Winnie go to Winnipeg,
Let Sidney go to Sydney,
Let Otto go to Ottawa–
I am not of that kidney.

Let Vera go to Veracruz,
Let Nancy go to Nancy,
But I'll stay home while others roam–
Abroad I do not fancy.

Uncle Norman

My eccentric Uncle Norman
Always keeps his uniform on,
Even when he has a nap
Or goes to bed,
And he looks a funny fellow
In his coat of black and yellow,
With his traffic warden's cap
Upon his head.

I once asked him why he wore it,
And he answered, "I adore it,
For it helps me sleep
Whilst counting traffic signs,
And I dream of parking meters,
Sporty chaps in their two-seaters,
And of booking them
On double yellow lines!"

Miss Flibberty-Gibbet

Miss Flibberty-Gibbet, please tell me,
Pray, why do you act like you do?
You pedal your bicycle backwards
And wear an old hat from Peru.

Miss Flibberty-Gibbet, I've seen you,
When everyone else is in bed,
Frantically pedalling backwards,
Peruvian hat on your head.

Miss Flibberty-Gibbet, one morning,
I'll follow and see what you do,
When you pedal your bicycle backwards
And wear that old hat from Peru.

Miss Flibberty-Gibbet, I'll get you,
And that, as they say, will be that!
Then I'll pedal your bicycle backwards
And wear your Peruvian hat.

Fritz, who Frolicked in the Foothills

There was nothing Fritz was fearing
When he went off mountaineering,
He left us amidst loud cheering,
Walking proud and tall.
Over rugged rocks he rambled,
Unconcerned he gaily ambled,
Like a mountain goat he gambolled,
Not afraid at all.

But Fritz made a fatal blunder
When he stopped a while to wonder
If the noise above was thunder–
What else could it be?
(All his life he'd lived on ranches,
Climbed up trees and swung from branches,
And not heard of avalanches.
What a tragedy!)

As Fritz stood in meditation
Pondering the situation,
Suddenly a sharp vibration
Filled him full of fear.
For nearby a falling boulder
Almost landed on his shoulder,
Fritz went hotter, then went colder.
Might his end be near?

All around him great rocks rumbled,
As towards his head they tumbled.
Poor Fritz staggered till he stumbled
And he lost his hat.
Then he started seeing double
And was soon in deeper trouble
When a half a ton of rubble
Sadly squashed him flat.

Thus from this world Fritz departed,
And it's left us broken-hearted,
But his trials have only started,
He is in despair.
For he once was six foot seven,
But now living up in Heaven,
He's a mere three foot eleven.
Isn't that unfair?

The Manatee

To test a sailor's sanity
Bring unto him a manatee *
And if he finds her beautiful,
Declare him fit and dutiful.

But if he finds her hideous,
This shows he's too fastidious,
And not the sort of matelot
Who's fit to fight a battle-o.

* It's sometimes said that sailors saw
This creature and mistook it for
A mermaid, back in days of yore.

36

My Uncle's Umbrella

Under my uncle's umbrella
Are Uncle Augustus and I.
My uncle's quite fat–
If it wasn't for that,
I'd manage to keep myself dry.

Silly Song

He: "One's tonsils are dispensable,
    Or so the surgeons say,
    So why not just be sensible
    And take *yours* out today?
    One's appendix is expendable,
    It's proved beyond a doubt,
    It would be moat commendable
    Of you to take *yours* out

She: "Your brain is quite ridiculous,
    As far as I can tell,
    So why not be meticulous
    And take *that* out as well?"

I Used to Climb Up Lamp-posts, Sir

I used to climb up lamp-posts, sir, at twelve o'clock at night.

I used to climb up lamp-posts, sir, and get to quite a height.

I used to climb up lamp-posts, sir, I knew it wasn't right.

I used to climb up lamp-posts, sir, but now I've seen the light.

Miss Evans

She dropped in for elevenses,
I heard the doorbell chime
At ten o'clock. "Good Heavens! Is…"
She muttered, "that the time?"

I wished she'd had some previous
Engagement which was urgent,
For patenting a devious
Device to save detergent.

But no, Miss Evans couldn't care
For anything like that!
She asked me if I wouldn't care
To take her coat and hat.

She eyed my favourite ornament–
The cup my brother won–
She didn't rate the tournament,
But said she'd have a bun.

I offered her Madeira cake
And coffee by the cup.
(Whenever she is near a cake
She gets the urge to sup.)

I played her tunes melodious
Upon my xylophone,
She found them all quite odious
And scoffed a further scone.

I got out my Monopoly
To see if she would play,
She licked her lips quite sloppily,
And said, "some other day."

She claimed that, "life's a mockery
With no one to harangue"
She criticised the crockery
And took my last meringue.

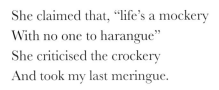

She ate my salmon sandwiches
And all my apple pie.
I shook her by the hand (which is
The way to say goodbye.)

She dropped in for elevenses,
But stayed to have her tea.
The thing about Miss Evans is
She "needs the company."

Gordon Glass

Every single time Miss Muffin
Puts a question to our class,
Who is always first to answer?
Need I ask, it's Gordon Glass.

He can tell you quite precisely
What's the boiling point of glue,
The capital of Venezuela,
The population of Peru.

And he knows his nine times table,
He knows the square root of pi,
He can add, divide, subtract or
Gordon Glass can multiply.

Gordon Glass has all the answers,
But one thing still bothers me:
Most our class are aged eleven,
Gordon Glass is thirty-three.

Who?

Who's always there come rain or shine?
From eight o'clock till ten past nine?
Who's back again at half past three
As we are going home for tea?
Who wears a coat that's long and white,
And cap with badge that's big and bright?
Who's always cheerful, always nice?
Whose banner bears a strange device?
Who teaches us the Highway Code,
And sees us safely 'cross the road?
Who is it makes the traffic stop?
O Lady of the Lollipop!

Bernard Ball

This is the tale of Bernard Ball
Who liked to skip and hop,
And when he saw a likely wall,
He walked along the top.

One day, quite near the village hall,
Beside the baker's shop,
He saw a likely-looking wall,
So walked along the top.

The wall was high and Bernard Ball
Came to a sudden stop.
He lost his balance on the wall,
And tumbled from the top.

It proved to be a fatal fall
From such a drastic drop.
How tragic, falling from a wall
Whilst walking on the top.

And so we buried Bernard Ball,
Who liked to skip and hop,
But now his ghost goes to that wall,
And walks along the top.

HERE LIES
Bernard Ball
RIP

The Dreadful Duo

Against my better judgement I've
Asked Jack and Jill to tea.
They said they'd come at half past five,
But whensoever they arrive
Will be too soon for me.

If you don't know these dreadful twins,
I'll tell you what they do:
They box your ears and kick your shins
And throw down their banana skins
As though you asked them to.

They never leave till nearly ten,
And when at last they go,
They say they'd like to come again,
And ask if you can tell them when,
To which you must say "No!"

Mr Burton

Mr Burton drives a bus:
He frequently delivers us
From the depot to the station,
Or some other destination,
Such as school or shopping centre.
(You just pay him as you enter.)

But on Sundays, Mr Burton
Hasn't got his busman's shirt on,
Or his busman's tie or hat on,
No, he's nothing quite like *that* on,
For on that day in his bungal–
Ow, he's Tarzan of the Jungle.

Something made of three wash leathers
Is his wardrobe in all weathers.
Meanwhile Betty (Mrs Burton),
Puts a sort of furry skirt on,
After which, she and her spouse
Stamp and hollo through the house.

All day long, behind closed curtains,
Thus amuse themselves the Burtons,
Jane and Tarzan every Sunday,
But at 8 a.m. on Monday,
He clocks in at the terminus,
And Mr Burton drives a bus.

Eve

If I'd *known* Eve,
I'd have told her
Of that fast
Descending boulder,
But as she was
Just a stranger,
It seemed wrong
To mention danger.

Florence

Florence fell into the ocean,
And caused such a grand commotion
That if I were any braver
I'd have been inclined to save her.

Bessie

As she worked the mangle, Bessie
Came unto an end most messy.
With the wash she got entangled,
Now she too is rather mangled.

Bruno the Sword Swallower

For years I was a follower
Of Bruno the Sword Swallower,
And to the world I endlessly would quote:
"His act is quite incredible,
He makes the sword look edible,
As inch by inch the blade goes down this throat."

But one dark day at Scarborough,
(I'd come from Market Harborough
With friends to visit Bruno at the fair),
The rain was sort of spitting down,
He said, "I'll do it sitting down."
So we provided Bruno with a chair.

He gulped his sword in gratitude
And never noticed that he chewed
A bit more than he really ought to eat.
"Be careful, Mr B!" we urged.
Too late! The tip, it re-emerged:
He'd riveted himself to his own seat.

Henrietta

Nature-loving Henrietta
Should have known a little better
Than to have continued reading
With an elephant stampeding.

Henry

When Henry from his ladder fell,
And broke his arm, and leg as well,
His wife was naturally upset–
He hadn't cleaned the windows yet.

Water Trough

I wonder if my pony knows,
When drinking from his trough,
It's really our old bathtub with
The enamel all worn off?

I wonder, *is* he unaware,
Or does he pause and think:
"Long years ago, here bathed Aunt Maud,"
Before he takes a drink?

The Lolloping Lollop

The Lolloping Lollop
Will meet you one morning,
And give you a wallop
Without any warning.

It's destined to happen,
There's no reason to doubt it,
But don't be concerned
And don't worry about it.

For Lolloping Lollops
Have one saving virtue,
They all say they're sorry
Soon after they've hurt you.

Water Skier

I'd like to be a water skier,
But I'm a little wobbly
When wearing skis and people tease
My knees for being knobbly.

Sylvester

Sylvester went upon the stage
To be a famous actor,
But couldn't earn a steady wage,
So now he drives a tractor.

Tiny Tony and His Pony

Tiny Tony had a pony,
He fed it tea and cakes.
Brother Brian had a lion,
He fed it juicy steaks.

Tiny Tony rode his pony
To the local park.
Brother Brian and his lion,
Followed after dark.

Tiny Tony and his pony
Vanished without trace.
Brother Brian and his lion
Licked each other's face.

My Vulture

I once had a little vulture,
But he didn't care for Culture,
And to let the whole world know it,
He would peck at any poet.

Though I begged not to do so,
He would squawk all through Caruso,
And what really seemed a scandal,
Hiccup all the way through Handel.

I once dragged him to a lecture
On Renaissance architecture,
But he found the subject boring,
So he spent the whole time snoring.

When at last I took my vulture
To a show of modern sculpture,
Twenty times he yawned, I counted,
So I had him stuffed and mounted.

Afterword

Poems, poems everywhere,
In my ears and in my hair,
In my shoes and in my socks,
In my desk and pencil box,
In my bath and in my bed,
In my heart and in my head.
Please read my books when you have time
And rid me of my life of rhyme.

NML/FF

Sweet William

Michael Pennington

Sweet William

Twenty Thousand Hours with Shakespeare

NICK HERN BOOKS
London
www.nickhernbooks.co.uk

A Nick Hern Book

Sweet William
first published in Great Britain in 2012
by Nick Hern Books Limited,
14 Larden Road, London W3 7ST

Copyright © 2012 Michael Pennington

Michael Pennington has asserted his right
to be identified as the author of this work

Cover photo by Laurence Burns,
designed by SWD (www.swd.uk.com)
Cover design by Ned Hoste, 2H

Typeset by Nick Hern Books, London
Printed and bound in Great Britain by
CPI Antony Rowe, Chippenham, Wiltshire

A CIP catalogue record for this book
is available from the British Library

ISBN 978 1 85459 568 3

MIX
Paper from
responsible sources
FSC® C013604
FSC
www.fsc.org

For my parents

Contents

Preface

Whatever their angle of approach, Shakespeare books could hardly be unaware of each other. So I have learned from – and had suspicions confirmed by – Peter Ackroyd, Andrew Dickson and Charles Nicholl, and by Professors Jonathan Bate, Stephen Greenblatt, James Shapiro and Stanley Wells. My thanks as always to Nick Hern, editor par excellence, and to Nick de Somogyi, a fine and genial Shakespearian sleuth who can spot a textual inaccuracy at twenty paces. It is hard to imagine this book getting to this point without Prue Skene; Mark, Louis and Eve Pennington have refreshed views of mine on the plays that I thought forever entrenched, despite or because of being, in two cases, fifty years younger than I am. There are many others who have encouraged me, at work and play and over a great space of time; they are too numerous to mention without offence to the unmentioned. I was about to say that they know who they are, but in many cases they don't; actors and writers are heartened by all sorts of people they never even meet.

As for the chronology and dating of the plays, I've always thought it was, beyond a certain point, something of a mug's game. So I haven't supplied a conventional list of speculative dates. Given the circumstances of Shakespeare's working life, the moment of a play's composition is likely to be immediately before its premiere; but the date of publication can be a very different and quite vexing matter. So while the birth of a handful can be happily identified by the date of their first recorded performances, that of others can only be established as being some time before a known event, such as publication, or after another, such as some topical reference in the play. In the face of only the vaguest consensus, I tend to fall back with a shrug: after all, unlike the scholars, I feel no special burden of proof here.

The search is in any case less interesting than you might think – or than it would be with another author. Outside of his Sonnets, Shakespeare's lived life seems to have left very little mark on his work; and as a writer he seems to have arrived fully formed, both inspired and fallible. Throughout his career the supreme and the rough and ready sit side by side: in among 'apprentice' works like *Henry VI* and *King John* lie masterpieces such as *A Midsummer Night's Dream* and *Romeo and Juliet*. Tone of voice is no more reliable: the great tragedy of *Hamlet* is immediately followed by the comic glories of *Twelfth Night*. Nor is theme: the treatment of marital jealousy in *The Comedy of Errors* (1594) has something in common with *The Winter's Tale* (1611). Throughout, Shakespeare maintains a resolutely private stance – what Chekhov later identified as 'autobiographophobia'. He wrote a series of comedies directly after his son's death; on establishing himself in London he bought a house in Stratford, and on the point of returning to Stratford he bought one in London.

Still, the rough sequence of events seems to have been this. Shakespeare arrived in London in 1592 and wrote plays for just over twenty years: occasionally, at the beginning and end, with a little collaboration. His debut may have been with *The Two Gentlemen of Verona* – or it could have been *Titus Andronicus*, or *The Taming of the Shrew*, or one of the *Henry VI* plays. Of the twenty-five or so he wrote in the first half of his career, roughly up until the death of Queen Elizabeth in 1603, a large proportion are history plays – indeed with the exception of *Henry VIII*, all his ten Histories lie in this decade. This period also features some box-office favourites – *The Merchant of Venice, Much Ado About Nothing, As You Like It, Julius Caesar*. In the second phase the pace slows down from approximately two to a little more than one a year – if you can call *Othello, King Lear, Macbeth* and *The Tempest* any kind of slowing down. When plague struck, as it regularly did and closed the theatres, Shakespeare wrote poetry – primarily *The Rape of Lucrece, Venus and Adonis* and the Sonnets which he finally collected together for publication in 1609.

In 1599 the Globe Theatre opened. In 1603 Elizabeth I died and James I succeeded – a most significant date to keep in mind, in my view. In 1609 Shakespeare's company began to use the indoor Blackfriars Theatre, though they continued to play at the Globe in the summer. The Globe burned down in 1613, and was rebuilt the following year. Shakespeare died in 1616. The first complete edition of his works was published in 1623. The new Globe was closed, as was the Blackfriars and all other London theatres, by the Puritans in 1642, and was probably destroyed in 1644. The Blackfriars was demolished in 1655.

The quotations in my text are not consistently taken from any particular Folio or Quarto, but are the versions I have myself become used to: editorial comparisons and textual variants are available elsewhere. The section at the end about phrases Shakespeare invented owes something, though not all that much, to Bernard Levin. I have T.S. Eliot to thank for the insight into Charmian's dying line in *Antony and Cleopatra*, and Philip Franks for his recollection of Donald Sinden's Benedick. All mistakes and eccentricities are, of course, my own.

Michael Pennington
November 2011

Introduction

In 1827 the composer Hector Berlioz went to see an English company perform *Hamlet* in Paris. He'd never seen a Shakespeare play before – in fact he spoke no English – but that evening he fell in love with the play, with the author, and with Harriet Smithson, the actress playing Ophelia:

> Shakespeare coming upon me unawares, struck me like a thunderbolt... I saw, I understood, I felt... that I was alive and that I must arise and walk.

I have little in common with Berlioz, but Shakespeare hit me like a hammer when I was eleven. I had the advantage of speaking English, but no more natural affinity with Shakespeare's world than might any other Tottenham Hotspur supporter of that age. The play was *Macbeth*, at the Old Vic Theatre in London, and it certainly wasn't my idea to go; and my parents, who took me, were only supposing in the vaguest terms that it would be Good For the Boy to see a Shakespeare play at some point before adolescence carried him off into the unknown.

Little did they guess. The show started with a bloodcurdling scream that came slicing out of a darkness which then lifted to reveal a blood-soaked soldier staggering towards us and collapsing; and a moment after that, from a tangle of dead trees and twisted branches behind him, the figures of the three weird sisters arose to ask when they would meet again in thunder, lightning or in rain. Two lines in, I was on the edge of my seat; and, the play being what it is, I stayed there all night. Macbeth was

played by the fine Paul Rogers; as he contemplated the murder of King
Duncan, he also saw what he was about to do to himself:

> Besides, this Duncan
> Hath borne his faculties so meek, hath been
> So clear in his great office, that his virtues
> Will plead like angels, trumpet-tongued, against
> The deep damnation of his taking off;
> And pity, like a naked new-born babe,
> Striding the blast, or heaven's cherubim, hors'd
> Upon the sightless couriers of the air,
> Shall blow the horrid deed in every eye,
> That tears shall drown the wind.

I couldn't quite work out this wonderful picture, but its power and fluency sounded like a great rumbling organ with all its stops open. A few
minutes later Macbeth saw his imaginary airborne dagger and followed it – slowly, slowly, slowly – towards Duncan's bedroom to do
the deed:

> Thou sure and firm-set earth,
> Hear not my steps, which way they walk, for fear
> The very stones prate of my whereabout
> And take the present horror from the time
> Which now suits with it…

Even then I knew that I was looking at an actor in property boots moving across a painted stage floor; but what I heard was the sound of their
weathered soles on the flagstones of Glamis Castle, and I fancied I could
feel the cold and the dark and the silence swirling around its battlements.
Why was this man, so terrified but so delighted, indulging his fancies
when he had such a single, brutal thing to do?

While he was about it, Ann Todd as Lady Macbeth thought she heard
something untoward:

> Hark! Peace!
> It was the owl that shriek'd, the fatal bellman
> Which gives the stern'st good night…

I caught the jagged phrasing: the shriek of the owl and the soft pounding
beat of a solemn bell, both sounds held in the same instrument like the
chanter and drone of the bagpipes.

Later on, darkness fell once more on the murderous but strangely
sympathetic couple as they prepared for their banquet:

> Light thickens, and the crow
> Makes wing to the rooky wood.
> Good things of day begin to droop and drowse
> Whiles night's black agents to their preys do rouse.

Nowadays I recognise with some affection Shakespeare's profligacy – with the crow established, he hardly needed the wood to be 'rooky' as well; but since he was bringing night onto an open-air stage in the middle of the afternoon he perhaps needed to rub it in a bit. And as always with him, there's a subtler possibility: the crow is solitary and the rook social, and Banquo, with only his son for company, is about to be mobbed by a flock of assassins. I also know now that what makes the passage work is the brooding rhyme of 'drowse… rouse', its broad vowels opening out from the tight consonants of 'makes wing… rooky wood'. All I was aware of then was that darkness was closing in on Banquo as it had on King Duncan; I heard wings flap above my head and had the distinct sensation that I was growing up fast. Not to mention wanting to know how they did all the blood, and quite how that empty seat at Macbeth's dinner table had become scarily filled without my noticing.

It's remarkable how often in this play we are asked to imagine dreadful things just out of sight. Once Lady Macbeth, her sleeping eyes blindly open, had left the stage, I could almost hear her breath stop while Macbeth looked at us as if through a doorway of hell:

> I have liv'd long enough; my way of life
> Is fall'n into the sear, the yellow leaf…

I had no idea what 'the sear' was, but it had a tearing sound, like something that would never be mended again. But I knew well enough about the yellow leaves. Only a few hours before – a lifetime by now – I'd seen them as I trudged home unwillingly (for once) *from* school, knowing I had to go to this damned Shakespeare play that evening. It was quite a nasty autumn night, and the leaves from the plane trees on our street had blocked up the gutters under yellow streetlamps that made the pavements look yellow too. So this time it wasn't at all the grandness of Shakespeare's language that caught me but its near-at-handness, its easy presence in my world. Especially as I heard the bleak abstracts that followed:

> And that which should accompany old age,
> As honour, love, obedience, troops of friends,
> I must not look to have; but in their stead,
> Curses, not loud but deep, mouth-honour, breath,
> Which the poor heart would fain deny, and dare not.

The play had begun with a scream, but now Macbeth's self-damnation was in whispered, ordinary words: though I was only eleven and certainly hadn't killed anyone, I understood what he felt about his life falling like autumn leaves.

Back home again and safe, I was like a child possessed, and my parents must have wondered if they'd ever hear comforting talk of Tottenham Hotspur again. I hooked *Macbeth* off the shelf and straight away, that night, started reading it aloud. And for days, weeks and months to come I kept trying Shakespeare that way – for years really, as I still can't read him in silence. I began to feel the oscillations in the language and the headlong narratives, events tumbling impatiently over each other as if intervening scenes in real time had been cut out. I saw a mind full of scorpions, a woman sensing devils murmuring in the room around her, the dead rising shrieking from the earth; but the play's most famous speech, about the tale told by an idiot, is, once it gets going, almost monosyllabic, a bulletin from a man glimpsing infinite, purposeless tomorrows. At the same time I was trying to find out whether the sound, so splendid but so intimate, would work coming off my tongue as well. And in fact it did, sort of, and so that was a first lesson learned: even a speech like that belonged to me, with my childish treble going on adolescent croak, and not just to the experts.

Now I'm an expert of sorts myself, having at a rough estimate spent twenty thousand hours of my life so far performing Shakespeare, leave alone the time taken rehearsing, talking, thinking and writing about him. So I know quite a bit about the torque of the engine. But sometimes during a performance I see a bespectacled eleven- or twelve-year-old down near the front, and it doesn't half make me raise my game. That's when I realise that all I've learned over the years doesn't add up to a hill of beans unless I can do something very simple with it: pass on to him or her that same intoxication of sound and meaning, its sudden impact on ear, eye and stomach.

✦

In between, Shakespeare has been as pervasive in my life as white noise. If Jaques was right about the Seven Ages of Man, then having spent my First in routine mewling and puking, encountering the plays in my Second had made me not so much the whining schoolboy as a thoroughly narrow-minded adolescent who had soon, to his own satisfaction and unthreatened by any audience, played everything from the Bawd in *Pericles* to Old Adam, from Titus Andronicus to Falstaff's Page – which I suppose has saved a lot of time learning the lines later. So, when the Old Vic put on the three parts of *Henry VI* for a short run that lay entirely inside my boarding school's term-time, you may imagine my shock at being refused leave by my headmaster to go home for a single day and night one weekend so that I could see a couple of them. He acknowledged that it would be 'a valuable experience' for me but was afraid, he explained to my father, of 'setting a dangerous precedent'. A dangerous precedent? Oh, happy dream – scores of young adolescent males rushing to see Shakespeare's least popular history plays rather than knocking each other's heads off on the rugger field. I still remember the dates we'd asked for, since I spent the hours of the performances facing more or less east, imagining the whole thing from the middle of Wiltshire; meanwhile my father, though terrified by his son's interest in show business, never forgave the headmaster for his elementary failure of vision, for such an illiberal reflex.

As for the Third of the Seven Ages, I was the lover in due course, sighing like furnace as Mercutio and Berowne, Shakespeare's great young fantasists I played at the RSC during the 1970s; and by the military Fourth, I was a hardened campaigner, sometimes bearded like the pard and frequently uttering strange oaths, asserting my own and Michael Bogdanov's views through our maverick outfit, the English Shakespeare Company. This was when I really started to learn something, for instance from playing in *Richard III* in East Berlin in 1989, towards the end of the Honecker regime, to an appalled silence: the glimpse of Richard's iron fist gleaming inside his velvet glove was not the merry irony it can be to Western audiences but a horrible daily fact. The silence would be broken minutes after the curtain each night as local actors, and not only actors, stormed backstage and wouldn't let us leave till we had all drunk and talked together for several hours.

Around the same time, I directed *Twelfth Night* with a Tokyo company in Japanese. I got on well with everyone except Toby Belch, the company's oldest member, whom I found very difficult until we went for a drink one night soon before the opening. Amidst the smoke of the *yakitori* barbecue and the fizzle of the Suntory he told me what of course I should have guessed: he was old enough to have served in the War and his reaction to all English-speakers, including directors and playwrights, was, he'd thought, forever prejudiced. Now, he declared as we reeled aerated out into the Tokyo night, Shakespeare had finally brought us together.

Another time I helped an eleven-year-old boy play Juliet's father Capulet in a workshop in a London comprehensive; as he uttered that terrible attack on his daughter for refusing to marry Paris, the boy suddenly grasped the pain not of being a misunderstood young lover (easy) but of being the middle-aged parent whom nobody seems to obey. I was also indirectly involved in organising a production of *The Tempest* in Maidstone high security prison, to be played by lifers who had never imagined Shakespeare to be a friend. They were visibly enfranchised by the physical sensation of speaking his language – not only by Caliban's repeated cries of 'Freedom... high day... freedom' but by his ache to offer his talents to unworthy masters, in his case a drunken butler and a clown:

> I'll show thee the best springs; I'll pluck thee berries;
> I'll fish for thee, and get thee wood enough...
> I prithee, let me bring thee where crabs grow;
> And I with my long nails will dig thee pig-nuts;
> Show thee a jay's nest and instruct thee how
> To snare the nimble marmoset.

As he spoke, the actor – as the prisoner had become – craned for a view out of the hall's high windows, even though it would only give him a vista of more prison cells. Caliban's dream was to be able to live in the moment, moving faster and seeing more than anyone else; his interpreter's was to take this one chance to join a different, forgiving world. No wonder the warders on duty were instinctively uneasy – this isn't a freedom that can be taken away by the slam of a door.

Having thus been round the block with Shakespeare several times – pausing at Buckingham Palace and the British Academy and dodging the rats falling from the rafters in Mumbai – in my Fifth Age (and never mind the fair round belly) I've been touring a solo show, *Sweet William*. A sort of Golden Anniversary of that night with *Macbeth* at the Old Vic, it's a many-coloured coat of prejudice, information and instinct, co-written by Shakespeare and myself. Like an earlier show I did on another great writer, Anton Chekhov, *Sweet William* approaches its elusive hero with due caution, palpable affection and even a sidelong sense of kinship – not as a writer of course, but as someone I have, after all, known all my life. Consequently the evening is not so much a daisy chain of Greatest Hits (it certainly doesn't include the Seven Ages of Man) as biography tangled with autobiography, elaborated with performances of many unfamiliar pieces as well as some famous ones.

It may also feature in my Sixth and Seventh ages, so please watch this space. At the time of writing, *Sweet William* has played over a hundred performances – up and down Great Britain, in various London theatres (including the former home of Ben Travers's Whitehall farces), in Romania, Hungary, Spain, Scandinavia and the US. The most common front-of-house poster design has a picture of myself with Shakespeare's face behind me; he has deep rings under his eyes, as if tired of being talked about so much. Abroad I work sometimes with surtitles and sometimes with a simultaneous translator; both methods are extremely rewarding when they work, but they can be fraught with imprecision. You don't want an audience, its eyes trained on the surtitles, laughing at the punchline of a joke before you've delivered it – or, conversely, after you've moved on to the next bit of narrative. Simultaneous translation involves a relationship of curious intimacy with the translator, as if you were being haunted by your own shadow, and often turns the auditorium into a kind of beehive, with two hundred pairs of headphones at full tilt. Both methods oblige you, for your collaborator's sake, not to change anything or make any accidental cuts on the night: both require a slower pace of delivery, especially if, as sometimes, the foreign language is of its nature less swift than English. (Our monosyllabic 'love' translates into two syllables in Catalan, three in Hungarian and stretches to four in Swedish.) The challenge is to speak slowly but very interestingly – not so easy, especially when you hope to give the effect of spontaneity.

The intimacy of most (but not all) of the spaces chosen for *Sweet William* more or less guarantees an unusually friendly audience – why would they be there if they didn't like Shakespeare and weren't tolerant of me? Sometimes they return my greeting at the beginning of the show enthusiastically; sometimes they seem on the brink of answering back during it; sometimes they stay behind for a while at the end to chat about anything that's intrigued them. The generations are – very agreeably – mixed. There was a woman not long ago who applauded when she sensed a cherished speech on its way, as if recognising the opening chords of a favourite song. She even murmured her way through one with me, each phrase a nanosecond ahead of me, which would have been difficult had it not been so charming. I felt I'd invented some new kind of entertainment akin to community singing.

Such experiences nicely demonstrate a point I make during the show. Shakespeare's theatres held upwards of two thousand people, but since their stages were little bigger than what we would describe as studio spaces, his actors probably moved with ease from the grandly rhetorical to the televisually intimate. It's not enough to say such a thing: I have to demonstrate it in my practice and prove that anything can be done in alternative ways. Depending on the venue, the heroic can become intimate and the confidential blossom. The Guthrie Theater in Minneapolis holds seven hundred; though I had always imagined my show in a more concentrated setting, the excerpts flowed naturally into every distant corner.

Two hours alone is an odd contest with yourself, like holding your breath for almost too long. Or spending a whole match having to keep possession of the ball and never passing it. And it's lonely. It happens that the great Victorian actress Ellen Terry took her solo talk-and-performance Shakespeare show on the road when she was the same age as me – she had the same agent looking after her too, Curtis Brown. 'Sixty-three one-night stands... it's enough to kill a horse,' she complained; and when she opened in Melbourne she was surprised to find, on coming out for her second half, that the audience had gone, imagining the evening done.

She also admitted that 'Familiar faces are the only faces I understand... it takes so long to read the truth in new faces.' It's as good a description of homesickness as I know. It was in friendly Minneapolis, in seventeen degrees below, that the chronic solitude of the soloist bore down most on me. At the end of the evening I would go to the bar, logically enough, and hope – as much out of desire for company as vanity – that some member of the public would say hullo. Instead, as it eventually emptied, one or two would come over and hesitantly enthuse, politely saying that they hadn't wanted to disturb me as I had my drink. Oh please, disturb me... Then I would return to the apartment and the washing up in the sink. This is not a plea for sympathy – as a boy I told my mother I could put up with the barmier aspects of the profession – just a bald fact that Ellen Terry would have understood.

I can't help thinking Shakespeare would have enjoyed his status as international visa – he who never toured abroad – especially the steep contrasts. Dromio of Syracuse's utterly non-PC account in *The Comedy of Errors* of being pursued by a woman so fat that he could imagine her as a globe played a little less comfortably in Colorado Springs than at home: only just tolerant of the obesity joke, the audience did however like him saying that, among the countries represented in her, America inclined deferentially to the 'hot breath' of Spain. Surprisingly, Chicago and New York didn't pick up the Bush-ism of James I taking the credit for sniffing out the Gunpowder Plot ('God has inspired me to foresee the conspiracy and root it out'), but Minneapolis did. My only regret about my US dates is that, to get the laugh, I have to turn myself into a fan of Manchester United rather than Tottenham Hotspur, the former being the only English football club everyone there knows, David Beckham having playing for Los Angeles. I imagined certain childhood heroes – Ron Reynolds, Ted Ditchburn and Alf Ramsey (and indeed my parents) – shocked by my expedient treachery.

I'm sometimes asked if *Sweet William* changes much from night to night, or week to week. Well, not much, any more than a play does, but it's also true that over the months I've discarded and replaced, rephrased and rewritten a little, since around the existing script is a host of alternatives, probably enough to make up another show. Or, it has now occurred to me, a book. This volume has its roots in *Sweet William*, but is in no way the script. All the plays figure somewhere here, some of them briefly (especially if I've done whole books on them before), others at length when they particularly serve the story, with no special favours done to the more popular end of the canon. I'm more or less following the chronology of Shakespeare's life – more or less: when particular themes present themselves, I double back or jump forward in time to pursue them. The narrative of Prince Hal and Falstaff, by some miracle, is both a great love story and a piercing anatomy of England, so it's dealt with, unapologetically, at considerable length. In fact it is noticeable to me in general how often the Histories crop up: but then they account for about a quarter of the canon and are in some ways the heart of the matter.

The theatre rejoices in its transience, but you sometimes need to get an experience fixed. The published versions of Shakespeare's plays that we depend on are a very different and much longer matter than what was actually performed, which was variable, sometimes depending on the weather and whatever was in the news that morning. The received wisdom is that he himself never felt the need to publish, but I'm not so sure – there is a suggestion that he cooperated a little in the preparation of the posthumously produced First Folio (blithely cutting some of his best stuff, including a major soliloquy from *Hamlet*). His Sonnets are obsessed with 'devouring time' and 'sad mortality'; so if he did help, it may have been his effort to have the last word – to be, so to speak, definitive for the moment. In that respect, if none other, we may be alike.

I

The Rose of Youth

Sweet William – Poor Inches of Nature – William Page –
Moth – Arthur – Marina – Perdita and Mamillius

L ike distant conversation, we can hear his colleagues commenting on
his pleasant nature, his industriousness, his ability to write so flu-
ently that he hardly ever had to make a correction. This wasn't an
intellectual celebrity like Ben Jonson or a hellraiser like Kit Marlowe.
One of his earliest editors, Nicholas Rowe, described William Shakespeare simply as

> A good-natured man, of great sweetness in his manners, and a
> most agreeable companion

– while the antiquarian John Aubrey confirms that he was

> a handsome, well-shaped man, very good company and of a very
> ready and pleasant smooth wit... not a company keeper... he
> would not be debauched, and if invited to, writ he was in pain...

Aubrey's first, vivid phrase seems to bring Shakespeare quite close to us;
the second suggests that this amiability was something he put on for
politeness's sake. And the intriguing final comment leaves it unclear
whether his pain was of the moral kind or a tactical move on any particular night – like pleading writer's cramp perhaps – to avoid offending his
friends. Aubrey in any case was a notorious gossip, the kind that trusts
his source at a remove or two: he can't be quite sure of his facts but he
has talked to a friend who is. And elsewhere he slightly undermines his
own evidence by subscribing to the idea that the reason Shakespeare was

friendly towards the children of the Davenant family, even giving them 'a hundred kisses', was because one of them was his own son by the wife. Or perhaps he was just a theatrical type who kissed everybody. Rowe is even less reliable, a scholar so absorbed in the novelty of editing the plays that he yearns to find the writer's character behind them. And since both men were writing long after Shakespeare's death in 1616 and didn't know him – Aubrey having been born in 1626 and Rowe in 1674 – their point of vantage is hardly better than our own.

At a still greater distance, we too have our ideas about what William Shakespeare was like, or what we would like him to have been like. The continuing slew of biographies – some from specialist Shakespearians (but rarely practitioners), some from fiction writers, some from established biographers feeling they should at last turn to Shakespeare – keeps the urge half-satisfied. Some of the best – James Shapiro's *1599* and Charles Nicholl's *The Lodger* – go round to work, assembling their portrait by describing everything except Shakespeare himself: they look at the rooms he may have lived in, the streets he probably walked, the political circumstances in any particular month, and leave a Shakespeare-shaped hole in the middle. So we catch a glimpse, just a glimpse, of someone turning a corner ahead of us or standing at the top of the stairs, the whisk of his cloak as he hurries past, keeping close to the wall.

Sooner or later we demand, like Dickens's Gradgrind, some incontrovertible facts. There aren't many to be had, but not so few either. Shakespeare's father was John, a glover, small businessman and by moonlight a moneylender; his mother was Mary Arden, from a Catholic family in the village of Wilmcote, just outside Stratford-upon-Avon. Mary had brought some money to the marriage, and just as well – John's career was to be a chequered thing. Both parents signed their names with a mark, but that was not so unusual at the time; annoyingly for myth-makers, it doesn't mean that Shakespeare's loquacity was a compensation for illiterate parents.

William was Mary's third pregnancy but her first child to survive; there were to be five more children, four of whom would reach adult-hood. The house in which he was born, on a spring day in 1564, was on the north side of Stratford, where the Birmingham Road now begins, in Henley Street, opposite where the Food of Love Café currently stands, cheek by jowl with Mistress Quickly's Tea Room and Iago's Jewellers – the latter perhaps the most ominous yoking of ideas in the Bardolatry trade since the closure of Timon's Restaurant. It seems that by local cus-tom, a fortifying portion of something sweet – butter or honey – would have immediately been put on the tongue of the newborn Shakespeare, he who would so often be known as honey-tongued.

The entire structure tumbles to the ground if you elect to believe, as some do, that Mary Arden returned for her confinement to her family house in Wilmcote: if so, the whole Shakespeare industry should be mentally transported five miles along the road with her. And it is obliterated completely if you incline to the view that the Man from Stratford was not the author of the plays at all, but a front man who deprived the suddenly modest Earl of Oxford, or Francis Bacon, or Christopher Marlowe, or Queen Elizabeth, or Sir Walter Ralegh, or Robert Cecil, or the Earl of Southampton, or Amelia Lanier (also a candidate for the Dark Lady of the Sonnets), or Sir Philip Sidney, or James I of due credit for breaking off their own careers to write thirty-seven superior plays anonymously. I don't plan to deal with that controversy any further in this book because it bores me, not least because it seems unlikely that when Ben Jonson described Shakespeare as the Swan of Avon he didn't mean that his friend lived in Stratford; or that Oxford contrived to write *King Lear* after his own death. The current answer to the latter problem is that the play must have been revised by various hands after Oxford died to make it worthy of performance, because otherwise it couldn't have been written by Oxford. The splendid circularity of this reasoning is of a piece with the snobbish idea that a Warwickshire grammar school boy was less qualified to write *Julius Caesar* than a university-trained aristocrat.

If you venture to accept the authorised version of events, then a few days after his birth, on April 23rd or so, Shakespeare's father would have taken the future author of *Hamlet* in his arms and, accompanied by the godparents, or 'gossips', carried him along Henley Street to the Market Cross, then right along the High Street, perhaps left down Sheep Street to the open fields that ran down to the river; then right, past the site of the future Royal Shakespeare Theatre, to Holy Trinity Church for his baptism service. Amazingly to us, his mother didn't attend the ceremony. The author of the Book of Leviticus suggests to the children of Israel that mothers are still impure in the aftermath of childbirth; the idea was taken up by the Christian Church, though by the sixteenth century there was a kinder explanation for the exclusion: Mary would have waited at home for forty days before being 'churched' because there was a danger of being taken by the fairies otherwise. Then she would be welcomed back into the community with thanksgiving for her survival. Shakespeare meanwhile would have been dressed for the occasion in a little white linen robe anointed with oil and balsam; this was the chrisom cloth, and it had a secondary use – if a baby died within a month of birth the garment could be reused as a burial shroud. This was much to the point in Stratford that year: as the summer warmed up, plague would carry off nearly 250 of the town's 1,500 citizens, and only one baby in three would survive. So the new arrival must have been a reasonably tough nut.

✦

> Poor inch of nature,
> Thou art as rudely welcome to the world
> As ever princess' babe…
>
> – *Pericles*

The mature dramatist didn't have much to say about coddling, swaddling or infancy in general. It's as if he couldn't wait to get his youngsters away from their apron strings – though he clearly enjoyed the idea of the teenage Juliet having to listen to her Nurse reminisce about sitting under the dovehouse wall and suckling her, minutes before she meets her sexual destiny in Romeo and becomes a tragic heroine. His other significant nursing is corrupted: Lady Macbeth intriguingly refers to a childbirth in her past, but swears she would have torn the child from her breast if she'd thought Macbeth would break his promise to murder Duncan.

Having survived the Plague Year, Shakespeare's own early childhood seems to have been happy enough in the pleasant honey-coloured house in Henley Street – probably much as it is now, except that in its wild garden the foul smells of skins being tanned by his father for gloves would have mingled, in a steep Shakespearian contrast, with the

> Hot lavender, mints, savory, marjoram,
> The marigold, that goes to bed with the sun
> And with him rises weeping.

However, his own stability contrasts with the condition of his imaginary children, who generally have a rough time, the more so for their customary intelligence. The first to utter is probably Lucius in *Titus Andronicus*: his job in the play is to cheer up his grandfather Titus, who has recently cut off his own hand, and to look after his aunt Lavinia, who has just been raped and had both hands cut off and her tongue cut out:

TITUS: This poor right hand of mine
Is left to tyrannise upon my breast…
Then thus I thump it down…

> [*To* LAVINIA.] Thou shalt not sigh, nor hold thy stumps
>   to heaven...
>
> LUCIUS: Good grandsire, leave these bitter deep laments:
>   Make my aunt merry with some pleasing tale...
>
> TITUS: Peace, tender sapling, thou art made of tears...

If this is the sort of talk Lucius has to put up with from his grandfather it might have been better if he rather than Lavinia had lost his tongue. The miserable little group go off at the end of the scene to the edifying prospect of Titus reading

> Sad stories chanced in the time of old

– with the warning that the boy will have to take up the narrative when Titus's eyes get tired.

Then there are the little Princes in *Richard III*, who end up in the Tower of London with a cushion over their faces; but on the evidence of what we see of them –

> I want more uncles here to welcome me...
> Fie, what a slug is Hastings

– I find them so obnoxious that I'm almost as glad as Richard to see the back of them. These are the kind of Shakespearian kids that turn you into Miss Trunchbull from Roald Dahl's *Matilda*. Benedick in *Much Ado About Nothing* is given a Boy who contributes only one irritating turn of phrase, like a tiresome teenager:

> BENEDICK: Boy –
>
> BOY: Signor?
>
> BENEDICK: In my chamber-window lies a book; bring it hither
>   to me in the orchard.
>
> BOY: I am here already, sir.
>
> BENEDICK: I know that; but I would have thee hence, and here
>   again.

However, this part and moment were redeemed forever in John Barton's 1976 Royal Shakespeare Company production of the play set in the Raj, when the Boy became an infinitely patient Indian servant (Paul Whitworth) who, knowing his master's liking for an afternoon read in his hammock, already had the book ready in his hand. So 'I am here already, sir' became 'I have anticipated your every wish'. Not troubling to look at him, Donald Sinden's Benedick irritably dispatched him as if he were an idiot. Rather than embarrassing his master, the servant gently walked to the back of the stage and after a moment returned to present the book.

Young John Talbot in *Henry VI Part One* has loyally become a soldier at the side of his bellicose father, also called John: so he can never escape his shadow, and they die together on the battlefield. In *Macbeth*, a play no child should find himself in, Lady Macduff's son is appealing because of his superb defiance of the murderer sent to dispose of him:

> Thou liest, thou shag-eared villain...
> He has killed me, mother: run away, I pray you!

Myself, I blame the parents, or at least the fathers. Talbot might have considered a safer profession for his son; Macduff perhaps shouldn't have run away to England, leaving his family behind him.

Such children, doomed by adult ambition or narcissism, are caught up in stories too big for them: they are there more or less for an instant effect, pathos usually. However, there are others who are present for a more substantial reason. Lucius in *Julius Caesar* makes a single pluck on the heartstrings because he falls asleep while playing a tune to his master Brutus. He then slumbers through the appearance of Caesar's Ghost in the tent: it's an affecting thing to see the dictator of the known world, the doomed revolutionary and the oblivious boy all there together in the same frame. Lucius may also be a means of pointing up how much better Brutus treats his servant than he does his wife. Having just reported the death of Portia, more or less killed, we feel, by his neglect, he now reproaches himself for being too preoccupied to notice Lucius's tiredness:

> If thou dost nod, thou break'st thy instrument;
> I'll take it from thee, and good boy, goodnight.

However, a few become masters of their destiny, or at least of their immediate future, such as the schoolboy William Page, who appears briefly in Shakespeare's only play about the contemporary middle class, *The Merry Wives of Windsor*, where his job is to show up his elders' lack of imagination. For Windsor we might read Stratford. At about five, William Shakespeare would, willingly or unwillingly, have gone for a couple of years to his elementary ('petty') school, and then trudged along the High Street to King Edward VI's new grammar school at the top of Chapel Lane. There he joined a class of about forty boys, all studying a full twelve hours a day with a small break for bread and beer, six days a week, no long holidays. He learned how to turn prose into verse – a gift that would stand him in spectacular stead later when he borrowed Plutarch's description of Cleopatra's barge from Thomas North's translation:

> The poop whereof was of gold, the sails of purple and the oars of silver which kept stroke in rowing... there ran such multitudes of people one after another to see her that Antonius was left post alone in the market place.

He gave this wings simply by adjusting the phrasing to make it metrical and adding a breath of genius here and there – the winds become 'lovesick' because of the perfume of the sails and the solitary Antony sits 'whistling to th' air'. And as for Cleopatra's own person:

> It beggar'd all description; she did lie
> In her pavilion – cloth of gold, of tissue –
> O'er-picturing that Venus where we see
> The fancy outwork nature.

He also studied the art of rhetoric – the matter of taking an argument and making both sides convincing – which would come in handy for young Prince Arthur in *King John* as well as other debates that still keep audiences on the edge of their seats. Since Latin was all the rage among parents of every class, he duly learned how to translate it into English and back – an unremarkable achievement for children of the time that has misled some into believing that only a university man could have written the plays. Shakespeare wore his Latin as lightly as one now might elementary French: he inevitably knew a great deal of it, perhaps as much as a university graduate today. Ben Jonson's comment that he had little Latin and less Greek would have been more aptly applied to his forever shaky history and geography.

A recent RSC production of *The Merry Wives* attracted the wrath of one critic, outraged that the 'integral' scene of the Latin lesson endured by William Page had been cut, rather as if To Be or Not to Be had been excised from *Hamlet* – a speech which, come to think of it, doesn't contribute much to the plot either. The fact is nothing could be less integral than the episode in which Sir Hugh Evans examines his young pupil: its real interest lies elsewhere. As commentators are fond of pointing out, Thomas Jenkins, Shakespeare's Latin teacher at King Edward's, was a Welshman like Sir Hugh, whose student, by happy chance, is called William. This, by the way, is not the only appearance of William in the works of William; in *Henry IV Part Two* he seems to have survived school so successfully that he's about to graduate from university:

> SHALLOW: I dare say my cousin William is become a good scholar? He is at Oxford still, is he not?
>
> SILENCE: Indeed, sir, to my cost.
>
> SHALLOW: He must then to the Inns of Court shortly...

William then transmogrifies into a lovelorn shepherd in *As You Like It*, who has been 'born i' the forest' but who also describes himself as 'not learned' – which is in a way true of Shakespeare, who was born near the Forest of Arden and whose intelligence was not academic. These three plays were written within three years, so this was obviously a running gag offered by the playwright to his loyal audience.

In *The Merry Wives* it's a day off school, presumably a Sunday, but William is to have extra tutoring at his father's behest – no doubt this is the reason he has to be encouraged to 'hold up your head; answer your master'. His main task is to be the declension of the Latin word for 'this' – 'hic haec hoc' – which allows Shakespeare an accent joke:

> EVANS: What is your accusative case?
>
> WILLIAM: Accusativo, hinc.
>
> EVANS: I pray you, have your remembrance, child,
>   accusativo, hung, hang, hog.

The right answer is 'hunc (hanc/hoc)', so Hugh seems to have developed a sudden nasal congestion not particularly typical of a Welshman. It's also hard to see how a Latin teacher could follow a nice phrase about remembrance with a perfectly rendered Italian word, only then to make his Latin incomprehensible; but with a joke in hand, Shakespeare will sacrifice anything, especially if he can involve a regional or a foreigner (there is a funny Frenchman in the play as well). Or if he can make fun of the ill-educated – Hugh's mistake lets in Mistress Quickly for a clumping joke:

> Hang-hog is Latin for bacon, I warrant you.

In the same vein, she then mistakes the Latin word 'caret' for the vegetable. And if there can be a hint of what Shakespeare's editors would call impropriety, so much the better; for good measure Mistress Quickly turns in a couple of double entendres when Evans asks William for some declension:

> EVANS: What is your genitive case plural, William?
>
> WILLIAM: Genitive case?
>
> EVANS: Ay.
>
> WILLIAM: Genitivo – horum, harum, horum.

This time it's the right answer, but there may have been a snigger both in William's reaction to 'horum' and in 'genitive' being linked with 'case', since, in case you hadn't guessed, 'case' was a slang word for vagina. It is certainly a gift for Mistress Quickly:

> MISTRESS QUICKLY: Vengeance of Jenny's case; fie on her! Never name her, child, if she be a whore.
>
> EVANS: For shame, 'oman.
>
> MISTRESS QUICKLY: You do ill to teach the child such words…
>
> EVANS: 'Oman, art thou lunatics? Hast thou no understandings for thy cases and the numbers and the genders?

Oh dear. It would be a pleasure to meet William Shakespeare in heaven, but I'd have a couple of bones to pick with him. This is the man Voltaire said showed 'not the least glimmer of good taste', the friend of whom Ben Jonson sorrowfully reported:

> His wit was in his own power; would the rule of it had been so too.

However, behind the scene's seaside-postcard humour lurks an important Shakespearian idea: that language is for those whose imagination is still free, who can hear the sudden music of one word meeting another, rather than for the totalitarian Malvolios and Hugh Evanses who would order and control it:

> EVANS: What is lapis, William?
>
> WILLIAM: A stone.
>
> EVANS: And what is a stone, William?
>
> WILLIAM: A pebble.
>
> EVANS: No, it is lapis; I pray you remember in your prain.

Aching on the wooden bench of King Edward's and looking forward to the beer-break, any pupil might take refuge in his imagination: he might well, like Edgar in *King Lear*, see a stone not just as a stone but as part of the 'unnumber'd idle pebble' on Dover beach chafed by the 'murmuring surge', or as a thing thrown off 'the raging rocks and shivering shocks' invoked by Bottom. However, from Hugh Evans's point of view language is not to do with such fripperies: it is only the vehicle for translating Latin into English and back again. He would presumably approve of a contemporary manual of pedagogical practice that instructed the pupil to

> Take the horn book in thy hand: stand upright. Hold thy cap under thy arm. Hearken attentively how I shall name these letters. Mark diligently how I move my mouth. See that you rehearse them so…

In other words, there is only one right way. When we irritably watch mouths categorically moving on Prime Minister's Question Time; or vainly attempt a phone conversation with an internet provider; or shudder at being encouraged to have a nice day by a complete stranger; or, within the arts, rebel against our paymasters' talk of meeting the diversity challenge through clusters and cohorts and walking the walk, we are inheriting Shakespeare's fight to stop language being wickedly drained of meaning.

✦

A most acute juvenal, voluble and free of grace…

– Love's Labour's Lost

It is always a mistake to vex a budding writer, and Shakespeare felt enough resentment towards his teachers to go on taking small revenges. His next mockable pedagogue is Holofernes in *Love's Labour's Lost*. This is a man who, as well as baffling everyone with Latin quibbles, is not impartial to a little bit of caning and takes a kindly custodial interest in the country wench Jaquenetta. In another part of the play his natural antagonist, the child Moth, is in fact page to the 'fantastical Spaniard' Don Armado (since the Armada the Spanish were good for a laugh). Moth is described by Costard the clown as 'not so long by the head as honorificabilitudinitatibus' (a word perhaps learned from Holofernes, but, more alarmingly, an anagram of a claim supposedly made in Latin by Francis Bacon that he had written the plays); but he is very long in terms of lines, the most substantial part for a child in Shakespeare. Moth has an answer for everything, sometimes a hoary old Shakespearian joke –

ARMADO: Who was Samson's love, my dear Moth?

MOTH: A woman, master

– and sometimes a gentle antithesis:

ARMADO: How hast thou purchased this experience?

MOTH: By my penny of observation.

His ability to run rings round everybody he meets draws a not altogether affectionate tribute from his master, a man himself not free of linguistic vanity, who may sometimes wonder about his wisdom in taking on a page so very ready to upstage him. In the end, Moth is humorously cast as

Hercules in a performance of *The Nine Worthies* put on for the royal lovers, only to be uncharacteristically 'put out of [his] part' by not being listened to by the women in the audience. Rather to our satisfaction, even Moth is thus defeated by the play's verbal profligacy, a great feast of language from which even he (as he says of Armado and Holofernes) could only steal the scraps.

It's tempting to imagine that Prince Arthur in *King John* might originally have been played by the same bright young actor who undertook Moth. It is hard to find a good enough boy to play either of them in our less linguistic times, but Shakespeare's company must have included young virtuosi for whom he could safely have written such parts, let alone the women they also performed. Arthur is Moth's natural cousin, but cast in a tragic light; he is still one of the major attractions of a play which, much more popular with the Victorians than it is with us, has the distinction of being the first known Shakespeare film: sections of Herbert Beerbohm Tree's 1899 stage production were shot, and a small fragment survives. Ellen Terry played Arthur for him at the age of nine (apparently in a pair of baggy pink tights and a little silver dress): presumably her evident girlhood made the story still more pitiful. In retrospect she would have been pleased to have done it: she later used to point out rather tartly – ignoring *Coriolanus* – that it's all fathers and daughters in Shakespeare, and Constance and Arthur are at least mother and son. The infant phenomenon was much loved for the performance, except by one German visitor, the novelist Theodor Fontane, who tellingly thought her 'intolerable... a precocious child brought up in the English manner, old before her years'.

Our problem these days with *John* is that its main interest lies away from the play's title role. Although the historical John was an exceptionally bad King, Shakespeare's denigration of him at the time would have had some shock value, as he was sometimes seen by Protestants as a semi-heroic figure for defying Rome like Henry VIII. Having tilted the scales in this way, Shakespeare, who may have been guarding his own Catholicism, then tilted them back again not only by omitting any reference to the humiliation of the Magna Carta, but by presenting the Papal legate Pandulph as a 'meddling priest', extravagantly ruthless, quibbling and devious. His King John is a listless casuist and manipulator, though he does get a superb death scene, poisoned in the orchard of Swinstead Abbey by a monk who is then so overcome with guilt that 'his bowels burst out'.

With *Richard III* in hand at the time and *Macbeth* ahead of him, some of the operating techniques of a man such as John do interest Shakespeare. All three are expert in the dropping of hints – Macbeth's briefing of the murderers of Banquo will be the best example, but John gets a fine Stalinist moment when, without explicitly going on the record, he conveys to Hubert that young Arthur, his nephew and rival to the throne, should be removed:

> I had a thing to say,
> But I will fit it with some better time…
> I had a thing to say, but let it go…

The clinching moment of this produces the most striking (and ostentatious) manipulation of a single verse line Shakespeare has yet achieved, a command issued to his actors to pick up their cues sharply:

JOHN: Death.

HUBERT: My lord?

JOHN: A grave.

HUBERT: He shall not live.

JOHN: Enough.
> I could be merry now…

In general, however, the victims of John's schemes are more engrossing than he is. In particular, his nephew Arthur is a diminutive source of big trouble. Arthur's mother Constance, an early study in the type of maternal dragonhood that Shakespeare would perfect in due course, is determined that he shall be King, despite the fact that the previous monarch, Richard I, has nominated his brother John to the job, as he was entitled to do. She behaves like the worst kind of show-business mother enraged that her boy isn't getting cast: throwing herself on the ground in front of the Kings of France and England, she wails and excoriates, to the embarrassment of Arthur, who is deeply uninterested in the matter:

> I am not worth this coil that's made for me…

She also laments at great length the special, though not unusual, misery of widowhood; and as for the driving love she feels for Arthur, she makes it clear that it is fortunate that the boy is 'fair' since she wouldn't love him if he wasn't.

The intemperate emotions of this mad world eventually wash over Arthur and drown him; but he struggles astutely, with some of the skills Shakespeare would have learned at King Edward's School. We perhaps see the boy now through sharper eyes than the Victorians did: Shakespeare's cunning lies in making him impossibly modest and lovable while giving him the instincts of a first-class advocate. Captured by his wicked uncle, he falls into the hands of Hubert de Burgh, historically a powerful landowner who pressured the King to sign the Magna Carta, but in the play a man who arrives from nowhere. Shakespeare, untroubled by history, simply borrows the name and defines him only by his grim task as Arthur's jailer and, John hopes, his executioner.

Mortal fear makes Arthur undertake some truly complex negotiations. For reasons that can only have been to crank up the horror, John has decided to have the boy blinded rather than simply cutting his throat. Arriving in the cell with a brazier and hot irons, Hubert is at first so implacable that even the executioner accompanying him recoils from the work, only to be reproached for his 'uncleanly scruples'. However, Hubert is to meet his match: the boy is smart in a Shakespearian way:

> Is it my fault that I was Geoffrey's son?

To make matters worse, he seems to have some unfathomable personal affection for Hubert:

> I would to heaven
> I were your son, so you would love me, Hubert…
> Are you sick, Hubert? You look pale today.
> In sooth, I would you were a little sick,
> That I might sit all night and watch with you.
> I warrant I love you more than you do me.

When the realisation of his fate comes, his love, turned to shock, shames his keeper:

> Have you the heart? When your head did but ache,
> I knit my handkercher about your brows…
> And with my hand at midnight held your head;
> And like the watchful minutes to the hour
> Still and anon cheer'd up the heavy time,
> Saying, 'What lack you?' and 'Where lies your grief?'

This unlikely account of Arthur's captivity certainly raises the sentimental ante. We may also notice that his tender sagacity is touched by an effortless snobbery: he points out en passant that as a Prince his love is worth more than that of 'many a poor man's son'.

Hubert, the historical aristocrat who has become, for Shakespeare's purposes, a good honest chap at heart in an impossible situation, plays a

straight bat as long as he can. But extreme emotion brings out the liti-
gant in Shakespeare, so Arthur out-reasons him for a hundred lines,
spinning metaphor and simile like plates on a stick. In imagery a little
too elaborate for Hubert, he claims that not only the blinding equipment
but the current age is made of iron, and both will surely be cooled by his
tears. He switches to passive aggression:

> Alas, what need you be so boisterous rough?
> I will not struggle, I will stand stone-still.
> For heaven's sake, Hubert, let me not be bound!...
> And I will sit as quiet as a lamb.

Wildly filibustering, he tries striking a bargain:

> Let me not hold my tongue, let me not, Hubert,
> Or, Hubert, if you will, cut out my tongue,
> So I may keep mine eyes: O spare mine eyes,
> Though to no use but still to look on you!

– and is finally saved by the bell:

> Lo, by my troth, the instrument is cold
> And would not harm me.

It's been a triumph of superior education, Hubert drawn into the mug's
game of quibbling with a young sophisticate. As a final sop to the working man, Shakespeare allows Hubert to get away with the whole dismal
affair: he spares Arthur's life, sustains an impossible fiction to the King
that the boy is dead, but then disowns it – to John's relief, since by then
he has himself fallen under suspicion of the imaginary deed.

It would be interesting to compare this treatment of the story with
what the older Shakespeare might have done with it; later on, he would
find regular satisfaction in having his intellectuals confounded by plain
speakers. But even at this stage, there is a stack of pleasing ironies around
the young prince. Utterly indifferent to the political intrigue surrounding him, Arthur is heavy with self-hatred:

> I would that I were low laid in my grave.

He eventually dies in an attempt to escape by jumping off the walls of
his prison – for obvious reasons a notoriously difficult scene to stage.
Before he does so, Shakespeare allows Constance to assume that he is as
good as dead, a false cue that provokes an astonishing lament from this
usually unsympathetic woman. Its writing hoists the play out of its noisy
turgidity into full-hearted Shakespearian verse:

> Grief fills the room up of my absent child,
> Lies in his bed, walks up and down with me,
> Puts on his pretty looks, repeats his words,
> Remembers me of all his gracious parts,
> Stuffs out his vacant garments with his form...
> O Lord, my boy, my Arthur, my fair son!
> My life, my joy, my food, my all the world...

As a grace note, Arthur turns out to be only one of two sons in *King John*: at the play's end, Prince Henry, the orphaned child of an equally unsatisfactory parent, John himself, suddenly appears. About to become, as Henry III, England's first child King, he compares himself, improbably but beautifully, to his father:

> I am the cygnet to this pale faint swan

– whereupon we hear an echo of the modestly elegiac Arthur, a boy in permanent pain, declaring his dearest wish:

> So I were out of prison and kept sheep
> I should be as merry as the day is long.

Advocate, victim, would-be shepherd: Arthur could have grown up to be something like King Henry VI, his near-contemporary in Shakespeare's portfolio.

✦

> Now grown in grace
> Equal with wondering...
>
> *– The Winter's Tale*

Arthur, like Moth, parries adult oppression with charm and wit. He comes from the early stages of Shakespeare's career; as he entered the Jacobean equivalent of old age, fatherhood and grandfatherhood made Shakespeare imagine children surviving all odds and even redeeming their parents. Those in *The Winter's Tale* and *Pericles* are no longer affecting snapshots but biographies of young heroes and – especially – heroines who turn their past to better account.

Ben Jonson thought *Pericles* – co-authored around 1607 by Shakespeare and a notorious pimp called George Wilkins – 'a mouldy tale'; but it was the first Shakespeare play to be revived after the Restoration of 1660, and its intermittent beauty has always kept it in the repertoire – just. Its starting point is as savage and arbitrary as the life of Wilkins himself, who appeared regularly in the Magistrates' Court, usually for abusing women, particularly prostitutes, in one case 'stamping' on one so she had to be 'carried away in a chair'. Still, the play, lapped in sea and sky, survives its clotted narrative as a hymn to compensating human kindness. It is ferociously difficult to stage, largely because of the multiplicity of characters and locations, as various as *Antony and Cleopatra* but much less skilfully manipulated; productions veer from a chamber style, with little setting and much doubling for most of the actors, to scenic extravaganza when budgets allow. Neither method guarantees either the play's intimacy or its gaudy grandeur.

The work having been shared by a great writer and an ordinary one, the *Pericles* experience is like reading two books superimposed on one another: absurd adventures told in trite rhyming verse are studded with moments of Shakespearian wit and grace. There's not much doubt who put into the mouths of three fishermen the thought that fish live in the sea

> as men do a-land; the great ones eat up the little ones

– or who, with *King Lear* behind him, lets Pericles reflect on human tyranny:

> The blind mole casts
> Copp'd hills towards heaven to tell the earth is throng'd
> By man's oppression, and the poor worm doth die for't

– or describe himself as

> a glow-worm in the night
> The which hath fire in darkness, none in light.

There it is again, that familiar cadence – the tension and release, the ellipsis, the philosophical QED, the pungent satire. On the other hand it is a mistake to assume that Wilkins wrote all the bad stuff: the description of Marina as a 'poor inch of nature' is known to be his.

As her name partly hints, Marina is

> born at sea, buried at Tarsus
> And found at sea again.

The storm into which she arrives appears to carry off her mother, and Pericles hopes that her life will be all compensation:

> Now mild may be thy life;
> For a more blusterous birth had never babe;
> Quiet and gentle thy conditions...

They aren't, however. Sold into a brothel in Mytilene, she defends her virginity with the radiant eloquence of Arthur contesting Hubert and with the same adroitness: in this setting her innocence and wit is enough 'to freeze the god Priapus'. She sends her disappointed customers away 'as cold as a snowball... out of the road of rutting for ever'; one of them, born again, runs off 'to hear the vestals sing'. She bribes the brothel's management and blackmails the Governor of Mytilene, who is visiting it incognito, into helping her escape; eventually he marries her, so that, having made his first appearance as a sexual customer, he is included in the play's final spiritual harmonies. Marina's talent and beauty gain her admittance to her grieved and reclusive father, whereupon he breaks a three-month silence and a fourteen-year abandonment of soap and razor, suddenly seeing her as

> Thou that begett'st him that did thee beget...

To the accompaniment of the music of the spheres and a vision of Diana, a Shakespearian scene of reunion, painful step by painful step, is enacted – paradoxically as moving as that of Lear and Cordelia because the actual suffering behind it is less strictly credible. It is like hearing a heavenly soprano line soaring over a confused theme.

So Marina survives the world's 'awkward casualties' to become an angel of redemption to her father – she also, if not exactly redeeming him, makes the Governor of Mytilene a very lucky man. The brief of Perdita in *The Winter's Tale* – written a few months after the birth of the only grandchild Shakespeare had during his lifetime – is even wider: to save just about everyone from themselves. Her name, like Marina's, tells her story. As a newborn baby she is dispatched by order of her father, King Leontes of Sicily, who doubts her paternity, to a mountainside in Bohemia to die, only to be found there by an Old Shepherd. At the same moment, a little further off, the Shepherd's son is watching Antigonus, who brought her, being torn apart by a bear as he starts his homeward journey – having left Perdita behind just in time, since presumably the bear would have made short work of her as well if it had found her. She grows up believing herself to be the Old Shepherd's daughter, and her appeal, like Viola's in *Twelfth Night* when disguised as a page, is in paradox: while thinking herself a

> poor lowly maid
> Most goddess-like prank'd up

she has the genetic humour and wit that Shakespeare associates with princely blood. As she presides over a Bohemian sheep-shearing festival,

Perdita's warmth and natural wisdom deeply influence everyone who comes into contact with her.

In his story *Beauties*, Anton Chekhov describes the experience of meeting an Armenian girl at a resting place during a journey across the steppe. Her beauty, while delighting everyone – the young narrator, the driver of his cart, his grandfather – also makes Chekhov feel that they have all somehow lost something important and necessary in life that they will never find again. Perdita stops people in their tracks in the same way: she is a force of nature, a miracle in herself. Polixenes, King of Bohemia and suspected by Leontes of fathering Perdita, and Camillo, who has escaped Leontes's court to join him, arrive to see if Polixenes's son Florizel, in love with Perdita, is indeed about to marry beneath him. They are enchanted by her candour:

> These are flowers
> Of middle summer and I think they are given
> To men of middle age. Y'are very welcome.
>
> CAMILLO: I should leave grazing, were I of your flock,
> And only live by gazing.
>
> PERDITA: Out, alas!
> You'd be so lean that blasts of January
> Would blow you through and through.

This goes beyond gallantry, pertness or flirtation. Flowers, of which she speaks with exceptional beauty and knowledge, are Perdita's currency; but like Marina she also has the talent to 'sing, weave, sew and dance', as testified by her adoring Florizel, who, though young, has something of the older writer's melancholy in him:

> What you do
> Still betters what is done; when you speak, sweet,
> I'd have you do it ever; when you sing,
> I'd have you buy and sell so, so give alms,
> Pray so, and for the ordering your affairs
> To sing them too; when you do dance, I wish you
> A wave of the sea, that you might ever do
> Nothing but that.

The yearning note in this deepens when Leontes is finally confronted by her, not knowing who she is. He responds instinctively, first with sorrow for what he has squandered, and then with a simple line that sums up the play's hard-won generosity:

> Welcome hither
> As is the spring to th' earth.

So Perdita is reunited with him and with her mother Hermione, and the parents are reconciled to each other. But there has been a real loss on the way, and, as the play closes with a strong element of the miraculous, it is a shock to remember it. Three Acts earlier, Shakespeare has delivered his most unsparing study of the internal agonies of childhood in the story of little Prince Mamillius, to whom Perdita is a posthumous sister.

The outward cause of Mamillius's conflict is his father's unreasoning jealousy of his mother. This storm breaks over his head as Hermione is preparing to give birth again – an anxious moment for any existing sibling, struggling to hold on to his identity in an unexplained world. Mamillius's perception of his parents' obscure battle for his soul wonderfully brings out the proto-Freudian in Shakespeare. Leontes, convinced that Mamillius is no more his than the new baby, does exactly what a troubled parent shouldn't do in such a delicate atmosphere – he involves the child in the argument:

> LEONTES: Mamillius,
>   Art thou my boy?
>
> MAMILLIUS: Ay, my good lord...
>
> LEONTES: Art thou my calf?
>
> MAMILLIUS: Yes, if you will, my lord...
>
> LEONTES: ...they say we are
>   Almost as like as eggs; women say so
>   That will say anything... Can thy dam? May't be?...
>   Mine honest friend,
>   Will you take eggs for money?
>
> MAMILLIUS: No, my lord, I'll fight...
>
> LEONTES: How now, boy?
>
> MAMILLIUS: I am like you, they say.
>
> LEONTES: Why, that's some comfort.

So without grasping why, Mamillius is having to look after his parent, and he shows an instinct for it: 'I am like you, they say.' His father's words dinning in his ears, he now goes to see his mother, awaiting her confinement with two of her ladies. As this scene opens, Mamillius must have done or said something disturbing: the first thing Hermione says to the women is

> Take the boy to you; he so troubles me,
> 'Tis past enduring.

They do what they can, each in turn:

> FIRST LADY: Come, my gracious lord,
>   Shall I be your playfellow?
>
> MAMILLIUS: No, I'll none of you.
>
> FIRST LADY: Why, my sweet lord?
>
> MAMILLIUS: You'll kiss me hard and speak to me as if
>   I were a baby still. I love you better.
>
> SECOND LADY: And why so, my lord?
>
> MAMILLIUS: Not for because
>   Your brows are blacker; yet black brows, they say,
>   Become some women best, so that there be not
>   Too much hair there, but in a semicircle,
>   Or a half-moon made with a pen.
>
> SECOND LADY: Who taught you this?
>
> MAMILLIUS: I learn'd it out of women's faces.

This is a shock: Mamillius has grasped the adult male prejudice of the time that black-browed women were promiscuous. He suddenly sounds like his suspicious father, with the same choppy, troubled style of speaking. Stepping in to help, the First Lady meets Mamillius's burgeoning misogyny:

> MAMILLIUS: Pray now,
>   What colour are your eyebrows?
>
> FIRST LADY: Blue, my lord.
>
> MAMILLIUS: Nay, that's a mock; I have seen a lady's nose
>   That has been blue, but not her eyebrows.

This 'mock' of his changes her tone, as if enough were enough, royal or no royal: she no longer calls Mamillius 'sweet lord' or 'gracious lord', and, perhaps as a punishment, chooses to be tactlessly sexy with him:

> FIRST LADY: Hark ye,
>   The queen your mother rounds apace: we shall
>   Present our services to a fine new prince
>   One of these days, and then you'ld wanton with us
>   If we would have you...

It's an obscure joke, somehow suggesting that with competition from a younger brother, Mamillius will become a serious flirt; if she did but know it, she is hitting him at his most defenceless. The taunt silences him, and his mother, who has perhaps heard it, sees that she is needed:

HERMIONE: Come sir, now
   I am for you again; pray you, sit by us,
   And tell's a tale.

MAMILLIUS: Merry or sad shall't be?

HERMIONE: As merry as you will.

MAMILLIUS: A sad tale's best for winter: I have one
   Of sprites and goblins.

HERMIONE: Let's have that, good sir…

MAMILLIUS: There was a man –

HERMIONE: Nay, come, sit down; then on.

MAMILLIUS: Dwelt by a churchyard: I will tell it softly,
   Yond crickets shall not hear it.

As he tries to make their world a circle of confiding warmth again, the scene is interrupted and they are separated, his terrors unbanished.

This jumble of the subconscious is the last we hear of the haunted boy: he doesn't appear or speak again. Later on, the oracle at Delphi, the next best thing to God, declares to Leontes that Hermione has been faithful all along, but Leontes calls the oracle a liar – and at that moment Hermione collapses as if dead, and we hear from a servant that Mamillius has died. Disabled by one parent, his heart broken over the other, Shakespeare's one young psychological victim, Mamillius is lost for good as Perdita will not be. No wonder we never heard that sad winter's tale he started to tell; in a sense it was his own.

✦

Shakespeare's son Hamnet died as he started *King John*; and though it is not the fashion to find autobiography in the plays, it is fairly clear that his own grief released an authorial generosity to, by any normal standard, Arthur's appalling mother. What is interesting is his entirely typical side-step: we, the audience, know that Constance's grief is based on false information, so dramatic irony taints the pathos. In fact Arthur has just triumphed over Hubert; by the time he hurls himself to his death, Constance, rather to our relief, will have died and gone out of the play – sparing her, us and perhaps Shakespeare himself from dealing with the real thing. As with his Sonnets, he has done a feint, blending life and imagination so that he can never be found out for sure. And then, as if disowning it all, he spends much of the next several years writing comedies.

Evasive as he is, however, from one angle we have hold of him. Consider: Shakespeare never saw a son of his become a man, while circumstances separated him from his own male siblings when they were younger than Hamnet. So many of the boys in the plays, Arthur and Mamillius most conspicuously, end up lost. On the other hand, when he died in 1616, he had seen his daughters Judith and Susannah into their thirties and married, and had been a grandfather for eight years. So Perdita and Marina, and indeed Miranda in *The Tempest*, survive into womanhood and marriage. Though Shakespeare would have found the authorial washing of dirty linen baffling, the clues are there if you look hard enough. His children are a mix of theatre opportunism and deep feeling. Benedick's Boy, the two Luciuses, and even Moth cash in on the idea of children for the sake of entertainment; but the doomed Arthur and Mamillius and the surviving Perdita and Marina offer a discreet window into Shakespeare's soul.

2

The Only Shake-Scene

John Shakespeare – Marriage and Flight – A Motley to the View –
London – The Two Gentlemen of Verona – The Comedy of Errors –
An Upstart Crow – Henry VI – The Rose

It's hard to give Shakespeare's children a precise age because of their exceptional, precocious fluency; but if Mamillius and Arthur are imagined to be dying at twelve or thirteen they are of an age with Shakespeare when his life received a jolt. His education seems to have ended then, cut short by his father's disgrace and bankruptcy. So his catapult into young manhood had the same velocity as that of other writer sons of poor or failed fathers – Dickens, Ibsen, Chekhov, Wells, Shaw – and the profusion of his achievement later – and, to state the obvious, the plays' interest in fathers and sons – suggests that in some sense he felt he was working for two. However, his only documented attempt to set the past to rights takes a conventional, not to say snobbish form: in success, he acquired a coat of arms and motto – 'non sanz droict' – to attach to the family name, as his father had tried and failed to do. In a life of determined anonymity, the ostentatious fact sticks out oddly.

John Shakespeare was a substantial figure in Stratford life – unofficially as usurer and entrepreneur, and officially as an alderman and then the equivalent of Mayor. It's not quite clear what went wrong for him in the late 1570s, though it may have had its roots in the family's probable Catholicism: his wife Mary came from her old Catholic family in Wilmcote, and John himself seems falteringly to have sustained the double life of the Elizabethan crypto-Catholic. In this game the very least that had to be done was to turn up in church and sing loudly as a good Protestant on Sundays even if you were practising your own religion at home. No doubt John was used to doing this – he had survived the tricky transition from Catholic Queen Mary to Protestant Elizabeth; however, obliged in his official capacity to 'destroy utterly' the images in Stratford's Guild Chapel because of their Catholic associations, it took him a telltale four years to get round to doing it, and even then he only covered them with limewash. At around the same time, in 1577, a commission was sent out to Stratford to track down recusants: John abruptly disappeared from the town council and tried to sell off his wife's inheritance and his lands to avoid their confiscation. Some say he compounded his problems with drunkenness and fines for non-attendance in church.

It was a bad moment for him to draw the heat. The Catholic community was already a milch cow as Elizabeth anxiously raised taxes to guard against national threats such as the Spanish Armada; meanwhile, her obsessive object of rivalry, the Catholic Mary Queen of Scots, was being passed from one castle prison to another like a hot potato. So to practise the old faith under Elizabeth's nervy eye called for deep discretion. Indeed, even at the best of times religious tolerance seems to have been a matter of which side of the bed the Queen got out on of a morning; for every William Byrd, a favourite despite his Catholicism on account of exceptional talent, there were a handful of potential martyrs suspected of being too close to Mary.

When John Shakespeare missed his step in this treacherous dance and his family took a tumble, William, cushioned till now by the free education available to the son of a public servant, found his life gaping in front of him. He straight away initiated a lifelong skill: he vanished. Just as his personality evaporates under scrutiny, Shakespeare physically dematerialises at many moments we would like to know more about. We have no idea what he did in the next six or so years until his marriage. Recent conjecture has it that he was encouraged by his family and teachers to go to Lancashire, a stronghold of the old faith, as tutor to the children of a wealthy Catholic family. There certainly is a William Shakeshaft documented as living with such a family at Hoghton Tower, near Preston; there are borrowings in that name of a volume of Ovid from the family's library, its margins annotated in what might be his hand. Elizabethan name spellings are notoriously approximate, and there's now enough support for the idea to justify the planning of a Globe-style theatre in the area. If the story is true, Shakespeare was learning from his father's mistakes: covering his recusant tracks more efficiently than John had, he remains as near-invisible to us as to the authorities.

He breaks cover to marry Anne Hathaway in 1582. We don't know whether he loved Anne or was dragged to the altar at gunpoint – she certainly was four months pregnant. Much as we might like to see this as a scandal, the truth was probably duller. The marriage may well have been approved, and the wedding ceremony was in some ways less important than the 'making sure' that preceded it, when the couple took hands in the hope that the other would 'use them well', after which they often went ahead and lived together. Susannah Shakespeare was born in due season, to a father just turned nineteen, who then, by the time he was twenty-one, saw twins arrive, Judith and the intriguingly named Hamnet – female-male twins like Viola and Sebastian in *Twelfth Night*, 'both born in an hour', but, life being unlike art in this, presumably not identical.

Soon after this Shakespeare left home, amicably or not, and he again stays off the radar until he resurfaces in London seven years later. Open season for conjecture again: military enthusiasts say he became a soldier, nautical fans a sailor; he may have been a country schoolmaster or even a government agent – this was a man who could convincingly think himself into any character he chose. My own theory reflects my bias likewise, though I'm not alone in it: having all his life seen travelling theatre troupes passing through Stratford (as an alderman John would always have got good seats), Shakespeare may have run away and hitched up with a company such as the Queen's Men, the major touring group of the day. He would thus have begun the life of an actor on the road – travelling, fitting up, playing, dismantling and travelling on – that Ben Jonson described in *The Poetaster* as

> going with pumps full of gravel after a blind jade and a hamper,
> and stalk upon boards and barrel heads to an old cracked trumpet.

The Queen's Men certainly visited Stratford when Shakespeare was twenty-three. One of their actors had been killed in a pub brawl at the previous date, Oxford, and there is a suggestion that Shakespeare offered himself as the replacement. I wonder what the audition involved, whether he was any good, or whether, under the circumstances, anybody would have done. Later on, tradition has it that he tended to play older parts – the Ghost in *Hamlet*, Adam in *As You Like It*, the King in *Henry IV* – so perhaps he was already what the modern industry calls Juvenile Character, the type of young actor who has to smile sweetly when he is told that he will come into his own later in life.

The attractively racy story is rendered a bit too good to be true by the fact that the dead actor was also called William. More convincingly, we know that in the repertoire of the Queen's Men there were anonymous old plays with suspiciously familiar titles – *The Taming of A Shrew*, *The Troublesome Reign of King John* – as well as versions of the *Titus Andronicus* and *Hamlet* stories. So it's tempting to imagine Shakespeare the actor spending a couple of years struggling to make such warhorses work on the stage, all the time dreaming of how their writing could be improved: after all, his own career would be based on recycling old tales. Perhaps he was the company member who kept complaining about the script – not a popular figure as a rule, but you can imagine the frustration in Shakespeare's case when you come across lines like these in a thing called *The Famous Victories of Henry V*, as the King urges his troops into the battle of Agincourt:

> Why then with one voice and like true English hearts
> With me throw up your caps, and for England,
> Cry St George, and God, and St George help us.

So Shakespeare as a touring actor – where's the evidence? Nowhere to be found. But I choose to find a clue buried deep inside his sequence of 154 sonnets, probably composed at various times between the late 1580s and 1609. These formal but intensely emotional poems are in any case notoriously interpretable. Assumed by some to be purely literary exercises with no personal content – one of Shakespeare's ways of keeping solvent and visible whenever plague closed the theatres – they can also be seen as providing a running commentary on his love life. A number are written with great erotic candour to a woman we've come to think of as the Dark Lady, but at least as many are addressed to a heartbreakingly beautiful young man who may or may not have been the Earl of Southampton – or more plausibly, William Herbert Earl of Pembroke.

Such is the general nervousness about coming face to face here with the reality of Shakespeare himself that in a 1640 edition all the amorous addresses to the young man were carefully re-gendered so that they were safely aimed at the woman. This homophobic travesty is finally counterbalanced by the remarkable claim of Katherine Duncan-Jones in her recent – and otherwise excellent – Arden edition of the Sonnets, that the poems have been so heterosexualised that we overlook the fact that only a 'lunar cycle' of 28 is addressed to the woman, leaving 126 to the boy. This is part, it must be said, of a numerological interpretation of the whole sequence, some examples of which ('our minutes' as a pun on 'hour minutes' in Sonnet 60) are unlikely to win many converts, while others (the first poem after 'three score and ten', i.e. Number 71, speaking of the time immediately after the poet's death) are intriguing. This kind of exercise will certainly separate sheep from goats among its readers, and is entirely typical of the Sonnet controversy. When it comes to the lunar cycle argument, it does strike me that since many of the 126 may on the face of it have been written to either man or woman ('friend' was used for a lover of either sex in Elizabethan English), and since it would perhaps be out of character for Shakespeare to keep a punctilious tally and allow himself only 28 to the woman for fear of breaking the menstrual norm, there could be a little pre-emptive reasoning involved here.

What there certainly is in the sequence – and here I go as well – is a little run about being away from home, travelling and then returning with or without a good conscience; and three poems in particular touch on a matter very familiar to actors. Rather, two matters: first, the suspicion that we cheapen our emotions by making a living out of them, and second, the uncomfortable truth that what an actor experiences on the stage can for the moment seem more powerful and authentic to him than the day-to-day. And as for life on the road, it's a fact that touring actors don't always behave as they might, though they probably do no worse in this regard than businessmen or airline pilots. In my experience there are two kinds of travelling actors. The first, let's call them the middle-aged marrieds, are in a permanent lather of homesickness, dispatching fretful emails and texts – somewhat like Shakespeare's rival Edward Alleyn, who at one point adds an anxious PS to a letter to his wife about the inadequacy of the one she's just written him:

> You sent me not word of my garden, but next time you will.

The others, usually young ones like Shakespeare, might meanwhile be available for romance. In Sonnet 109 the matter seems at first no more than a painful separation followed by a happy homecoming:

> O never say that I was false of heart,
> Though absence seemed my flame to qualify;
> As easy might I from myself depart
> As from my soul, which in thy breast dost lie;
> That is my home of love; if I have rang'd,
> Like him that travels, I return again;
> Just to the time, not with the time exchang'd,
> So that myself bring water for my stain…

So far so normal, even if a little shadowed by the dissonance of 'false... qualify... rang'd... stain'. But, as if he'd just given something away, in the next two sonnets the author explains to whoever has stayed at home that this was all to do with the peculiar nature of his work – the

> public means which public manners breeds.

In any case, he is still faithful in his fashion:

> Alas 'tis true I have gone here and there,
> And made myself a motley to the view,
> Gor'd mine own thoughts, sold cheap what is most dear,
> Made old offences of affections new;
> Most true it is that I have looked on truth
> Askance and strangely; but, by all above,
> These blenches gave my heart another youth,
> And worse essays prov'd thee my best of love.
> Now all is done, save what shall have no end;
> Mine appetite I never more will grind
> On newer proof, to try an older friend;
> A god in love, to whom I am confin'd.
> Then give me welcome, next my heaven the best,
> Even to thy pure and most most loving breast.

The ugly note won't go away – 'gor'd', 'sold cheap' and – above all – 'grind'. This is an unusual degree of self-dislike for an actor simply describing the paradox of his job: there is a distinct hint of sexual consolation on the road.

And what would you think of such a coded apology if you were Anne Hathaway – or the fair friend – stuck at home? Puzzling over the poem, if she did, she would come face to face with the glorious frustration we all feel about Shakespeare, always – his manipulation of metaphor to the point that it becomes an alternative reality. It would have been difficult for Shakespeare's nearest and dearest to know exactly what his sonnet meant. He could always claim the licence of storytelling: and with his general gift of the gab, I suspect he may have got away with it anyway.

If indeed he kept coming home to Anne, he didn't stay for long, and at twenty-eight he hit London for sure. Perhaps he approached from Stratford, south to Oxford and then south-eastwards to our Marble Arch (where the first thing that greeted him would have been Tyburn Gallows); he would then have had to elect, as per today's roadsigns, either Westminster or the City. Or perhaps, back from a tour with the Queen's Men, he came in from the south, more directly to where he would end up, through Blackheath and Southwark and over London Bridge; London Bridge, which was a little like the Rialto Bridge in Venice now, packed with houses and shops, a church and even a public lavatory hanging precipitately out over the river. A traveller entering the bridge from the south had to pass through a great gate, above which stood poles impaling the heads of executed traitors, glaring down at the new arrivals – one of them belonging to a remote Catholic cousin of Shakespeare's, John Somerville, who in 1583 had conceived a nutty plan to kill Queen Elizabeth, which he made nuttier by telling everyone about it in advance. So that was one family connection Shakespeare wouldn't have wanted to underline.

London was called a great theatre, the fair that lasts all year, and you could smell it as far away as Windsor. But apart from in the obvious ways, it must have been much as it is now: the perfect place to get lost in if you were on the run from something, as Shakespeare may have been from his family, but also the perfect place to be lonely in. Nobody knew you, and you were worth no more, as the saying went, 'than a piss in the Thames'. And rather as an Italian arriving in New York would at one time have headed for Little Italy, I can see Shakespeare gravitating towards the theatre district of Shoreditch (John Aubrey, for what he's worth, records him as living near the High Street) – an extremely rackety and Bohemian area where the playwrights Christopher Marlowe and Thomas Kyd lived, as well as the comedian Richard Tarlton, the pamphleteer Robert Greene (soon to be one of the inspirations for Falstaff), and the family of the young Richard Burbage, who would become Shakespeare's star actor. For by now his head is bursting with lines of his own that he wants other actors to speak, not those of worse writers he must struggle with as an actor himself; it's as if we can suddenly hear, piercing all the noise and filth and chaos and feculence of London in the 1590s, a new voice singing like a sweet violin:

> What light is light, if Silvia be not seen?
> What joy is joy, if Silvia be not by?
> Unless it be to think that she is by,
> And feed upon the shadow of perfection.
> Except I be by Silvia in the night
> There is no music in the nightingale;
> Unless I look on Silvia in the day
> There is no day for me to look upon.
> She is my essence, and I leave to be
> If I be not by her fair influence
> Foster'd, illumin'd, cherish'd, kept alive.

This simple catchy music comes from Valentine in *The Two Gentlemen of Verona*, possibly the first Shakespeare play to see the foggy light of London day. It's a lightweight exercise to be sure, but sometimes a deeper music begins to sound. Not only because Proteus, Valentine's best friend who falls for Silvia himself, confides in us with the appalled maturity of the treacherous Angelo in *Measure for Measure*, but because the betrayal causes the honest Valentine to start the long journey of a true Shakespeare hero through disillusionment, sorrow and anger to a pantheistic stoicism away from the eyes of men. It is the rite of passage endured by Posthumus in *Cymbeline* but without the self-reproach, or by a more amiable Timon of Athens. Valentine ends up living in the woods off his own resources, in the company of a group of outlaws:

> How use doth breed a habit in a man!
> This shadowy desert, unfrequented woods,
> I better brook than flourishing peopled towns.
> Here can I sit alone, unseen of any,
> And to the nightingale's complaining notes
> Tune my distresses and record my woes...

Shakespeare being Shakespeare, the play contains a deep contrast. As we wait for Valentine improbably to forgive Proteus his treachery – with such enthusiasm that he also offers him Silvia as a gesture of friendship – Shakespeare has brought a dog onto the stage. *The Two Gentlemen of Verona* may be mainly concerned with highly narcissistic love among humans, but a different kind of affection exists between Proteus's servant Launce and the miraculous Crab:

> one that I saved from drowning, when three or four of his blind brothers and sisters went to it... I have sat in the stocks for puddings he hath stolen, otherwise he had been executed; I have stood on the pillory for geese he hath killed...

But, Launce insists, the feeling is all one way: Crab's flinty heart in the face of these kindnesses is his running theme. He is shocked by the dog's callousness as he takes leave of his family before reluctantly setting off for Milan with Proteus (it is not only dogs who have unpredictable masters):

> my mother weeping, my father wailing, my sister crying, our maid howling, our cat wringing her hands, and all our house in a great perplexity, yet did not this cruel-hearted cur shed one tear.

However, nemesis seems to be in store for Crab: once in Milan, he is in danger of being sent by Proteus as a clandestine lover's gift to Silvia, who is the Duke's daughter. He saves his bacon with a uniquely canine revenge:

> LAUNCE: He thrusts me himself into the company of three or four gentleman-like dogs under the Duke's table. He had not been there – bless the mark – a pissing-while, but all the chamber smelt him… Did not I bid thee still mark me and do as I do? When didst thou see me heave up my leg and make water against a gentlewoman's farthingale?

Dogs were no strangers to the Elizabethan stage. It's thought that the jig that followed all performances of Shakespeare's plays (even *King Lear*) may sometimes have featured a troupe of dancing dogs. But had anyone made such a feature of one before? I doubt it. Shakespeare is starting something here which certainly had consequences: in *The Witch of Edmonton* (1621, Dekker, Rowley and Ford) the Devil turns up disguised as a dog.

Crab conforms to an important technique of vaudeville: precondition the audience and they will laugh at anything. I recently saw a very brilliant French mime who ventured to do impersonations of various types of cheese. There, you're interested already. He gave his Camembert a sort of shamefaced self-loathing, low and squat, as if his pungency embarrassed him; the English cheddar was rather upright and noble. From then on the mime could do no wrong. Yes, we cried, that's a Bresse Bleu exactly; oh yes of course, a Taleggio, I've always thought that. Crab works like that too: to the relief of subsequent casting directors, Launce's part is written in such a way that whatever Crab does, and is, is funny. Accused of ingratitude, whether he just sits there morosely, scratches and sniffs, bounds about, looks at the audience or blankly at Launce, it is equally good.

Shakespeare is of course well ahead of his time in this. A couple of centuries later Crab would have flourished in music hall as a speciality act – the Mind-Reading Dog or the Talking Dog; and he is perhaps a less manageable cousin of the ventriloquist's dummy, that other means of putting words into an uncomprehending mouth. Indeed the comedy of the vent lies in the cussed independence of the dummy, which may relapse into the same stubborn silences as Crab. And of course a real dog on the stage exemplifies the immemorial mournful warning of W.C. Fields never to work with anything on four legs. Though biddable for small tasks, a dog is not much of a dissembler; and a theatre holds as many interesting distractions as a toy shop does for a child. In a recent production at the Open Air Theatre in London's Regent's Park, the fact that a barbecue was cooking throughout the evening in the foyer bar led to some interesting chases for Crab – off down the grassy slope at the front of the stage and right up the central aisle to the front of house, pursued by Launce and sometimes members of the audience. The Rose, if that is where the first *Two Gentlemen* played, can hardly have been less attractive, with its rich mélange of aromatic refreshments – cheese, spice, meat pies and roasted thrushes.

Will Kempe, who played Launce, may often have used a dog in his act regardless of the play, so he deserves some credit for Crab. However, in co-opting the idea, Shakespeare may have improved the quality of Kempe's patter, and it could be seen as a way of taking control for good of an ungovernable clown who, to Hamlet's disgust, perhaps spoke a good deal more than was set down for him. It's not known whether Kempe was involved in what was also developing in Shakespeare's mind – the complex calculations of farce for *The Comedy of Errors*, which follows the fortunes of two pairs of identical twins. The romantic cadences of *The Two Gentlemen* were broken by Proteus's attempt to rape Silvia; and *The Comedy of Errors*, like all good farces, sails close to tragedy when a harmless quack, Doctor Pinch, is burned nearly to death, while mistaken identity leads one of the protagonists' wives to sleep with the wrong man – a final indiscretion that most later farceurs skilfully avoid. Or does she? It's left to you to guess, but if so this is a rare and striking example of female adultery during the course of a Shakespeare play.

Actually *Comedy* contains the germs of everything that came to obsess Shakespeare – the separation of families, the working of chance, the longing for a secular miracle. When Adriana denounces her husband Antipholus for his infidelity, it is with a moral outrage that might occur to Paulina in *The Winter's Tale* twenty years later, but also with the sexual explicitness of the mad King Lear, her imagery suggesting Antipholus has infected her with physical disease; she is then reproached by the Abbess for the destructive force of her jealousy very much as Othello will be by Emilia. The pile-up of mistaken identities is deeply perturbing, like the night in the forest for the lovers in *A Midsummer Night's Dream*; but it is also brilliantly constructed and extremely funny. At one point Dromio of Syracuse describes to his master, the other Antipholus, his life on the run from a woman who in fact has mistaken him for his twin brother and is now claiming him as her man:

DROMIO: I have but lean luck in the match, yet she is a wondrous fat marriage.

ANTIPHOLUS: How dost thou mean, a fat marriage?

DROMIO: Marry sir, she's the kitchen wench and all grease, and I know not what use to put her to but to make a lamp of her, and run from her by her own light...

ANTIPHOLUS: What complexion is she of?

DROMIO: Swart, like my shoe, but her face nothing like so clean kept...

ANTIPHOLUS: [And] she bears some breadth?

DROMIO: No longer from head to foot than from hip to hip: she is spherical, like a globe: I could find out countries in her.

ANTIPHOLUS: In what part of her body stands Ireland?

DROMIO: Marry, sir, in her buttocks: I found it out by the bogs.

ANTIPHOLUS: Where Scotland?

DROMIO: I found it by the barrenness, hard in the palm of the hand...

ANTIPHOLUS: Where England?

DROMIO: I looked for the chalky cliffs, but I could find no whiteness in them...

ANTIPHOLUS: Where Spain?

DROMIO: Faith, I saw it not; but I felt it hot in her breath.

ANTIPHOLUS: Where America, the Indies?

DROMIO: O sir, upon her nose, all o'er-embellished with rubies, carbuncles, sapphires, declining their rich aspect to the hot breath of Spain...

ANTIPHOLUS: Where stood Belgia, the Netherlands?

DROMIO: O sir, I did not look so low.

So there's an early profile of England's national poet: sizeist, sexist, apparently chauvinistic and extremely dirty-minded. The play is set in Ephesus sometime in the past, but really this is London in the 1590s, so full of foreigners that it was described by one visitor as sounding like a swarm of bees; a city that was probably more multi-ethnic than at any time afterwards until today. The writing of *Comedy of Errors* certainly coincided with a great deal of xenophobic activity in London. Anti-immigrant graffiti were appearing, in particular against the industrious Huguenots (French Protestants) who had escaped Catholic persecution in France and gained a foothold here, especially in areas like Shoreditch, which lay outside the city's jurisdiction. It's a familiar story: London's guarded welcome to these migrants had turned to resentment, particularly against those who seemed reluctant to integrate: the barely veiled threats of violence expressed a fear of lost jobs and resources. Shakespeare, sidestepping as ever, leaves the French out of Dromio's list; but still, if he was working for an audience that included Spaniards and Scots and Irish, this was a provocative piece of writing which nowadays might get him sued for incitement. On the other hand, if he was playing simply to an English crowd, they would surely have loved this sop to their ambiguous feelings about the strangers – part appreciation of an enriching culture, part fear of the outsider. So: inclusiveness and diversity, 1590s style; and who knows what Shakespeare might have come up with if he'd been writing *The Comedy of Errors* in a World Cup year.

Theatrically, however, he had arrived at exactly the right time: a contemporary visitor to London reported that 'to pass over grief, the Italians sing, the French sleep, the Germans drink, the English go to plays'. There had been no such thing as a theatre, in the sense of a permanent building dedicated to the job, when Shakespeare was growing up: actors had generally played in innyards, bear-baiting arenas, guild halls, off the backs of their carts. But now, although the Globe was still in the future, a short walk in Shoreditch would have brought him to The Theatre, the city's first permanent custom-built playhouse, erected in 1576 by Richard Burbage's father James and a businessman, John Brayne. Next to The Theatre was the Curtain; in Southwark there was the Rose, and, also south of the river, a playhouse (sometimes claimed as the earliest of all) at Newington Butts. The City of London was bordered by its ancient walls, and was a tiny area of perhaps four square miles, from Temple to the Tower, from Moorgate to the Thames; the new structures were going up just outside its limits to avoid the jurisdiction of the City Fathers, who were inclined to equate playhouses with brothels. Not unreasonably – many of the men who owned the first also presided over the second.

In the sensationally competitive new industry, the playhouses demanded product, as much and as fast as possible, to feed a daily changing repertoire – which a permanent company and an absence of sets made practical as long as the actors learned their lines fast. The writers had to work at speed, to collaborate if necessary and adjust their scripts on the hoof – no copyright law, no second, third and fourth drafts or preparatory workshops – and, once delivered, they had to be prepared to see them cut and revised according to the space they were to be played in and the actors involved. Not to mention the time of day. In summer a show would start at 3 p.m. (2 p.m. in the winter); so the Chorus in *Romeo and Juliet* is delivering a stern and precise warning to his cast as well as reassurance to his audience when he speaks of 'the two hours' traffic of our stage'. Apart from the minor alliteration, 'three' or 'four' would have fitted Shakespeare's verse line just as well, so two is exactly what he meant. Actually, a running time of two hours is simply not possible for that play without heavy cutting; performed at its published length, however fast, *Romeo and Juliet* might have left its audience as fearful of being abandoned in the dark as its heroine before her incarceration in the Capulets' tomb. So it seems certain that the printed versions of Shakespeare's plays that we now rely on are less what the audience generally heard than an omnibus edition of all possible variants drawn from their performance history thus far. In which case it's also possible that Shakespeare's tendency to pile on the similes and subordinate clauses was not so much a temperamental profligacy as a way of offering two or three alternatives to choose from. King John goes to his death in the grip of unimaginable fever –

> Ay, marry, now my soul hath elbow room...
> There is so hot a summer in my bosom
> That all my bowels crumble up to dust:
> I am a scribbled form drawn with a pen
> Upon a parchment, and against this fire
> Do I shrink up...
> And none of you will bid the winter come
> To thrust his icy fingers in my maw...
> The tackle of my heart is crack'd and burnt
> And all the shrouds wherewith my life should sail
> Are turned to one thread, one little hair;
> My heart hath one poor string to stay it by

– but perhaps the contemporary audience, as opposed to today's reader, only got one or two from this splay of wonderful images.

As it turned out, nobody was better equipped to deal with all these circumstances than Shakespeare; as a practising actor, he knew the hard realities better than most playwrights, who sometimes didn't bother to see their plays in performance at all. His instinct for both the demotic and the metaphysical was also timely: for the first time outside of the Mystery Plays, an audience was gathering not only to be entertained but to think. The structure of the new buildings both served and formed his writing: they all had much the same design, being round or polygonal and enclosing a courtyard open to the sky, with a three-sided stage sticking like a tongue into its centre. This platform was in an almost literal sense suspended between heaven and hell: the canopy above it, which was really there to keep the sun and the rain off, was known to everyone as the heavens, while the area beneath, reached through a trapdoor, was universally known as the hell. So whatever the story being told on it – comedy, tragedy, tragical-comical-historical-pastoral – the stage would have reflected, however lightly, man's position in the universe. Shakespeare's ability to allow comedy to take on mortal significance and to make mortality seem a joke was ideal for such a 'theatre of the world', which also generated an obsessive volume of theatre imagery within the plays.

Meanwhile his double profession as actor and writer – and so double income – must have irritated the hell out of the literary Establishment, such as it was; partly because the English don't much like all-rounders in the arts, but also because playwrights were notoriously badly paid, whereas actors, perhaps for the last time in history, were rewarded relatively well. Indeed the first we hear of Shakespeare in London comes from the infuriated Robert Greene, also annoyed perhaps for another, less worthy reason: like most of his colleagues, he was university trained, and here was a Warwickshire grammar school boy come to upstage them all – at least the reigning star Christopher Marlowe had made up for his poor background by going to Cambridge:

> There is an upstart crow, beautified with our feathers, that with
> his 'tiger's heart wrapp'd in a player's hide' supposes he is as
> well able to bombast out a blank verse as the best of you; and...
> is in his own conceit the only Shake-scene in a country.

Apart from getting himself a place in the history books which he might not otherwise have secured, Greene was giving Shakespeare free publicity here – with a small adjustment we can recognise the 'tiger's heart wrapp'd in a player's hide' as a line from the play we now know as *Henry VI Part Three*, which was showing at the time.

What had happened was this. As London's new arrival started looking about him, he must have seen that there could be a fashion for heroic two-part plays like Marlowe's *Tamburlaine*, premiered in 1587 and now (1592) entering its second printed edition. Accordingly his *First Part of the Contention of the Two Famous Houses of York and Lancaster with the Death of Good King Humphrey* – the play we now know as *Henry VI Part Two* – was published in 1594, having probably premiered around 1592; it was followed by *The True Tragedy of Richard Duke of York and the Death of Good King Henry VI with the Whole Contention Between the Two Houses Lancaster and York* (*Henry VI Part Three* to you and me) in 1595. The current critical wisdom is that *Henry VI Part One* was then, despite its name, a follow-up, completing a trilogy and capitalising on the success of the earlier two plays. This has some logic, if only because Shakespeare was nothing if not an opportunist: some years later, the Chorus would conclude *Henry V* with a fond reminder of the next episode of the story 'which oft our stage hath shown', thereby paving the way for a revival of these earlier plays. Only some logic, though: it is fairly clear that whereas *Part Two* and *Part Three* are Shakespeare's own work, there are several hands involved in the writing of *Part One* – which raises the question of why, having had a success with the first two on his own, he would have collaborated with inferior writers for what turned out to be quite a shaky prequel. It is also hard in the reading to believe that the first play written (*Part Two*, above) would have begun with Suffolk's arrival from France with Margaret and her marriage to Henry VI, with nothing about the new reign established first.

In truth, the only opening in the three plays that feels like a real beginning is that of *Part One*, which presents the accession of Henry V's young son – extremely effectively when staged, as often these days, within a continuous cycle of the Histories, so that the audience has, an hour or two before, seen the hero of Agincourt at the peak of his career and now returns to find his coffin at the centre of the stage. Shakespeare could never have envisaged such a literal image for the simple reason that he didn't have a full sequence in mind: the cliffhanging eight-play cycle that runs from *Richard II* to *Richard III* is all the more remarkable for the fact that, a little like George Lucas's *Star Wars*, it was created out of order. If you regard *Richard II* as chronologically No 1 and *Richard III* as No 8, most probably the order of composition was: 5–6–7–8–1–2–3–4.

In modern practice, the two parts of *Henry IV* and *Henry V*, despite being the last three written, hint at their historical successors the most readily; the two bookends, *Richard II* and *Richard III*, oblige the least, partly because they both have more of the star vehicle about them than state-of-the-nation play. However that is a minor problem compared with what to do about the general unevenness of *Henry VI* – especially *Part One*: such writers' committee jobs of the time, in which the authors tinkered with each other's work or lobbed in a scene or two of their own, are baffling to us in an age when most playwrights demonstrate acute occupational *amour propre*. But working on the result can be like panning for gold – for all their messiness, deep within the *Henry VI*s lies a seam of passionate narrative and metaphor that could only have come from one hand, even if that hand from time to time needs restraining, and the mind that prompts it calming down a little.

✦

PLANTAGENET: Hath not thy rose a canker, Somerset?
SOMERSET: Hath not thy rose a thorn, Plantagenet?

– Henry VI Part One

Henry V's coffin or not, *Henry VI Part One* opens with the funeral of the great warrior, a character Shakespeare will attend to a few years later. The play investigates such things as the efforts of his brother, the Protector Humphrey of Gloucester, to defend the King's pacific young son, now Henry VI, and those of the Earl of Suffolk to engineer Henry's marriage to Margaret of Anjou – Suffolk's *quid pro quo* for this service being Margaret's sexual favours. The Cabinet conspiracy that eventually brings Gloucester down leaves the new King, isolated in a loveless marriage, exposed to his political enemies as well. Crucially, there is a trivial scrap early on in the Temple Gardens in the Inns of Court in London which leads to momentous consequences: the division of the country into adherents of the red rose and the white, the two irreconcilable parties of Lancaster and York. There is more metaphorical play on the warlike and virtuous properties of the two factions than clear explanation of their quarrel. That has to wait for a helpful history lesson near the start of *Part Three* which reminds us that the whole royal inheritance issue links back to Henry IV's usurpation from 'that sweet lovely rose', Richard II – another matter that Shakespeare will return to in due course.

So the sins of the grandfathers are to be visited even on such peacemakers as Henry VI; and it is quickly evident that, born to carry a shepherd's crook rather than a sceptre, he is quite unable to resolve political partisanships. He is equally ill-equipped to emulate his father on the international stage. The French, smelling his weakness, are intent on reclaiming Henry V's annexations: domestic and foreign conflicts nastily intermesh when the military hero Sir John Talbot is brought down in the middle of his French campaign because of the failure of Somerset and York, locked into their roseate allegiances, to send him reinforcements. Talbot himself and the French champion Joan la Pucelle (Pucelle, meaning virgin, being the name that Joan of Arc gave herself) dominate the play in energy if not in intelligence; the image of the red rose and the white typify the play's style, which pitches irreconcilables against each other in primary colours, bludgeoning responses from the audience like an overamplified piece of musical theatre. The unswervingly loyal Humphrey squares up to the equally immovable Grand Guignol Bishop of Winchester; Somerset spits insults at York; the xenophobically handled Joan of Arc confronts the unimpeachably chivalrous Talbot.

Even if the pen is passing casually between Shakespeare, Thomas Kyd and Thomas Nashe, you know where it is at the good moments. In contrast to the surrounding din, the pious King Henry speaks with a limpid rationality, like quiet organ music –

> I see no reason, if I wear this rose,
> That anyone should therefore be suspicious
> I more incline to Somerset than York;
> Both are my kinsmen and I love them both...

The betrayed Talbot, the first of several fathers bereaved of their sons in battle, is allowed to lift off into sympathetic verse when he realises his loss –

> And in that sea of blood my boy did drench
> His over-mounting spirit; and there died
> My Icarus, my blossom, in his pride

– while La Pucelle shows surprising philosophical grace:

> Glory is like a circle in the water
> Which never ceaseth to enlarge itself
> Till by broad spreading it disperse to nought.

This is exceptional however: in general Shakespeare's treatment of Joan is a disappointing case of the writer as time-server, happy to reflect Tudor propaganda. She is even given a group of fiends who appear at her bidding but who in her hour of need, being fiends (and perhaps French as well), withdraw their help.

Since the height of his collaborators' achievement is Shakespeare's starting point, you would expect still greater unevenness; but in general it is as if a quango of writers were obeying an overbearing commission and trying to imitate each other. The shared aim is so direct that a man's unchanging character can usually be deduced from helpful introductions:

> KING HENRY: Is this the lord Talbot, uncle Gloucester,
> That hath so long been resident in France?...
> When I was young (as yet I am not old)
> I do remember how my father said
> A stouter champion never handled sword.

What more do you need to know? Henry VI is too young to rule; his father was a good judge of a soldier; Talbot is everything an English bulldog should be. Nobody confounds expectation, and there is little counterpoint between reputation and reality; no room for doubt, and no reason for the audience to question their preconceptions. *Henry VI Part One* is momentous in a slightly forced manner, unequivocally bustling forward; nothing much wrong with it in a way, but nothing much to be expected of it either – and nothing very interesting or complex to act in it, apart perhaps from the gently burgeoning title role.

✦

> For where thou art, there is the world itself...
> And where thou art not, desolation.

> *– Henry VI Part Two*

Part Two, however, returning to domestic politics, has real horsepower. Margaret of Anjou arrives to marry the young King without a dowry, having been shipped over from France at England's cost: the Earl of Suffolk, who has closed the deal, has, perhaps blinded by love, also sacrificed the English interest in Anjou and Maine to pacify her father. So naturally he's not popular at home, though less hated in this nest of vipers than the good, if self-satisfied, Duke Humphrey of Gloucester. When Gloucester's wife Eleanor is found to have been consulting necromancers, the scandal leaves him exposed to his enemies, and he is duly murdered at Suffolk's and Winchester's behest. (This sequence paid off particularly well in performance when Nancy Reagan was found to have been consulting an astrologer for advice on the presidential schedule.) Oddly though, the predictions from the discredited seance Eleanor has attended – that Suffolk's eventual death will be associated with water, that Somerset should 'shun castles' and that Henry will be deposed by York but outlive him before dying violently – will, though uttered by conmen, all turn out to be true. Buried too deep for the audience to remember in performance, this is an early moment of Shakespearian mischief.

With Gloucester's passing, the old regime is dead and gone, leaving ample space for Queen Margaret, already chafing at her husband's guilelessness, to stretch her wings. Meanwhile what little King Henry does in office is well-intentioned but incautious. He packs the Duke of York off to Ireland to quell a rebellion, an ideal opportunity for York to raise an army, return and make an assault on the Crown. The rest of the nobles are hardly more trustworthy: their disloyalty and opportunism are the play's commonplace, as the undesirability of the French was that of *Part One*. Nor does either play present us with any women we would want to spend more than five minutes with.

However there are some strong Shakespeare mechanisms already at work, particularly in the role of Henry VI himself. Deeply religious, with an unanswerable decency the court has to put up with without irritably catching each other's eyes, he is initially annoying for the audience as well. He mouths virtuous saws, fails to see through a clumsy trick practised on him by an apparently blind cripple claiming a miraculous cure, and reminds us at every opportunity of how unhappy power is making him. Gradually he accomplishes a series of kingly things, if rather in the manner of his times than ours: he condemns to death the 'witches' who organised Eleanor's seance, but Eleanor herself – being 'nobly born' – only to internal banishment; and he personally dismisses Gloucester, his favourite uncle, as a political liability. He is also smart enough to sense Suffolk's involvement in Gloucester's death before anyone else – except, that is, the citizenry on the streets, who with similar instincts reach the same conclusion and make short work of Suffolk.

In this matter of Gloucester you feel for the first time internal conflicts entirely missing from *Part One*. The grief Henry expresses even as he disposes of him causes his verse to bloom. Though still confined to convention, it has a rhapsodic, sharp-witted momentum:

> Ah uncle Humphrey, in thy face I see
> The map of honour, truth and loyalty...
> And as the butcher takes away the calf
> And binds the wretch, and beats it when it strays,
> Beating it to the bloody slaughterhouse,
> Even so remorseless have they borne him hence;
> And as the dam runs lowing up and down,
> Looking the way her harmless young one went,
> And can do nought but wail her darling's loss
> Even so myself bewails good Gloucester's case...

So the young Shakespeare is easing comfortably into his stride. Certain situations inspire him more than others – the iconic fall of a good man, the moment when a political dilemma becomes humanly intolerable, or when one or another kind of love is thwarted; the latter especially so when disappointment tilts into malediction. So the discredited Suffolk faces separation from Margaret:

> Now by the ground that I am banish'd from
> Well could I curse away a winter's night
> Though standing naked on a mountain top
> Where biting cold would never let grass grow
> And think it but a minute spent in sport...
> For where thou art there is the world itself
> With every several pleasure in the world
> And where thou art not, desolation.

The style of this is still constrained by the form Shakespeare has inherited: its insistent rhythm more or less dictates the emphasis and clinches the sense at every line's end – experimentation in the playing will cause the meaning to buckle. The *Henry VI*s lend authority to the insistence of some directors that a breath should only (and always) be taken at the end of a verse line. Actors sometimes chafe at this, but it does make sense in sixteenth-century Shakespeare – unlike his seventeenth-century manner, when he allows his arguments to expand and contract in the heat so that you can hardly sense the metrical pinions at all. An uncanny young musician, Shakespeare is starting with Dixieland before discovering free-form jazz; in the playing of Bach, he is an Edwin Fischer who turns into Glenn Gould.

Also in *Part Two*, in prose much less constrained, is something quite new – the galvanic story of the rebel leader Jack Cade. A likely recruit picked up by York in Ireland to cause trouble to the King, he is announced by his paymaster with a shortened blank verse line all to himself, a warning of things to come:

> I have seduc'd a headstrong Kentishman,
> John Cade of Ashford,
> To make commotion, as full well he can,
> Under the title of John Mortimer.
> In Ireland have I seen this stubborn Cade
> Oppose himself against a troop of kerns,
> And fought so long till that his thighs with darts
> Were almost like a sharp-quill'd porpentine;
> And in the end being rescued, I have seen
> Him caper upright like a wild Morisco
> Shaking the bloody darts as he his bells.

This fearsome figure is based on the real-life insurrectionist who led an army from Kent to London in protest against high taxes and weak government – and against the loss of France, to which he was specially sensitive as returning soldiers were pouring home through his county with dismal stories of the campaign. Arriving in London, the historical Cade struck London Stone and declared himself Lord Mayor before setting about looting the city; eventually he was captured, killed and quartered, and his head put up above London Bridge (perhaps to be succeeded a century later, the carrion crows having done their work, by Shakespeare's incompetent cousin John Somerville). King Henry was so alarmed by Cade that he retreated to Warwickshire, and in Shakespeare's play Cade puts the wind up him even after death: as Henry remembers him with a shudder, his mental picture, like York's farouche imagery, is unusually specific. Shakespeare tended to leave appearances to the imagination unless they were particularly good value theatrically, like those of Falstaff or Richard III. But Cade has

> A visage stern, coal black his curled locks,
> Deep trenched furrows in his frowning brow,
> Presageth war-like humours in his life.

However, there is one major – and characteristic – adjustment of the story. The original Cade had some support from the gentry and landowners as well: the idea that the current Establishment had squandered Henry V's achievements was also common in court circles. Shakespeare ignores that and makes Cade's a thuggish and illiterate popular uprising with all associated ills.

I played Cade in the 1980s, and liked him – as an actor, I mean: we put him into a Union Jack T-shirt, gave him a skin-tone like Johnny Rotten's and the nastiest machete-like weapon I could arm myself with; his porcupine darts and curly black locks became the spiked hair of a punk hero in a hellish shade of copper. 'You're going to get your fuckin' head kicked in,' whooped my followers – this was a couple of years after the riots at the Heysel stadium in Brussels at the European Cup Final which resulted in a five-year ban on English clubs' participation. As a matter of interest it was also three years after the Miners' Strike, which had Cade's county at its heart.

As a debased Hotspur, a junior in *Henry VI*'s cast of malcontents, Cade is a weird compound of reactionary and revolutionary politics, of the demotic instinct (as long as he is in charge of it) and sheer preposterousness. The audience is certainly not encouraged to take him very seriously at first. He arrives declaring a romantic claim to the throne as the son of a lost twin fathered by Edmund Mortimer, obliged by his disinheritance to take up manual labour. In knockabout style, he is discredited at every turn by his own right-hand man, Dick the Butcher:

CADE: My father was a Mortimer.

DICK: He was an honest man and a good bricklayer.

CADE: My mother a Plantagenet.

DICK: I knew her well, she was a midwife...

CADE: Therefore am I of an honourable house.

DICK: Ay by my faith, the field is honourable, and there was
he born, under a hedge.

However, Cade soon develops a tawdry splendour, not least because of his knack with an audience: cheerfully admitting in asides that his story is all a pack of lies, he crudely anticipates Richard III's collusions. He is an admirer of Henry V, and thus a conservative in his populist clothing, inheriting from the great man's legend an instinctive jingoism; he dislikes the Italians and the Dutch, and invents a typical Frenchman as 'Monsieur Besmoncu' (literally 'kiss my arse'). For the time being, he is content to dub himself a knight, and, out of respect for Henry V, to let Henry VI reign as long as he, Cade, is made the King's new Protector (imagine them together).

But this is a man with a long-term vision: England under the eventual Jack the First will be a utopia in which there is no money except his own, with which he will start a running tab for the whole nation. All his subjects will wear one uniform and therefore 'agree like brothers', especially in their worship of 'me their lord'. His horse will graze in Cheapside, he will exercise *droit de seigneur* on the women of England; all lawyers will be put to death, and his crowning piece of legislation will be an upgrade for the Cornhill drinking fountain, notorious for its feeble flow; the new order will be that

> the Pissing Conduit run nothing but claret wine this first year
> of my reign.

He also insists on a ban on reading and writing, and it is less enjoyable to watch him hanging a harmless clerk for being capable of signing his name. He gives his lieutenants licence to kill at random and open all the prisons, drags the King's messengers through the streets at his horse's heels, and makes the decapitated heads of his victims kiss each other: this is a tatterdemalion Robespierre linking Terror with Virtue. Still, there is a certain thoughtfulness in him, and his muddled argument against educational inequality arises from a respectable enough levelling instinct:

> Ah thou Say, thou serge, nay, thou buckram lord... I am the
> besom that must sweep the court clean of such filth as thou art.

> Thou hast most traitorously corrupted the youth of this realm
> in erecting a grammar school; and whereas before our fathers
> had no other books but the score and the tally thou hast caused
> printing to be used, and contrary to the king, his crown and
> dignity, thou hast built a paper mill... thou hast men about thee
> that usually talk of a noun and a verb, and such abominable
> words as no Christian ear can endure to hear.

Eventually he is abandoned by his followers and makes a run for it. It is hard not to feel something for him when, going to ground in Kent and so halfway back to his native earth, he hides in a gentleman's nursery garden, living on grass and salad leaves:

> These five days have I hid me in these woods, and dare not peep
> out.

Treated kindly by the owner but unable to understand such a thing, he gives his life away by provoking him:

> I'll make thee eat iron like an ostrich, and swallow my sword
> like a great pin...

It's a strangely picturesque death ('tell Kent from me, she hath lost her best man'), gallant in a completely futile way. The King and everybody else may feel Cade deserves to be decapitated, buried in a dunghill and sent to hell; but it's clear that he has stirred Shakespeare's curious imagination without dislodging his lifelong distrust of the working man as a political force.

✦

> I have no brother, I am like no brother;
> And this word Love, which greybeards call divine,
> Be resident in men like one another
> And not in me. I am myself alone...
>
> *– Henry VI Part Three*

However jerky the momentum of the first two plays, there's never been much doubt about the furious energies of *Henry VI Part Three*. It is an inferno stoked with knotty political debate and remorseless betrayal; not just what *King John*'s Bastard will call a 'mad world, mad kings, mad composition', but England on the rack, action and reaction endlessly rotating, the plainsong of the King and his leaderless commons just audible above the noise.

Like its predecessors, *Part Three* needs cutting. It comes with a heavy burden of early Shakespearian imagery – improbably eloquent soldiers talk ad nauseam of lions, serpents and hinds, of wolves surrounding lambs; but with ruthless pruning unexpected benefits appear, and the fact that almost everyone sounds much the same paradoxically becomes part of the play's strength. It is as if the company has become sisters and brothers in liturgical verse, trying to remake an England in the image of Henry V: the language in which to mourn or celebrate the national idea is shared by everyone, from the nobles to the two gamekeepers who finally arrest King Henry.

In its third part, *Henry VI*'s earlier rituals of filial revenge deteriorate into self-righteous spitefulness. Young Clifford, a figure looming out of the fog of civil war as if he had been created by it, goes on a rampage to avenge his father's death at the hands of York; as he predicted at the end of *Part Two* his emotions have been neatly and unthinkingly transferred by that event:

> Even at this sight
> My heart is turn'd to stone, and while 'tis mine
> It shall be stony...
> Henceforth I will not have to do with pity.

He and Queen Margaret, now grown into one of Shakespeare's biggest hitters, capture York, stand him on a molehill, torment and kill him: later, York's three sons, completing a pointless circle of violence, take copycat revenge by murdering Margaret's son Edward before her eyes. Like Clifford, they are driven not by principle but a Pavlovian rage, and hardly behave like brothers at all: by now allegiances mean nothing, *amour propre* everything. It's what Nietzsche called 'sublime malice'. So the erratic middle brother Clarence announces his disapproval of brother Edward's choice of wife by briefly becoming a Lancastrian, then changes back again. Edward's champion Warwick, on hearing of Edward's decision – and thus made a fool of in the middle of wooing a French princess on his behalf – joins up with Queen Margaret on the spot, to the amazement of the French court and no doubt the amusement of the audience. The red and white roses, once so loyally plucked in the Temple Garden, are swapped at will or tossed insouciantly aside: changing sides with farcical speed, protagonists wearing one favour speak with the same barefaced oratory as they did moments ago when wearing another. Whereas you could once believe – just – that some principle of royal succession might be at stake, such matters are barely mentioned at all: there seems to be no moral position of any kind, just the gloomy criminal determination to do your utmost and to take leave with belligerent fatalism:

> Thus yields the cedar to the axe's edge,
> Whose arms gave shelter to the princely eagle...
> Why what is pomp, rule, reign but earth and dust?
> And live we how we can, yet die we must.

Still just audible at the heart of the violence is the music of King Henry himself, who never stops telling the truth. In an extraordinary and experimental scene – the play's only famous one – he sits on a molehill to confide gently in us, his only possible friends, that his wife and the raging Clifford

> Have chid me from the battle, swearing both
> They prosper best of all when I am thence...

He is joined by the anonymous figures of a Son Who Has Killed His Father and a Father Who Has Killed His Son: the Son has been pressed into battle by the King, the Father by the Yorkists. Both now dread what their women – respectively mother and wife – will say about the cross-party catastrophe they've perpetrated. Rather as music takes over in opera because language can't suffice, the scene modulates into a formal trio of sorrow (or in visual terms a religious triptych), condensing the nation's accumulated suffering. At its centre Henry, who has already come as close to nihilism as he dared –

> Would I were dead, if God's good will were so

– finally loses the deference of a believer and his pacifism breaks its banks:

> O that my death would stay these ruthful deeds!
> O pity, pity, gentle heaven, pity!
> The red rose and the white are on his face...

'O pity, pity'... 'Desdemona, dead, dead'... 'O false Cressid, false, false, false!' These are precious moments in Shakespeare where language fails, a pause in which Homer is unable to sing.

✦

Almost 400 years after the *Henry VI*s were first played, their venue, the Rose Theatre, in Southwark by the Thames, was excavated, in a pause between the clearance of the site and the building of an office block. During the weekend before the bulldozing many of our profession headed down there and pitched camp, led by Peggy Ashcroft – a cross for the occasion between Shakespeare's Queen Margaret and King Canute – and filibustered to anyone who'd listen. The braver spirits lay down in the road to stop the bulldozers working on Monday morning – much to the amusement of the drivers, who naturally backed off and went for tea. The upshot was that the Rose was spared, and the office block built on stilts above it.

Brief journalistic reports then mentioned the odd pipe, hazelnut, and, rather improbably, armadillo shell having come to light. A good deal more than that surfaced as time went by. Listen to this: fragments at least of candlesticks, chafing dishes, pipkins and porringers (one inscribed 'Drink and eat but do not forget God'), money boxes for the take, rings, German, Spanish and Dutch ceramics, glass urine sample bottles such as Falstaff sends to the doctor, buttons, ribbons and sleeves, nearly seven hundred headdress pins, a ring inscribed 'Think of me God willing', beads, highly coloured by the manganese inside them, a two-sided ivory comb with some teeth broken off (just like yours and mine), an iron razor with a handle of antler bone, a glass make-up mirror, a spoon with the maker's name, a long-handled iron fork or 'sucket for sweetmeats' (imagine poking Turkish Delight out of a box), dice, fish hooks, Elizabeth I coins from 1d to 6d, gaming tokens, a cannon ball, the bones of thrush and fish and dog and brown bear, and – most eloquent of all – shoes: smallish and round-toed, both slip-on and laced, simply stitched in all shapes and sizes, babies', women's and men's, all bent with use, one with a hole in the toe perhaps to accommodate a bunion, boots both buskin and full length. Green turtle shells (they ate the meat and threw away the shell) and other evidence of conspicuous consumption, fruit seeds, many glass beakers, clay pipes with the makers' initials on them, some standing for Bachelor and Culpepper (they smoked them once and threw them away), hazelnut shells (both refreshment, and at various stages used as hard core in the surface of the yard). It's like one of those comic Shakespearian lists of pedlar's wares or the accoutrements of someone's horse, with a sudden short punchline at the end. Oh yes, and a thousand iron nails.

Here, in its mixture of audience accessories and, no doubt, stage props, was the real whiff of an afternoon show four hundred years ago. When the *Henry VI*s played here, they were an enormous hit: London had never heard anything quite like them before. On 3 March 1592, one of the trilogy is cheerfully recorded in the accounts of Philip Henslowe, the theatre's manager, as taking £3.16s.8d. This is a favourite anecdote, but actually it's only part of the story: even with an audience paying as little as ld it's hardly a full house in a theatre we know to have held nearly 2,000, which would therefore have been able to take about £8. Important to add that Henslowe, in building the Rose, had had to cope with a Mr John Chomley who had a house on the site and astutely claimed 50 per cent of the take, and Henslowe may have been recording only his half.

At any rate it was better than a play of Marlowe or Kyd had ever done. Shakespeare had learned much from these two contemporaries, but there was something else: within his surging language, a more human voice was prodding away at the audience. The overall rolling style was certainly reminiscent of Marlowe's, but already Shakespeare held a card in his hand that Marlowe never had; his ability, in the words of Feste in *Twelfth Night*, to sing both high and low.

He plays it in the early stages of *Part Three*. First Queen Margaret kills York's youngest son Rutland – another luckless Shakespearian child – who, coming face to face with the unequivocal Clifford, has none of Prince Arthur's luck with Hubert:

> RUTLAND: Ah, let me live in prison all my days…
>
> CLIFFORD: Thy father slew my father; therefore die

– whereupon Rutland expires with a Latin tag on his lips. The Lancastrians then capture his father, stand him on his molehill, and with the aid of a paper crown and a napkin dipped in the boy's blood Margaret exacts this revenge:

> What, was it you that would be England's King?…
> Where are your mess of sons to back you now?
> The wanton Edward and the lusty George,
> And where's that valiant crookback prodigy,
> Dickie your boy, that with his grumbling voice
> Was wont to cheer his dad in mutinies?
> Or, with the rest, where is your darling Rutland?
> Look, York, I stain'd this napkin with the blood
> That valiant Clifford with his rapier's point
> Made issue from the bosom of the boy;
> And if thine eyes can water for his death
> I give thee this to dry thy cheeks withal…
> I prithee grieve to make me merry, York.
> What, hath thy fiery heart so parch'd thine entrails
> That not a tear can fall for Rutland's death?…
> Stamp, rave and fret that I may sing and dance…
> York cannot speak unless he wear a crown.
> A crown for York! And lords, bow low to him.

The power of her onslaught is in its sheer lack of qualification. She makes a precise equation between York's grief and her merriment: his desperate pummelling of the earth would translate automatically into song and dance for her. In the theatre, such reckless, mysterious absolutism is riveting. What is the purpose of the awful ritual, and who is its audience? Thus far in the war Margaret has no personal loss to avenge – she simply sees York's designs on her husband's crown as a blasphemy, light years from any justified claim. If she is demonstrating something to her followers she is setting the bar very high – so much so that a good production will allow her companions to support her with varying degrees of enthusiasm, concealing any doubts if ever her eye swings onto them.

Margaret's exultant, brutal transgressiveness – like that of Marlowe's Tamburlaine – becomes, as it turns out, the only weapon in York's tethered hands: she so distorts human values that he can swiftly turn her boasts back onto her. He sees that her failure of grace and self-control shames her sex:

> She-wolf of France, but worse than wolves of France,
> Whose tongue more poisons than the adder's tooth!...
> But that thy face is visor-like, unchanging...
> I would essay, proud Queen, to make thee blush...
> 'Tis beauty that doth oft make women proud,
> But God he knows thy share thereof is small.
> 'Tis virtue that doth make them most admired;
> The contrary doth make thee wonder'd at.
> 'Tis government that make them seem divine
> The want thereof makes thee abominable...
> O tiger's heart wrapp'd in a woman's hide!
> How couldst thou drain the life blood of the child
> To bid the father wipe his eyes withal
> And yet be seen to wear a woman's face?...
> Bid'st thou me rage? Why, now thou hast thy wish.
> Wouldst have me weep? Why, now thou hast thy will...
> That face of his the hungry cannibals
> Would not have touch'd, would not have stain'd with blood;
> But you are more inhuman, more inexorable,
> O ten times more, than tigers of Hyrcania.
> See, ruthless Queen, a hapless father's tears;
> This cloth thou dipp'st in blood of my sweet boy
> And I with tears do wash the blood away...

For a moment it's as if he had won: it is so devastating that Margaret has to shut his mouth the only way she can, by slicing off his head. When the moment comes, perhaps she feels it almost as a defeat.

As the Rose began to surface, the other surprise was that it was very small. It held 2,000 people; but the courtyard, let alone the stage within it, was only about twelve metres across. So could it be that Margaret and York, for all their extremity, played as quietly as we now might in a theatre of three hundred? No doubt the actors knew how to barnstorm, but with the audience right on top of them, they may also have mastered what we would recognise as a delicate, cinematic style. We have the idea that Elizabethan actors were hams – maybe we confuse them with the Victorians – but I would bet that Shakespeare's company knew very well how to handle the extremes he presented them with – or if they didn't they quickly learned to.

If so, coaxed into the scene rather than assaulted by it, the spectator could have spotted the characters' interplay as if in close-up. Any audience spends as much time looking at the addressee as at the speaker: perhaps they saw Margaret, once the paper crown was in place on York's head, turning against the image she had created – she is married to the notoriously weak Henry VI, who might well be characterised as a king in a paper crown. They could have observed her face and the grades in her voice as she pushed and pushed for a reaction from York, which – in retaliation – he withholds; and how, when he finally lets her have it, it withers even her. As he mops Rutland's blood all over his face York's passion is so eloquent that the mute Earl of Northumberland, perhaps a father himself, is moved to tears. Will Margaret, a mother, also weaken and spare York? Nothing in the lines implies it, but it could be seen subtly to cross her mind, and the fact that she silences him so suddenly suggests the miserable cost to her of her own life, the sheer difficulty of keeping her own company.

Under such scrutiny, complicated possibilities swirl into, around and between the lines; the actors are no longer dealing with a predicated rhetorical form but with as many variations as the situation might present in life. I think that the reason Shakespeare moved so quickly beyond Marlowe and Kyd was that the actor in him instinctively understood the scope of the playhouses he was working in. Marlowe could certainly have delivered the grandeur of the she-wolf of France and the tiger's heart in a woman's hide; but I don't think he would have had the versatility to suggest the petty grumbling voice of Dickie, cheering on his dad from the terraces, or managed the surprisingly simple effect of York's tears mixing with the bloodied handkerchief, the one diluting and thinning the other like stained laundry under a tap. Shakespeare outstrips his contemporaries by registering not only the corrupt heroics of the scene but its intimate detail.

In time, his knack of switching from mid-shot to close-up in a split second will become one of his best effects. A character reaching an emotional emergency will, instead of taking off into the descriptive blue, be stunned into banal monosyllables, idiosyncratic fragments, almost off the point. In *Macbeth* Malcolm reacts to the news that his father is murdered with 'O, by whom?'; Laertes to his sister's drowning in *Hamlet* with 'O, where?'. In the final moments of *King Lear*, Lear stumbles on with the dead Cordelia in his arms, and just as he's about to die himself he has a little trouble with his own or her clothing and has to appeal to a mute attendant soldier:

> Pray you, undo this button; thank you, sir.

In a related way, in *Henry IV Part Two*, Mistress Quickly says goodbye to her beloved Falstaff, who is leaving for the wars:

> Well, fare thee well; I have known thee these twenty-nine years
> come peascod time, but an honester and truer-hearted man –
> well, fare thee well.

The detail is in the twenty-nine years – not a round thirty or twenty-five, and in fact not quite twenty-nine until 'peascod time', when the peas finally form in their pods. And I don't see Marlowe being empathetic enough to let her start with 'fare thee well', then struggle to express her love for Falstaff, see that she hasn't the language for it, and end up where she started.

What a gift this kind of detail is for the actor. As soon as language develops such a range, a whole new acting style – flexible, vernacular, intimate – can grow up alongside it. However, the trick took time to perfect: Shakespeare doesn't always pull it off in the 1590s. In the scene from *Titus Andronicus* in which young Lucius tries to look after his inordinate handless grandfather, Titus's brother Marcus suddenly strikes a dish with his knife; asked what it is he is aiming at, he admits it is a fly. Titus becomes furious, feeling that the world doesn't need further violence towards the innocent:

> But how if that fly had a father and mother?...
> Poor harmless fly,
> That with his pretty buzzing melody
> Came here to make us merry. And thou hast kill'd him.

Then Marcus has a rhetorical brainwave:

> MARCUS: Pardon me sir, it was a black ill-favour'd fly
> Like to the Empress' Moor; therefore I kill'd him.

TITUS: O, O, O!
>   Then pardon me for reprehending thee
>   For thou hast done a charitable deed.

The Empress Tamora and her black lover Aaron are the family's sworn enemies; and the fly is now seen, with effortless racism, as taunting the whiteness of the Andronici. Apart from the lousy verse – the line about the fly's father and mother may be Shakespeare's worst – it's a not unpromising idea, this crazy distortion brought on by grief; it's just that it's clumsily delivered, the fly crushed by the weight of its sudden significance as much as by Marcus's knife.

However, flies are just the start of it: in *Henry VI* and its sequel, Shakespeare finds an easy means of introducing guttering candles, barking dogs, thorny woods at night, looking glasses and ladies' laps, even the specially good strawberries in the Bishop of Ely's garden, into his epic account of England's continuing crisis. And he has sensed something else, related to this and still more important. One day it will lead to the electrifying moment when Hamlet dismisses Rosencrantz and Guildenstern, turns and says 'Now I am alone' – to two thousand people. Exhausted by the wrong kind of company, the troubled Prince of Denmark means it literally. But he is also dropping out of his part and letting the play change from one thing into another. It's as if some figure on a platform comes down into the crowd, weaves through it and approaches you alone, fixing you with his eye. It may be good or bad news, but there is no escape.

Already sidling into *Henry VI Part Two* and *Part Three* is someone very like this: a vaudevillian of implacable logic who takes psychological subtlety and audience manipulation to a new level. Armed with Shakespeare's technique and sheer force of personality, dwelling on every detail of his own anatomy with fascinated shock, he repeatedly steps out of the action and buttonholes us, simultaneously scaring us and articulating our own malevolent desires. As he does, he moves the entire history project into another light.

3

Myself Alone

The Soloists – Richard III – King John

The buttonholing soliloquy was not a new idea. Kyd and Marlowe had made use of it, and Shakespeare had tried it with Proteus in *The Two Gentlemen of Verona*. In *Henry VI Part Three* he extends the convention hugely. The actor, using a new linguistic range, can now treat the audience either as confidential friends or as an alien crowd, whisper in their ears or rattle the roof. The rule seems to be that if a single character is alone with us, we get the truth: a Shakespearian soliloquiser never lies. What would be the point? He knows we won't betray his confidence to anyone because we're not in the play that he or she has stepped half out of. I was once challenged on this by a scholarly type who claimed that Iago tells the audience a lie when, attempting to justify himself to us, he claims to suspect that his wife is sleeping with Othello. I don't think so. Iago is jealous of everyone, and his obsessive invention of a preposterous new intrigue tells us a good deal about the state of his mind, which is at least as suspicious as Othello's.

In the audience, the inside knowledge we gain from a soliloquy gives us a new, if limited, authority. We are now better informed than the other characters in the play but powerless to influence events: we can no more help Viola, trapped in her secret love, than save the victims of Richard III. The qualities of introversion and secrecy, of not quite saying what you mean or meaning what you say, come into their own in a later theatre than Shakespeare's; but Brutus, Hamlet and Bottom share their preoccupations with disarming candour. It is impossible to escape from heroes or villains so eager for company.

Especially villains. At this early stage of Shakespeare's career it is not the good guys who get his best attentions in this but the outsiders, loners and transgressors. The likes of Proteus, and Aaron in *Titus*, get most of the soliloquy time, dark figures who warn us of Edmund and Thersites to come – or of Iago, who, rather than Othello, compulsively talks to the audience. The less compunction they show about what they are up to, the more fascinated we are. We are taken by their simultaneous lack of empathy with their victims and chumminess with us: for some reason we find this flattering. Later, we will gather more clearly than anyone inside the play that Macbeth is able to unseam his enemies from the nave to the chaps in the line of business but can't cope with the consequences of the one murder he really wants to do. By contrast, Richard III, so forsaken by love from the start that he seems to have no human feelings at all, finds it only too easy.

Richard of course is what York's grumbling boy Dickie turns into. By the beginning of *Henry VI Part Three* he is already pushing himself out of the patchwork. Within a few minutes of the play's opening, he throws a decapitated head onto the floor of Parliament; as if in answer, three suns briefly appear in the sky to symbolise his and his brothers' rise. Innocent of scruple, he shows this reaction to his father's death:

> I cannot weep, for all my body's moisture
> Scarce serves to quench my furnace-burning heart...
> Tears then for babes; blows and revenge for me.

Bereavement sets Richard free: while his brothers Clarence and Edward become conventional fighting soldiers, he blossoms into a self-knowing, self-wondering force of nature. With the triumvirate of York brothers in the ascendant, he reluctantly accepts the dukedom of Gloucester after observing that the title is ominous: well, yes, indeed. The Lancastrian Margaret calls him a 'valiant crookback prodigy', the first of many startling epithets he will inspire. He continues to be admired by everyone on his own side as a trusted comrade-in-arms, a brave soldier, long-suffering under his physical disabilities and a much loved brother. But don't be deceived. He watches his sibling Edward leave the stage and turns to us; as his face changes we realise that his enemies know him better than his friends:

> Would he were wasted, marrow, bones and all,
> That from his loins no hopeful branch may spring
> To cross me from the golden time I look for...

This is a sound we haven't heard in Shakespeare before – the antihero sucking energy from his own solitude. Why does he have to? Because

> love forswore me in my mother's womb:
> And for I should not deal in her soft laws,
> She did corrupt frail nature with some bribe,
> To shrink mine arm up like a wither'd shrub;
> To make an envious mountain on my back...
> To shape my legs of an unequal size,
> To disproportion me in every part,
> Like to a chaos, or an unlick'd bear-whelp
> That carries no impression like the dam...
> For I have often heard my mother say
> I came into the world with my legs forward...
> The midwife wonder'd, and the women cried,
> O Jesus bless us, he is born with teeth...

In blistering, almost interactive soliloquy, he lays out his wares, speaking of himself with something like awe: we're complicit from the start. He rakes his audience, cajoling and implicating, his language swaying and straining against the metre:

> Then since this earth affords no joy to me
> But to command, to check, to o'erbear such
> As are of better person than myself,
> I'll make my heaven to dream upon the crown...
> And yet I know not how to get the crown
> For many lives stand between me and home;
> And I, like one lost in a thorny wood
> That rents the thorns, and is rent with the thorns,
> Seeking a way, and straying from the way,
> Not knowing how to find the open air,
> But toiling desperately to find it out,
> Torment myself to catch the English crown;
> And from that torment I will free myself
> Or hew my way out with a bloody axe.
> Why, I can smile, and murder while I smile...
> And wet my cheeks with artificial tears,
> And frame my face to all occasions...
> Can I do this, and cannot get a crown?
> Tut, were it further off, I'd pluck it down.

Being 'sudden if a thing comes in his head', he impulsively visits King Henry in the Tower; no one else has the will to do what he can in a moment. Henry knows the meaning of his arrival: his Christian charity falters and he reiterates Richard's account of himself:

> The owl shriek'd at thy birth, an evil sign;
> The night-crow cried, aboding luckless time;
> Dogs howl'd and hideous tempest shook down trees...
> Thy mother felt more than a mother's pain
> And yet brought forth less than a mother's hope.
> To wit an indigested and deformed lump,
> Not like the fruit of such a goodly tree.

It is very exhilarating to hear this from such a saintly mouth, before it is as abruptly silenced by Richard as Richard's father's was by Henry's Queen on his molehill. Chucking the body 'in another room' the killer hurries away to find brother Edward, with the war over, finally installed on the throne; by now we know Richard's real plans for him too. There they stand, the whole clan, with a Queen and a baby for King Edward as well. York is gone but his sons, standing side by side, represent three aspects of him: 'lascivious Edward', the golden boy with a special weakness when sexually attracted; 'perjured Clarence', unreliable, witty and self-centred; and 'misshapen Dick', his deformity seen by Shakespeare's audience as matching the sickness in his heart. So, with barely a pause in his conversation with us and in no doubt at all of his capability, Richard shunts *Part Three* onto the play that will bear his name.

✦

> The Cat, the Rat, and Lovel the Dog
> Shall rule all England under the Hog...

> – Contemporary lampoon used in
> Laurence Olivier's film of *Richard III*

For all its energy and popularity – and the vitality of the protagonist's relationship with us – *Richard III* suffers from a certain division of focus. The debate about civil war, rights of succession and the consequences of the past rumbles on, but a little distantly, overtaken by Shakespeare's fascination with his new character. One with enormous box office appeal, too: Richard III probably gave Richard Burbage his first star part for the Lord Chamberlain's Men, formed when the theatres reopened in 1594 after a long period of plague, and the role has remained a magnet for actors ever since.

But the audience does have to keep adjusting: is this a thriller with the villain as star or a historical play for a company? Characters talk

compulsively about the past when we'd rather they got on with the plotting, murdering and recoiling; but if they didn't, we would feel the lack
of a context in which such an exotically toxic plant as Richard has
grown. The back story is reiterated mainly by Margaret and the play's
other widows, Queen Elizabeth and the Duchess of York, who forever
lament their lost families; as they are largely unknown to an audience
which hasn't been at the *Henry VIs*, this is not a potent theatrical device.
The leader of the Chorus, Queen Margaret, in retirement after the civil
war, observes how

> prosperity begins to mellow
> And drop into the rotten mouth of death.

She has taken on the role of ringside prophet, where her complaints are
sometimes as wearing for the audience as for the court. Rather as the
discredited seance in *Henry VI Part Two* turned out to be accurate,
Margaret, routinely condemned by everyone as mad, correctly predicts
each of their fates: all who die at Richard's hands will remember her
prophecy in their last moments. Those of us who do know how things
have come to this pass listen patiently, perhaps regretting that we are no
longer in Richard looking at a soldier of some vitality, but, by a damning
consensus, at a 'poisonous bunch-backed toad', a 'bottled spider', an
'abortive rooting hog' – one whom stage practice increasingly presents as
a man who could never inspire the beginnings of trust or indeed last five
minutes on a battlefield.

By now Shakespeare seems primarily interested in Richard's diabolical technique as he discovers that he can succeed not so much by
brutality but force of intellect and will. Like Iago, he operates through
showmanship, skilful delegation and opportunism. Part of his equipment is that he is, in the best totalitarian traditions, an intellectual – in
the sense that a strategist and salesman can be an intellectual. He can
play wit-games with the best; he is classically trained, a master quibbler
and well briefed in the law. His chutzpah immediately reveals the cracks
in both his brothers' personalities. He allows 'ancient prophecies, libels
and dreams' to reach the ears of King Edward to the effect that someone with the initial G will disinherit him – but manages to divert
attention from G for Gloucester to G for George of Clarence. As a result
Edward, 'sickly, weak and melancholy' from an unnamed 'evil diet' (as
obvious a euphemism for syphilis as I can think of), sentences Clarence
to death, only to recant – too late, because Richard has swiftly taken
advantage of the original edict, laying the blame on the family of

Edward's Queen, Elizabeth. Edward despairs: in a last breath of superb equivocation, he blames the entire court for Clarence's death because none of them tried to change his kingly mind at the moment of sentence. He is dying because, unlike Richard, he cannot endure his own breaches of brotherly love, so in effect Richard has murdered him from a distance as well. As for Clarence himself, one of the play's few respites from Richard's overbearing character is a wonderful speech in prison describing a guilty dream in which his malevolent brother pitches him into the sea and he meets all his wartime victims in its depths; he is rewarded for the telling by the arrival of Richard's two murderers, who are no more nor less murderers than Clarence has been himself. (His pleas to them for his life are as long drawn out as Arthur's in the near-contemporary scene with Hubert in *King John* – Shakespeare liked this type of last-ditch resourcefulness.)

Richard goes on to discredit the entire opposition. He claims everyone is illegitimate, including his dead brother; he cites witchcraft at the drop of a hat; with Edward out of the way, he insists that the Queen and her family have been responsible for his own physical deformities, which of course long pre-date her. In *Henry VI*, as a cripple bonded to his womanising brother, it was a miserable thought to him that to

make my heaven in a lady's lap

was harder to achieve than 'twenty golden crowns'. Now, in his own play, he finds himself in full sexual flow, transformed into 'a jolly thriving wooer' by his remarkable success with women, who fall over like ninepins before him. First Anne, wooed over the coffin of her father-in-law (and Richard's victim) Henry VI, agrees to marry him despite her certain knowledge that he has also killed her husband, young Edward Prince of Wales; later in the play Edward IV's widow, flattered by his appeal to her social ambitions, and perhaps by his provoking description of her daughter's womb as a 'nest of spicery', brings her to his side in Anne's place. Richard has found the key at last: no wonder he now considers himself 'to be a marvellous proper man' and sets off to hire forty tailors and become a dedicated follower of fashion.

As he edges ever closer to the throne, the Mayor and citizenry of London have to be dealt with: in theory at least, they must accept him as King rather than Edward IV's son and heir. Richard handles this part of his project like a master. The Mayor is first privately presented with full evidence of his intent – the severed head of Hastings, who has stubbornly continued to support young Edward: a clear enough hint of

potential sanction, like the horse's head in the movie producer's bed in
The Godfather. While looking into the dead man's hollow eyes the Mayor
finds himself changing his long-held view that Hastings was an honourable man and accepting the fiction that he conspired against Richard
and so deserved to die. The adjustment is exemplary: the Mayor goes so
far as to say he expected no better of the man in view of his choice of
girlfriend:

> Now fair befall you! He deserv'd his death…
> I never look'd for better at his hands
> After he once fell in with Mistress Shore.

It's a short step from that to his promising to warn the public of the justice of Hastings's death, so that blame should not fall on Richard. Then
the scrivener called in to draft the indictment of Hastings notes – alone
with us but no doubt with an eye over his shoulder – that by the time
he'd finished the work Hastings had already been dead five hours.

A long virtuosic sequence follows in which the people are persuaded
to accept Richard – a scene notable for their complete silence and the
mock-piety of the candidate. Sporting a prayer book between two monks
as if parodying Henry VI, he declares his unwillingness to be forced 'to a
world of cares' till the very last moment – till they are about to give up
and go home, in fact. It is quite a funny scene for an audience that has
never actually experienced surveillance and censorship; but I have played
in *Richard III* in parts of the world where a dictator prepared to subvert
religion and a people for whom freedom of choice is a distant memory
seem a poor joke. For this is totalitarianism in detail, planning and effect;
corralled at Baynard's Castle in the City of London (now, ironically, that
place of connectivity, a telephone exchange), the citizens feel the air bris-
tling with possible reprisals if they don't oblige. Hushed and nervous, we
see through them the dawning regime of Richard III with absolute clarity: he will make ordinary people outsiders in their own lives.

Richard only becomes King two-thirds of the way through the play,
which is so inordinately long that his Coronation could almost be its end;
and, were it not for the interminable scene in which the three Queens again
lament their fate (a typical Shakespearian Act Four longueur), there would
be very little of his reign being dealt with. Shakespeare has been mainly
interested in the campaign of barefaced cheek whereby he got there – so
what's left except some routine form of remorse? Or if not remorse, a
deepening flaw. Richard always thought his strength derived from being
'myself alone'; but cut off from human counterpoint, he eventually found

he needed help. His best luck in this line has been his alliance with the 'high-revolving witty Buckingham', his one relationship in the play.

Not that this was any kind of love affair, being based on Buckingham's need to back the right political horse and Richard's need for Buckingham's brains. This man, a terrific early study of the supple political fixer, is bribed by a future promise of land when Richard becomes King, and offers himself as his spin doctor. He masterminds the removal of Edward's young children from sanctuary so that Richard can imprison them in the Tower and then presents himself at Baynard's Castle as spokesman of the citizens (to their cowed surprise). The velvet glove on Richard's iron fist, Buckingham will always be able to reinterpret his activities for the increasingly alarmed electorate. Richard can get no further without him; and when, on the throne, he ignores his promise of land to Buckingham and insists that he dispose of his nephews in the Tower (where they are hardly a threat any more), he loses him.

Buckingham is of course rapidly dispensed with – he raises a futile rebellion and then goes the way of all Richard's critics; but Richard is the victim too, significantly losing his touch once Buckingham is gone. With so many murderous projects and marital strategies in hand, he begins to show signs of disorder – forgetting to brief his servants on what errands they are to run before dispatching them, beating up messengers and issuing paranoid threats. With the fulfilment of his hopes, it is as if his personality, lacking sustenance, begins to disintegrate. This is not the same as second thoughts: in a play full of murderers with some conscience – Clarence's two killers, and the Princes' three – Richard, with undiluted sadism, asks to know the exact 'process' of the children's death. Truly imagining witchcraft everywhere, he pays attention to quibbling prophecies just as he once encouraged Edward to do. He ends up at Bosworth Field with not even a semblance of companionship, contradicting his existential toughness by seeing significance in the sun's refusal to rise over the battlefield. Here he is visited on the night before the conflict by his victims' ghosts (as characteristically predicted by Margaret) and deals with his terror by means of a rattled casuistry, in a speech not unlike the effort of Richard II in Pomfret prison to assemble a human personality for himself. Unable to shed his self-dramatising character, Richard III has less success: unlike his namesake he gives it up as a bad job and goes to a less gallant death, pleading for a horse.

Only now, having done his duty by Richard's fall as well as his rise, does Shakespeare remind us of the overarching purpose of his History project: he is getting a little close to his own time, so it contains more than a degree of time-serving. The entire sequence closes with Henry of Richmond pledging national reconciliation. Richmond is technically a Lancastrian, but he is resolving civil war by marrying a Yorkist, the daughter of Edward IV. Together, as Henry VII and Elizabeth, they will found a new dynasty, the Tudor, the one under which Shakespeare's audience lived, and for whom the more disgraceful the portrait of Richard III could be made and the more heroic that of Queen Elizabeth's somewhat ambiguous grandfather Henry VII, the better. As he addresses the nation Richmond sounds hauntingly like Henry VI on his molehill:

> England hath long been mad and scarr'd herself;
> The brother blindly shed the brother's blood;
> The father rashly slaughter'd his own son,
> The son, compell'd, been butcher to the sire...

We sense both the cruel length of the struggle and how convenient the resolution is. The people of England can be imagined standing eloquently silent before Richmond, thinking their own thoughts, just as they did when, citizenry without a chance, they were hoodwinked by Buckingham and Richard at Baynard's Castle. As Richmond speaks, the recently dead tyrant suddenly seems a distant part of history. It is England that counts after all; the brothers and sisters, the tradesmen, officials and the powerless people. Their weaknesses have been exposed and mercilessly exploited; worst of all, as with most tyrannies, they themselves have opened the door to the tyrant. Now there is a hint of hope, or at least stability: *Richard III* has turned out to be a state of the nation play after all.

✦

> For he is but a bastard to the time
> That doth not smack of observation.

– King John

There is another early Shakespearian outsider, not a destroyer but one who enters the system and could even become a national hero – the king indeed – were it not for an awkwardness about his birth less painful than Richard's disability but more decisive. He operates in a play titled after a cutprice Richard III: King John never comes alive as King Richard does, because facility with an audience is given not to him but to Philip Falconbridge.

Falconbridge's separateness is defined by honest illegitimacy. He stands alone in front of the audience for *King John*, acting as their touchstone, and in many ways makes the play bearable, rendering its turgid rhetoric human when he can. He is a boisterous swill of Shakespearian motifs. He taunts his enemies much as Gratiano does Shylock; his fantasising about life at court – disdaining to recall people's names, sucking his teeth and engaging in chit-chat with foreign visitors – sounds like Malvolio dreaming of life as Olivia's husband, or perhaps the popinjay courtier despised by Hotspur on the battlefield in *Henry IV* – though Falconbridge also sounds like Hotspur himself. In his dogged, conventional patriotism, he oddly prefigures Henry V as well.

This is the first of Shakespeare's two big Bastards – the other being the far more destructive figure of Edmund in *Lear*, at the other end of his career, whom Falconbridge also mildly resembles in his dedication to his own interests. He is all paradox: a careerist who despises *Realpolitik*; a plain speaker who acknowledges expediency; opportunistic but loyal to the Crown even while disgusted by the craven accommodations of the King. An entirely non-historical inspiration, he is boldly imagined as the product of a brief amour between Richard the Lionheart, King John's brother, and Lady Falconbridge, conceived while her husband was away fighting on Richard's behalf. Lady Falconbridge is thus, like Adriana in *The Comedy of Errors*, that rarity in Shakespeare, an unfaithful wife; but Adriana did it by mistake, and Lady Falconbridge before the play begins, so perhaps it doesn't count. In any case her son shows a proper appreciation of her daring:

> Madam, I would not wish a better father:
> Some sins do bear their privilege on earth
> And so doth yours; your fault was not your folly.

Being thus descended 'one way of the Plantagenets' and referred to as the Bastard at almost all times, Philip arrives in the play to have the matter of his inheritance settled; but he is distracted from his claim by an impetuously awarded knighthood and an invitation to go to war with the King, to whom his cheek (and perhaps his skill with rhyming couplets) recommends him:

> Why, what a madcap hath heaven lent us here!

Having inherited his father's way with the ladies, he is also taken up by King John's and Richard Lionheart's mother Queen Eleanor (of Aquitaine), his grandmother in the eyes of God. He declares that he had

never wanted to 'be Sir Nob'; but intrigued with court life, prepares to
relaunch himself as an aristocrat. His game plan is that of any Shakespearian schemer:

> this is worshipful society
> And fits the mounting spirit like myself...
> Well, whiles I am a beggar, I will rail,
> And say there is no sin but to be rich;
> And being rich, my virtue then shall be
> To say there is no vice but beggary.

He arrives on the French battlefield with an odd mixture of bellicosity
and pacifism – on the one hand decapitating the relatively harmless Duke
of Austria, but also advising the French and English to end their stupid
squabbling over the succession and to unite. Perhaps he is licensed
because of his fearsome loyalty to the King's cause, or perhaps because
he is the one actual son of the Lionheart to be seen – if he were only
legitimate, the crown would be his, rather than either John's or Arthur's.

In peacetime, Falconbridge takes on the questionable role of the
King's fixer. Not that there is much diplomacy involved. One of his
assignments is to ransack the churches on John's behalf, at which point
our belief in him as a moral compass may falter a little:

> JOHN: See thou shake the bags
> Of hoarding abbots; imprison'd angels
> Set at liberty; the fat ribs of peace
> Must by the hungry now be fed upon...
>
> BASTARD: Bell, book and candle shall not drive me back,
> When gold and silver becks me to come on.

However, the conflicts in his role become critical. He is disgusted by
the possibility that John may have caused Arthur's death, but equally
so by the defection of John's lords, and he sees England sliding towards
civil war:

> I am amaz'd methinks, and lose my way
> Among the thorns and dangers of this world...
>   England now is left
> To tug and scamble and to part by th' teeth
> The unow'd interest of proud swelling state;
> Now for the bare-pick'd bone of majesty
> Doth dogged war bristle his angry crest
> And snarleth in the gentle eyes of peace...
>   and vast confusion waits

> As doth a raven on a sick-fall'n beast
> The imminent decay of wrested pomp.
> Now happy he whose cloak and cincture can
> Hold out this tempest...
> A thousand businesses are brief in hand,
> And heaven itself doth frown upon the land.

This speech is in quite a new register, of experience and passion, and for me clinches the Bastard's supremacy in the play.

It also exemplifies Shakespeare's growing ability to characterise through styles of speech: the vocal mix in *King John* is strikingly sophisticated for such an early work, much more so than in *Henry VI* or *Richard III*. John himself needs to be played by an actor unafraid of verse bordering on the nightmare-florid. The big public scenes call for unforced declamation in end-stopped lines from everyone; whereas Hubert is the plain man, sympathetic but with limited range. The Bastard goes well in a country dialect as befits his mobility in life; the part needs an actor with a gift for making verse the natural means of direct speech, and he develops a poetic timbre of his own, which we trust in a way we do not quite the others.

His final summary is the nearest thing to a familiar quote that the play contains:

> This England never did, nor never shall
> Lie at the proud foot of a conqueror...

However, like many familiar lines this has been wrenched a little from its context. The jingoism fades with the rest of the sentence:

> But when it first did help to wound itself...
> > Nought shall make us rue
> If England to itself do rest but true.

Falconbridge has seen that a society can be destroyed not by enemies but from its own depths. He has travelled from opportunism to political insight, from the rough and tumble of pageant drama to presidential authority, hinting at the depth of sorrow of *Henry VI*. A combination of passionate orthodoxy and renegade independence, this is perhaps Shakespeare's first real hero, both inside the play and outside it, narrating. If one Shakespearian genealogy – Richard III, Iago and Macbeth – calls for actors of dark charisma whose complicity with us has a sexual shimmer, the Bastard starts another, of those who make easy, sympathetic cause, pointing the way directly to Hamlet and Viola.

In their different ways Henry VI, a stranger in his own kingdom, the butcher Richard and this benevolent Bastard all use a privileged position to testify to the state of the commonwealth. However, the greatest and most congenial outsider of all is looming and he will not be standing alone as they do: he will be linked to an insider who seems to share his values but in fact is only borrowing them. As well as continually talking to the audience (in the new medium of prose soliloquies), he will have some purchase in the Establishment, though in the end it will slam its doors on him. With a new trilogy of plays Shakespeare is about to look back in historical time to complete his sequence, analysing Britain through an unexpected prism – the connection between a wayward heir to the English throne who allows himself to be a temporary transgressor and a lying alcoholic and cheat who hopes that he will eventually stand at his side.

4

The Tide of Blood

Henry IV Part One – Henry IV Part Two – Henry V

The King of England wants to lead a Crusade to the Holy Land. But there is a delay: first he must contain an uprising at home, led by the Welsh and about to be joined by a young warrior from the north, Harry Hotspur, whom he wishes his own son resembled more closely. The rebels believe the King has no right to be there, having stolen the crown from his predecessor, Richard II.

No sooner has he announced his intentions than a young man is reproaching a fat older one for asking him the time:

> Thou art so fat-witted, with drinking of old sack, and unbuttoning thee after supper, and sleeping upon benches after noon, that thou hast forgotten to demand that truly which thou wouldst truly know. What a devil hast thou to do with the time of day?

So where are we? If this story is being told on a bare stage in 1597, the audience can't be quite sure of its bearings. Is this slangy conversation beginning in the room the King has just left? If so, how can such a disreputable figure as the fat man be so close to the seat of government – how did he get in, where are the guards? And is he being fairly described? Now that he speaks, he sounds more like a university don:

> we that take purses go by the moon and the seven stars, and not by Phoebus, he 'that wandering knight so fair'…

The reference is a little learned for most of us; this is no derelict on a park bench. He is pitching for the cultivated listener, and in fact seems better equipped to do that than his young friend, who only declares that the old man has enough 'grace' to be 'prologue to an egg and butter': why is he speaking like this, and is he even a friend?

The well-spoken stout party continues:

> Marry then, sweet wag, when thou art king, let not us that are squires of the night's body be called thieves of the day's beauty; let us be Diana's foresters, gentlemen of the shade, minions of the moon...

Within the sophisticated diction, a startling reference to the future: can a young man who keeps such company really be in line for the throne? And why does the thought suddenly sadden the older man:

> 'Sblood, I am as melancholy as a gib-cat, or a lugged bear.

The future king is quickly roused to a competitive riff, as if the two of them were suddenly in a comedy show:

> – Or an old lion, or a lover's lute.
> – Yea, or the drone of a Lincolnshire bagpipe.
> – What sayest thou to a hare, or the melancholy of Moorditch?
> – Thou hast the most unsavoury similes...

Whatever this relationship is, it clearly has its rituals which partly reveal and partly hide the truth. The next routine is on the theme of the Wronged Innocent:

> Thou... art indeed able to corrupt a saint: thou hast done much harm upon me, Hal; God forgive thee for it! Before I knew thee, Hal, I knew nothing; and now am I, if a man should speak truly, little better than one of the wicked.

Compulsive banter suggests both intimacy and its opposite; mock-insults delight until they suddenly hurt. Perhaps there is some instinctive truce between these two; perhaps the larkiness is covering something up.

Before we can find out, a new character appears, replacing the fat man. Ned Poins has infiltrated the Palace as well: clearly Hal runs his own fiefdom within it. Poins's mission is the stealing of purses. Early the next morning a group of pilgrims will be travelling from London to Canterbury with their holy offerings, and simultaneously traders coming into London with bags of cash; a well-organised gang should be able to manage a double heist at the point where the two groups intersect at Gadshill near Rochester. It is the sort of thing Hal himself has just suggested to his fat friend:

> Where shall we take a purse tomorrow, Jack?

But, in what sounds like a regular ritual, he now demurs:

> What I, rob? I a thief? Not I, by my faith

– before agreeing:

> Well then, once in my days I'll be a madcap.

'Madcap' is putting it mildly: armed robbery is quite some undertaking for the heir apparent to the Lancastrian throne.

Then Hal changes his mind again. But this is another feint, his means of finding out more. There is, Poins confides, a way to have a good night of it without exposing him: he and Poins will be out of sight when Jack and their other friends make the assault, but once the victims have fled, they will set upon the thieves in disguise and steal the winnings. Then they will all meet up at suppertime in the Boar's Head pub and hear the 'incomprehensible lies' Jack will inevitably spin on the adventure. With that degree of security in place, Hal commits himself.

Left alone, he becomes more candid, answering an unasked question:

> I know you all, and will awhile uphold
> The unyok'd humour of your idleness;
> Yet herein will I imitate the sun,
> Who doth permit the base contagious clouds
> To smother up his beauty from the world...
> So when this loose behaviour I throw off,
> And pay the debt I never promised,
> By how much better than my word I am
> By so much shall I falsify men's hopes...

This bulletin treats the audience only a little more confidentially than his friends: it's a promise to the first and a threat to the latter. It is also a very rare type of Shakespearian soliloquy, addressed not only to us but to the play's offstage characters – in effect, paradoxically, excluding both.

✦

The combined vitality and caginess of Hal's companionship is obvious; but whether it is really friendship remains a puzzle. Perhaps, burdened as he is by his position, he can't really afford such a thing. As for the fat man, if any single character can be said to dominate the inspired tour of pub, court, rebel camp, battlefield and apple orchard that is about to make up the two parts of *Henry IV*, it is Sir John Falstaff. Like Hal and Hal's other father-figure King Henry, he is presented by Shakespeare not so much as a role, more a biography, one side of an emotional triangle played out at epic length. Saloon-bar philosopher, selfish, drunk and disorderly, Falstaff is a reprobate of every kind; but his transgressions are essentially against outmoded codes of honour and timeserving attitudes to life. And he is full of surprises: the erudition of his opening lines, for one thing. His knightly title is probably inherited rather than earned, but he is educated. He has moved in court circles all his life: Shakespeare even asserts (unhistorically, and therefore intriguingly) that as a boy he was page to the unfortunate Sir Thomas Mowbray, banished as a security risk by Richard II after – by royal hint – killing Richard's uncle and critic, Thomas of Woodstock. Later in *Henry IV Part One* he will share the battlefield with King Henry on something like equal terms, and be at home in the company of the Lord Chief Justice in *Part Two*. So he is close to big events, and he has mobility: everyone has to appreciate his pedigree, however at odds it seems with his current arrangements.

And there is love inside Falstaff – the adventurer's love of life, but also paternal love for his young protégé, his royal Hal. His self-interest in this is obvious: but whenever Shakespeare allows us to think that the attachment is tactical, he swiftly underlines that he also sees Hal as the son he's never had. And beneath all Falstaff's extemporisations we will come to recognise a profound anxiety: he can never resist asking for reassurance about his future. Always the same burning question: What will happen when Hal becomes King Henry? Apart from at one devastating moment, Hal will never give him a straight answer. While he waits, Jack Falstaff is perhaps the best company in Shakespeare.

✦

The Boar's Head was a real venue, in Eastcheap, a street near London Bridge and the site of London's meat market – the tavern actually sat where King William Street would be built, replacing the western part of Eastcheap, in the nineteenth century. As one of the central locations in *Henry IV*, it expands in the imagination, an extravagantly detailed world created entirely from words. There are drawers (bartenders) zig-zagging through the rooms, trying to keep up, their work sometimes complicated by a Prince of the realm playing silly tricks on them. There could be a couple of fellows playing backgammon in the corner. There are regulars and roaring boys, snugs you instinctively wouldn't sit in because you can sense they are a regular client's domain, chancers and tarts. There are sidebars called the Half Moon and, downstairs, the Pomgarnet. These being the days before the sex industry was ghettoised, its world has insinuated itself within this one: Mine Hostess's main anxiety is that the authorities should not come after her for running a bawdy house, and sure enough there are upstairs and back rooms worked by the likes of Doll Tearsheet.

It is always a pleasure for *Henry IV*'s audience to get back to the Boar's Head from the outside world, which is not to say it's a safe or reassuring place – throats get cut, pockets picked, it is as violent as London itself. Its lawlessness may in the end be as imprisoning as the orthodox life, but for the moment it seems to represent freedom. At least all the entertainment is human – no amplification and no flashing lights. All the same there is live music every night, one of the bands intriguingly called Sneak's Noise. The names are familiar, but try to hear them afresh – Mistress Quickly, Doll Tearsheet, Falstaff and Bardolph, Pistol and Poins, Francis and Ralph – an extravagant brew of predominant humours and commonplace trades. Also mentioned but just out of sight are Goodwife Keech the butcher's wife, local officers of the law called Fang and Snare, a rival pub called the Lubber's Head in Lombard Street, Master Dommelton the tailor and Master Smooth the silkman, Dumbe the Minister and Tisick the Deputy. You can smell the stale beer, the sickly sweet wine, the fug, the illicit ramshackle air of an old riverside pub. Above all it is Jack Falstaff's kingdom, where he can call for any entertainment and enjoy, apart from momentary rebellions by the management, unlimited credit.

> HAL: Why thou clay-brained guts, thou knotty-pated fool,
>   thou whoreson, obscene, greasy tallow-catch...
>
> FALSTAFF: Away, you starveling, you eel-skin, you dried
>   neat's tongue, you bull's pizzle, you stock-fish...

The insults now have some point. Poins's plan has gone perfectly: the travellers were robbed by Falstaff's gang, who were robbed in turn by Poins and Hal – either at or in the company of Gadshill, since Shakespeare seems unable finally to decide whether that is a person or a place. As the facts begin to come out, the characteristic dance of Falstaff and Hal is brilliantly continued. In the intervening hours Falstaff has taken time to distress his clothes and weaponry: his demeanour hints at a great injustice nobly borne, his shield is dented and his sword hacked all about – 'Ecce signum! [Behold the proof]'. In his superbly self-righteous account of the robbery, he pours scorn on all 'cowards and runaways' such as he takes Hal to be; but the Prince's defection has given him a great opportunity to exaggerate the affray, so that the number of his victims (zero) is multiplying in the telling – from a dozen to sixteen, to twenty-two and to some fifty or even fifty-two; and if anyone were to accuse him of economy (or its opposite) with the truth, then he is 'a bunch of radish'. (An insult also used, as it happens, for a bad actor in Japanese Kabuki theatre.) Drawing from this continually recharged glass, Hal joins him in hyperbole:

> HAL: ...this sanguine coward, this bed-presser, this horseback
>   breaker, this huge hill of flesh...
>
> FALSTAFF: ... O for breath to utter what is like thee – you tailor's
>   yard, you sheath, you bow-case, you vile standing tuck...

It occurs to us to ask – might Falstaff ever overstep? Hal is not above changing the terms of any conversation to assert his status, but he seems to practise that technique on everyone but Falstaff; if we can read his love for the old man from nothing else, there is the fact that he never, until the very end of the story, pulls rank on him. For the time being, the older man's licence seems unlimited, though we will gradually realise the melancholy reason: it is based on a dream. He can say what he likes, go as far as he wants: nothing, either way, will affect what awaits him in the end.

As for the robbery, the audience on- and offstage waits for the pay-off. Hal points out that he himself has the swag he stole from Falstaff, 'here in the house', and the bottom falls out of the story. If he can turn *this* around, it will be a Falstaffian Olympic Gold, and he does it without drawing breath. He ran away advisedly:

> Why, hear you, my masters, was it for me to kill the heir-
> apparent? Should I turn upon the true Prince?... Instinct is a
> great matter, I was now a coward on instinct.

It's a masterstroke, and Falstaff's stock rockets. He immediately gets a reward, from Hal and Shakespeare: he is given the job of dealing with a nobleman from the court, Sir John Bracy, arriving with news of Hotspur's incursions and trying to summon the Prince to court. Hal gets Falstaff to send him packing: if the outside world has the effrontery to track him to his special headquarters here, it deserves to be humiliated by his trusted lieutenant. You can imagine Falstaff's relish for the job. Returning and still flushed with his triumph, he calls for more risqué entertainment. It is to be an improvised play. Hal allocates the parts: he will remain himself but Sir John must play the role of his father the King and

> examine me upon the particulars of my life.

The main attraction presumably will be Falstaff's satirical performance as King Henry, though it's noticeable that even to have the initial idea suggests Hal's need to justify his way of life to an audience.

This presents a question to the director: How public is this bar in which the heir to the throne relaxes? Falstaff has asked Mistress Quickly to 'clap to the doors' for the play so they can be a little more intimate, and Shakespeare's stage directions nominate only the actual speakers in the scene as being present. So perhaps they are in a private room with their closest allies. Even so, the idea that casual drinkers are about to witness the Prince extravagantly satirising his father is startling. You could almost sympathise with King Henry: like the lapses of our present heirs to the throne, Hal's carelessness about being overheard is remarkable.

As always in Shakespeare, the artifice of the play within a play releases essential truths. Two real-life figures will hover behind this performance – the present King and the king Hal himself will become; and the device will answer many of our questions about Hal and Falstaff. Playing the royal father, Falstaff can warn Hal of the dangers of his current life but notably exclude himself from blame. As for the quality, his acting as the pinched and pedantic King seems surprisingly good – Mistress Quickly for one is impressed:

> Jesu, he doth it as like one of these harlotry players as ever I see!

This is enough to make Hal, nothing if not competitive, reverse the casting: if he plays his father himself while Falstaff simpers as Hal, he will be able to warn the 'old white-bearded Satan' indirectly that he has no special licence to be a

> villainous abominable misleader of youth.

There could be a momentary embarrassment, politely covered. The watchers presumably love Falstaff entirely and the Prince only guardedly; will Hal's acting in the same role be as funny as their favourite's? Surprisingly enough, it is, though less inventive, less good-natured and more driven by zeal – and as usual there is only one joke in it, fatness:

> There is a devil haunts thee in the likeness of an old fat man...
> that trunk of humours, that bolting hutch of beastliness, that
> swollen parcel of dropsies, that huge bombard of sack, that
> stuffed cloak-bag of guts, that roasted Manningtree ox with the
> pudding in his belly.

The change of role also gives Falstaff-as-Hal the chance to edge towards his own obsession, pleading his case a little. Sir John is surely, he says, as good a companion for him as any young man's father could wish. But the nagging question of the future won't settle. Suddenly Falstaff makes the mistake of breaking the convention: with great subtlety Shakespeare stops him acting. Planting his own name like a tree in every line, he no longer addresses King Henry but Hal himself, the new King:

> ...No, my good lord, banish Peto, banish Bardolph, banish Poins; but for sweet Jack Falstaff, kind Jack Falstaff, true Jack Falstaff, valiant Jack Falstaff, and therefore more valiant being, as he is, old Jack Falstaff, banish not him thy Harry's company, banish not him thy Harry's company: banish plump Jack, and banish all the world.

It is as if an actor were to forget the name of his colleague's character and address him by his real name; except that in Falstaff's case it is not a mistake but a cheat brought on by anxiety to find out the truth. He is immediately punished: Hal, affronted by such a breach of the code, comes out of character too and stuns him with the bleakest monosyllables:

> I do, I will.
>
> [*A knocking heard.*]

Where could the improvised play possibly have gone from here? It has fallen to the ground and lies there in silence. The director has some interesting options: either to let Hal's last words briefly echo before the knocking breaks in; or to bring the new sound in sharply, so that his line might or might not have been heard quite correctly.

This sound of knocking in the wings invariably means trouble in Shakespeare – for lovers, for the bloodied Macbeth – just as in Agatha Christie a ring on the doorbell means someone come to change the course of the plot. Here it unblocks an impasse: the pub is being raided, Falstaff is under suspicion of the Gadshill robbery, and the law is after him. Hal bundles him behind a curtain (where, unperturbed, he immediately falls asleep) and, shifting easily into princely verse, covers for him, dispatching the respectful officer. He performs this gesture of loyalty without breaking his stride; in the scene's last moments, he also lets us know that he will discreetly arrange the repayment of what was stolen. It is an impressive moment of rectitude in a cycle of transgression, and for a moment we see Hal's two personalities simultaneously: the authoritative prince dealing with the police, and the black sheep the same police would do well to keep an eye on.

✦

Logically enough, the edgy burlesque in the Boar's Head has been the prologue to an actual interview between Hal and his father: now, perhaps under the hammerbeam roof of Westminster Hall (built by the usurped Richard II), its themes are played out in a chillier key. King Henry has a talent for identifying his personal anxieties as those of the nation, and he wastes no time. His two bargaining counters to shame Hal with are the dead King Richard and the very much alive Harry Hotspur. At the start of the play he expressed the wish to his Cabinet that Hotspur and Hal had been exchanged at birth; now he viciously declares to Hal's face:

> He hath more worthy interest to the state
> Than thou the shadow of succession.

Thick and fast the accusations come. The unruly Hal lacks any sense of the public relations aspect of being a member of the Royal Family – and this is without the King's knowing the full extent of it at the Boar's Head Cabaret (with Special Royal Guest) the previous night. His son seems to be God's punishment on him for

> some displeasing service I have done.

Well, there are secular voices a-plenty, led by Hotspur, murmuring what that displeasing service might have been – Henry, as Bolingbroke, usurped both Richard II's crown and life and now faces vociferous public judgment on his actions.

This remarkable evasion is the first in a series of pitiless and largely specious manoeuvres. What, Henry would like to know, if he himself had behaved like Hal, alienating the great and good and missing important meetings? Moving on to his own virtues, he elaborately extols his approach to public relations: this seems to be the sum of life's wisdom he means to pass on to his son. It is all a matter of modesty and a low profile:

> By being seldom seen, I could not stir,
> But like a comet I was wonder'd at,
> That men would tell their children 'This is he'…
> And then I stole all courtesy from heaven
> And dress'd myself in such humility
> That I did pluck allegiance from men's hearts.

In this way he kept his 'person fresh and new'. Richard II, by contrast, was a 'skipping King' who, like Hal,

> ambled up and down
> With shallow jesters and rash bavin wits...
> Grew a companion to the common streets,
> Enfeoff'd himself to popularity...
> So, when he had occasion to be seen
> He was but as the cuckoo is in June,
> Heard, not regarded.

He might have added that with masterly passive-aggression he simply waited for the deserted Richard to drop the crown into his lap; that he dispatched his life with an unattributable hint to an assassin (like King John's to Hubert); and that he then banished the assassin just as Richard had banished Mowbray for much the same service.

Henry expounds his banal lesson in public relations so vigorously that we might miss the fallacy: the comparison with Richard II is misleading. Richard often appeared in public on ceremonial occasions, but he wouldn't have been seen dead in the Boar's Head. His capering with Bushy, Bagot and Greene was mostly conducted behind Palace doors, and he never showed Hal's demotic instincts. But history's repetitions, however falsely interpreted, obsess King Henry, and anything about Richard is useful if it mortifies Hal. He goes on to claim that his son is in the same position as Richard was when Bolingbroke arrived home from banishment with his army, which is nonsense: Hal is near the centre of government whereas Richard's mistake was to go to Ireland, leaving a weak deputy in his place. He also adds a twist of paternal blackmail: everyone is sick of the sight of Hal except him, the father, who has

> desir'd to see thee more.

This elaborate half-nelson shows his fascination with technique and betrayal of fatherhood. The account of himself is so spun that you can hardly sense the man beneath, who is in fact riddled with furtive guilt, acknowledged to himself mainly in the dead of night. He will, sadly, never admit as much to Hal; if he did, Hal, bound to him, would have less to rebel against. As it is, we see the extent of the son's problem: though revolted by his father's tactics, he knows they are skills he will one day have to have at his own disposal.

Now it's Hal's turn. He has already declared that he is the victim of the press ('base newsmongers') – sounding very much like one of our own princes complaining of the *paparazzi*. However, in Hal's time, the behaviour of the heir to the throne was not the relative triviality it is today; it affected England's central nervous system and its government's

ability to function. Hal capitulates rapidly and promises to do better –
perhaps sincerely, or perhaps, to judge from his terseness, just to get out
of the room. Certainly there seems little point in trying to make a case
to such a father:

> I shall hereafter, my thrice gracious lord,
> Be more myself.

This is not enough for the suffocatingly garrulous King, who clearly listens
to nothing his son says, even an apology. He prefers to go on and on about
Hotspur's rising popularity as if that too were Hal's fault. Hal has to shift up
a gear, and he plunges into a promise that he will take Hotspur on

> And in the closing of some glorious day
> Be bold to tell you that I am your son;
> When I will wear a garment all of blood
> And stain my favours in a bloody mask...
> The which if I perform and do survive
> I do beseech your majesty may salve
> The long-grown wounds of my intemperance.

He's borrowing his father's diction, and it's a little overdone. It meets a
rather ungracious approval:

> A hundred thousand rebels die in this;
> Thou shalt have charge and sovereign trust herein.

No concession, no acknowledgment of Hal's individuality, just chilly
pragmatism: Henry has perhaps heard such good intentions before. He
immediately moves on to planning, giving his son a job to do in the forthcoming campaign and troops to do it with, and that's all. This, clearly,
has been his super-objective from the start: to manoeuvre him into the
front line.

   In its way this scene between father and son has been more coded
than Hal's and Falstaff's guying of it – the same situation and the same
speeches, and in this tenser acoustic the degree of empathy is no easier to
measure. All Hal's meetings with his father threaten to widen the distance
between him and Falstaff, but so far they do the opposite – though they
also remind Hal of the exact length of the spoon he needs for supping
with the devil. It is clear to us that the relationship of blood father and
son is deeply compromised; where warmth and intimacy are called for,
qualities that Falstaff at least simulates, Hal is in acute need. The world
he was born to is measly and calculating, but inescapable; Falstaff's is
everything that appears free and life-enhancing, but underpinned by the

desire for advancement. Which is the more constricting? If we left the Boar's Head with dawn approaching and Hal contemplating his future among empty bottles and discarded furniture, it might be that, left alone now, he kicks the King's desk in savage frustration.

As if to sharpen Hal's conflict, the country is about to go to war – with itself, significantly. He has to give this some thought. Much as his instinct would be to slip out of the palace to prop up the bar with his friend before the end of the day, there is a small pause while he works out how to navigate the next stage. He has already, in the Boar's Head, given notice to Peto (or was it Poins – they seem to be interchangeable) that he will take care of him if need be, and – perhaps a little guilty about those awful monosyllables 'I do, I will' – of Falstaff as well, by giving him a commission in the forthcoming campaign. Apart from a financial allowance, this will give Falstaff the chance to lay up some official good-will. Now Hal must decide whether to keep his word to him and implicitly double-cross his father.

✦

For Falstaff, Hal's visit to Westminster has been a worry: like a lover, he waits anxiously in the Boar's Head. Worse, he has only Bardolph, so uninspired after Hal, to play off. Fretful and insecure, he even feels he is losing his physical substance:

> Do I not bate? Do I not dwindle? Why, my skin hangs about me like an old lady's loose gown; I am withered like an old apple-john...

Has he made a mess of his life? He talks up his imaginary salad days:

> I... went to a bawdy house not above once in a quarter of an hour, paid money that I borrowed three or four times, lived well, and in good compass, and now I live out of all order, out of all compass...

Bardolph, struggling to keep up, sees an opening:

> Why, you are so fat, Sir John, that you must needs be out of all compass; out of all reasonable compass, Sir John.

He's forgotten that in Falstaff's kingdom there is only room for one star – one of whose specialities is the fertile exaggeration of small truths. In the case of Bardolph, this is his spectacularly red nose, a gift for Falstaff. Even in alcoholic depression his improvisation is like rolling thunder:

FALSTAFF: Do thou amend thy face, and I'll amend my life. Thou art our admiral, thou bearest the lantern in the poop, but 'tis in the nose of thee: thou art the Knight of the Burning Lamp... I never see thy face but I think upon hell fire... When thou ran'st up Gadshill in the night to catch my horse, if I did not think thou hadst been an *ignis fatuus*, or ball of wild-fire, there's no purchase in money. O, thou art a perpetual triumph, an everlasting bonfire light, thou hast saved me a thousand marks in links and torches, walking with thee in the night betwixt tavern and tavern...

BARDOLPH: 'Sblood, I would my face were in your belly.

FALSTAFF: God-a-mercy, so should I be sure to be heartburned...

Falstaff has little in common with Mercutio in *Romeo and Juliet*, but the tone is exactly that of Mercutio when, with Romeo often absent now he has met Juliet, he is left with only Benvolio for company. It just doesn't feel the same; anxiety underlies the brilliant inventiveness, making it spin free of any ratchets. His harassment of Bardolph is not entirely affectionate: the audience is uncertain whether his linguistic warmth comes from good heart or malice. But it is certainly funny. No wonder Hal gravitates towards this sort of thing: it suits his taste for the exuberantly unkind, even if he can never quite match Falstaff's prodigality.

Falstaff's luck is holding: Hal arrives, with his commission and good cheer. Even after the paternal drubbing, or perhaps because of it, he reassures his friend that he has not been won over. In fact, realignment is a matter of sly revenge:

I am good friends with my father, and may do anything.

So Falstaff gets his job and regains his favourite company. The immediate future looks good: with Poins, Peto, Bardolph and him in tow, Hal will be turning up for the battle with his own coterie, a provocative reminder that he does things on his own terms. The minor embarrassment of Falstaff's interjections during official parleys will be the price of bringing an anarchist friend along to the party; and who knows what relief the friend may bring? And perhaps Sir John himself is ready to adapt to the times, re-entering the official world of money and some sort of purpose.

We may find Falstaff's involvement with the military a little surprising – as much so as the realisation that Richard III, extravagantly crippled as he is sometimes made, has been much cherished as a war hero in an age of hand-to-hand conflict. For all his dilapidation, Falstaff too is competent to lead a platoon into battle. He is part of an ongoing English tradition – the disreputable regimental type who passes as a gentleman in peace, the rake who can step up to the line in a national emergency. Evelyn Waugh must have loved him.

As he moves out of London, he begins a new transaction with the audience, whom he has never addressed directly before: now he will rarely stop, with a vigour that sustains both this play and its sequel. From now on he will be living mostly out of doors, on the country roads and the field of battle: it is a highly original effect. You might think of Falstaff as some exotic plant blooming in the dark, the great outdoors both too healthful and too dull for him: in fact he is intensely interested in his changing surroundings, on which he trains the sharpest of philosophical eyes. Conscripting soldiers on the road to Shrewsbury, we find him applying his idiosyncratic methods to the national crisis. He immediately allows his victims to buy their way out of service, leaving himself 'heinously unprovided' for the battle but three hundred pounds richer. None of this profit finds its way to Bardolph, now his lieutenant, who nevertheless has to provide the petty cash to keep his master in the liquor he demands en route. Cheerfully admitting to his novel approach, Falstaff's sense of metaphor is intact as his morals are not:

> If I be not ashamed of my soldiers, I am a soused gurnet... a mad fellow met me on the way and told me I had unloaded all the gibbets and pressed the dead bodies. No eye hath seen such scarecrows.

But he has the insight of the true conman: he sees that this is the fall-out of a lethargic time. Too much leisure – what Hamlet calls 'the imposthume of much wealth and peace' – has left England in need of the flurry of a good war. His men are

> discarded unjust serving men, younger sons to younger brothers, revolted tapsters and ostlers, trade fallen, the cankers of a calm world and a long peace...

He also knows that 'the better part of valour is discretion', and once on the battlefield he becomes a walking reproach to the bellicose nonsense around him. Coming across the body of a dead lord and struck by its 'grinning honour', he disposes of the illusion of glory in a few famous seconds:

> Can honour set to a leg? No. Or an arm? No. Or take away the grief of a wound? No. Honour hath no skill in surgery then?

> No. What is honour? A word. What is that word 'honour'? Air.
> A trim reckoning! Who hath it? He that died o' Wednesday...
> Therefore I'll none of it; honour is a mere scutcheon; and so
> ends my catechism.

This comes winging down the centuries, of course; within Shakespeare's work, it belongs to a strain of military commentary, direct to its audience, that continues with the Boy in *Henry V* and then finds its bitterest form in Thersites in *Troilus and Cressida*. Heard at every opportunity here, it is a relief: the wasteful sight of the flower of England, Hal and Hotspur, combating to the last breath is accompanied by the fact of Falstaff the survivor lying fatly doggo a few feet away, feigning death to avoid dismemberment by the ferocious Earl of Douglas.

The country's move onto a war footing, like all such extremities, throws relationships into a new perspective: perhaps its real benefit is not territory or power, but a broadening of generosity in the survivors. Certainly, Falstaff's camaraderie with Hal warms up again. After an unpromising start: in the moments before the battle, as everyone contemplates what lies ahead, Falstaff's craven Eastcheap philosophy is grating:

> HAL: Say thy prayers and farewell.
>
> FALSTAFF: I would it were bed-time, Hal, and all well.
>
> HAL: Why, thou owest God a death.

However, having dispatched Hotspur, Hal sees his old friend apparently dead too. Eyes closed and breath held, Falstaff hears this, which he might be able to interpret as affectionate:

> Poor Jack, farewell;
> I could have better spar'd a better man;
> O, I should have a heavy miss of thee
> If I were much in love with vanity.

Left alone, though afraid that 'this gunpowder Percy' might be shamming like him and will leap to his feet, he sees an opportunity. He stabs Hotspur's corpse, and begins to shoulder it. Hal returns with his brother John to find his friend incandescently alive:

> if your father will do me any honour, so; if not, let him kill the
> next Percy himself.

We know by now that one of the glories of Falstaff is his stamina in the face of the truth. He knows he's making his claim to John in front of Hotspur's actual conqueror, but no matter for that:

HAL: Why, Percy I killed myself and saw thee dead.

FALSTAFF: Didst thou? Lord, Lord, how this world is given to lying. I grant you, I was down and out of breath, and so was he, but we rose both in an instant, and fought a long hour by Shrewsbury clock.

Hal, as delighted as he was by Falstaff's account of the Gadshill robbery, shows real class as a friend:

PRINCE JOHN: This is the strangest tale that ever I heard.

HAL: This is the strangest fellow, brother John.
Come, bring your luggage nobly on your back;
For my part, if a lie may do thee grace,
I'll gild it with the happiest terms I have.

Pleased with the old man, but also reconciled with his father, whom he has himself saved from death, Hal goes on to report Hotspur's death neutrally – just 'the noble Percy slain'. It's a surprising sign of grace, by far the warmest Hal is to Falstaff in either play. We get a first glimpse of a hero with a liberating sense of the absurd, even a guarded magnanimity; a little touch of the Henry V to come. Reborn on the battlefield, he has fulfilled one duty without betraying another, and the amoral gallantry of his gesture to Falstaff ensures that *Part One* closes with the question of their friendship still open. Hal is marginally in credit with his overseers while leaving his own preferences intact. It will not always be this easy; but for the moment it is hard to believe that in the end he will only resolve his dilemmas by savagely guillotining half of his life.

✦

The heavens thee guard and keep, most royal imp of fame!

– Henry IV Part Two

Whether Shakespeare resolved to add a second part to *Henry IV* after the success of the first or always had it in mind, we'll never know. The second possibility suggests a due sense of the scope of what he was undertaking; the first would be an entirely typical response to having a popular hit – that is, simply to deliver more of the same, with plenty of Falstaff. Whichever it was, the further exploiting of Sir John's talents in *Part Two* happens to suit the development of his and Hal's story, since it thrusts him to the front of the picture and the subdued Hal – his father sickening and the succession imminent – for the time being to its back. Largely separate, the two of them operate less contentedly: the air is still heavy with their relationship, but we only see them together once before the play's climax.

The vague report that he has done good service at Shrewsbury in disposing of Hotspur has gained Falstaff a modicum of his despised 'honour': Hal – the one person who knows how undeserved the honour is – has rewarded him with a young Page to attend him. It is not a gesture Falstaff seems to relish, since the boy's diminutive size only emphasises the opposite in him: out walking, he feels

> like a sow that hath overwhelmed all her litter but one.

He's not usually so sensitive about his size; this is a note of energetic discontent reminiscent of his exchanges with Bardolph in *Part One* and now becoming dominant. Throughout the play Falstaff will continue to talk like a forest fire, but he is more peppered with mortal intimations: he has the gout, perhaps the pox, and the doctor has been looking at his water. His comic self-loathing extends to contempt for a tailor who, no doubt sensing his 'consumption of the purse', requires some security before making him a new cloak – aptly enough in a story which will end with Falstaff's bankruptcy. The other dominant chord waiting for resolution is his preoccupation with the absent Hal.

As he looks at the comic resources that served him well in *Part One*, Shakespeare's vision of Falstaff as the supreme escapologist strikes him as too good not to repeat. So, recalling his manipulation of the warm-hearted Mistress of the Boar's Head, Ursula Quickly, he allows her to bring a breach of promise action against her 'honeysuckle villain'. She claims that in a moment of weakness under her affectionate hands – as she dressed a wound apparently inflicted by a boisterous Prince Hal – Falstaff has promised her marriage and confirmed it with a kiss. True or not, the incident points up both her tenderness – she remembers every detail, including his oath sworn on a 'parcel-gilt goblet' and her stopping him eating a dish of prawns in case they slowed his recovery – and his tongue-in-cheek brutality. He declares to the Lord Chief Justice:

> My lord, this is a poor mad soul; and she says up and down the
> town that her eldest son is like you. She hath been in good case,
> and the truth is, poverty hath distracted her.

The Lord Chief Justice is a frustrated man. He is after Falstaff for various small misdemeanours; after the Gadshill robbery he summoned him to account for himself, only to find that the national emergency had given him temporary immunity. Now, his military prestige is allowing him to parley from a position of security. The Lord Chief Justice must feel the forces of darkness are conspiring to stop him doing his job, especially since Falstaff's wit is moving at twice the speed of his. In two scenes he faces a dazzling repertoire of Falstaffian diversions, which include tactical deafness and frantic concern for the King's health, the state of the nation and the Lord Chief Justice's (imaginary) personal ailments. It is a series of wrangles the latter can only lose:

> LORD CHIEF JUSTICE: Well, the truth is, Sir John, you live in great infamy.
>
> FALSTAFF: He that buckles him in my belt cannot live in less.
>
> LORD CHIEF JUSTICE: Your means are very slender, and your waste is great.
>
> FALSTAFF: I would it were otherwise; I would my means were greater and my waist slenderer.
>
> LORD CHIEF JUSTICE: You have misled the youthful prince.
>
> FALSTAFF: The young prince hath misled me; I am the fellow with the great belly, and he my dog.

He should never have got into it, of course, and he finds himself rhythmically bullied like a bear forced to dance:

> FALSTAFF: My lord, I was born about three of the clock in the afternoon, with a white head, and something a round belly. For my voice, I have lost it with hollaing, and singing of anthems.
>
> LORD CHIEF JUSTICE: Well, God send the prince a better companion!
>
> FALSTAFF: God send the companion a better prince!

But there is a sting in all this that Falstaff, for all his temporary elevation, doesn't sense. If he only knew it, the law lord is another proxy father for Hal and is fighting the old one to the death. So the real meaning of their dealings lies buried: bested though he is now, the Lord Chief Justice will soon usurp Falstaff's place in Hal's affections. For the moment we can't see this either.

The object of the paternal competition between the man of law, the fat knight and the King of England sits in his lodgings, strangely becalmed. Back from the wars, Hal has subsided into discontent: he is rangey, irritable, not settling. There is also some sense of incognito: Bardolph thinks he has only just come back to London, while Mistress

Quickly believes he is in Wales. Perhaps he has secluded himself to avoid Falstaff and immerse himself in his conflicting feelings about his father. He is 'exceeding weary', might do this or that. He affects to despise himself, a royal, for having a yen for 'small beer' – and indeed for small companionship, such as with the endlessly attentive Poins.

Poins, as ever his aide-de-camp and guarantor in the unofficial world, is the closest the prince gets, 'for fault of a better', to friendship: but he is also, when Hal pleases, like a put-upon manservant. So he is acceptable in any of Hal's moods. He rarely takes more than discreet offence, and is used to Hal's silliest conceits – such as the embarrassing moment in *Part One* when, excited by the ludicrous camaraderie of the working class, he played a practical joke on a 'puny drawer' in the Boar's Head which had him running in different directions to take contradictory orders. But now Poins is genuinely stung by his famous friend's wilful melancholia:

> How ill it follows, after you have laboured so hard, you should talk so idly.

Not to mention Hal's harping on Poins's inferior social position:

> By this light, I am well spoke on, I can hear it with my mine own ears: the worst they can say of me is that I am a second brother, and that I am a proper fellow of my hands, and these two things I confess I cannot help.

On this bracing moment of disharmony a familiar music breaks in. Bardolph and Falstaff's new Page arrive with a letter from Falstaff, the Page by now so at home that he is making Bardolph jokes: he claims to have once been unable to see Bardolph's face because it was protruding from a red curtain. The letter is a sort of nudge. Falstaff 'commends' himself to Hal by claiming that Poins is telling everybody that Hal is to marry his, Poins's, sister. This is low-level mischief to cause half-hearted outrage, a simple ploy to get Hal back to 'the old place... in Eastcheap'; and like an unreformed drinker gleelessly falling off the wagon, Hal can't resist it for long. He does need a livelier sparring partner than Poins, just as Falstaff needs someone other than Bardolph. It won't be a reunion exactly: rather, Hal fancies spying on the old man in his den as he disports himself with Doll Tearsheet. He can't at first think how to pull off this listless and unsociable trick. Poins suggests they disguise themselves as drawers, and Hal leaves with a small joke on the usual theme:

> From a prince to a prentice? A low transformation! That shall be mine...

If in *King John* Shakespeare was finding a way to counterpoint styles of speech – the Bastard's and the King's particularly – he tells much of the story of Hal and Falstaff by contrasting their timbres, which are parallel but distinct. Both originate in the speaker's self-image; but while Falstaff's metaphorical bounty flows in such an intoxicating tide that we forgive him most things, Hal's style is more angular, unsettling, sometimes atonal: nothing like the same richness, only a certain adroitness. It is also less secure. Sometimes he mimics his formal father; sometimes he relaxes into Falstaff's argot; only occasionally so far does he speak in his own unmistakable register. As a result he is as difficult to warm to as Falstaff is to resist: we find ourselves indulging Falstaff for cheating the law and a vulnerable woman while judging Hal coldly for his honesty about the future. Though he warns us to 'let the end try the man' we wonder how this dark and complex individual will achieve any heroic status at all.

At this point it's not clear whether the two of them will still be connected enough to move the play forward. But it is evident that such complicated men are better together than apart: each is uneasy without the other, and the unease spreads to us. It's an uncompleted equation: Hal's waywardness needs some of Falstaff's renegade charm, and without Hal, Falstaff's lack of principle has no real counterpoint.

✦

Time and again *Henry IV Part Two* recapitulates its predecessor in a minor key. Even the Boar's Head scene in the new play is again 'Act Two Scene Four', though the second version has little of the same energy. To enliven it Shakespeare finds it necessary to introduce two new characters – Doll Tearsheet and the braggadocio Pistol, a phoney military captain who replaces his heroic alter ego Hotspur from *Part One* (in fact the parts are often played by the same actor). Pistol is said to live

> upon mouldy stewed prunes and dried cakes

– ever the countryman, Shakespeare loved fruit as a symbol of putrefaction. Doll meanwhile is politely described by the Page as a kinswoman of Sir John's but perhaps more accurately by Hal as

> such kin as the parish heifers are to the town bull.

Insulted as she was in front of the Lord Chief Justice, Mistress Quickly has nevertheless invited Falstaff to dinner again and offered Doll as a sweetener. His response has been to get the poor woman to pawn her wall hangings and plate to subsidise more nights on his tab.

Doll arrives in the Boar's Head having drunk 'too much canaries... a marvellous searching wine', so she doesn't seem likely to be the unalloyed treat Mistress Quickly has promised him. Her first line insists that she is

> Better than I was. Hem!

'Hem' in Shakespeare generally suggests a cough or a burp – here we might stretch it to a puke into a bucket. At the same time Falstaff arrives issuing instructions to 'empty the jordan', so evacuation seems to be the order of the day – an unpromising start for romance. But Falstaff and Doll are clearly old adversaries in what passes for love: Mistress Quickly declares

> you two never meet but you fall to some discord; you are both,
> i' good truth, as rheumatic as two dry toasts: you cannot one
> bear with another's confirmities.

As a professional, Doll's ability to feel affection is presumably somewhat blunted. She lives an unhealthy life, her body commandeered not only by clients but by her madam in return for a modicum of security little better than that of a slave. She is certainly in no humour for Falstaff's routine double entendres about bent pikes and surgery, the result of the venereal disease she bestows on her clients – he omits to mention whom she might have contracted it from in the first place. Still, she sees that this may be their last meeting:

> Come, I'll be friends with thee, Jack, thou art going to the wars,
> and whether I shall ever see thee again or no, there is nobody
> cares.

Meanwhile Pistol, whom Falstaff mysteriously acknowledges as his 'ancient' or ensign, is the kind of client Mistress Quickly, who has to 'live among my neighbours', wants to keep off her premises. To her he is no more than a swaggerer (having just discovered the word, she uses it eight times in two short speeches). Bursting into the bar, Pistol goes into yards of rumbustious alliteration and pidgin Latin verse: this is what he does whenever he feels in need of bolstering up, which is most of the time. Often thought to be a mischievous portrait of Christopher Marlowe, he is like an explosion of cheap fireworks, more noise than splendour; and his company soon wears thin on Falstaff, who for once 'would be quiet'. The histrionic posturing also drives the hungover Doll into a paroxysm:

I scorn you, scurvy companion. What, you poor base rascally cheating lack-linen mate... you mouldy rogue... you cutpurse rascal, you filthy bung... you bottle-ale rascal, you basket-hilt stale juggler, you!

Consider the case of Doll. She has a preference for men to present themselves exactly as they are, and she is skilled at seeing them that way rather than as they would fancy themselves to be. Suddenly patriotic as working girls can be, the fraudulent two points on Pistol's shoulder strike her as a slur on all good soldiers:

You a captain! You slave, for what? For tearing a poor whore's ruff in a bawdy-house!

Insecure as he is, Pistol can only match her moral indignation by defensive yelling, so that he has to be driven out by the suddenly fearless Falstaff, his ragged tail between his legs.

There is a gentle truce between Doll and Falstaff as she rewards the old knight's minor chivalry with appreciative sexuality. Her attentions – played, interestingly enough, against music – are unexpectedly touching:

DOLL: Ah, you sweet little rogue, you! Alas, poor ape, how thou sweatest! Come, let me wipe thy face; come on, you whoreson chops: ah, rogue, i' faith, I love thee, thou art as valorous as Hector of Troy... and ten times better than the Nine Worthies: ah, villain!

FALSTAFF: Ah, rascally knave! I will toss the rogue in a blanket.

DOLL: Do, an thou dar'st for thy heart: an thou dost, I'll canvas thee between a pair of sheets.

But her vitality only increases the old man's foreboding:

DOLL: When wilt thou leave fighting a' days and foining a' nights and begin to patch up thine old body for heaven?

FALSTAFF: Peace, good Doll, do not speak like a death's head. Do not bid me remember mine end... I am old, I am old.

DOLL: I love thee better than I love e'er a scurvy young boy of them all.

FALSTAFF: What stuff wilt have a kirtle of? I shall receive money o' Thursday; shalt have a cap tomorrow. A merry song, come, it grows late, we'll to bed: thou'lt forget me when I am gone.

DOLL: By my troth thou'lt set me a weeping an thou sayest so. Prove that ever I dress myself handsome till thy return...

Their short exchange has an odd dignity: neither of them normally gives anything away without a return, but now they go beyond their usual limits into something like love's generosity. We feel that Sir John, though he has no ready cash, really would give her these gifts if he could; and that Doll, though a professional amnesiac, will never forget her 'whoreson little tidy Bartholomew boar-pig'.

Unknowing, they are sharing the stage with a far more compromised object of Falstaff's love, his unofficial son. For some reason, and for Doll's benefit, Falstaff denigrates Hal as 'a good shallow young fellow' and, especially, Poins – 'hang him, baboon'. In fact, the humour is a little measly on both sides:

> POINS: Is it not strange that desire should so many years outlive performance?
>
> FALSTAFF: Kiss me, Doll.
>
> HAL: Saturn and Venus this year in conjunction! What says the almanac to that?

Summoned in his drawer's disguise for a nightcap, Hal demands an explanation. Falstaff's efforts in this greatly lack the ingenuity of the equivalent scene in *Part One*:

> Didst thou hear me?... I did not think thou wast within hearing... No abuse, Hal, o' mine honour; no abuse... no abuse, Ned, in the world, honest Ned, none... I dispraised him before the wicked, that the wicked might not fall in love with thee...

There was a time it wouldn't have taken him so long to come up with a good line.

For all the bonhomie, Falstaff and Hal suddenly seem miles apart. Abruptly called to court for military duty, just as he was in *Part One*, Hal leaves the scene (and much of the rest of the play) with pious blank verse:

> By heaven, Poins, I feel me much to blame,
> So idly to profane the precious time...
> Give me my sword and cloak; Falstaff, goodnight.

Falstaff, on the other hand, prepares for his departure for war as if he were himself the future Henry V:

> You see, my good wenches, how men of merit are sought after;
> the undeserver may sleep, when the man of action is called on.

Quite where he is going at this time of night is unclear: no sooner has he left than he sends word that Doll should come to him before he leaves, so this sombre scene has a cheerful kick in its tail. She should probably scamper off among the cheers of the clientele in the pub: she is going to entrust a shaky old vessel to the seas and will need all the encouragement she can get.

So a reunion from which much might have been expected has merely sputtered along; its merriment laboured, its eavesdropping device routine, the unmasking of Falstaff not particularly funny. The thrill has gone, no doubt about it. Pistol and Doll have brought a new vitality to the Boar's Head, but neither of them has anything to do with Hal: indeed Hal's attachment to Falstaff looks a meagre thing next to the affection between the old man and the young working girl. It may be that this improbable, unforced feeling of theirs is what the scene has been drawing attention to: the reprobate and the tart now look better together than the Crown Prince and his favourite knight of the realm.

✦

Appropriately enough, the road divides: Hal and Falstaff will not meet again until the moment outside Westminster Abbey when Falstaff stands face to face with King Henry V. Perhaps with the sense of having lost something irretrievable, he plunges into old England, into a world of Cotswold apple orchards and quiet pathways. His mission has only a light narrative meaning – much to the Lord Chief Justice's chagrin, he has an official commission to take on a new pack of rebels led by the Archbishop of York – but an important thematic one. In many ways it is an elegy for Hal, a mourning rite before its time.

Again the countryside seems to release something in Falstaff, and he talks directly to us, with unique colour and perceptiveness, his instincts undimmed by the Gloucestershire sun. On his way to Yorkshire, he makes this rather wide detour to visit an old acquaintance, the country Justice Robert Shallow, who may be able to provide him with local recruits. Again Shakespeare has seen an opportunity – to expand Falstaff's description of his recruits in *Part One* – and he warms to it as he didn't quite to its predecessor, in some of the most remarkable tragicomic writing he ever did. Justice Shallow lards the process of conscription with memories of the great days of their early acquaintance (much more vivid to him than to Falstaff): amateur theatricals around Clement's Inn, or the night when they had some kind of orgy in the Windmill pub in St George's Field in Southwark and Shallow's only regret was that Jane Nightwork, his favourite, 'never could away' with him.

The scene in Shallow's orchard is a delight: you can smell the apples, feel the sun and relish a new tempo of conversation, rambling and nostalgic. But it only works properly if it is accompanied not by comedy rustics but real young men standing listening, desperately trying to think of pretexts to avoid being recruited. Under the apple trees, they are looking death in the face, while Shallow ruminates about old acquaintances now dropping off the metaphorical tree – 'Is old Double dead?'. These young men are not going to grow as old as Double. First, like Pompey Bum in *Measure for Measure* and other working-class characters in Shakespeare, they have to put up with jokes about their names; then, without the means to bribe their way out, they have to accept their fate as cannon fodder as certainly as if they were headed for Ypres or Passchendaele. Bullcalf has a 'whoreson cold, sir, a cough' but is chosen because he can roar so loudly; Mouldy, despite his plea that he's needed to look after his aged mother, is told that his name insists he be 'used'; Shadow is chosen because he may give Falstaff relief from the heat. Behind Falstaff's back Mouldy and Bullcalf manage to bribe Bardolph, who like his master is giving himself preposterous airs; in this way Falstaff loses the two recruits who might have done him some good. Francis Feeble, gently teased for his profession as a ladies' tailor, is the only one who rises to the challenge philosophically:

> By my troth, a man can die but once; we owe God a death.

The last phrase is well-chosen: Falstaff may remember Hal saying the exact same thing to him before the battle at Shrewsbury.

However far he travels, all the old man's mental roads now lead back to his adopted son. He finishes three scenes – two in Shallow's orchard, one on the Gaultree Forest battlefield – with a prose soliloquy dedicated to Hal, for our ears only. They represent the best of him, even though his ostensible behaviour is at its familiar worst. Surely Hal would enjoy this puncturing of Shallow's nostalgia, as deadly as his interpretation of military honour at Shrewsbury:

> This same starved justice hath done nothing but prate to me of the wildness of his youth... and every third word a lie... I do remember him at Clement's Inn, like a man made after supper of a cheese-paring; when a' was naked, he was for all the world like a forked radish... yet lecherous as a monkey, and the whores called him mandrake...

You wish Hal could be there to hear this. It's part of Falstaff's tragedy that at the very moment he would most appeal to Hal's affections and intelligence, he is slipping away.

In the battle against the rebels (a dreary bunch compared to Hotspur's army – insurrection can be a dull business), Falstaff has a rare stroke of luck and is reminded of Hal once more. He comes face to face with Sir John Coleville of the Dale, a 'most furious knight', who on hearing that he's dealing with the hero of Shrewsbury immediately surrenders without a blow. This time Falstaff is not allowed credit for the capture: the cold-blooded Prince John of Lancaster, who has taken his brother Hal's place on the battlefield, denies it him – so unlike Hal, who allowed his friend the glory of killing Hotspur. We dislike John by comparison, with a dislike that intensifies as he carts the surrendering Coleville off for execution and then tricks the rebel leaders under pretence of a truce and has them summarily killed as well. We can see that John is more his father's son than Hal, whose reserves of gallantry he certainly lacks, and that he perhaps represents a new world. The obvious contrast triggers another Falstaffian extemporisation. The trouble with this 'sober-blooded boy' John is that 'he drinks no wine', an oversight that always leads to the 'male green sickness' whereby a man can only father daughters. Continual drinking is the secret of life, and somehow guarantees the future of the nation:

> Hereof comes it that Prince Harry is valiant; for the cold blood he did naturally inherit of his father, he hath like lean, sterile, and bare land, manured, husbanded and tilled, with excellent endeavour of drinking good and good store of fertile sherris, that he is become very hot and valiant. If I had a thousand sons, the first humane principle I would teach them should be, to forswear thin potations and addict themselves to sack.

There is no evidence that Hal is a heavy drinker: linking the two things Falstaff loves most, this is really a wistful message from a father to a son who has not quite followed his example:

> A good sherris sack hath a two-fold operation in it. It ascends me into the brain; dries me there all the foolish and dull and crudy vapours which environ it; makes it apprehensive, quick, forgetive, full of nimble, fiery and delectable shapes; which delivered o'er to the voice, the tongue, which is the birth, becomes excellent wit. The second property of your excellent sherris is the warming of the blood; which before, cold and settled, left the liver white and pale, which is the badge of pusillanimity and cowardice; but the sherris warms it, and makes it course from the inwards to the parts extreme: it illumineth the face, which, as a beacon, gives warning to all the rest of this little kingdom, man, to arm…

On his circuitous way home from Yorkshire, Falstaff drops in on Shallow again, largely to fleece him (he will by the end of the play owe him the equivalent of £200,000 in our money). But he is uncharacteristically muted, and would clearly prefer to get away than endure the Justice's hospitality one more night. As his host prepares supper, all he can manage is an odd formality:

> You must excuse me, Master Robert Shallow.

There is only one man who would make the evening tolerable for him, one whose face would be literally creased up with joy:

> I will devise matter enough out of this Shallow to keep Prince
> Harry in continual laughter... O, you shall see him laugh till
> his face be like a wet cloak ill laid up!

As it is, we watch him with increasing apprehension. Surrounded by merriment, he takes an after-dinner digestif in Shallow's orchard, accompanied by a pippin of Shallow's own grafting. It is 'the sweet o' the night', wine is flowing, Shallow's relative Silence peppers the scene with tipsy songs. Shallow, in the overbearing way of the well-oiled, keeps commanding everyone to be merry; Bardolph and Shallow's man Davy swear to be friends for life and to meet up in London one of these days. This kind of sixes and sevens would swiftly, under Falstaff's rule at the Boar's Head, have become a bacchanal; but here he says virtually nothing, like a tolerant outsider putting up with boring drunks:

> 'Fore God, you have here a goodly dwelling, and a rich...
> There's a merry heart, good Master Silence.

What is he waiting for? Why the forced politeness? Why, for the first time, a verbal frailty to match his physical ageing?

It's as if he knew what is happening elsewhere. For if Hal has indeed been sick at heart it has not been for him. While Falstaff has criss-crossed the nation, its future King has been journeying into the dark machinery of government, settling his accounts. When we left the Boar's Head, the tone was already shifting and history on the move. While Doll was attending to Falstaff, a mile or so away the King was lamenting that he could not achieve what she – one of his thousands of poorest subjects – would soon sink into, a modicum of rest:

> O sleep! O gentle sleep...
> O thou dull god, why liest thou with the vile
> In loathsome beds, and leav'st the kingly couch
> A watch-case or a common 'larum-bell...

This is a good example of how Shakespeare manages the profound links between widely different parts of his story: he is holding the young tart and the King of England in the same frame. The royal pyjamas and the momentary sexual accommodations of Falstaff are all part of the same organism.

From this point on it is as if the actor of Hal has a new part to play. Can this really be the Eastcheap regular who, re-entering the action and seeing his father comatose and the crown on his pillow, sounds such a note:

> O polish'd perturbation! Golden care!
> That keep'st the ports of slumber open wide
> To many a watchful night! Sleep with it now!

Yes it can, because Shakespeare has been careful to bring him on with an inappropriate joke typical of his old life:

> How now? Rain within doors and none abroad?

In fact it was innocent – he was rejoicing at the rebels' defeat – but it was possible for his brothers to interpret it as callousness to the mortal matter in hand. Hal has never been able to convince anybody, even Poins, that he has human feelings for his sick father: he well knows how the world sees him.

But as he sits beside the bed, believing him dead already, his new speech glistens with destiny. Whatever you think of royalty, in the theatre it is a brilliant thing to see this reprobate beginning to lean into the slipstream of history – his vision sharp, his tone economical and resonant:

> My gracious lord! My father!
> This sleep is sound indeed, this is a sleep
> That from this golden rigol hath divorc'd
> So many English kings...

When Henry wakes up and finds the crown gone with Hal into the next room, it must seem to him that natural succession is yet another theft. Richard II once teased him, inviting him to seize the crown while continuing to grip it himself; now it has been seized again, by his son. He turns on Hal, and they begin a long wrangle of reproach, protest and grief. To the delight of modern audiences, Hal is advised to distract attention from domestic controversy by going to war abroad as soon as possible – and in the end there is a profoundly moving reunion, a catharsis for audience and characters. We didn't realise till now how much we had invested in these two lonely men, father and son; it is as if, all said and done, we needed them to come to terms. More, if the three *Henry*s are played in a day, this scene comes up at about teatime, when the audience's blood sugar might otherwise be dropping, so it is perfectly placed.

One effect is to make Falstaff's world seem trivial for the first time. Hearing the news of the King's death in Shallow's orchard, he is already shuffling his Cabinet:

> Master Robert Shallow, choose what office thou wilt in the
> land, 'tis thine. Pistol, I will double-charge thee with dignities

– and he plunges into the storm like a burlesque King Lear, darkness about to descend on his life. He is still travelling towards London as Hal forms his own cross-party Truth and Reconciliation Committee. The Lord Chief Justice, apprehensively ready 'to welcome the condition of the time', is amazed that this is no longer the Hal who once punched him and even had to be sent to prison, but a young leader eager to listen to a new father. Hal keeps hammering the crucial word home:

> You shall be as a father to my youth...
> My father is gone wild into his grave
> And in his tomb lie my affections...
> Now call we our high court of parliament...
> That the great body of our state may go
> In equal rank with the best-govern'd nation...
> In which you, father, shall have foremost hand...

Somewhere between rhetoric and poetry, his speech asserts the audacity of hope:

> The tide of blood in me
> Hath proudly flow'd in vanity till now;
> Now doth it turn and ebb back to the sea...

At last this is the metaphor he was struggling for when he overdid his speeches to his father in *Part One*: the dread moment of losing him has set Hal free.

In a street outside Westminster Abbey, at two in the afternoon, Falstaff is out of breath: with his motley group, dressed to kill, he stands in prime position from which to 'leer' upon the new King as he comes by:

> O, if I had had time to have made new liveries... 'tis no matter:
> this poor show doth better; this doth infer the zeal I have to see
> him.

Shallow is in a permanent rictus of nodding:

SHALLOW: It doth so.

FALSTAFF: It shows my earnestness of affection.

SHALLOW: It doth so.

FALSTAFF: My devotion.

SHALLOW: It doth, it doth, it doth.

At last the Coronation procession passes. Hal acknowledges his old friend all right:

FALSTAFF: God save thee, my sweet boy...

HENRY V: My Lord Chief Justice, speak to that vain man...

FALSTAFF: My King, my Jove! I speak to thee, my heart.

HENRY V: I know thee not, old man; fall to thy prayers;
How ill white hairs become a fool and jester...

For twenty-five sharp, bright lines the message slices into Falstaff. Understand this: everything he represents is an old dream of Hal's he has awoken to despise; at his time of life he should (a low blow) look to his health; no, he may not answer back; he is to be banished with 'the rest of my misleaders'. You would think Hal were an innocent victim of circumstance. But this is forever how politicians editorialise in front of the cameras:

For God doth know, so shall the world perceive
That I have turn'd away my former self,
So shall I those that kept me company.

Falstaff is to receive a small unspecified allowance 'for competence of life', and in return he is not to come within ten miles of Hal again; in the unlikely event he reforms, his case will be reviewed. And since the essentials in this long story have always been told in monosyllables – 'I know you all... I do, I will... I know thee not' – there are two final ones – 'Set on' – and he's gone.

One certainty about Falstaff has been his ability to face down the devil, but he is no match for this. As the crowd stares at him there is not a slither of ambiguity to grip on to, no hint of humour to lighten it, no complicity. Perhaps this is why executions in public used to be favoured rather than in dignified privacy: to appease any anxiety, what Hal needed to do had to be seen to be done. His old friend is on his knees in the front row of the crowd, laughed at, being looked away from, his cap in his hand. He even, in a gesture towards good faith, acknowledges something he never would have done before:

Master Shallow, I owe you a thousand pound...

But even this genial part of the pack is turning on its wounded member, and Shallow shows no more mercy than Hal:

> Ay, marry, Sir John: which I beseech you to let me have home with me.

Falstaff briefly rallies:

> I shall be sent for in private to him. Look you, he must seem thus to the world… I shall be sent for soon at night.

In theory he could be right: he's grasped the possible politics, and deals can be done. But we can't wait. Within moments, as Shallow negotiates for at least £500 of his £1,000, John of Lancaster (of all aggravations) returns with officers and the little party is bundled off, away from view and possible sympathy, to prison.

As for our own sympathies, there's little doubt where they will lie; but sympathy is not really the point. There is an absolute consistency to what has happened, and Hal's willingness to take the moment by the neck commands an awed respect. But the breaking of the old man's heart was almost audible. Hal's Falstaff, scholar and soldier, lord of misrule, one of life's virtuosi, a counterfeit father who even delighted in being teased for being fat, has had the colour drained from him. Falstaff's Hal, ruthless and as isolated as if he were an orphan, was unable to escape the inevitable. Hal and his pernickety father have continued England's history; Falstaff, embodiment of licence, will soon die in an upstairs room of the Boar's Head, fidgeting and muttering. If Falstaff's love for Hal was always compromised, why is this scene so very affecting? Because we too had begun to fool ourselves; it is the kind of self-deception we all know.

And in this education of a prince, has there been no cost for the prince – did he really have no feelings for the old man? Were those nights in the Boar's Head only a matter of acquiring the common touch as an investment in the future? If he had no belief in Falstaff's values, did he need to spend quite so much time among them? Was there even a chink of light in his bleak final speech, or a painful subtext? It can be played so, as long as the speech keeps coming, its surface official and even: the absolute priority for Hal is that it should be as impermeable as it would need to be if replayed on television later. But beneath the code, both men know that what is being disposed of is a thing to be mourned but not revisited; a necessarily dealt wound that won't close up; a loss hard to define, but impossible to make good.

✦

God save thy grace, King Hal, my royal Hal!

– Henry IV Part Two

The historical Henry V was never connected with anyone called Falstaff; and he went to war in France a couple of years later, and not, as brother John says at the end of *Henry IV Part Two*, 'ere this year expire'. But in Shakespeare's next instalment, *Henry V*, naturally enough, the events come tumbling over each other. Within moments there are changes all round: Doll Tearsheet has disappeared, one dreads to think where, but Pistol seems to have survived intact and is now Mistress Quickly's husband. Her marital status was always confusing – as confusing as the identity of Gadshill or the difference between Poins and Peto. Married to someone in *Part One* (where she describes herself as 'an honest man's wife' and Falstaff instructs her to love her husband), then suing Falstaff for breach of promise in *Part Two*, she has now hitched up with her despised swaggerer – much to the fury of Corporal Nym, who in the vague mores of this world thought he had a promise from her.

There is, in the squeaky-clean new reign, a general anxiety in this part of town. Before the end of *Part Two* there was an incident in which a man died after being beaten by the two women and Pistol: the police arrested Doll Tearsheet (who vainly pretended a mitigating pregnancy with a cushion) while Mistress Quickly, her shoulder put out of joint in the struggle, subscribed to a prevailing myth –

> O the Lord, that Sir John were come! He would make this a
> bloody day to somebody...

Now, more than ever, she has to watch her reputation:

> we cannot lodge and board a dozen or fourteen gentlewomen
> that live honestly by the prick of their needles, but it will be
> thought we keep a bawdy house straight.

Which of course is what the Boar's Head has in part always been: in the new dispensation Mr and Mrs Pistol are a pair of old disreputables setting up a bed and breakfast where a brothel used to be. But the tide is against them, and against all their friends. The new character, Nym (a word that meant 'thief'), has a very eccentric manner of speaking which he'd like to think gnomic, and his character is well nailed later in the play by Falstaff's perceptive Page:

> He hath heard that men of few words are the best men... but his few bad words are matched with as few good deeds, for he never broke any man's head but his own, and that was against a post when he was drunk.

We may not quite be able to get interested in Nym, because our tastes have changed. The Chorus has declared Henry V's reign open with the bright possibility of an unprovoked war against France. The new King has heeded his father's deathbed advice to

> busy giddy minds
> With foreign quarrels

– and we, like 'all the youth of England', are more on fire about the national news than about the love life of the lowlife.

The youth of England perhaps, but not the elderly: in the shadow cast by the new Sun King a quiet death is in progress. With patriotic racket in the streets and Nym and Pistol trying to beat each other to death with rhetoric, tucked away in an upstairs room lies a dwindling figure that would never have flourished in this new regime, even had the King not 'killed his heart'. Mistress Quickly always knew that Falstaff would 'yield the crow a pudding one of these days' and that even Bardolph's famous red face wouldn't warm the bed he is dying in. In an epilogue at the end of *Part Two* Shakespeare promised more Falstaff in *Henry V*; now he has realised what damage that could do to the new play and coolly reneged.

Mistress Quickly has been at his side when the moment came, and from the utterly authentic way she speaks you feel that Shakespeare too has done somebody such a service:

> A' made a finer end and went away an it had been any christom child. A' parted e'en just between twelve and one, even at the turning o' the tide; for after I saw him fumble with the sheets and play with flowers and smile upon his fingers' ends, I knew there was but one way; for his nose was as sharp as a pen, and a' babbled of green fields.

Feeling his feet, knees and upward, she found that he was 'as cold as any stone'. Now he's gone she is at tender pains to defend his reputation:

NYM: They say a' cried out of sack.

MRS QUICKLY: Ay, that a' did.

BARDOLPH: And of women.

MRS QUICKLY: Nay, that a' did not.

> BOY: Yes, that a' did; and said they were devils incarnate.
>
> MRS QUICKLY: A' could never abide carnation; 'twas a colour he never liked...
>
> BOY: Do you not remember a' saw a flea stick upon Bardolph's nose, and a' said it was a black soul burning in hell?

There's no doubt whose doing the tragedy is:

> NYM: The King hath run bad humours on the knight... the King is a good king: but it must be as it may; he passes some humours and careers.

This tentative elegy for times past is the last we will hear of love in *Henry V* until its very end. The agent of Falstaff's decline, unambiguously assertive, will strip the new play of affection. Its absence is very clear, together with an attempt, partly successful, to cancel the past. Back in *Henry IV*, rather as if he was emphasising that Tony Blair's having played lead guitar would make him a better Prime Minister, the Earl of Warwick promised the dying King that the memory of Hal's old friends would

> as a pattern or a measure live
> By which his grace must mete the lives of others,
> Turning past evils to advantages.

Evil or not, their memory is uncelebrated and his meting of lives notably robust. Henry moves through the play like a scythe, connecting with one area of the brain only. His one declared moment of conscience comes the night before Agincourt, when, unsure of success, he seeks to make amends in heaven for his father's usurpation with a desperate programme of public works. Even here it is difficult to distinguish sincerity from self-justification. There is just one other moment when love – or nostalgia, or acknowledgment of things gone – might have been glimpsed. During the campaign Captain Fluellen brings Henry news of the execution of an old friend who has predictably disgraced himself by robbing a French church:

> one Bardolph, if your majesty know the man: his face is all bubukles, and whelks, and knobs, and flames of fire...

Bardolph's nose brings back a happy memory to the audience, and we turn with interest to Hal, protagonist in the Gadshill robbery and other illegalities. This is not a moment when he needs to dissemble. Everyone knows about his past, he is not on show as he was outside the Abbey; rather he is in the mud and the cold and the chaos of battle with his men. He could afford a little warmth. But here is what he says:

We would have all such offenders so cut off...

At such moments, *Henry V* feels to be quite a different play from its pred-ecessors; not a panorama of England but England as a bullet with a single trajectory.

Leaving for France, we also leave behind the supremely rich lan-guage, the subtlety and multiplicity of *Henry IV*. King Hal is a logician and a rhetorician – not just in his stirring speeches, but because of his ability, now applied to a dubious cause, to construct an argument and see it this way and that, a skill Shakespeare learned at the feet of Thomas Jenkins at King Edward's School. It is a gift Hal used to employ to wrongfoot everyone around him: then it helped him keep his distance as a prince, but now it is taken as kingly good humour. You can never be sure of the man: he both despises and stands on ceremony, makes his subjects nervous then reassures them. Most rulers do this, as anyone who has met the Royal Family can confirm: they allow you to be impressed by the distance between you, then affect to narrow it with chumminess. Hal will alternately punish an honest soldier, Michael Williams, for ques-tioning his motives in going to war (a confidence Williams made to Hal when he spied in disguise on his people to check their morale), then reward him with a glove full of gold.

In this new, harsh light, Hal's brilliant career as the scourge of the French is an energetic but chilly thing. Next to his loyal and warm-hearted fellow Welshman Fluellen, he looks like a specially cold fish. Part of this is due to some Shakespearian debunking. No sooner has the King urged the English unto the breach than there is Bardolph getting a laugh out of it:

On, on, on, on, on! To the breach, to the breach!

Pistol meanwhile is given the interesting task of representing the entirety of the battle of Agincourt by beating the hell out of an unarmed French prisoner while stealing his money and mocking his accent: that's how Shakespeare chooses to represent the iconic battle in a play that some still think of as an anthem for England.

When it finally comes, love will be in an odder, more disguised form. Making a treaty with the defeated French, Henry insists on marrying the French Princess Katherine (whose sister, oddly enough, had been Richard II's child bride) to bind the two kingdoms together. This is pure political bargaining: Katherine is simply

our capital demand, compris'd
Within the fore-rank of our articles.

So she has less than no choice, and the normally eloquent Henry, wearing his wooer's hat, seems not much bothered:

> If I could win a lady at leapfrog, or by vaulting into my saddle with my armour on my back... I should quickly leap into a wife. But before God, Kate, I cannot look greenly, nor gasp out my eloquence, nor I have no cunning in protestation...

It's an unpromising start, but then his tone shifts a little:

> If thou canst love a fellow of this temper, Kate, whose face is not worth sunburning, that never looks in his glass for love of anything he sees there, let thine eye be thy cook. I speak to thee plain soldier... And while thou livest, dear Kate, take a fellow of plain and uncoined constancy, for he perforce must do thee right, because he hath not the gift to woo in other places... A good leg will fall, a straight back will stoop... a fair face will wither, a full eye will wax hollow – but a good heart, Kate, is the sun and the moon, or rather the sun and not the moon, for it shines bright and never changes, but keeps his course truly.

It is easy enough to believe that having done what he has to the French Henry might have difficulty confronting his own face in the mirror in the mornings. And where was his 'plain and uncoined constancy' when he broke Falstaff apart or hanged Bardolph and Nym for the sort of petty theft he used to approve himself? And what has a good heart to do with the moment when he had his French prisoners killed at Agincourt – not, as was glossed by Gower, in response to the French killing of English boys, but simply as a means of releasing the prisoners' guards into active service?

But this is a character who has conditioned the actor to listen for deeply buried subtext; and do you hear what I hear? The talk of mortality, of the sun and moon, is a new music, faltering and tentative, coming late in the day. Perhaps Hal sounded a little like this by his father's deathbed, but even then there was a veil of self-consciousness. He has made no real concession to his other life since the moment when, for good fellowship, he gilded Falstaff's lie about killing Hotspur – at the very moment he needed the credit himself. Those now seem like less constricted days, when a good heart might have been all a man needed – no watchfulness, no strategy, no spin. Certainly, the mild trangressiveness of the Boar's Head was nothing compared to this toxic world of death and collateral damage. In the wistfulness of Henry's surprising lines, or rather between them, a fat figure drawn in the russet and sandstone colours of old England begins to re-form and perhaps stirs in his memory. This is what the cost has been, and also what we've been waiting for.

The effect of course is to open Henry up a fraction, so that Katherine can begin to assess him as a human being and even feel something for him. Quietly, the scene begins to change shape. As if sensing her, Hal does something truly unexpected – he tries to speak in French. At first he makes a real hash of it:

> Je quand sur le possession de France, et quand vous avez le possession de moi… vostre est France, et vous estes mienne

– but then, gifted with tongues, he speaks as if he'd known the language all his life:

> La plus belle Katherine du monde, ma très chère et divine déesse…

For the first time in three plays he risks falling on his face. The effort is charming and funny, but more than funny: the conqueror is trying to speak the language of the conquered, and finding that he perhaps can. This, after all, is the beginning of love, this stepping into someone else's territory, trying to speak their language, making a start. If a fat knight and the Prince Royal can find something in each other that neither can elsewhere, or the same fat knight and a tart tell each other the simple truth, why not a captive with no English and her conqueror?

> You have witchcraft in your lips, Kate; there is more eloquence in a sugar touch of them than in the tongues of the French council.

The historical fact is that the marriage between Katherine and Henry, which Shakespeare places in the immediate wake of Agincourt, would continue to be a political football in the struggle between French and English. It was only consummated five years later, and, in an irony Shakespeare must have liked very much, it turned into a love match: in the remaining two years before Henry's death (by another irony he'd contracted dysentery during the French campaign) they found deep feelings for each other. The influence of this manipulated Frenchwoman on English history was considerable: having thus been mother to King Henry VI, Katherine remarried, to Owen Tudor, and became grandmother to Henry VII, who brought peace to England after the Wars of the Roses, sixty years after this. But in imagination, she and Hal, however cynically set up, immediately create peace; and Shakespeare attributes it to a movement of character – to the ability of a calculating man to surprise himself, to release himself from his own power, to give in the act of taking.

This would undoubtedly get Falstaff's vote, and I fancy there is a distant guest at the wedding. Sometimes passers-by or derelicts take a break from the struggles of the open air and wander into a church, chancing on a ceremony of marriage or a funeral. They generally don't disrupt them. As King Hal and Katherine of Valois solemnise their vows in the ancient cathedral of Troyes, I see a huge hill of flesh hunkered down approvingly in a remote pew. He may have yielded the crow his pudding; but somewhere along the way he may also have taught the future King of England how to love.

5

Love, Love, Nothing But Love, Sweet Love

Fools for Love – Love's Labour's Lost – The Merchant of Venice –
The Taming of the Shrew – Much Ado About Nothing –
Romeo and Juliet – A Midsummer Night's Dream

Grace comes in odd forms in Shakespeare. When Falstaff drives Pistol out of the Boar's Head, Doll Tearsheet and he share their moment of blind, hopeful sweetness, candid and tender. Who would have thought Shakespeare would have given such a scene to such a pair? But then who would have thought that Henry V would have fallen for Katherine, or that the overwhelming violence of *Henry VI Part Two* would be the site of one of Shakespeare's great love affairs? The extravagant passion of Margaret and Suffolk is lit up by lightning flashes:

> MARGARET: O could this kiss be printed in thy hand
> That thou mightst think upon these by the seal
> Through whom a thousand sighs are breath'd for thee…

> SUFFOLK: A wilderness is populous enough
> So Suffolk had thy heavenly company…
> Where from thy sight I should be raging mad
> And cry out for thee to close up mine eyes
> To have thee with thy lips to stop my mouth.

It's Shakespeare's most full-blown writing in this manner so far, and the psychology is delicate as well. Accepting the inevitable, Margaret sounds a little like Juliet when Romeo is banished and she almost wants him gone so she can start her real suffering:

> So get thee gone that I may know my grief;
> 'Tis but surmis'd while thou art standing by...

And as they finally fall apart, their verse divides as well:

> SUFFOLK: Even as a splitted bark, so sunder we;
>   This way fall I to death.
> MARGARET: This way for me.

The love stories in these history plays are conditioned by extreme circumstantial pressure: Shakespeare has become an expert on the unpromising soil in which the emotion can grow. But he knows the inside story as well: any relationship can be snagged not by circumstance but by the lovers' individual DNAs. Jaques's glib reduction in *As You Like It* of man's journey through life to seven images for seven ages suits his own lachrymose nature but misrepresents Shakespeare himself, who insists that a human being's temper and impulses are forever mixed. It's not just a matter of the third age forever frozen in the act of choosing the perfect rhyme for his mistress's eyebrow: in love, personality readjusts at every moment, one state of mind elides into another, and every combination can be explosive.

This is becoming interesting enough for him to take the subject to the centre of a play rather than being an incident within it. Then, the third and fourth ages seem to interplay particularly well: a whole evening can be devoted to how a lover may turn murderous. Troilus, betrayed by Cressida, no longer sighs like an amorous furnace but rages like a forest fire:

> You vile abominable tents
> Thus proudly pight upon our Phrygian plains,
> Let Titan rise as early as he dare
> I'll through and through you...

Conversely, the most straight-arrow soldiers have amorous sinews; Coriolanus's arch-enemy Aufidius greets him like this:

> Let me twine
> Mine arms about that body, where against
> My grained ash an hundred times hath broke,
> And scarr'd the moon with splinters.

And of course love can make a fool of a man. The triple pillar of the Roman world Mark Antony becomes a strumpet's fool simply because he is unable to leave Cleopatra alone, not seeing that the world he thinks well lost is what he has spent his soldier's life battling for. Less tragically, the magnificently decrepit figure of Don Armado in *Love's Labour's Lost*, as intent as the rest of the Court of Navarre on spiritual improvement through sexual abstinence, is tempted by the country girl Jaquenetta. He celebrates his falling-off with a battery of quixotic military images:

> I do affect her very ground (which is base) where her shoe (which is baser) guided by her foot (which is basest) doth tread…Cupid's butt-shaft is too hard for Hercules' club… the passado he respects not, the duello he regards not; his disgrace is to be called boy, but his glory is to subdue men. Adieu, valour, rust, rapier, be still, drum, for your manager is in love; yea, he loveth.

By no accident his splendid folly lies alongside a ravishing speech delivered by his fellow votary Berowne:

> A lover's eyes will gaze an eagle blind,
> A lover's ear will hear the lowest sound
> When the suspicious head of theft is stopp'd;
> Love's feeling is more soft and sensible
> Than are the tender horns of cockled snails;
> Love's tongue proves dainty Bacchus gross in taste;
> For valour is not love a Hercules
> Still climbing trees in the Hesperides?
> Subtle as Sphinx, as sweet and musical
> As bright Apollo's lute, strung with his hair,
> And when love speaks, the voice of all the gods
> Makes heaven drowsy with the harmony.

The catch here is the outrageous moral equivocation: Berowne's only aim is to find a pretext for his companions and himself to break their solemn vows of celibacy. Blood rushing to their heads, they charge off to conquer their women as if taking up Armado's discarded weaponry:

> KING: Saint Cupid, then! And soldiers, to the field!
>
> BEROWNE: Advance your standards, and upon them, lords!
> Pell-mell, down with them…

Berowne the lyrical equivocator, Armado the sentimental warrior, Troilus lethal in rejection: even in full sail Shakespeare was ever the ironist. This was a writer who so understood the unruliness of human existence that he let an anonymous lord in *All's Well That Ends Well* declare that

> The web of our life is of a mingled yarn, good and ill together.

✦

Although Jaques promises both men and women as 'mere players', he delivers only men, all occupied in rather a limited choice of careers. He doesn't seem interested in the women, whom elsewhere Shakespeare frequently makes more watchful, more self-aware and less benighted than the men. Berowne's lover is Rosaline, a woman of sharp moral sense as well as wit: in the end she sends him into retreat for a year so that he can grow up by undertaking community work among the sick. Her philosophical alertness corrects the lyrical exuberance of the play, in which the men not only don't get the girls but have their perjury punished by such penances, with only a hint of earned happiness in the future. They may not pass their tests; or perhaps the women end up more or less accepting them in the lost and intriguingly titled later play *Love's Labour's Won*.

Rosaline's is a short part sometimes seen as a precursor of the big female fighters who star in the classic comedies of the 1590s – Beatrice in *Much Ado About Nothing*, Portia in *The Merchant of Venice* and especially Katharina in *The Taming of the Shrew*. Squaring up to the men, these women achieve, if not Rosaline's control of her situation, at least some bargaining power. In *The Merchant*, set in a world hostile to human tenderness, Portia's suitor Bassanio – a man of limited wit and ingenuity – coldbloodedly borrows money from his male admirer, Antonio, to win her by entering an absurd competition about three caskets devised by her father. Made a hostage to fortune by this alarming ceremony, Portia is eventually matched with Bassanio and makes herself indispensable by saving his Antonio's bacon with a famous advocate's quibble. Beyond the trickery of the bloodless pound of flesh lies a perception Bassanio and his friends would never have had. Portia has seen the flaw in the alienated Shylock, lying exactly where his strength seemed to be. Shylock has a vitality shared by no one else on the stage, but his emotional weakness is that he is prepared to murder a friend of the man who eloped with his daughter. Blinded, he blunders into Portia's trap instead of taking the money. The interest here is in how, because of her ingenuity, love's worm quietly turns in Bassanio's moral darkness. Like most people in the play Portia is a thoroughgoing racist, but she is talented; in the end, observing a Christian and a Jewess beginning to make a new future together, she and Bassanio begin to feel a non-mercenary stirring for each other. But there is no doubt that it is Portia who will wear the not very attractive trousers.

✦

Of all mad matches never was the like.

– The Taming of the Shrew

If *The Merchant* is racially tense, *The Taming of the Shrew* is sexually so –
extremely. This is a play which has always changed colour in the available light. In recent times it has gained a new lease of life in the theatre
from a very modern sense that the story of Petruchio and Katharina may
be more than that of a male bully and a bad-tempered woman unpleasantly slugging it out for domination, with the male winning by force of
muscle. The most extreme version of the new argument is that these two
individualistic people, instinctively rebelling against a venal world, find a
private language with which to build a mutually respectful relationship.
The truth may be a little short of this, and a little less pleasing, but it's a
fruitful idea.

Like Bassanio, Petruchio looks to 'wive it wealthily' – in spite of the
fact that his father has recently died and left him all his estate anyway.
Perhaps he fancies to live off his wife and use his legacy for his own pleasure. This being a moment – *The Merchant, The Two Gentlemen, Romeo* –
when Shakespeare thought immediately of Northern Italian towns for
his settings, Petruchio arrives in Padua, on a wave of violence only a little moderated by rhyming verse. He immediately boxes his servant's ears
for a forgivable mistake; but then his future prey, Katharina, makes her
debut by punching her sister Bianca, their father's favourite. Still, the
combative lovers are, in the early stages at least, hard to resist; they certainly stand in relief to the exceptionally dreary subplot of the wooing of
Bianca, which involves characters as confusingly named as Gremio
(Petruchio having a servant called Grumio), a host of aliases and
assumed names to remember, and a notable shortage of grace, wit or
affection.

Petruchio's methods are those of a courtly lion-tamer. On his first
meeting with Katharina he declares himself astonished at the popular
view that she has a limp, since she seems to him as upright and slender
as a hazel twig. Her famous raucous complaints are like the song of a
nightingale to him, her frowns are

morning roses newly wash'd with dew.

Really, he is very polite. His warning that if she hits him he will hit her
back (it's the one thing he will never do) is considerate; and he feels it is

only fair dealing to reassure her that, 'will you, nill you', he will marry her and bring her

> from a wild Kate to a Kate
> Conformable as other household Kates.

So his determination to stand for no nonsense is warmed by imperturbable praise. His inspiration is that there are two Kates, the one the world knows and the one that he senses to be in hiding; and he dares her not to be intrigued. The fact is that he knows that a self-confident, farsighted male will always win out as long as he avoids complacency or disrespect.

This single scene of supposedly formal wooing is very funny. His backhanders are matched by the ingenuity of her insults; but Shakespeare is also at pains to scatter clues to their instinctive recognition of each other – at the very least, they find a shared taste for rude jokes about tongues and tails, coxcombs and combless cocks. The giveaway is Katharina's wordlessness when her father returns to hear the scene's outcome: she briefly calls Petruchio

> A madcap ruffian and a swearing Jack

but then relapses into silence as her father sets about the practicalities of the wedding with what she would normally see as a shopkeeper's haste. It seems that some deeper bargain has been struck.

On the wedding day Petruchio does not so much stand Kate up as bring her down to earth. He turns up for the ceremony looking like a tramp, in

> a pair of boots that have been candle-cases, one buckled, another laced; an old rusty sword ta'en out of the town armoury, with a broken hilt and chapeless, with two broken points...

He and his horse are as one: the latter is like Lee Marvin's crapulous nag, mimicking his master in drunken decrepitude, in the movie *Cat Ballou*. Petruchio's is

> hipped with an old mothy saddle, and stirrups of no kindred, besides possessed with the glanders, and like to mose in the chine, troubled with the lampass, infected with the fashions, full of windgalls, sped with spavins, rayed with the yellows, past cure of the fives, stark spoiled with the staggers, begnawn with the bots, swayed in the back, and shoulder-shotten, near-legged before, and with a half-cheeked bit, and a head-stall of sheep's leather...

> BAPTISTA: Who comes with him?
>
> BIONDELLO: O sir, his lackey, for all the world caparison'd like
>   the horse...

It's lucky that you don't then have to see these strange ailments: no production could make them half as funny.

Taking his place at the altar rail, the dishevelled bridegroom declares, unanswerably, that:

> To me she's married, not unto my clothes.

He causes the officiating priest to drop the Bible by uttering a great enthusiastic oath to confirm that he will have Kate; then he kisses her with 'such a clamorous smack' that the church echoes with it. He punches the priest and calls for wine, all of which he drinks except for what he throws into the sexton's face: this is all somehow done for love. He makes off with his bride, leaving the wedding guests to have the reception without them. To her relief perhaps: he is removing them both from a world which they resent, a fakery in which fathers love their daughters imperfectly and well-wishers think only of money.

So far, so good; but things take a darker tilt once the pair are free of their past. Till now Shakespeare has used the convenience of slapstick to justify the play's violence, usually accompanying it with rhyme. With marriage the gloves come off. Petruchio lets his wife lie in the mud when her horse collapses exhausted under her. At his country house he bullies his servants mercilessly; he throws the dinner around and will neither feed nor sleep with his new bride; and not a rhyme in sight. If it is one thing for a man to flatter his wife with a great kiss at the altar, it's quite another to behave like a pig in front of the servants, who are lax only because he's made no particular demands on them before. For their part, they have, naturally enough, taken on his values, and they hit each other a good deal; one of them, Grumio, is a mini-Petruchio, taunting and tormenting the new mistress in her hunger. It feels like the Addams Family mansion.

Eventually Petruchio feeds Kate, perhaps on the principle of softening up the animal for the kill; but he denies her every new piece of clothing that she wants, dangling it before her and snatching it away to keep her in a permanent posture of begging. Then, chillingly, he turns to us to report on his 'reign'; significantly he does this from on high, the Elizabethan stage's commanding upper level. We must understand that the whole affair has been a matter of breaking in a horse or a dog; this being a soliloquy, he means what he says, and he dares us to reply:

> He that knows better how to tame a shrew,
> Now let him speak, 'tis charity to show.

But he is safe by now because he knows we've enjoyed ourselves, however grudgingly: this is much like Richard III's audience ending up on his side without meaning to.

At length Kate and Petruchio return from their honeymoon, the devil continuing to get the sweetest tunes:

> PETRUCHIO: Well, come, my Kate; we will unto your father's
> Even in these honest mean habiliments:
> Our purses shall be proud, our garments poor,
> For 'tis the mind that makes the body rich:
> And as the sun breaks through the darkest clouds,
> So honour peereth in the meanest habit.
> What, is the jay more precious than the lark
> Because his feathers are more beautiful?

Being by Shakespeare, this attractive speech is followed by its opposite; a dismal piece of bullying as Petruchio insists that it is seven o'clock rather than two:

> Look, what I speak, or do, or think to do,
> You are still crossing it...
> It shall be what o'clock I say it is.

What is the writer up to, bringing things to such a dark point – and letting a little poetry in at the same time? Why, nothing, he would shrug: he is an entertainer, using what comes to hand. But as in *The Comedy of Errors*, his piercing insights into men and women are jostling with his instincts for knockabout. Confoundingly, under Petruchio's totalitarianism Kate begins to sound like an adult, matching her husband's cadences:

> Why, sir, I trust I may have leave to speak,
> And speak I will; I am no child, no babe;
> Your betters have endur'd me say my mind,
> And if you cannot, best you stop your ears.
> My tongue will tell the anger of my heart
> Or else my heart concealing it will break...

They start off back to Padua, their ghastly holiday over. Petruchio insists that the moon is the sun and vice versa and that the old man approaching them on the road is a beautiful girl whom Kate should embrace in greeting; then he changes his mind and makes him an old man again.

Kate, who a few moments ago was developing the limpid integrity of a Hermione or her namesake in *Henry VIII*, also shifts tone: as if she'd suddenly got the point of the unsavoury game, she obliges him with wit and panache, rather as Polonius indulges Hamlet by pretending a cloud looks like a weasel and a whale:

> Pardon, old father, my mistaking eyes
> That have been so bedazzled with the sun
> That everything I look on seemeth green;
> Now I perceive thou art a reverend father;
> Pardon I pray thee for my mad mistaking.

Her acquiescence is not so much a surrender as an intelligent means of taking control, and the sudden compliance takes the wind out of Petruchio's sails. What is he to do with such obliging behaviour?

Back in Padua they encounter the subplot, and we see why Shakespeare has left it so stupid. Its slapstick, involving a mirthless disguise to raise money for Bianca's marriage, stands in steep contrast to Petruchio's modulation as he turns gently to Kate:

> Prithee Kate, let's stand aside, and see the end of this controversy.

They watch what they have saved each other from. Petruchio might take Kate's arm as carefully as in the Elizabethan ceremony of hand-fasting, when the lovers answer each other's prayer for mutual good treatment. It is a most surprising exchange, and Kate says almost exactly the same thing as Petruchio just has:

> Husband, let's follow, to see the end of this ado.

Put the lines side by side and you see what Shakespeare has done – the key, the rhythm, the inflection and phrasing are the same. Perhaps too the word 'husband' – affectionate, prosaic and normal – is what he has been waiting for:

> PETRUCHIO: First kiss me, Kate, and we will.
>
> KATE: What, in the midst of the street?
>
> PETRUCHIO: What, art thou ashamed of me?
>
> KATE: No sir, God forbid, but ashamed to kiss.
>
> PETRUCHIO: Why then, let's home again. Come sirrah, let's away.
>
> KATE: Nay I will give thee a kiss; now pray thee, love, stay.

PETRUCHIO: Is not this well? Come, my sweet Kate,
  Better once than never, for never too late.

This singular reconciliation makes the play's famous final moments, when Kate stands before two pairs of newly-weds to expound the duties of a wife, especially ambiguous. Here the production finally shows its colours without necessarily sounding the depths of Shakespeare's mystery. When Kate declares

Thy husband is thy lord, thy life, thy keeper

is her tongue in her cheek, or is this what she has painfully decided? Is her public deference a coded message to her husband, reminding him of a bargain he had best not fail in?

Has she changed Petruchio? Perhaps, by making him see her for what at heart she really is. On the other hand, for all the roughness of their courtship, it is possible that these two understood each other from the first moment – she seeing exactly what he was up to, he allowing her anger to exhaust itself on him. And whatever the reality of their marriage is to be, it can hardly be as ominous as that of Bianca's with Lucentio. Bianca has seemed independent-minded in its palatable, father-pleasing version, well this side of her sister's truculence. But now as a wife and far from tamed, she begins to display some of Kate's unruliness in her resentment of the men. The point is obvious – difficult in a small way, she will end up unhappier than her genuinely conflicted sister. As for Kate, whether her speech bodes 'peace... and love and quiet life' or only the continuation of Petruchio's 'awful rule', it will certainly be true to itself.

Rocking on an awkward hinge, *The Taming of the Shrew* mixes cruelty with farce, sometimes leaving out the farce. For all its outlandish rituals, it expresses Shakespeare's intense curiosity about men and women, as if he were wondering out loud how to disarm their mutual defensiveness. Nerve and imperturbability may help a man get over his fear of a woman; humour may ease a woman's anger. It's a modern commonplace that as soon as you ask whether men should be cavemen, or if women are happier leading or being led, or how much of either, you offend someone: Shakespeare gleefully confounds our narrow programming. But we can surely agree that a good partnership defines its own terms. Some characters in the play are scandalised by Kate's and Petruchio's union; but the mad-brained rudesby and his shrewish wife are not to be judged by expert outsiders, and finally Petruchio speaks for them both:

If she and I be pleas'd, what's that to you?

✦

BENEDICK: I do love nothing in the world so well as you:
    is not that strange?

BEATRICE: As strange as the thing I know not...

– Much Ado About Nothing

There is an odd convergence between *The Shrew* and *Much Ado About Nothing*. Petruchio and Benedick have no relatives in their plays, while Katharina is a neglected sister and Beatrice the niece of a man who is fonder (and less frightened) of his daughter. There is something of the fully grown orphan in all four of them – all redeemed by their mother wit, and all a liability to their friends, who want them to see that two joined solitudes can be better than one. The difference is that Benedick and Beatrice, for all their vitality, lack the relative self-knowledge of Petruchio and Kate: *Much Ado*, though more popular, is a less searching play, not so provocative, more reassuring.

I confess that if there is a Shakespeare that I like less than I feel I ought to, this is it. Aside from the more arcane academic interpretations – that no-thing is a euphemism for vagina, or that the play is about not(h)ing things down – the title is apt enough: *Much Ado* can be a little disappointing. It is full of characters done slightly better elsewhere – Leonato aspires to Capulet in *Romeo and Juliet* but lacks his devouring energy; Claudio could be an early study for Troilus were it not for his extreme unimpressiveness on every front. The play's broad comic relief, Dogberry, is a one-joke character along the lines of Sheridan's Mrs Malaprop, though, like a stammerer suddenly made fluent by a crisis, he touchingly regains his grip on the English language when he realises that real villainy is at hand and reports it to Leonato. The comic mechanism depends on our accepting a degree of obtuseness in the otherwise gifted Benedick and Beatrice in never acknowledging that their mutual aggression is defensive: obviously the reason they could 'talk themselves mad' is that they are very much bothered by each other. There is even a complicating factor – an ambiguous passage which suggests that Benedick once won Beatrice's heart 'with false dice': the poignancy makes them rather sillier for not, it seems, understanding their own behaviour now.

But if plot were everything *Hamlet* wouldn't be famous, and if we all understood ourselves better we wouldn't need the theatre at all. *Much Ado* has always held the stage, largely because of the two scenes in which Benedick and Beatrice separately overhear their friends discussing how much loved each is by the other (the first, with Benedick, is much better rendered than the second – even Shakespeare had difficulty making the same joke twice). And there is good judgment in it – in a romantic comedy the audience likes to be ahead of the characters, urging them to see what is as plain as the nose on their faces.

Shakespeare's ironic view is that the difficult love of the two touchy wits is likelier to last than the conventional romance of Claudio and Hero. The latter is conducted on the classic lines of *Romeo and Juliet*, though Claudio is not as manly as Romeo and Hero less imaginative than Juliet: they go through all the standard crises of malicious intervention, but unlike that of Romeo and Juliet, the instinctive trust between them is very inadequate. The mind of the deeply unheroic Claudio is full of far more disloyal thoughts than those of which he accuses Hero; the reconciliation feels rigged up; and, as if unimpressed by the writing, Claudio is signally ungrateful for his undeserved good luck in getting his fiancée back from the grave – all he has to say, ambiguously, is 'another Hero!'

Two-thirds of the play is in prose, while Claudio and Hero carry the burden of its verse, which is not particularly distinguished. However, the dialogue of Benedick and Beatrice shimmers with wit and vision. For most of the action they use each other as target practice, but are then obliged to work side by side to avenge Hero when Claudio rejects her in church on their wedding day. Collaborating on this project takes their minds off themselves for once, and they find they are more deeply engaged than they thought. As at an equivalent point in *The Shrew*, their language becomes terser and more direct, its metaphorical flair replaced by limpid prose or measured verse. It is as if love, to present itself fully, needs a painful project to work on, preferably on someone else's behalf. At the end they find they are inseparable – like Miss Adelaide in *Guys and Dolls*, Beatrice even develops a love-struck cold – and feebly attempt to disguise their vulnerability with jokes about cuckoldry and with the affectionate dismissiveness that might well prove a good basis for a marriage and in any case fools nobody.

✦

I would I were thy bird.

– Romeo and Juliet

If Shakespeare often saw love as a practical truce that keeps the world turning, he also knew that it could transform its surroundings and cause the young to teach their elders. The tragedy of the world's most famous love story, written somewhere between *The Shrew* and *Much Ado*, lies in the destruction of what was already perfect. There is no question but that Romeo and Juliet are ready for and meant for each other. When they meet, by chance at a party, they immediately construct a perfect sonnet together, beginning 'If I profane with my unworthiest hand' – right there, off the cuff, amidst the noise of the dancing. This has often been pointed to as a Shakespearian pleasantry: in fact it is a masterstroke. For these lovers fit together as ideally as perfect lines of verse: in a sense they *are* the verse, emotional content wedded to formal perfection. Outlandish as the idea may sound, the fact that in 1845 Charlotte Cushman played Romeo with her sister Susan as Juliet is not so bizarre: they are like two halves of an egg.

Their difficulties all lie beyond themselves and not at all within their characters. So their story is impressively simple, perhaps uniquely so in Shakespeare – its irony lies not in itself but in its consequences. United at last, they lie in bed after their only night together as long as they dare, their ears sharp for Juliet's mother approaching the door. That's the excitement of being young and forbidden: it happens in parents' houses all the time. But they are in special danger: Romeo of the Montagues has been banished for the murder of Juliet's Capulet cousin Tybalt. The degree of anxiety that Romeo should now be gone quickly shifts to and fro between them. First Juliet declares they still have plenty of time together; when he agrees and recklessly decides to stay, she urges him to go, for that really was the morning lark they both heard and no nightingale. This inconsistency is not a conceit: it is, in the brief time available, proof of what they could have become if life had given them the chance. It is a baffling thing that apparently well-adapted lovers can nevertheless drain each other's strength and individuality; but Romeo and Juliet have the gift of becoming strong or weak as the other is weak or strong, each in turn shouldering the necessary weight. Their combined strength remains constant: they would have made good parents.

Less than ten years later, Shakespeare will write a very similar morning scene for Troilus and Cressida after they've spent their one night together: but their tenderness is compromised by his complacency and her uncertainty about how best to talk to him now they are intimate.

They are interrupted not by a parent but by a hefty piece of political strategy (the exchange of Cressida for a Greek prisoner of war) to which they are unequal – partly because of their inexperience but more because of the vicious reality of warfare, with which their integrity will not be able to compete. That grim insight lies ahead; for the present Shakespeare's interest is in a couple who, despite impossible circumstances, have everything going for them. Given that the source story Shakespeare used, Arthur Brooke's *Tragical History of Romeus and Juliet*, is highly critical of the lovers for 'thralling themselves to unhonest desire' (and disrespecting their parents), it is specially interesting that nothing makes you question the integrity of Shakespeare's Romeo and Juliet. Instead he pitches their idealism into pervasive violence – in some sense to be refined by it. Capulet's cruelty to his daughter is physically explicit and her mother's acquiescence in it equally destructive; Tybalt's blood is on Romeo's hands, though that at least was in defence of his best friend Mercutio, a somehow manly fault in a culture which daily causes fights to break out over nothing at all. These miseries distil and perfect Romeo's and Juliet's feeling for each other.

Since they have no internal faultline, the lovers have eventually to be defeated by a Shakespearian accident – a messenger unable to deliver a letter because of a suspected epidemic. And their rapture has always to compete with a mocking world, its cadences lapping against the ugly outcrops of Capulet and Tybalt, Mercutio's obsessive debunking of romance and the *petit guignol* Apothecary, 'in tattered weeds, with overwhelming brows', who sells Romeo his poison. The figure of the Nurse grounds much of the action in a day-to-day bustle of rope ladders and bad news, not to mention the need to rest her back before delivering her urgent messages. These are the cross-rhythms against which love has to hold its tempo. No sooner has Juliet swallowed her sleeping draught and been extravagantly mourned by her family than a group of musicians turn up to play at her wedding. Finding there is no job for them to do and therefore no cash, they have an argument with a household servant before sensing that there might still be some advantage in a wedding that's turned into a funeral:

> SECOND MUSICIAN: Hang him Jack; come, we'll in here: tarry
> for the mourners and stay dinner.

As for the lovers themselves, their eroticism is sustained by constant improvisation, and by youth's peculiar talent for visualising its dilemmas: adolescents can be obsessed with death even if they are not threatened by it as these two are. The tendency of Romeo and Juliet to see visions is anticipated from the start by the apparently cynical Mercutio, who, to instil in Romeo enough bravado to gatecrash the Capulets' party, evokes the world of dreams with his extempore account of Queen Mab, midwife to the fairies. Romeo, infected, immediately responds by sensing that

> Some consequence yet hanging in the stars
> Shall bitterly begin his fearful date
> With this night's revels, and expire the term
> Of a despised life closed in my breast
> By some vile forfeit of untimely death.

Later that night, irredeemably in love in Juliet's garden, he looks upwards and for the first time notices a detail:

> Lady, by yonder blessed moon I swear
> That tips with silver all those fruit-tree tops...

He is like his author: he has seen reality anew and repainted it. Juliet, more than a match for him, applies her intellect – can he really be invoking something that changes its shape every night?

> O swear not by the moon, the inconstant moon,
> That monthly changes in her circled orb,
> Lest that thy love prove likewise variable...

The play's casualties are not just the lives of its heroes but their talents.

Later, as he finally climbs out of her bedroom window, Juliet is shocked by what she sees:

> O God, I have an ill-divining soul;
> Methinks I see thee, now thou art so low,
> As one dead in the bottom of a tomb...

The hallucination revisits her the night before her enforced wedding to Paris. She is to take a potion which will make her mimic death until Romeo comes to her family tomb to save her – an idea almost as foreign to her as it is to us. Shakespeare takes time to touch in the fact that Juliet, although a married woman, is still a child facing the dark: an impulse to call her mother and Nurse back again pushes her over the end of one line into the next, which is then syncopated, its natural rhythm abandoned:

> I'll call them back again to comfort me:
> Nurse! What should she do here?

The thrill of it awakens a luxuriant second sight. She feels the temperature in her bedroom changing: the air thickens, the phial of narcotic clutched in her hand swells and heats up like a forbidden thing. Her body has anticipated its exact effect:

> I have a faint cold fear thrills through my veins
> That almost freezes up the heat of life.

As she looks at the modest liquid, her verse is completely silenced; the rest of the line is blank, four bars tacet:

> My dismal scene I needs must act alone.
> Come, vial.

She marvels that it will go straight to her brain before she knows it, her breath dying on her lips. How can this be? The idea of such a drug is familiar to us: we wonder in the same way about anaesthesia, how it won't allow us to count as far as ten, how we might be the unlucky one in several thousand who is immobilised but still sensitive to pain:

> What if this mixture do not work at all?

Ever practical, Juliet lays a dagger beside her on the bed. Then another fantasy tempts her:

> What if it be a poison, which the Friar
> Subtly hath minister'd to have me dead,
> Lest in this marriage he should be dishonour'd
> Because he married me before to Romeo?

Well, yes, human beings being what they are. What, after all, does she know of these men? Her husband is a murderer, her father threatens to beat her up for having her own opinions, so what price a herbalist Friar? But then again:

> How if, when I am laid into the tomb,
> I wake before the time that Romeo
> Come to redeem me? There's a fearful point!

It's as if she were casting about for the most powerful means to stimulate her imagination. Once in the tomb, she will suffocate on the smell of death, she will surely run mad. It takes some seventeen lines to complete the fearsome litany; she hears unearthly shrieks while she, like a lost soul in Goya's *Madhouse*, plays games with the dead bodies:

> And in this rage with some great kinsman's bone
> As with a club dash out my desperate brains...

And all the time there will be Tybalt's festering corpse, lying over there in his bloody sheet. The fantastic idea of him rising up to stalk Romeo like the walking dead catapults her into action. She must hurry to save her husband:

> Stay, Tybalt, stay!
> Romeo, I come, this do I drink to thee.

Brought to this point by her own imagining, she throws back the poison without another thought.

Romeo learns the news of Juliet's narcolepsy while standing in the street in Mantua, where he is feeling the fragile cheerfulness of the traveller:

> If I may trust the flattering truth of sleep
> My dreams presage some joyful news at hand.

Compared to her ghoulish fantasies, his of her are sweetly conventional: Juliet has visited him in his dream and laid such kisses on his lips

> That I reviv'd and was an emperor.

This is not quite of her order of imagination, but then, freed by banishment, he has been under less pressure recently. When 'reality' arrives in the form of Balthasar's news, his heroic terseness stands in contrast to his wife's unrestrained fancies:

> Is't even so? Then I defy you, stars.
> Thou know'st my lodging; get me ink and paper,
> And hire post-horses; I will hence tonight.

A few stage minutes later he steps into Juliet's tomb, armed with a real poison, and stands over her body, astonished that in death she can look so lovely, and so exactly as she was before:

> here lies Juliet, and her beauty makes
> This vault a feasting presence full of light...
>   O my love, my wife!
> Death, that hath suck'd the honey of thy breath,
> Hath had no power yet upon thy beauty:
> Thou art not conquer'd; beauty's ensign yet
> Is crimson in thy lips and in thy cheeks,
> And death's pale flag is not advanced there...

In Shakespeare beauty of speech often arises from a mistake: this is like Constance's lament for a son we know is still alive. Romeo's language continues to sing: he is mistaken but deeply and beautifully in tune:

> Ah, dear Juliet,
> Why art thou yet so fair? Shall I believe
> That insubstantial death is amorous
> And that the lean abhorred monster keeps
> Thee here in dark to be his paramour?
> For fear of that I still will stay with thee,
> And never from this palace of dim night
> Depart again; here, here will I remain
> With worms that are thy chambermaids; O, here
> Will I set up my everlasting rest
> And shake the yoke of inauspicious stars
> From this world-wearied flesh. Eyes, look your last,
> Arms take your last embrace, and lips, O you
> The doors of breath, seal with a righteous kiss
> A dateless bargain to engrossing death.
> Come bitter conduct, come, unsavoury guide,
> Thou desperate pilot, now at once run on
> The dashing rocks thy seasick weary bark.
> Here's to my love. O true apothecary,
> Thy drugs are quick. Thus with a kiss I die.

Widely separated in the play, this speech of Romeo's and that of Juliet before she drinks the poison enact their relationship more deeply than a further love scene could have done. As they balanced each other's intimate weaknesses, they have deferred to each other's strengths in their separation. Her power of imagining has been greater than his, but he has made up for it with a special potency in grief; her delicacy was the counterweight to his command of their last moments. He dies with a long protective hymn on his lips; she hurriedly and without beauty, on the point of a knife. Their misfortunes, like Benedick's and Beatrice's project, created a call and response between female sensibility and male protectiveness, male recklessness and female care. They were completely equipped for it; death's interception was banal.

The whole play has posed a series of questions. What if the poison didn't work, asked Juliet; what if the Friar was deceiving her; what if she woke up too soon? In the end Shakespeare makes the whole play a query: what if the course of history could be changed through love alone? Romeo and Juliet, on either side of an impossible divide, cause their two families, at each other's throats for as long as anyone can recall (we can read that as two halves of the world), to sit down and begin to talk peace at last. I have seen the play done as a *folie à deux*, in which the director assured us such love couldn't have lasted. I've heard it said that Capulet's and Montague's plan to build statues to their dead young heroes is no more than a public relations exercise, a competition in insincere grief. I call that an imaginative failure, fear of an outlandishly optimistic idea. It is, certainly, frantically difficult to find young actors with the emotional generosity and grace for these parts: but really, Romeo and Juliet are undebunkable. Both of them are improved by love, made wittier, wiser, more able to apprehend life – not least because Shakespeare allows them a small handful of inglorious moments: Romeo's earlier extravagance in grief, the touch of punctiliousness in Juliet that makes her ask at what time the next day she should send her Nurse to confirm the wedding schedule he has in mind. Once they are dead it may seem a dramaturgical mistake to have Friar Laurence take the time to tell the Prince the whole detailed story we've been watching all evening, but you can see what Shakespeare was up to: he needed to cool matters down and ask his bigger question about the parents' responsibility and whether the wider world is in safe hands after all.

✦

HERMIA: Methinks I see these things with parted eye,
    When everything seems double.

HELENA: So methinks;
    And I have found Demetrius, like a jewel,
    Mine own and not mine own.

                                        – *A Midsummer Night's Dream*

The following year (probably) Shakespeare sets love's compass further askew for an audience that may well have remembered *Romeo and Juliet*. *A Midsummer Night's Dream* is a story of love in a deeper sense than is understood by its rather erratic quartet of lovers – just as *Twelfth Night* is about a deeper form of harmony than who marries whom in the end. In the *Dream* love is close to madness; the play's intoxication is both chemical and romantic, and in the end more comprehensive than either. Surviving its hallucinations is an optimism that goes way beyond the idea that love is blind or that men are asses.

Early on in the play Lysander observes, unexceptionally, that the course of true love never did run smooth. He might have said that its terms are often more unpromising even than they were in *Romeo*, when love sprang up from enmity, or in *The Comedy of Errors*, where the clock ticked on towards a death sentence and a family reassembled itself just in time. In the *Dream* Egeus, the father of Hermia, who wants to marry against his wishes, is less impressive than Capulet but still more violent, so that Hermia is confronted with an extremity no other disobedient child in a Shakespeare comedy faces – state execution. Her true love for Lysander is also under siege from the unruly desire of her best friend Helena for him. Meanwhile Duke Theseus, the heroic aggressor and rapist of myth, is trying – more comically than most productions allow – to recommend himself to the terse Hippolyta, a disgusted Amazonian prisoner of war he has decided to marry and who he somehow thinks might come to admire him in time. In fairyland, King Oberon's love for Queen Titania is being poisoned by an emotion well down on the human scale – his male vengefulness in a child custody dispute between them, which he will take so far as to make her humiliate herself by falling in love with a donkey.

So the relationships between men and women in both worlds are all over the place: in this play the love is not at all where you think it will be. Shakespeare introduces early on the carpenter Peter Quince and the weaver Nick Bottom, who have real passion in them – not for any individual but for the theatre. They are amateur actors, and on the whole theirs is a generous enthusiasm: as Stanislavsky would have said, more to do with what they can offer to the theatre than what the the-atre can do for them. Falling foul in mid-rehearsal of Oberon's vengeful designs on Titania, Bottom is famously translated into an ass, but then blessed with everything that a fairy queen can give – junior fairies to sing and dance for him, bees' thighs lit by glow-worms to see him to bed and butterfly wings to waken him – all in a language so erotic that, as always in Shakespeare, it improves on any physical rep-resentation.

The paradox is that this absurd and nightmarish situation works on Bottom as true love would do: his imagination is as released as Romeo's was in the orchard as he instructs the fairy Cobweb to steal a honey-bag from 'a red-hipped humble-bee on top of a thistle'. His sense of wonder survives waking from his dream of Titania:

> Methought I was – there is no man can tell what. Methought I was – and methought I had – but man is but a patched fool if he will offer to say what methought I had.

Quickened sensibility leaks into his restored life, and may well, among other things, make him into what he would most want to be – a better actor.

The mysterious power of this affection between a fairy queen and a man with the head of an ass is so convincing that even Oberon is overcome by whatever passes in the fairy kingdom for remorse – or perhaps by envy for the unlikely liberation he sees. He is reconciled with Titania, and together they fly through the night to bless the house of three pairs of aristocratic newly-weds. Two of these couples have emerged from a night of utter confusion in the woods in which they've been rendered laughably (and in the women's case most painfully) out of control of their loyalties by fairy magic; they articulate a hesitant return to life of such surpassing beauty that among other things it conjured some of his loveliest music from Benjamin Britten. Married at the same time as Theseus and Hippolyta, they attend a wedding-night entertainment devised for them all by Quince's Dramatic Society of tinkers, tailors and joiners. The show is the old love story of *Pyramus and Thisbe* – Shakespeare's final joke, since some of his audience would have remembered it being used more stirringly in *Romeo and Juliet* the previous year. Their various reactions to the performance crystallise their relationships: Theseus begins to see Hippolyta as an equal, and the young women, in their silent reproach of their husbands' facetiousness, start to exert proper control over their immature, barracking partners.

Nevertheless the working-class actors rapidly learn that an aristocratic crowd can be the unkindest of all. Although he comes out on their side in the end, to some extent the treatment of these 'Mechanicals' may have been Shakespeare's genial revenge on all amateurs: professionals still dread the opinionated member of the local Dramatic Society anxious to buttonhole them in the bar and say, in the tones of Bottom the Weaver, that their *Hamlet* was better than the one they've just seen you in.

Thoroughly heckled, the performance goes unluckily. It reaches a nadir when the figure of Moonshine appears, played by the tailor Robin Starveling. The only pleasure for him in this alarming task is that he has escaped his original casting as Thisbe's mother, but the new role is onerously prop-bound – as well as remembering his lines, he has to carry an emblematic thorn bush and lantern with him to explain his part. On the big night he has added to this problem by bringing his dog along, perhaps as a sort of security blanket. This nameless mutt doesn't get as much exposure as Crab in *The Two Gentlemen* – Starveling is laughed off the stage within moments – but he does give his master, shouted down by the courtly hooligans, the chance of a little grace under pressure:

> All that I have to say is to tell you that the lanthorn is the moon,
> I the man i' the moon, this thorn-bush my thorn-bush, and this
> dog my dog.

Although there's no particular evidence for it, the theatre tradition is that the props go missing and the under-rehearsed actors lose their lines and then their collective nerve – until near the end, something changes. The tenderness that Shakespeare has felt towards their efforts becomes a discreet hymn to the imaginative power of theatre in those who don't quite recognise their own abilities. Thisbe, played by a young bellows-mender called Flute, comes upon the dead body of Thisbe's lover Pyramus:

> Asleep, my love?
> What, dead, my dove?
> O, Pyramus, arise.
> Speak, speak; quite dumb?
> Dead, dead? A tomb
> Must cover those sweet eyes.
> These lily lips,
> This cherry nose,
> These yellow cowslip cheeks,
> Are gone, are gone;
> Lovers make moan,
> His eyes were green as leeks...
> Tongue, not a word,
> Come, trusty sword,
> Come, blade, my breast imbrue!
> And farewell, friends,
> Thus Thisbe ends,
> Adieu, adieu, adieu.

The play would originally have been performed on the three-sided stage of the Curtain or The Theatre; on this platform between heaven and hell stands Flute, a young man who's perhaps never appeared in a play before. The audience knows he is embarrassed at the idea of playing a woman and perhaps thought him silly for that, since all the women's parts in Elizabethan theatre were played by male actors – but he is an amateur, so how would he know that. When he was cast he protested that the part was impossible for him as he had a 'beard coming'; a hoary old stage tradition obliges him to pause after declaring that he has this beard before qualifying it with '...coming' because of his colleagues' amazed look at his hairless chin. The stage business is so theatrically hallowed that it is quite a relief once in a while to see the line played through simply. Better still, just before the performance, Flute chides Quince for saying Bottom is a 'paramour' instead of a 'paragon' – a mistake natural enough because of the unfamiliarity of the words, but Flute's scandalised reaction –

A paramour is – God bless us! – a thing of nought

– testifies both to the state of his nerves and the idea's proximity to the awful gender-bending he is about to undertake.

Now he has watched his colleague Starveling being cruelly mocked, and to his utter misery finds himself standing as the bereaved Thisbe, wearing what once seemed to him an acceptable wig, before an audience thirsty for blood. He has nowhere to go except the text and his own heart. At the moment of speaking his banal lines he is, I should say, taken by Thisbe's heartbreak and at that moment becomes an actor, in other words someone who puts themselves into someone else's shoes. The onstage spectators no longer interrupt, and Shakespeare's actual audience, then and now, quietens down as well. Flute's unexpected sincerity is dissolving all the boundaries among them – between foreigners and clerks, lords and carpenters, apprentices, illiterates and poets; they're all held for a moment on the same intake of breath. His language is simple, naive, almost comic – and best of all, it's a countryman's language, the author's natural accent.

Shakespeare is closing this beautiful play – as gorgeous but in some ways as impenetrable as a perfect diamond – with two things he by now does especially well: the soliloquy and the unlikely nature of love. But he has added a very large third: the theatre platform as an instrument of change in its audience. He did this once before. In *Love's Labour's Lost* the same sort of arrogant young males heckle an honourable performance of *The Nine Worthies* by the villagers, and are eventually silenced by the actor of Hector, Don Armado, answering back:

> The sweet war-man is dead and rotten; sweet chucks, beat not
> the bones of the buried; when he breathed, he was a man. But
> I will forward with my device...

In the Mechanicals' *Pyramus and Thisbe*, the actors likewise find pride in their work, the onstage audience learns some respect for honest endeavour (not the same as talent but perhaps more moving), and, I should say, in the dance that follows, take hands with the working men to celebrate their evening together. The fairies, watching from their hidden corners, see that this group finally has enough love in it to be worthy of blessing, and they move through the house promising the couples faithfulness and unblemished issue.

Shakespeare is halfway through his career: *Hamlet* lies ahead, together with darker forms of comedy, and love will be still less straightforward. The century will soon turn over: but at this tipping point, and long before he has thought of the phrase himself, he's found a touch of nature to make the whole world kin, and the perfect platform to do it from. We have laboured to recreate the physical experience through four centuries of theatre architecture, forests of audience surveys and expectations of acting that find reconciling the epic and the detailed hard in a way Shakespeare would never have understood. At its best all this is not just a laborious search for historical accuracy, but rather the hope of capturing something still more tantalising, Shakespeare's particular mystery: his way of making us all one with his music both high and low, his range, immediacy and metaphysical delicacy.

Interval

The State We're In (Part One)

If you are spirited away, eyes closed, to a theatre performing
Hamlet and open them to witness three actors playing the title
role, a woman playing Polonius, Ophelia in the nude and the set
a rusty bedstead – then you are probably in Germany. If Hamlet
is over forty – it's probably France, if Ophelia is over forty – it's
probably Russia, and if you are unsure what play you are
actually watching – it's probably America, the land of 'the
concept'. And if Fortinbras is wearing a Bosnian, Georgian,
Iraqi, or Afghan uniform – then of course it is England.

Terry Hands, director,
in conversation with the author, 2007

How Paul Rogers and Ann Todd actually sounded as the Macbeths
on the night I was dragged to the Old Vic in 1955 is beyond recovery. However, a rough idea of how things stood at that time can be
caught from John Gielgud's contemporary recording of *Hamlet* with the
Old Vic Company, many of whom were also in the *Macbeth*. Gielgud
himself was quite another matter, but what can be heard from most of
the cast is a manner very typical of the decade or so after the Second
World War: a brisk and genteel prettiness in the women, as if they weren't
quite speaking with their own voices (think of Celia Johnson in *Brief
Encounter*), whereas the men undoubtedly were, with a sound that was
generally staunch, officer-class and heterosexually sensible (think of Cyril
Raymond as her husband in the same film). Working-class characters
were generally patronised.

Gielgud of course, like all originals, stood outside fashion. A miracle of speed and feeling, his is the only performance which sounds as if it comes from a deep place within him and that he will perish if he doesn't let it out. His secret was less the fabled beauty of his sound than the visceral force that made its beauty possible. He seems to be in a state of rapture, the language harrowing him like fire: for all his breeding and fastidiousness, I have never known a performer put so much passion into the act of speech as Gielgud did. I say that even though I was startled once to be told by Princess Margaret after a charity concert that Gielgud was quite the worst verse-speaker she had ever heard. Well, there we are. For a good half-century he seemed to many people Shakespeare's personal representative on earth, releasing a quite new sensibility into the sturdy world of classical acting.

And forever loved for his foibles: as reactive as a highly strung thoroughbred, Gielgud seemed to think and speak at the same rate, and offstage, his ability to give offence because of a more or less complete inability to reflect before he opened his mouth is the stuff of legend. Of all his legacies, this impetuosity as actor and man may well be the greatest. Appropriately it was a quality reminiscent of Shakespeare himself, in whom, according to his colleagues and editors Heminges and Condell:

> mind and hand went together, and what he thought he uttered
> with that easiness that we have scarcely received from him a
> blot on his papers.

There is a story (and there is a special category for Gielgud stories, one that invisibly blends the apocryphal and the real) that he was once directing Laurence Olivier and things weren't going well. Then Gielgud had an inspiration: beaming with his new idea, he advised him to play the part 'like a second-rate Hamlet' – which would have been fine except that Gielgud suddenly looked aghast, and apologised for his tactlessness. So you could say he even dropped bricks when he didn't.

I am one of the diminishing band of witnesses not only to his fire and impetuosity but to the very different appeal of Olivier, live and in full flood; the volcanic power, the courage, the delicate intuition, the ability to spring any number of physical surprises – a talent that a live audience elicited from him far more readily than a camera. Witnesses to them as men too. On my first afternoon with Gielgud, he courteously enquired what parts I was playing at Stratford that year, before declaring that each and every one of them was unplayable, quoting the most outrageous examples of failure he could remember. It was his version of noblesse oblige. I encountered

Olivier's variant on this when, at the very moment we first set eyes on each other, he noted by way of greeting that I had highlights in my hair for the Hamlet I was then playing, just as he had had in his 1948 film. In the face of such pleasant making of common cause it would have been graceless of me to observe how much more subtle mine were than his had been.

As a teenager I had seen Olivier as Coriolanus and Titus Andronicus, and left feeling relief that I had managed to train-spot what were clearly historic events – not least because of the famous Coriolanus death fall, in which he swung upside down from a bridge, held by his ankles. That moment was really what I was waiting for: in that sense he infantilised us all. I was mightily impressed by both performances, not without a sense of remoteness: I felt a little uninvolved, just a bit had. Though only fifteen, this seemed to me very unlike the Hamlet of Michael Redgrave, who even at fifty touched the heart with his scathing, tender intelligence, or the essential modesty of Ralph Richardson's enormous talent, or the idiosyncrasy of that great text-prospector Paul Scofield, able to make the imagination fly with some apparently random cadence, not even, perhaps, to be repeated the next night. I felt there was something tyrannical and unyielding in Olivier's supremacy over his audience. Perhaps significantly, though he was unmatched as Shakespeare's self-confident heroes – Henry V, Richard III – he avowedly disliked the 'complainers': the inner collapse of a Lear or Hamlet tended to evade him, and his best studies of failure lay outside Shakespeare, as Archie Rice or Chekhov's Doctor Astrov.

These two great figures stand in interesting contrast. Gielgud inherited from William Poel and Harley Granville Barker at the turn of the century a belief in speed and clarity of speech, as well as an odd cross-influence from the witty, naturalistic ease in commercial comedy of Seymour Hicks and Gerald du Maurier. His Shakespearian passion was temperamental – he was a Slav, Polish on his father's side, and a great-nephew of Ellen Terry. Olivier on the other hand seemed to come from nowhere, and his innovations were artistically bolder. In 1938, having read the work of Ernest Jones, Freud's biographer, he decided that Iago nursed a repressed sexual desire for Othello; this horrified and disgusted Ralph Richardson, who was playing the Moor – and no doubt made Gielgud giggle when he heard about it. Olivier, however, was in this well ahead of his time, expressing what most of us now see as perfectly feasible. Gielgud, though a star actor-manager, insisted on having strong ensembles around him, while Olivier, jealous of his reputation, didn't often care to share the stage with his peers, and for a long time wouldn't play Othello in case Iago stole the play from him. Olivier continues to glow because of his films, but Gielgud is a mystery to many young actors, and I doubt if Gielgudian, an epithet still potent when I started working, would still be seen as a compliment. The wisdom of the time was that Gielgud gave you the music of Shakespeare, and Olivier, recklessly, the reality. I'm not so sure. There were times when Olivier's brazen tenor seemed the voice of Shakespeare himself; and others when Gielgud, mercurial and generous, seemed closer to the emotional source.

✦

As for the map that they were redrawing, there is a CD of 'Historical Shakespeare Performances' now on the market. Both actors are included, relative newcomers surrounded by the real old-timers – Henry Irving, Herbert Beerbohm Tree, Sarah Bernhardt. Gielgud's early Hamlet sounds like a Gielgud imitation, which at least shows he wasn't brilliant right from the start; Olivier's on the other hand is vulgar but terrific – as is John Barrymore, an American who puts most of the English actors to shame as Macbeth. This may have something to do with the cinema: both he and Olivier had swiftly grasped how to confide in the camera – or microphone – and applied it to Shakespearian soliloquy, so they suddenly seem way ahead of the game. Listening to these partly remastered cylinder recordings sounds fun, but it's quite hard work, particularly if you find hearing Shakespeare done badly not so much entertaining as depressing. You must first get over the fact that the men sound like country squires and the women like questionable duchesses. Some of this is to do with the phonetic manners of the time:

Who calls m' villin, breaks m' pate across…

– but it's more than that. Sybil Thorndike is great when reading Lady Macbeth's letter but tiresomely histrionic when she imprecates. Even Ellen Terry, whom one so wants to be good, is a bit disappointing: recorded in 1911, you can hear the sensibility of a modern actress struggling to escape a traditional deliberateness of speech and, for us, excessive vibrato. Excessive not only to us in fact, since Caruso had done much to kill the fashion in opera some years before. Johnston Forbes Robertson is among the most natural performers, but as Hamlet he seems to view his dilemmas as a curiously amusing business and no more; still, he was the actor who drew from Bernard Shaw a view of how Shakespeare should be played – 'on the line and to the line, with the uttering and acting simultaneous, inseparable and in fact identical' – which is as good as it gets.

Tree is said to have been better at make-up than speaking, and he's certainly laborious at the latter. And slow. And loud. Irving, as determined as Garrick before him to make the theatre socially respectable, sounds ridiculous and pontifical as a result: I'd far rather have heard the great rogue and vagabond Edmund Kean half a century earlier than these sanctimonious vowels. All of them play very fast and loose with the text – as Henry V, Frank Benson tells his troops not to dishonour their fathers rather than their mothers in the speech that he starts as

> Once more unto the breach, once more, dear friends
> Or [*pause*] fill the walls up with your English dead

and carelessly ends with

> God for England, Harry and St George.

Every time he is about to depart like this from the familiar text there is a little hesitation that I know well comes from momentarily losing your lines. It's a pity that there are, as far as I know, no recordings of Eleanora Duse or of the young Edith Evans – though the latter did tape a good performance of her younger self playing Millamant in *The Way of the World* some thirty years after the event.

As you strain to hear the voices through the dustbowl of mechanical noise you begin to think about a society irredeemably class-bound, in which the actors seem in no sense asked to reflect real life but to make some kind of daft oratorio out of it. What, you wonder, did people go to the theatre for? No mirror was being held up to nature that I can glimpse. I'd like to say the reason is simple, that the orotund style was inevitably created by the size of the auditoria; but that's only partly true. Irving enthusiastically expanded the Lyceum to 1,700 seats and Tree's Her Majesty's held 1,400; but I suspect the expansive gestures and broad vocal strokes were a cultural expectation, like the extravagant stagings to which audiences also looked forward, as some do these days to a new operatic *mise en scène*.

✦

Both Gielgud and Olivier had more or less finished with live Shakespeare by the mid-1970s: and since then, despite moments of nostalgia, audiences and performers have changed a good deal. I suppose as young actors the two of them may have encountered the occasional bore who remembered Irving effortlessly filling the huge Lyceum, implying that they couldn't; likewise a couple of later generations, including mine, have patiently suffered comparisons with the Mount Rushmore figures that they became. Now, the great bells are sounding less loudly at last and the anecdotes are less pervasive, even the tellers finding them a bit beside the point. It may even be coming to light, though there is some spluttering about it from the over-eighties, that today's leading actors are as good as Gielgud and Olivier were, and the range of talent and standard of ensemble playing infinitely better.

As in all things, fashion slithers this way and that, and it's sometimes hard to say whether the industry leads the audience or the other way round. In some ways audiences never change any more than does the structure of the human heart: but there are circumstantial differences all the same. Even those who haven't grown up with television look to stage actors not just for some emotional top-up – beautiful speaking or physical daring – but for an accuracy to ordinary life that matches what they can now see every night in ruthless close-up on the screen. The current taste is to eavesdrop, spotting motive or change of heart in the flick of an eyebrow or a moment's hesitation in speech. Any self-respecting classical actor knows how to do this, and most nowadays are as at home in front of a camera as on a stage.

It follows that bespoke new playing spaces have appeared to serve a closely scrutinising audience – sometimes on a scale less than a tenth that of Irving's Lyceum. (Gielgud, who had a streak of self-consciousness even at his best, wouldn't have liked this at all.) The contraction of theatre into pubs and rooms during the late 1960s and early 1970s was rapid and exciting. These venues were initially intended for new and experimental work, but the question of whether you could cram a neglected epic or a Shakespeare into them soon arose. I joined the Royal Shakespeare Company just in time for this. In these days of barter and opportunism, it is hard to imagine the idealism that flowed through the debate: we were like a not very unworldly monastic order, bent over points of doctrine, preparing a new version of the Bible.

Stratford-upon-Avon does encourage this kind of concentration. It stands at an odd convergence of three influences: the spirit of Shakespeare, which can be quietly felt by the river and the church where he is buried; an intensive production line for the plays with the best resources he could hope for in a town in which many people have spent their working lives in such specialities as medieval armour or the stitching of Elizabethan shoes; and finally, the worst excesses of tourism. It is thus both hallowed ground and a circus. The occasional crassnesses thrown up by this are well known; but it remains the place where you most aptly combine watching the swans with debating how best to do Shakespeare.

The question by the Seventies was: were *King Lear* or *A Midsummer Night's Dream* best served by traditional houses such as the old Royal Shakespeare Theatre, built in 1932, with its tricky perspectives and its 1,300 seats (a bit optimistic in these days of television), some of them a long way from the stage? More and more actors – and by no means the least experienced ones – were saying it was difficult to act subtly or to speak quietly in such a space. Well, the RST certainly had its problems and was beginning to decay physically, but several generations had learned to overcome its difficulties: I started my own story there as a supernumerary, watching Ian Holm as Richard III control his audience with a whisper or silence them with a look in his eye, eagerly working out how it was done.

Stratford's alternative theatre, The Other Place, opened at the end of 1973, with seating for 150. It was really a prefabricated shed, formerly a rehearsal room and storage space. Not nearly as well appointed as it later became, it had a corrugated iron roof that expanded noisily in the sun and effectively passed on the winter's cold, its audience wrapped around a stage you sometimes had to approach through the customers' toilets. Referred to as The Tin Hut (while the RST was known a little less affectionately as The Jam Factory), its original purpose was for intimate work, but the Shakespeare question soon arose. Many miracles then took place – Buzz Goodbody's *Lear* and *Hamlet*, *Macbeth* directed by Trevor Nunn. As the latter worked here he was already, as Artistic Director, imagining a third possibility, a small-scale touring operation which would travel to gymnasiums, arts centres and schools round the country with Chekhov and Shakespeare. And a fourth, which was to become the Swan Theatre, a Jacobean-style thrust stage loosely based on Shakespeare's Blackfriars, its audience on three sides, on which it was proposed to explore the less familiar Elizabethan and Jacobean plays. Both ideas have flourished; the Swan has proved triumphantly successful, and is now used for every kind of play. In the middle of this the National Theatre in London opened its doors, asking the old question again by offering the epic Olivier stage (1,160 seats) or the intimate Cottesloe (400) as alternatives for the classics, not forgetting the Lyttelton (890), which is now the only surviving proscenium stage in the portfolio of our two national companies. Everybody wanted to work in the Cottesloe, fewer in the Olivier. Peter Hall as Artistic Director found that he was always having to do productions in the two big houses himself because most of the directors he invited in only wanted to work in the smallest: on the other hand when he directed three late Shakespeares he himself insisted on the Cottesloe.

His preference was logical enough: he knew that by now audiences were as likely to be caught by the sinewy arguments and subversive ironies of the writing as by the ring of a beautiful line. They want to be part of the argument, and sometimes find the body politic as engrossing a subject as the hero: indeed there are passages in the history plays so shockingly topical – often on the subject of foreign policy – that they laugh bitterly aloud. Instinctively democratic, they specially enjoy seeing an eloquent hero capsized by a Player, a Gravedigger or a Fool. They will still go to one of the tragedies for the sake of some incandescent performer – just about – but will come out of *Lear* feeling short-changed if, as well as the suffering of the perplexed old man, they haven't felt more than a twinge of sympathy for Goneril and Regan, driven to an insane revenge by his paternal bullying. In *Hamlet*, they may also reflect that, guilty or not, Claudius is a better proposition for Denmark than either the belligerent old King Hamlet or his over-complicated son – who will leave his country stripped and ready for annexation by Fortinbras of Norway, whose approaching drums threaten to drown his famously beautiful death speech. Alert to comedy's darker seams, they will appreciate *A Midsummer Night's Dream* all the more because it starts with such an unnerving premise – the possibility that her father Egeus will have Hermia killed for disobedience. Preferred actors are classless; in fact the trace of a regional accent is welcome, some tough grain pushing through the polish. By the same token, the idea of Great Acting by a theatre aristocracy is sceptically viewed, since many unsung heroes can be great for a moment, in one part, on one night of the run; audiences well understand that it may take ten actors, not one, to expose the breathing heart of the play.

All of this is easier to achieve at close quarters, and does something to make up for the downsides of contemporary theatre – the suspicion felt towards it by many young people and its voyeuristic obsession with celebrity. And the distractions, many to do with the fear of exchanging one kind of connectivity for another. The call of the mobile phone has become irritably tolerated even in small auditoriums, whereas a mere dozen years ago it was greeted with general horror and the ushers would come charging down the aisles (doubling the disturbance) to apprehend the offender. Now the little tune goes more or less ignored by everyone except the owner, who may even take the call. Occasionally actors protest from the stage when this happens, but less and less so, and we most of us have developed some kind of technique – and there are several – for dealing with it without breaking up the play or ourselves. Perhaps these techniques will soon be taught in drama schools. And in the small theatres, the front row may put plastic mugs and sometimes their feet on the edge of the stage: what would John Gielgud have made of that? Much the same I suppose as a senior actor of my acquaintance who used to tell the young spectators slumped in the front row of the stalls in the Gielgud Theatre in the West End to sit up straight. A little unfairly, as looking steeply upwards at the stage from there made it quite a natural thing to do; tough on me too as, onstage beside him, I had to decide whether my character had heard that part of his speech or not. It may be that at such times the rough and tumble of Elizabethan theatre, which we so earnestly seek, is closer at hand than we think.

✦

This argument about scale underlines the fact that Shakespearian acting has largely become a matter of finding out how real you can be without screwing up the poetry. We are obsessed with the intricacies of character, those lumpy protrusions and paradoxes with which we face the world, even though Shakespeare would barely have understood the word beyond its meaning of handwriting:

CLAUDIUS [*reading*]: 'Tis Hamlet's character...

The problem is that Shakespeare's methods are very anomalous: he sometimes feels slap bang up to date, and sometimes very remote indeed, the other side of a great gap in time. In a way that we might condemn in a modern playwright, quite commonly everyone in a Shakespeare play sounds like Shakespeare, speaking with his wit, beauty or style even when this is 'out of character'. Gertrude's famous description of the drowning of Ophelia – 'There is a willow grows aslant a brook' – is lovelier than anything else she says in the play, and there has been no previous evidence that she could ever come up with such a thing. The fact is that this is probably writer's opportunism: she is, for the sake of pathetic effect, being visited with Shakespeare's gift of tongues, and it would not have occurred to him to justify it in any other terms. However, our conditioning makes us wonder what he's trying to tell us. Is Gertrude calling up unsuspected talents to construct a tremendous gloss on an event she has watched happen but has been content not to stop? Has she perhaps pushed Ophelia in, even? You may laugh, but I've been at those discussions. In *As You Like It*, the repentance of the usurping Duke is the most enormous improbability: on his way to the forest with an army to kill his brother, he meets an unseen 'old religious man' and 'after some question with him' abandons his plan, gives back the dukedom and becomes a hermit himself. In character terms one would have to conclude that he was bipolar, but even if the actor played that convincingly, we would still notice how snugly his change of heart comes moments before the harmonious ending.

In these cases Shakespeare is very unlike a modern writer. He seems to regard 'character' as fluid or even non-existent until the moment of speech – few people make much impact in Shakespeare unless they're voluble – and even then as expendable if some more poetic purpose can be served. But sometimes he does just the opposite, leaving idiosyncrasies embedded in the language as strikingly as Chekhov and his successors – Mistress Quickly and Falstaff are full of them, she with her verbal repetitions and he with his particular style of elaboration. The characters' linguistic choices in these cases are a clue both to their fundamental nature and what is happening to them at that moment. In the second scene of *Hamlet*, the lights flare and Claudius explains to his court how it is that he has taken over both crown and queen two months after his brother King Hamlet has died. The effect on the audience is to chase away the doubts the jumpy opening scene on the battlements has created: there are no mysteries and the note is no-nonsense, practical, the goods without fuss if also without much nuance. There have been problems, yes, but Denmark must pull together and get behind him – and never mind that young man in ostentatious black over there. We watch him with eyes attuned by the television interview to how swiftly a politician can call up his data and override interruptions: Claudius's trick throughout is to forestall opposition by the simple expedient of rarely finishing a sentence at the end of a line of verse. There's simply no space for anyone to interrupt or even think: dazzled by an operator on this form, we can't quite get at the reality but we certainly respect his talent.

You can see something of the same technique at the beginning of *Measure for Measure*, but used to create uncertainty rather than confidence. The Duke of Vienna's name is Vincentio, though oddly enough, like Claudius, he is never given it in Shakespeare's text, only in the list of characters. Dispensing with introductions, Shakespeare gives him the staccato first word:

DUKE: Escalus.

ESCALUS: My lord?

And whereas Claudius glides affably through warm antithetical waters, the Duke wades through mud, his horizons austere and foreshortened:

> Of government the properties to unfold
> Would seem in me to affect speech and discourse
> Since I am put to know that your own science
> Exceeds in that the lists of all advice
> My strength can give you; then no more remains
> But that, to your sufficiency, as your worth is able,
> And let them work.

Only one metaphor ('the lists of all advice'), and a strange bump in the metre – 'But that to your sufficiency, as your worth is able' – which might be significant. Its momentary clumsiness may be saying something about the Duke's difficulties in coming to the point – or perhaps that, mentally congested, he would have been happier speaking in prose. This is not an orator like Claudius, more an exhausted chairman delegating power – or, if you like, an obfuscating fixer getting off the hook. On the other hand you might decide that Shakespeare intended nothing of the sort and that this odd line is an editor's slip: but in front of an audience there's not much point blaming the editor. You choose what's useful to you, what might give you the 'character'.

Shakespeare sometimes expresses psychological depth in very formal writing. On the walls of Flint Castle, King Richard II realises he's losing the crown he thought was his by divine right, and imagines his future:

> I'll give my jewels for a set of beads,
> My gorgeous palace for a hermitage,
> My gay apparel for an almsman's gown,
> My figur'd goblets for a dish of wood,
> My sceptre for a palmer's walking staff,
> My subjects for a pair of carved saints,
> And my large kingdom for a little grave,
> A little little grave, an obscure grave.
> Or I'll be buried in the king's highway,
> Some way of common trade, where subjects' feet
> May hourly trample on their sovereign's head;
> For on my heart they tread now whilst I live,
> And buried once, why not upon my head?

Nothing complicated about the verse: almost every line starts a new thought and ends by completing it, and the emotion Richard feels is obvious to the audience. The actor's first danger is using too thick a wash: sorrow, sorrow, sorrow. Shakespeare never does that – if he wants someone to be completely overcome, he makes language collapse altogether. Generally, suffering makes his characters more eloquent (as it doesn't always in life), just as falling in love speeds up their brains (as it always does in life) and makes them wittier than before.

What the audience is finding out is that Richard's nature is to exchange one fantasy, the illusion of divinity, for another, the life of the anchorite. They are moved by his peculiar courage, his willingness to invent while his heart is sinking. Without a vocation till now, Richard has suddenly found it, and his grief has a desperate painterliness, the pain measured not by luxuriance but precision. His talent, and comfort, is to make those objects as visible as Macbeth's yellow leaf once was to me. So the actor has to match Richard's skill with his own. Within the word 'wood' is a nucleus waiting to be cracked open like a germ of wheat: the idea has to be sent on its way so that in a flash we see the grain of the dish, its uneven colour, its lopsidedness perhaps – just as we have to see the thirteen other common nouns in the seven lines of verse. On the nights the actor fails, it will be in not hitting the plumb centre of the word, allowing emotion to twist it into an exclamation, not a fact. By any standard it's quite difficult, and if I could absolutely say how the balancing act of passion, cadence and accuracy is done, my own success rate would be 100 per cent. Like serving well at tennis, a very complicated process of coordination leads to a simple, rapid result. It is difficult for a performer to get bored in a long run with Shakespeare: you never can be sure from one night to the next, and you're qualified for nothing but starting again the next day – in the words of Samuel Beckett, Try Again, Fail Again, Fail Better.

I see I've found more examples of character revealed by language than subsidiary to it. Of course: these are the best moments in Shakespeare, when he convinces you that these dazzling images could only have come from the mouth they have. For the falling King Richard, the props of devoutness and poverty – rosary beads, a walking stick, two quaint medieval carvings – are so vividly realised that you too feel them in your hand. When, in *Troilus and Cressida*, Achilles admits:

> My mind is troubled, like a fountain stirr'd,
> And I myself see not the bottom of it

we certainly couldn't have put it better ourselves: this dark swirling of his mind – his uncertainty about himself, in fact – is exactly what is intriguing about him. Later, with Hector's blood on his hands, he realises that the impact on the Trojan War of what he has done will not be seen till the morning:

> The dragon wing of night o'erspreads the earth,
> And, stickler-like, the armies separates.

We can hear the crackle of disengagement in the falling dark and see Achilles brooding on Hector till dawn. After his shaming threat of revenge on Titania, the amazing beauty of Oberon's conjuration of the wind riffling the wild thyme on a bank he knows reasserts his fairy dignity; the horrible squeaking of the 'shadow like an angel in bright hair dabbled in blood' is – obviously – the jolt that would make Clarence start up time after time in a night sweat; Juliet's vision of Tybalt all green with mould in his tomb is partly that of a child. Shakespeare is a puzzle: if he can do psychological subtlety in such blazing language, why does he at other times not bother with it at all?

✦

To be called a Shakespearian actor might seem an archaic compliment these days, but perhaps it still means something. Stamina, suppleness, imagination and a relish for argument; a sharp ear for a key-change or the sudden thump of a monosyllable in the verse; an instinct for the antithetical structures of the prose. And perhaps a certain slyness. In 1974, in the midst of President Nixon's lying on television, I was at the RSC playing Angelo in the politically satirical *Measure for Measure* – the play was done a lot around that time. As deputy Duke of Vienna, Angelo attempts to seduce Isabella, a highly religious young woman, in return for a reprieve for her imprisoned brother, sentenced to death for sexual intercourse with his fiancée. In this difficult undertaking Angelo tacks about, hoping that Isabella will take his point without his having to say anything too gross:

> Admit no other way to save his life –
> As I subscribe not that, nor any other,
> But in the loss of question – that you, his sister,
> Finding yourself desir'd of such a person,
> Whose credit with the judge, or own great place,
> Could fetch your brother from the manacles

> Of the all-building law; and that there were
> No earthly mean to save him, but that either
> You must lay down the treasures of your body
> To this suppos'd, or else to let him suffer...

She continues to look enquiringly at him. Then he runs out of legalistic hypotheses and blurts out:

> What would you do?

Given the enormity of what he's suggesting, I found this funny: Angelo is a man trained to present a case in court but in no way to talk to a woman. I did the last line as slangily as I dared, edging towards 'What wouldja do?' The gaucheness got – I still think – a legitimate, tense laugh. However, if it were now, I probably wouldn't make quite such a point of it, and I might even up the rhythm a bit – just a bit. It was a little too flip perhaps, though in a way right for the time, a time when a certain brutal practicality was assumed to underlie an efficient political speech.

On the other hand, not long ago I saw an actress playing Lady Macbeth in Chicago dealing with

> We fail?
> But screw your courage to the sticking place
> And we'll not fail.

All my life I've heard these lines grandly declaimed, full of dark foreboding and perverse heroism. But this time it was as if she were arguing with her infuriating husband about whether the car would break down – not in the sense of trivialising her feelings, but because for the moment her annoyance was the same. It was the first time the lines had really made sense to me: Lady Macbeth has only one voice to speak with, and you don't have special inflections for killing a king. And she had done no harm to the verse, that resilient, flexible thing. What made her choice right, and mine in 1974 – on balance – wrong?

Maybe no more than my own changing taste. When Puck declares

> Now the hungry lion roars
> And the wolf behowls the moon

should the actor use the animal sounds onomatopoeically, allowing a bit of roar into the first phrase and a keening note into the second? I don't like it, though I've seen good actors do such things, and have probably done them myself. On the other hand when Romeo says in his distress that Juliet will think him 'an old murderer' the cuteness of it seems to me

delightful, as if Romeo is imagining his lover intimately ticking him off.
Likewise when Macbeth declares that he has

> bought
> Golden opinions from all sorts of people

the slangy swing the last phrase nowadays has seems to me entirely worth
using.

A little shamefacedly, an actor in Shakespeare will be drawn to
anachronistic moments like these to test the limits of how up-to-date the
material can sound. The answer is, invariably, more up-to-date than
you'd think. If he or she can find as conversational a form as possible for
all the tension and release, the lightness and weight in the verse, without
betraying the soft, heavy beat, the way the melodic line sometimes strains
against the rhythm (not to mention the equally taxing architecture of the
prose) – and then find a way of doing all of it in a very wide range of theatre acoustics… well, I'd say the job was done.

✦

Hamlet asks a lot of us:

> The purpose of playing… was and is to hold, as 'twere, the
> mirror up to nature; to show virtue her own feature, scorn her
> own image, and the very age and body of the time his form and
> pressure.

In a slightly odd series of images ('scorn'?) the last is the most seductive,
with its hint of deep cultural applicability. When Paul Rogers played
Claudius in Gielgud's recording of *Hamlet* it was 1956. What the young
man in black (actually over fifty years old, but never mind) would object
to in him would have been his very self-confidence, the lack of healthy
doubt; what might be attracting Queen Gertrude meanwhile would be
the oddly potent male mixture, like a strong tobacco, of aggression and
homeliness. Claudius's kind had won a war only a decade ago and were
uninterested in the moral anxiety of a young intellectual who might soon
turn into John Osborne's Jimmy Porter or go on CND marches.

A decade or so later, this antagonism came to a head in the Paris
événements and the American student uprisings. In leafy Warwickshire, I
had, as very small beer indeed, joined the RSC and was watching Brew-
ster Mason's Claudius dealing with David Warner's red-scarfed student
Hamlet. He was like the sports coach reproaching a young intellectual

to whom he'd had to give a place on the team because of parental pressure, and who might let him down. What Warner's Hamlet objected to in this was the meretricious role-playing – Claudius is far from being a sporting man – and spun rationale, typical of his parents' generation. Its personal habits too: this Hamlet was clearly teetotal while Claudius's chicaneries were lubricated by a deal of hard drinking and sexual *oeillades*. Whereas Rogers had bluffed Hamlet out by force of pseudo-common sense and fair play – urging him to get over himself, in fact – Mason understood his prey well enough, but was implicitly appealing to the rest of the court to agree that the job now was to take up the reins of government firmly, even if that involved a little blurring of scruples.

In the 1990s I came to play Claudius myself under the same director as Mason, Peter Hall. By now the issue was barely political at all (as it would once have been with him) but musical – it was a matter of whether you could avoid breathing within a blank verse line, but always did so, if only for a nanosecond, at its end. Everything else – character, political nuance, relationship – could be trusted to follow from this discipline, and whatever Shakespeare meant would be out there for all to see, unedited. In a move worthy of Claudius himself Hall turned to me on the first morning's rehearsal and asked me as an old friend for a demonstration of his methods with the King's opening speech. This presented a bit of a problem to me, as I wasn't sure I agreed with him. Then I remembered the dictum of another, earlier teacher, the director Tyrone Guthrie, that a man can't call himself a man until he can do half a dozen lines of verse on a single breath. And so I did it, seven lines in fact. Hall was jubilant, but the Cheshire Cat performance actually allowed everyone to draw whatever moral they pleased. What with his pre-emptive strike and my studied neutrality, we had, in effect, played Claudius with each other.

There's a truth underneath such anecdotes: for one thing, directors change their minds over time, and so do actors. In my case two things had happened. First I now had enough technique not to show if I was breathing at all and so could accommodate the director in front of his cast; and as it happened I had also (as Hall had in the 1960s) been drawn into a specifically political – sometimes heretical – approach of my own to the plays, one which I still largely have. Accidentally concurring with Margaret Thatcher about the nobility of small businesses, I had in 1986 got my hands on the means of production and founded with Michael Bogdanov the English Shakespeare Company – a rather grand name and, considering that Bogdanov and I are both Celts, a misleading one. Our modest proposal, which rapidly became quite a big business, arose from frustration with what we saw as the lack of small-p politics in the Shakespeare work around us. Having lived through the free-for-all of the Seventies – by turns doctrinaire and formless, wilful and puritanical – I for one was offended by the new 1980s bombast issuing from Shakespearian addresses that should have known better; and since bombast reflects uncertainty, this said something about the loss of nerve afflicting every branch of the arts during Thatcher's period of disabling. One can't blame the Iron Lady for everything, but hers was a prime example, worthy of the citizens in *Coriolanus*, of banishing the thing you don't understand (and therefore fear); the theatre community responded with a loss of self-esteem expressed as contempt, like the patricians in the same play.

The ESC's work was based on a conviction that everything in Shakespeare, however beautiful, is full of argumentation, and every line a point of view in a transfixing debate. So *Romeo and Juliet* is not just a beautiful love story but a bold question about whether love can change the world. Is it better to have a bad man who's a good king, like Claudius, or vice versa, as Hamlet, with his tendency to be paralysed by the opposing sides of an argument, would perhaps have been? Is Othello a victim or a fool? What is to be done? Do the ends justify the means? Like the first Elizabethans crammed into their playhouses, looking at a platform suspended between heaven and hell, audiences want to take part in an urgent conversation which they can perhaps only get in the theatre, one in which they're encouraged to change sides as often as they like, but find it impossible to sit on the fence for long.

John Gielgud was one of the ESC's Patrons for a while, but politely resigned at the sight of the modern dress that we became famous for: on the other hand he insisted that he was deeply impressed by the standard of the verse speaking. The modern dress notoriety was all right since everyone needs a trademark, but really it was only a small part of the point. As far as possible, we were trying to provoke a political debate through Shakespeare's language without, I hope, losing any of its beauty. Picking up whatever iron filings were in the air, we presented Henry V's invasion of France like the Falklands campaign; *Richard III* was played out in a series of boardrooms with IBM computers and dispatch cases, into one of which Hastings's head fitted surprisingly well and shockingly. Later on in our trajectory, Coriolanus found himself in 1989 Bucharest, in the smoky committee rooms and excited alleyways of revolutionary politics. The people's repeated chant of 'Demokratie!' was both inspiring and inane; the set was dominated by a huge fallen statue of Coriolanus's head, suggesting that of Stalin or Dzerzhinsky and emphasising every-one's tendency in the play to see him as an icon, not a man.

I shall be forever glad of the style we achieved at our best, something between heroism and hectic argument. There was very little Received Pronunciation: wherever possible our actors worked in their natural accents, so that a Geordie or a Scot were, unless the casting absolutely forbade it, encouraged to use the voice they thought and felt in. (I in any case have a belief that Celts make the best Shakespearian actors – some-thing to do with an unforced poetic sense, ancient passion, an attraction to the very heart of a word.) In this we were, after all, mimicking Shake-speare's own company, who must have sounded like a Tower of Babel – actors drawn from all over the country at a time when people from one village might hardly understand those from another.

The ESC was an enterprise both progressive and nostalgic. In his book *Will and Me* Dominic Dromgoole flatteringly describes us as the rock 'n' roll company of the time, carousing and breaking hearts across five continents, and indeed we were in one sense old-fashioned rogues and vagabonds of the road. But I'm proudest of a more subtle thing from those years; the sight of young actors, not trained for the classics and with all the compressed diction of television acting, moving into a new 1,500-seat theatre every Monday, checking out the acoustic for a couple of minutes like roadies at a microphone, before going on in the evening with, as well as their colloquial instincts, the open throats and full vow-els of opera. At this point we seemed to be looking back into the best of our traditions and forward into something quite new.

In due course the ESC ran out of steam, as perhaps it was always going to after a spectacular start in which we toured the Shakespeare History cycle from *Richard II* to *Richard III*. This was a sequence that hadn't been seen since the groundbreaking RSC version of 1964: even since then, no one has had the temerity to tour it, week in and week out, through the UK and all round the world, occasionally doing marathon weekends of all the plays in the fifty-two hours between Friday and Sun-day nights. Winding up six years later, we left the debate about the rights and wrongs of the playing of Shakespeare – forever changing and sub-jective, forever echoing the political moment – to be conducted by bigger organisations with more money to do it with. We did good work still, but our political bite had softened. We had always been better at argument than at states of mind – though oddly enough the pastoral energies of the Bohemia scenes in *The Winter's Tale* suited us well, as did the tenderness of Lady Mortimer singing in Welsh to a husband who can't understand her in *Henry IV Part One*. Certainly our aims were more important than the production details which scandalised a few – I've lost count of the number of times we riposted that productions of Shakespeare were all in modern dress till the middle of the nineteenth century. Critics of this ignored our use of costume from earlier periods as well, sometimes within the same scene, and a choice of music that ranged from Gregorian Chant and Byrd, Handel and Monteverdi, through to Philip Glass, Louis Armstrong and Status Quo. And if nothing else, we had the wit, at the moment in *Richard III* when King Edward IV dies, to have a newspaper seller yelling 'Ed's dead – King shuffles off mortal coil'. You could hardly object to that when, as Gielgud said, we were also speaking the verse so well.

6

The Great Globe Itself

Hong Kong – The Globe – Hamlet – As You Like It –
Measure for Measure – Julius Caesar –
The Merry Wives of Windsor – Othello

In 1988 the ESC was invited to play its cycle of History plays at the
Hong Kong Festival. We duly arrived with our mixed bag of offensive
weapons – medieval broadswords, machine guns and ammo belts,
ancient pistols and nasty knives. All harmless props, of course, but the
Hong Kong police became so nervous that they required us to pack it all
up and deposit it in the police station after the show each night. Thus it
was that our two stage managers, a boy with some resemblance to Keith
Richards of The Rolling Stones and a girl with the demure bespectacled
prettiness sometimes seen on the faces of female urban terrorists – the
Baader Meinhof look – terrified a series of Hong Kong cabdrivers by
flagging them down with kitbags full of machine guns on their shoulders;
and indeed were seen taking a ferry into Hong Kong Harbour after the
last performance to dump all the unused ammunition in the water.

Something about this adventure made me feel close to Shakespeare.
In late 1598, a man named Giles Allen, the owner of The Theatre at Holy
Well in Shoreditch, complained to Queen Elizabeth that a mob had
attacked his property, armed with

> Swords, daggers, bills, axes and such-like... In very outrageous,
> violent and riotous sort, to the great... terrifying... of your
> Majesty's loving subjects there near inhabiting.

Listen to this Elizabethan language, how flat it can become when out of Shakespeare's hands: at best, Allen sounds like one of those over-protesting official types in the History plays – a Mayor, say, or some enraged cleric – with whom Shakespeare's mind wasn't quite engaged. As for the murderous weapons, the swords and daggers and axes, Allen, like the Hong King police, had no way of knowing that they were only theatre props normally used in the likes of *Henry VI* and now brought out of store to make the right impression. For the disturbance was being led by William Shakespeare on behalf of the Lord Chamberlain's Men, the company of which he was now a shareholder, and included his colleagues and no doubt some hired heavies; it also featured the leading actor of the day, Richard Burbage, together with his mother. At least the invective used in the affray will have been of a higher standard than Allen's flabby rhetoric.

Behind and around this exceptional event lay a mesh of complications. Twenty-two years earlier, James Burbage, Richard's father, had built The Theatre (its footprint has now been found just off New Inn Street near Shoreditch High Street). The name was not as boastful as it now sounds: as a generic term 'theatre' was still as unfamiliar as 'cyber-café' was in the early 1990s, so it was a novelty. This was where the Lord Chamberlain's Men normally played, as had the Queen's Men, Shakespeare's probable first colleagues, before them. The Lord Chamberlain's company was formed in 1594 by the then incumbent, Lord Hunsdon, who – rather as the Arts Council of the 1980s proclaimed a few 'centres of excellence' to be preferable to the old multiplicity of local repertory theatres – saw it as a way of rationalising London's diverse theatrical factions. Then, in 1596, Hunsdon died. His successor, Lord Cobham, was far less supportive, understandably resenting the fact that Shakespeare had mocked his Lollard ancestor Sir John Oldcastle by making him the model for Sir John Falstaff in *Henry IV*. Indeed the Falstaff figure seems to have been called Oldcastle in early performances of *Henry IV* and was hurriedly renamed Falstaff by the time of the publication of *Part One* in 1598. However, intriguing traces of the name persist in *Part Two*, which ends with a somewhat grovelling apology by a Dancer declaring that, in the matter of Falstaff, the real Oldcastle had 'died a martyr' (as indeed he had, by Puritan reckoning) and 'this is not the man'.

Cobham's reign was shortlived. He died a year later, in 1597, to be succeeded by another Hunsdon, which must have been a relief. The company will have felt they would once again have a powerful voice behind them as James Burbage attempted their relocation from The Theatre to an indoor venue, a disused Dominican monastery in Blackfriars. So far his plan was being stalled by local residents who feared 'the gathering together of all manner of lewd and vagrant persons' and the sound of drums and trumpets drowning the sermons.

By late 1597 the lease on The Theatre had expired and it had reverted to Giles Allen as the freeholder. And the elder Burbage had died as well, leaving Shakespeare's company rudderless. They had even begun selling some of the plays for publication, which, in the absence of our copyright protection laws, was seen as the end of their controllable life. They also had no home, and were moving here and there in London like the self-exiled Royal Shakespeare Company of the early 2000s after they had severed their link with the Barbican. To pursue the analogy, The Theatre, which they could no longer get into, was standing as mockingly empty and unused as Tony Blair's Millennium Dome at the equivalent time, once the party was over. Desperate times, desperate measures. The actors managed to convince themselves that they had a moral right to the physical materials of The Theatre, and perhaps to the land it stood on. They had had such a right under their now-expired lease, so it was an arguable point at least. Perhaps they felt able to continue insisting because of a deep Shakespearian conviction that their performances had somehow impregnated its wood: if neither brass nor stone nor gilded monuments could outlive their powerful rhyme, what price conveyancing documents? Eventually, on the first day off during their Christmas residency at court in 1598, despite thick snow on the ground and the frozen Thames, they assembled at The Theatre, scared off the bystanders as described, dismantled the entire building, loaded all its timbers onto wagons, rolled the wagons down Bishopsgate and hid everything in a warehouse near Bridewell Stairs on the river bank. The whole process took four days of their five-day break from court performances, and presumably involved an intense system of security to lock up the area at night, perhaps including fierce-looking actors with axes. Allen was supposed to be away on holiday, but they could never be sure who was looking after his interests in his absence. Indeed, questioned by one suspicious onlooker, Peter Street the builder claimed that he was merely taking down some of the wooden supports to have a good look at them before putting them back.

The whole business was especially critical for the five actors who had already taken the unprecedented step of becoming shareholders in a speculative new plan to erect a theatre across the river in Southwark, not far from the Rose (where their rivals, Edward Alleyn's Admiral's Men, were now in residence), and likewise beyond the city limit defined by the Thames. The five were, between them, to contribute half of its building costs in return for a share of the eventual profits; so, in adapting their plan to this new, albeit slightly cheaper opportunity (the timbers already existed), they couldn't afford a wrong step. One of them was Shakespeare, who, tied to the new idea, had changed his domestic arrangements to be permanently on site. It wasn't his first such move. In the mid-1590s he had gone from Shoreditch to Bishopsgate, near the Church of St Helens, quite a respectable area. Soon after, we feel a momentary warmth of proximity: in 1596 he was in trouble with the taxman there over an unpaid bill of five shillings of what we would call Council Tax. However he managed to be out when the knock came on the door: he is listed in the 1597 records as a defaulter, either 'dead or gone out of there'. As it happens, his son Hamnet had died in August 1596, and in early 1597 he had bought a big house, New Place, in Stratford; so he clearly 'went out' of Bishopsgate quite regularly, and in Stratford our sense of intimacy fades. By the time the authorities called again about the same debt, in 1598, he had made his move to Southwark in preparation for his new business, and was living close to the Clink prison. This is where we find him now; after his flirtation with respectable Bishopsgate, he was once again among the racier type of neighbours who had surrounded him when he first arrived in London.

Bit by bit over the first months of 1599 the dismantled Theatre, moved piecemeal across the river, was reassembled on the chosen site. The land in Southwark was swampy and the weather unhelpful as flood followed frost, but by the summer the Lord Chamberlain's Men were able to open the new Globe Theatre, the playhouse that had risen from the marshes. In time and motion terms that sounds like good going to me, and I salute Peter Street, a forgotten hero, for seeing it through.

Installed in his custom-built new premises, the company's house playwright, in the person of *Henry V*'s Chorus, showed a drift towards false modesty:

> But pardon, gentles all,
> The flat unraised spirits that have dar'd
> On this unworthy scaffold to bring forth
> So great an object. Can this cockpit hold
> The vasty fields of France? Or may we cram
> Within this wooden O the very casques
> That did affright the air at Agincourt?
> O pardon!

Well, of course they could, as they knew very well. For several years to come this 'wooden O', secured by guerilla tactics between losing one theatre and not being able to move into another, would be the stage that Shakespeare imagined every time he sat down to write, and when he stood up to act that's where we in turn imagine him. Onto a perfect platform, which without scenery looked almost exactly the same from play to play, Rosalind could step in the middle of a London afternoon and announce to three thousand people:

> Well, this is the Forest of Arden

– or Viola could ask a Sea Captain

> What country, friends, is this?

and be told

> This is Illyria, lady

– or the armed Prologue to *Troilus and Cressida* could inform us that

> In Troy there lies the scene.

And of course, geography was only the start of it. Soon Hamlet, who has seen a Ghost and is pretending to be mad, will walk towards his audience and denounce himself:

> O what a rogue and peasant slave am I

– and then, in a series of hammerblow questions, wonder whether his emotions are any more authentic than those simulated by the professional actor he has been watching:

> Is it not monstrous that this player here,
> But in a fiction, in a dream of passion,
> Could force his soul so to his own conceit
> That from her working all his visage wann'd,
> Tears in's eyes, distraction in's aspect,
> A broken voice, and his whole function suiting
> With forms to his conceit? And all for nothing?
> For Hecuba!
> What's Hecuba to him or he to Hecuba
> That he should weep for her?

This is a Pirandellian trick before its time: Hamlet is himself a fiction, made real by a player, whose performance in the part could be described in the same terms – what's Hamlet to Burbage or Burbage to Hamlet?

> What would he do,
> Had he the motive and the cue for passion
> That I have?

I, the fictional Hamlet the Dane, that is:

> Am I a coward?
> Who calls me villain? Breaks my pate across?
> Plucks off my beard and blows it in my face?
> Tweaks me by the nose, gives me the lie i' the throat
> As deep as to the lungs? Who does me this?
> Ha?

Well, surely the customers sometimes answered back: these are real questions being asked of actual witnesses. On our later, less helpful stages actors have tried to catch the tone of this: but while speaking to the audience in broad daylight may have been second nature to the Elizabethan performer, we have had to relearn the trick – as players at the new Shakespeare's Globe have done. The actor has to become as brave as a stand-up comedian, in this case without the laughs. When he fails to make contact it will be because he has kept the question half-closed, throwing a glance over the serried ranks in a rhetorical, excluding way that keeps him safe from interruption: but what is the point of Hamlet's questions, fraught as they are with contradiction and self-criticism, unless he looks us in the eye, treats us as equals, and gives us at least half a chance to reply before moving on to someone else? It's not so easy when peering into a dark auditorium of course, but with an audience lit by the same sun and breathing the same air, it can be thrilling.

With *Hamlet*, Shakespeare pushed his monologue form to the limit and the audience were involved as never before. The hero's relation to them is perhaps what finally distinguishes the play. It is not simply a matter of the soliloquies themselves: it's the renewed intimacy we feel with him as he re-enters the action afterwards. The Globe, which made this possible, had been built by actors for acting, which was more than a matter of putting the dressing rooms in the right place. It's been said that by a simple cunning, the stage was angled so that the afternoon sun – if it was out – hung behind the performers and shone into the faces of the long-suffering spectators. However, by stepping well forward towards them, an actor about to soliloquise could, with luck, begin to bring himself out of the shadow of the building and be better back- and top-lit by the sun. I don't really believe this – you'd need light coming from the front of house onto the speaker as well – but maybe audiences were more tolerant then, and I'm happy to believe that all the proportions of stage and auditorium were the fruit of experience. The company knew what they needed by now and will have corrected anything that hadn't seemed right for them at The Theatre.

The Globe surely represents the high summer of Shakespeare's career, between the clamour of its predecessors and, eventually, the pensive experimentations of the Blackfriars. It is possible to overstate the new theatre's effect on his writing; but the Globe was clearly the best of its kind, and the effect of no longer responding to given spaces but working in his purpose-built home may have been as much psychological as physical: like someone who constructs their own house or designs their own clothes, he had no one to blame. He responded by vigorously developing everything that specially interested him and in which he'd already smelled success.

The further possibilities of implicating the audience are obvious in the play with which the Globe probably opened, *Julius Caesar*: the theatre spectators more or less standing in for the citizens of Rome and being worked by Antony and Brutus would presumably have had the actors among them exhorting them with the scripted lines. This is a real step forward from the crowd scenes of *Henry VI* and *Richard III*: and there is also a new depth of confidentiality in the monologues that paves the way for Macbeth, Leontes and Angelo. Brutus's have a deeper introversion than did Prince Hal's; Hamlet's are as challenging as Richard III's but their method is more sophisticated. Also, something about the new theatre's intimacy – probably to do with proportion rather than size – seems to allow for such illuminating naturalistic details as Caesar's deafness, Lear's difficulty with the buttons on his clothes, and perhaps a close-up of Cleopatra's asp. The dialectic becomes sharper too: the equivocal nature of the characters of Caesar, Antony, Brutus and Cassius, four protagonists all claiming our attention in quick succession, makes it difficult to take sides in their story, so to that degree the Globe becomes a debating chamber, just as in the same season the jingoistic fanfares of *Henry V* are riddled with scepticism about the self-justifications of warfare.

One of the features of a debating chamber is that all privileges are left at the door. So, most interestingly of all, Shakespeare indulges a mischievous tendency to turn expectation on its head: this is to be the period of intelligent plain men and discredited wits. There is, I should say, no example in Shakespeare until now of an uneducated or working-class character genuinely besting his 'superior' in argument. Poins becomes irritated with Hal, but has to defer; Flute wins round his audience as Thisbe but it is a harmonising rather than a divisive effect; in *Love's Labour's Lost* Constable Dull, an unaffected man with the kind of judgmental name Shakespeare would not use again, sheds a pleasant sidelight on the windbags around him but it's hardly a criticism. However, in the heady months of the Globe's opening season, we find a shepherd confounding a courtier in *As You Like It*; then an honest soldier in *Henry V*, Michael Williams, standing up unapologetically to the King for having criticised him in a conversation in which the King was disguised; and shortly after that a Gravedigger puts the super-articulate Hamlet to shame. There's hardly a play from now on when something of the sort doesn't happen. Why this should coincide with the move to the Globe I don't know, but once you've spotted it, it is unarguable.

In *As You Like It* the shepherd Corin is dealing with the courtly affectations of Touchstone, the supposed wit of the piece, who is compelled by the plot to live – 'the more fool I' – in the Forest of Arden. Corin invites Touchstone to give his impressions of country life. Touchstone replies with routine paradoxes – it's a good life because it is solitary, but vile because it is private; it's pleasing because it's in the fields, but tedious because it's not in the court. And, as if he's actually said something substantial thereby, he sniffily asks Corin if he for his part is capable of 'any philosophy'. If that's all philosophy adds up to – a mocking way of stating the obvious – it seems a no-brainer to Corin, so he borrows the method; he knows that

> he that wants money, means and content is without three good friends; that the property of rain is to wet, and fire to burn; that good pasture makes fat sheep and that a great cause of the night is lack of the sun.

So he can antithesise with the best. Touchstone, feeling a disadvantage, tries to unnerve him:

TOUCHSTONE: Wast ever in court, shepherd?

CORIN: No, truly.

TOUCHSTONE: Then thou art damned.

CORIN: Nay, I hope.

TOUCHSTONE: Truly thou art damned, like an ill-roasted egg, all on one side.

CORIN: For not being at court? Your reason?

TOUCHSTONE: Why if thou wast never at court, thou never saw'st good manners; if thou never saw'st good manners, then thy manners must be wicked, and wickedness is sin, and sin is damnation. Thou art in a parlous state, shepherd.

Corin is a match for that too: skilfully addressing him by his simple name ('Not a whit, Touchstone') he easily closes the argument:

> Those that are good manners at the court are as ridiculous in the country as the behaviour of the country is most mockable at the court.

And as for himself:

> Sir, I am a true labourer, I earn that I eat; get that I wear; owe no man hate, envy no man's happiness; glad of other men's good, content with my harm; and the greatest of my pride is to see my ewes graze, and my lambs suck.

In some desperation, Touchstone keeps on with a riff about the wickedness of making a living from 'the copulation of cattle', but really he has been floored by natural, intelligent humour.

Among other things Corin has issued a warning to theatre practitioners which is still often ignored: the less verbal characters in Shakespeare are not necessarily clodhoppers. They can be thoughtful men and women of few words. But you still see the likes of Corin and Constable Dull patronised in performance, which is weirdly out of step in a culture priding itself on being more democratic than Shakespeare's. He may have believed in Ulysses's hierarchical system of 'degree' in society when it suited him and he may have lived in London most of his life, but he is not about to insult Warwickshire, where the Forest of Arden was situated: even in the capital's new theatre, the countryman in him is stronger than the metropolitan.

The triumph of Corin becomes an insistent effect: from now on the star of the show is always liable to be caught out by someone going about their daily business. In *Twelfth Night* a professional jester, Feste, outsmarts Olivia and Malvolio; in *Antony and Cleopatra* the Queen has her suicide mildly debunked by the man who sells her the asp. No sooner does the troubled Duke Vincentio in *Measure for Measure* go among his people than he runs into trouble of this kind. As a sabbatical, he disguises himself as a nameless travelling friar to see how the other half lives: in fact, in some ways he represents Shakespeare's most intent enquiry yet into a leader's actual capacity to govern. Cast adrift, he is startled by his subjects' uncontrollability, which forces him to improvise his way out of every problem. He has often been played (particularly at times when the very worst is thought of politicians), as a ruthless manipulator who abdicates to frame his ambitious younger deputy Angelo and then hangs around to watch him make a hash of his job. It's a dull reading of the part, since as fixers go the Duke has none of the wicked panache of Richard III or the drive of Iago, and watching his self-satisfied progress can make for a long evening. In fact, far from being the one with all the answers he has virtually none of them; his trajectory should be hesitant, sometimes desperate, full of inspirations he never thought himself capable of.

Angelo meanwhile sets about enforcing Vienna's more unpleasant laws, such as capital punishment for sex before marriage. Things come adrift when, thunderstruck by desire, he tries to strike his dirty bargain with Isabella. She indignantly refuses to sleep with him, her brother Claudio's death sentence is confirmed, and in Act Four the jilted Angelo waits for Claudio's severed head to be delivered to him. Working in the prison, the Duke/Friar sees that he has a tragedy to avert and may rapidly have to find a substitute head – or a substitute body from which the head can be cut. And so emerges from Shakespeare's imagining the briefly great figure of Barnardine:

> A man that apprehends death no more dreadfully but as a drunken sleep: careless, reckless, and fearless of what's past, present and to come.

He's a foreigner, 'Bohemian born', nine years already on Death Row – nobody can quite remember what for – utterly unmoved by the approach of death but equally unimpressed by a string of unsuccessful appeals for clemency. According to the Provost in the prison, he is maddeningly at ease with his situation:

> He hath evermore had the liberty of the prison; give him leave to escape hence, he would not; drunk many times a day, if not many days entirely drunk

– a condition that the Provost and his team have sometimes tried to take advantage of:

> We have very oft awaked him, as if to carry him to execution, and showed him a seeming warrant for it; it hath not moved him at all.

From the Duke's point of view Barnardine is the perfect replacement for Claudio, and in fact Angelo has fortuitously asked that he at last be executed a little later the same day. So the Duke suggests switching the victims and sending Barnardine's head to Angelo. The Provost's reasonable objection to this –

> Angelo hath seen them both, and will discover the favour

– drives the Duke, at the very edge of his resources, into a most unfriarly pragmatism:

> O, death's a great disguiser, and you may add to it. Shave the head, and tie the beard; and say it was the desire of the penitent to be so bared before his death; you know the course is common.

In the event the stubborn Provost is won over by the broadest of hints as to the Friar's real identity – he is in unlikely possession of the ducal seal on a letter: it is a surprise he absorbs without comment. Barnardine is called up from his cell:

> POMPEY: Master Barnardine! You must rise and be hanged, Master Barnardine...
>
> BARNARDINE: A pox o' your throats! Who makes that noise there! What are you?
>
> POMPEY: Your friend, sir, the hangman. You must be so good, sir, to rise and be put to death.
>
> BARNARDINE: Away, you rogue, away. I am sleepy...
>
> POMPEY: Pray, Master Barnardine, awake till you are executed, and sleep afterwards...

That at least gets him on to the stage:

> He is coming, sir, he is coming; I hear his straw rustle

– whereupon the Duke steps in to minister:

> DUKE: Sir, induced by my charity, and hearing how hastily you are to depart, I am come to advise you, comfort you and pray with you.
>
> BARNARDINE: Friar, not I; I have been drinking hard all night, and I will have more time to prepare me, or they shall beat out my brains with billets. I will not consent to die this day, that's certain...
>
> DUKE: But hear you –
>
> BARNARDINE: Not a word: if you have anything to say to me, come to my ward; for thence will not I today.

His ward is presumably that pile of straw, and back he goes to it, a model of marvellous mad dignity, having brought the play to a standstill. The Duke can only comment starchily:

> Unfit to live or die. O, gravel heart!

He and the author now have a problem, which is solved by the lucky chance that a 'most notorious pirate' whose hair colour is like Claudio's has just died in the prison, and might do instead. The laughable coincidence draws further attention to the basic helplessness of the Duke.

None of this is enough to make Shakespeare a Marxist, but these are more than just good theatre jokes. Watching the hero – ruler, King, alpha male – being embarrassed so regularly, we realise not only Shakespeare's comic sense but also, I would say, his inclination. With Othello, Macbeth, Lear and Coriolanus beginning to jostle for his attention, he seems less inclined to take such men at their word. Being a tragic hero seems to involve behaving very stupidly at some point, a prerogative Shakespeare generally sees as male.

✦

O these men, these men...

– Othello

So once again, this is where the women come in, a new sequence stepping up to the plate to confront the blunderers. At the Globe, they are getting gradually older, no doubt being played by maturing child actors, and they are often dealing with more elaborate personalities. Soon they will stand in the dock, where Hermione's dignity in self-defence will shame Leontes, and Queen Katherine's pride reproach Henry VIII. For the moment, they seem simply more practical than the men. In the sunlight of *As You Like It* Rosalind saves Orlando from the hash he would undoubtedly have made of their wooing had it been left to him, regulating its pace and controlling its terms, often against her own impulses. Taking on the advisory part of the boy Ganymede, she coaches Orlando in lovemaking. He little knows that he is already wooing Rosalind herself:

> ROSALIND [*playing Ganymede playing Rosalind*]: Why, how now, Orlando! Where have you been all this while? You a lover! An you serve me such another trick, never come in my sight more.
>
> ORLANDO: My fair Rosalind, I come within an hour of my promise.
>
> ROSALIND: Break an hour's promise in love!... I had as lief be wooed of a snail...

ORLANDO: Of a snail!

ROSALIND: Ay, of a snail; for though he comes slowly, he carries
his house on his head...

An hour! This man certainly needs all the help he can get – does he not
know that even Juliet was anxious to make Romeo, for all his fine talk,
stick to his schedule:

JULIET: Romeo!

ROMEO: My dear!

JULIET: What o'clock tomorrow
Shall I send to thee?

In *Julius Caesar* the stakes are high and the demands of conscience
pressing. Brutus, sleepless at night, is wandering about in daytime 'musing
and sighing', missing his meals. We know why: he's planning Julius Caesar's
assassination. Being a man, his first line of defence on being questioned by
his wife is that he's not feeling so well, but Portia is immediately onto that
– if he's sick he wouldn't be mooching around in the garden in the
evenings, making matters worse. No, Brutus has something on his mind,
and if ever he admired her beauty or pledged his love to her, she has a right
to know what it is. Otherwise she is 'Brutus' harlot, not his wife', living

in the suburbs
Of your good pleasure.

No, no, says Brutus, still deflecting: she is his 'true and honourable wife'.
This is still more maddening: he is patronising her as incapable of sharing a difficult secret. Either way it has driven her half crazy:

I have made strong proof of my constancy
Giving myself a voluntary wound
Here in the thigh; can I bear that with patience
And not my husband's secrets?

At this point the scene lurches from something easily recognisable – what
secrets to keep and not to keep in marriage – into startled silence. Such
has been Portia's despair at being 'protected' that she has taken a knife
and gashed herself not far from the most intimate area of her body. It is
something that Edmund in *King Lear* will later do to his arm, but he's
anaesthetised by his own ruthlessness; Portia's extremely painful gesture
– lonely, desperate and purposeless – shames and shocks. The cynical and
unmarried Cassius might call it passive-aggressive; Brutus is clearly
meant to take her self-harm as a measure of her isolation.

And it does her no good. Her husband, momentarily awed by the gesture, begins to see what he's done to her:

> O ye gods,
> Render me worthy of this noble wife

– but is saved from a change of heart by one of those fortuitous Shakespearian 'knockings within': his fellow conspirators have arrived. Portia is bundled away without a word, only aware that a succession of strangers is assembling in her house in the middle of the night. Her sickly husband seems to have a lot of doctors.

The chance that Brutus might regain his humanity in the face of his wife's self-harm has evaporated. Principled idiot that he is, he goes on to kill Julius Caesar the next day, then fails to get public support for what he has done; he has initiated a tragedy in which everybody will die, including himself. For Portia, you can only imagine her life after the night of the self-wounding: the shock of finding her husband with Caesar's blood on his hands the next day, then the flight from Rome, a civil war – with Brutus unlikely to become more confidential with her as the crisis deepens. In the end we hear that, disabused by these terrible events, she has 'fallen distract'

> And, her attendants absent, swallow'd fire.

In its context, her death has the function only of disabling the quarrel between Cassius and Brutus, so moved is the former by the latter's loss; they become firm allies once more, fight on and are destroyed. Shakespeare has shone a brief light on an innocent bystander and then, as Brutus himself does, consigned her to the shadows again. But it has been enough for us to see the human cost of regime change in those who least deserve to pay it.

Sometimes, rather than wounding themselves, the women keep their counsel, but their acquiescence is likely to be tactical. This is especially so when they are confronted by the men's odder proposals. In *Twelfth Night*, Viola, dressed as the boy page Cesario, is allowed bluntly to contradict Duke Orsino when he rails against women. It is quite a surprise, the result of her being sorely tried. On the one hand she is entitled to speak, being for the moment a man; on the other hand, Cesario is only a page. When all is revealed in the final scene, Orsino, chastened, proposes to Viola; she says nothing in reply, and in fact remains silent for the rest of the play. We aren't much troubled by this because we know she loves him (she told us so in a soliloquy); but at the end of *Measure for Measure*, Shakespeare does

a similar thing with a more ominous feel. The Duke has managed to tie up
the loose ends of the plot and is about to bring the curtain down when he
turns to Isabella and says, almost as an afterthought:

> Dear Isabel,
> I have a motion much imports your good:
> Whereto if you'll a willing ear incline,
> What's mine is yours and what is yours is mine.

The unexpected suggestion silences Isabella for good. No wonder. She's
been through a great deal at the hands of men – the Duke himself has
spent the evening fooling her into thinking he was a man of the cloth – so
his proposal sits in the air much more tensely than Orsino's did. What is
she thinking and what will she do? Any production has to present something visually – Isabella can be compliant, shocked or resentful – but in
strict terms of the text there's no information. Such ambiguous silences
are the women's means of survival, buying them time to reflect: a capacity which, combined with humanity and good judgment, makes me feel
that the female principle in Shakespeare is often well ahead of the male.
If the women don't become tragic icons with quite the noisy regularity
of the men, it must be because they are less like fools.

✦

> They are not ever jealous for the cause,
> But jealous for they are jealous; 'tis a monster
> Begot upon itself, born on itself.

> *– Othello*

And few things are more foolish or ghastly, comically embarrassing or suddenly murderous than male sexual jealousy. If possession defines a man's
control, jealousy confounds it, leaving him looking distinctly worse than
the woman. Later, with Posthumus in *Cymbeline*, Leontes and Othello, the
consequences of the fixation will be entirely negative; in the meantime, an
innocuous story, *The Merry Wives of Windsor*, gives Shakespeare an opportunity to look for the first time – and at no great tragic cost – at this great
upender of male dominance. In the case of Master Ford, respectable
burgher of Windsor, the author's tongue is still in his cheek and the possibility both of farce and a happy ending is acknowledged.

It seems that Shakespeare broke off halfway through the composition
of *Henry IV Part Two* to write, perhaps by royal request, an extra Falstaff
play. In it, the supreme ingenuity and wit of Sir John, perfected in the

alehouses of old England and defeated by Lancastrian succession, is transferred wholesale into sixteenth-century suburbia. It is as odd as if the Bastard Falconbridge from the 1200s were to turn up in *Henry IV*. *The Merry Wives* asserts the essential harmlessness of the English attitude to sex; the humiliated Falstaff is finally absorbed into the bourgeois community, having done no damage in his determined pursuit of two married women – his interest in them having been, in the best traditions of English farce, less carnal than financial.

Ford's manic need to spy on his wife is helpful to the plot as a farcical means of forcing Falstaff to hide in a laundry basket prior to being dumped in the Thames, and then to disguise himself as 'the fat woman of Brentford', an innkeeper for whom Ford harbours an unaccountable hatred. This makes Falstaff's perhaps the only true drag act in a Shakespeare play. But it is what happens in Ford's head that intrigues the writer. He is defined by his jealousy as if it was a medieval humour – he is 'jealous for he is jealous'. He arrives in the play without preamble, 'crotchets' already in his head:

> PISTOL: Sir John affects thy wife.
>
> FORD: Why, sir, my wife is not young.

For that he deserves all he's going to get. But beneath his disrespect, and subconsciously creating it, lies the fear that his is 'a fair house built upon another man's ground'. He decides to disguise himself as Master Brook and – 'very preposterously' in Falstaff's opinion and ours – hires Falstaff to test Mistress Ford's loyalty by presenting this Master Brook's suit to her. So the husband is spying on his own wife by means of the man he rightly suspects of having designs on her. Falstaff's contempt is expressed by an old Shakespeare joke: giving his opinion of Ford to Brook, he draws from the bottomless spring of Shakespearian insults:

> Hang him, mechanical salt-butter rogue! I will stare him out of his wits... Master Brook, thou shalt know I will predominate over the peasant, and thou shalt lie with his wife.

But this is as nothing next to Ford's increasing capacity for self-insult. In the first of a trio of marvellous prose soliloquies, he expresses his pride in his condition as if it were an intellectual achievement:

> I will rather trust a Fleming with my butter, Parson Hugh the Welshman with my cheese, an Irishman with my aqua-vitae bottle, or a thief to walk my ambling gelding, than my wife with herself... Then she plots, then she ruminates, then she

devises... God be praised for my jealousy!... Fie, fie, fie!
Cuckold, cuckold, cuckold!

In the second he sees himself performing a public service by teaching his
fellow husband Master Page to

> hear this shower sing in the wind... I shall be rather praised for
> this than mocked.

Then in an heroic rallying cry he calls himself to arms:

> Master Ford, awake! Awake, Master Ford! There's a hole made
> in your best coat, Master Ford!

Unlike Shakespeare's later victims of the disease, there is some reason
for his fear: Falstaff is indeed after Mistress Ford among others, as Cassio
is not after Desdemona or Polixenes after Hermione. Confronted in the
end by the integrity of his wife, Ford acquires some self-knowledge and
touchingly foresees his own epitaph: future cuckolds will be

> As jealous as Ford, who searched a hollow walnut for his wife's
> leman [sweetheart].

He apologises and is, like Falstaff, reconciled to the company, glad to
rejoin the cosy world of Windsor after his escapade on the wilder shores
with Othello and the rest.

It is hard to imagine the two unlucky wives in *Othello*, Emilia and Desdemona, contemplating Master Ford of Windsor, but they would sum up
his condition in a trice. As examples they have before them both Emilia's
husband Iago and the great archetype of jealousy, Othello himself:

> ...Nay, we must think men are not gods
> Nor of them look for such observancy
> As fits the bridal.

This is said by Desdemona, whose world is being destroyed, as it was
once created, by Othello's affection. Her compliance has been rewarded
with something related to but not at all the same as love; she is a true
victim as Mistress Ford, happily, is not. With a bitter wisdom she sees at
last that there are men who 'puddle' their 'clear spirit' by letting the small
things in them overwhelm the greater:

> Men's natures wrangle with inferior things,
> Though great ones are their object. 'Tis even so;
> For let our finger ache, and it indues
> Our other healthful members even to that sense
> Of pain.

Othello, taking the dilemmas of Master Ford and twisting them much tighter, is a play quite without mercy. It differs from the other major tragedies in that there is no recourse to or mention of the gods or the super-real; there are no Kings, no toppling states, no pitting of oneself against the heavens. In a tightly knit military garrison an intricate net of personal resentments is unravelled: the overbearing Mediterranean sky beats down on Iago's victims, but it is as if the Globe's roof has been low-ered and clamped shut. In fact the play is least comfortable when Othello, grandiosely appealing for heaven's justice, tries to make it meta-physical – condemning himself instead to the frosty judgment of the literary critic F.R. Leavis who declared him a self-dramatising man filled with 'an obtuse and brutal egotism'.

Well, that's all very well, but Othello is perplexed in the extreme in a way most of us can understand. The majority of people don't have to avenge a murdered father and aren't driven mad in a storm, but if ever there was a place any one of us could visit, it is where Othello finds him-self. Perhaps for that reason, by an old-fashioned definition of things prevalent when I was grudgingly studying and Professor Leavis was lec-turing, the play doesn't quite cut the mustard: tragedy was supposed to lead to general catharsis. As well as being scolded by Leavis, Othello, standing in the ruins of his life, suffers from a staunchly British – and in his case faintly racist – form of criticism: a man should not be so untrust-ing of his wife. A story that involves only the humiliation of a gullible man, the argument runs, inspires scorn but not pity. This seems to mean that Othello should, like a good chap, have trusted Desdemona (that is, taken her more for granted?), and, assuming her safely locked up, should have risen above the awkward side effects of new and passionate love. I would rather say that a wife so taken for granted might be the more likely to rebel. Emilia issues some timely warnings:

> 'Tis not a year or two shows us a man;
> They are all but stomachs, and we all but food;
> They eat us hungerly, and when they are full,
> They belch us...
> 　　　　　　Let husbands know
> Their wives have sense like them; they see and smell,
> And have their palates both for sweet and sour,
> As husbands have...

An American colleague of mine (female) recently did a production which hinted that, because of the pressure of unexpected events in the early stages of the play, the marriage of Othello and Desdemona may not have been consummated and so has remained in a certain way insecure. Desdemona, in extremis, seemed to wonder whether she wouldn't have done better to stay in Venice and accept the attentions of Lodovico ('a proper man... he speaks well'). This reference to Lodovico became not just a pretty piece of girlish musing but ached with a sense of a good life lost. I like this idea very much: it makes Desdemona less of a male ideal of wronged innocence and more of a human being.

It is the depth of Othello's passion that makes him vulnerable, not his wisdom on the subject. He has certainly not had time to achieve the even tempo of married love; also, as a Moor, he is an outsider in a white world. This is partly compensated for by the honour of being its champion: he is like an iconic sportsman with his roots in another culture – think of Zinedine Zidane, the ultimately disgraced Algerian hero of the French World Cup football team. So his success is ritualised while his deeper sense of exclusion is unaddressed. He speaks well, to be sure, but he lacks the white man's courtliness; he is attractive to women but a little old for his wife. He is sexually proud; he would

> rather be a toad
> And live upon the vapour of a dungeon
> Than keep a corner in the thing I love
> For others' uses

– but he demeans himself by spying on his wife behind a curtain, completely mishearing a male joke about a prostitute and assuming it refers to her. Serve him right, in a way; but by then his love has become a madness.

What Othello hasn't noticed is that he is at the centre of an interlocking pattern of male jealousy, in which the most afflicted man, Iago, has an unusual capacity for cruelty and high intelligence. Iago instinctively knows on what flank to attack, and is unlikely to be caught out since he is clearly the very best of Othello's friends. Perhaps taken up with his own glories, it hasn't occurred to Othello that Iago – no doubt highly capable, a veteran of campaigns in Rhodes and Cyprus – may have been specially hurt by Othello's passing him over for promotion in favour of Cassio, so that he ended up as a mere ensign (even the soubriquet, 'ancient', is depressing), rather than a lieutenant as he had hoped. Into the wake of Iago's shock has flowed, possibly for the first time, the noxious slurry of racism: he now refers to Othello as 'the thick lips'.

There is, in fact, no trace of racism in the play where there is not already a personal grievance. In Desdemona's father Brabantio the unacknowledged sexual jealousy of a parent has spawned racial hatred. At the start of the play he suffers the indignity of being roused from his bed by Iago and Roderigo yelling at him from the street that his daughter is submitting to an 'old black ram', then of going to her bedroom to find she has thumbed her nose at him and gone, perhaps leaving a body-shaped bundle in her bed. So he now sees Othello, her secret choice of husband, as a sort of shaman, the spinner of

> spells and medicines bought of mountebanks.

The attitude of the Duke of Venice (to whom Brabantio appeals) and his War Cabinet is quite different: to them Othello is 'noble' and 'valiant'. Even when the heroic Moor disgraces himself in the later stages of the story his colour is not commented on: Shakespeare has perceived that this ugly slur is generally provoked by a grudge about other things.

So Othello's obtuseness lies not in being deceived by his ancient but in failing to sense the details of the world around him. Samuel Taylor Coleridge saw Iago, most implacable of destroyers, as a demon of malignity without motive. The phrase has stuck, but it flatters him. His motives are banal and clear, and he keeps reminding us of them, in relentless and voluble soliloquy. He is jealous of Cassio, not only professionally but because he chooses to think Cassio may have slept with his wife Emilia, and for good measure he thinks Othello may have done so as well. He also, almost on principle, desires Desdemona himself and is envious of Othello that way too. So he knows from his own experience the monstrosity he is about to conjure up:

> The green-ey'd monster that doth mock
> The meat it feeds on.

The difference is that his weakness gives him not Othello's myopia but uncanny insights and speed of reaction.

In this unpleasantly simple logic lies the cruelty of the play: it is driven by the intense desire of one gifted man to make everyone around him as unhappy as he is. Rather than metaphysics, *Othello* shows the operation, moment by moment, of an exceptional mind dedicated to utter destruction. The miserable fact is that, as most audiences will quietly acknowledge to themselves, Iago's campaign is so brilliantly and opportunistically executed, such a masterly blend of planning, improvisation and happenstance, that you would have to be inhuman to withstand it. The process is as logical and clear as the daylight in which the Globe audience observed it; as clear as it would be on a pair of close-up cameras, for this is very modern writing.

Even more than Richard III (though with less pleasure), Iago makes his own luck. A drunken rout he has engineered to discredit Cassio results in the latter needing to be reinstated in Othello's favour: his obvious champion in this is the well-disposed Desdemona, the best kind of great man's wife. In her happy new-married confidence, she naively declares that she will use her sexual power to persuade Othello to reinstate Cassio: until he is forgiven, Othello's

> bed shall seem a school, his board a shrift.

It must be hard for Iago to believe his good fortune: this is exactly the kind of thing that, with a little briefing by himself, will start Othello wondering about her motives. Cassio discreetly scampers away on seeing Othello approaching, and Iago redraws his body language:

> I like not that...
>   I cannot think it
> That he would steal away so guilty-like
> Seeing you coming.

If Cassio's link with Desdemona was a gift, Iago has, with this comment, skilfully created another. When Desdemona moves in to start her plea, it is an unseasonable moment in Othello's working day, but then she has the new wife's privilege. Asked to call Cassio back, Othello keeps putting her off:

> Not now, sweet Desdemona; some other time

– but on she prettily goes, pursuing her obsession in the way of a child who can think of nothing else but the treat in store – 'tonight... tomorrow... Tuesday... Wednesday'. Iago sees (and perhaps Othello senses) that this is as much a matter of her own gratification as of justice for Cassio:

> DESDEMONA: I wonder in my soul,
>   What you could ask me that I should deny,
>   Or stand so mammering on. What! Michael Cassio,
>   That came a-wooing with you, and so many a time
>   When I have spoke of you dispraisingly,
>   Hath ta'en your part.

Another opening: Cassio seems to have held the privileged position of go-between for the lovers. So he is locked into a curious intimacy with them both, knowing each's secrets better than the other does: he is used to appeasing their momentary doubts and routine annoyances.

Listening to this charming stuff, a misogynist such as Iago might reflect on how wifely manipulation can shade into emotional blackmail. However, in Othello the misogynist still lies buried, and it all works to his delight, as if he were being tickled – though tickling can also make you want to cry out with discomfort. He promises he will deny Desdemona nothing, and indeed will

> come to thee straight

– perhaps for the pleasure of a shared siesta.

It is the thought of this kind of pleasure no longer being sacred that will, in the next few minutes, bring Othello to his knees. The great central scene in which, step by step, Iago destroys his peace of mind has a sizzling overture. As the uxorious husband watches his wife leave, you see how close his rapture borders on anguish:

> Excellent wretch! Perdition catch my soul
> But I do love thee! And when I love thee not,
> Chaos is come again.

Iago's initial technique is to present himself as a discreet and modest thinker, hesitating to declare or over-interpret:

> IAGO: Did Michael Cassio, when you woo'd my lady,
>   Know of your love?
>
> OTHELLO: He did, from first to last; why dost thou ask?
>
> IAGO: But for a satisfaction of my thought;
>   No further harm.

The word 'harm' is well chosen, and Iago watches it being taken. As if still preoccupied with that, he gives himself a new characteristic – an irritating deafness to the matter in hand:

> IAGO: I did not think he had been acquainted with her.
>
> OTHELLO: O yes, and went between us very oft.
>
> IAGO: Indeed!
>
> OTHELLO: Indeed! Ay, indeed; discern'st thou aught in that?
>   Is he not honest?
>
> IAGO: Honest, my lord?
>
> OTHELLO: Honest! Ay, honest.
>
> IAGO: My lord, for aught I know.
>
> OTHELLO: What dost thou think?
>
> IAGO: Think, my lord?

OTHELLO: Think, my lord! By heaven he echoes me,
  As if there were some monster in his thought
  Too hideous to be shown.

In this way Othello has been made to take the initiative. New nerve patterns begin to form in his brain: the 'hideous monster' is not so much in Iago's thought as something coaxed from Othello's subconscious. He begins to misread facial expressions, for the worst: whatever Iago's expression has just been will have been quite subtle, but Othello somehow saw him

  contract and purse thy brow together,
As if thou then hadst shut up in thy brain
Some horrible conceit.

A cold, toxic anxiety starts to move through Othello. Iago sees that it will be best accelerated by more indirectness: asked

      if thou dost love me
Show me my thought

he answers only the first half of the question:

IAGO: My lord, you know I love you.

OTHELLO: I think thou dost…

IAGO: For Michael Cassio,
  I dare be sworn I think that he is honest.

'I dare be sworn I think…': the line creaks with manufactured effort, and the little linguistic turn, which makes the oath provisional only, causes a limp in the metre. Othello's better self will suddenly have no more of it:

  I think so too.

For the moment he is on top again, applying a full stop: Iago, who deals in ellipses and hesitations, has to think quickly. A pleasant aphorism may keep the discussion alive:

      Men should be what they seem.
  And those that be not, would they might seem none.

But Othello is able to defend himself: he has got the hang of this way of saying something with nothing:

  Certain, men should be what they seem.

He has suddenly become a little less permeable. Iago works harder still –

IAGO: Why then I think Cassio's an honest man.

OTHELLO: Nay yet there's more in this...

Success: Othello has opened his flank again. Now Iago preposterously stands on his rights: a man is not obliged to share his secret thoughts. In fact his are specially unworthy since

> it is my nature's plague
> To spy into abuses, and oft my jealousy
> Shapes faults that are not.

In other words, Othello was right not to promote him and shouldn't listen to him now. His is a flawed personality, and he should remain silent for both their sakes:

> It were not for your quiet nor your good...
> To let you know my thoughts.

All he knows is that in this close-knit military community, reputation is all-important:

> Good name in man and woman, dear my lord,
> Is the immediate jewel of their souls.

Suddenly Iago has edged into the bedroom. He has sensed that honeymoon heat has made Othello more easily threatened than he would normally be. So perhaps he can afford one crucial, unambiguous word:

> O beware, my lord, of jealousy...

Perhaps too he is returning Othello's gaze for the first time, man to man. The feint about 'good name' was the start of a brilliant strike. Within the next twelve lines he will have linked 'man and woman' with, daringly, 'cuckold'. But then Othello shows a sort of amorous statesmanship:

> I'll see before I doubt: when I doubt, prove;
> And on the proof, there is no more but this:
> Away at once with love or jealousy.

He seems to have regained some initiative, but in fact he is already in check.

Othello's frankness seems to Iago to deserve the same: the honest servant can at last call things by their proper names. Othello should simply keep his eyes open – after all, they are living in adultery's natural home:

> In Venice they do let God see those pranks
> They dare not show their husbands...

And another thing: isn't there something odd about a woman who

> Seem'd to shake, and fear your looks

as a symptom of loving him? Could she possibly be one of those who are not quite 'what they seem'? And – the killer punch:

> She did deceive her father, marrying you.

Immediately, we and Othello recall Brabantio's logic:

> Look to her, Moor, if thou hast eyes to see;
> She has deceiv'd her father, and may thee.

Othello becomes monosyllabic. Hearing it, Iago is sorry: he is guilty of too much love, he has upset him, he is probably wrong. If Desdemona's honest, then

> Long live she so! And long live you to think so!

Another low blow in the line's second half, and Othello is winded all over again. Then Othello hands him the race card:

> And yet how nature, erring from itself...

Iago doesn't even let him finish:

> Ay, there's the point.

He wouldn't have mentioned such a thing unprompted, but was it not perverse for a white girl not to look at suitors

> Of her own clime, complexion and degree

– instead marrying both above her (a general), and beneath her (a black man)? That's not the way that 'nature tends'; it even deserves an expletive:

> Foh! One may smell in such a will most rank,
> Foul disproportion, thoughts unnatural.

Most of the job is done. Iago makes to leave – and returns. Why? Good acting, a performance of having second thoughts. On reflection Othello should not think about it any more (what a joke); he should definitely assume Iago is wrong till some proof presents itself. This is a sharp instinct: the thing must be kept from exploding while Iago manufactures some evidence. Now both men have their burdens. Othello may need to unwish the past; Iago, caught in his own net, can't escape until everybody is dead.

Despite some poetic glories, nothing else in *Othello* quite matches this extraordinary scene – the emotion so minutely observed on a new stage which allows Iago to step forward and confide in us as well. But if this intricate central passage was perfect for the Globe, much of what follows is a form of melodrama. The embarrassing ignominy of Othello's decline is matched by some grotesquerie in the storytelling, such as Iago's invented dream in which Cassio whispered to him in his sleep as if he were Desdemona and even started to mount him – not with the vocal shudders of a man half asleep but with the elegant diction of a Shakespeare:

> 'Sweet Desdemona,
> Let us be wary, let us hide our loves';
> And then, sir, would he gripe and wring my hand,
> Cry 'O sweet creature' and then kiss me hard.

Then there is the silly business of the lost handkerchief Desdemona had from Othello, a sacred object bred by holy silkworms. Considering its pedigree, he has been remarkably careless of it: maddened by Desdemona's physical proximity he dashed it to the floor as she used it to bind his forehead – an odd way in any case of treating the headache he said he had. It is discovered by Emilia, who ingratiatingly gives it to Iago, who leaves it in Cassio's quarters, where it is found by Bianca, an entirely unnecessary character variously described as his mistress and as a prostitute on the army's coat-tails. Back the 'minx's token' comes to Cassio just as Iago is making him laugh at Bianca while Othello, incompetently eavesdropping on them (how Shakespeare loves such a scene, complete with asides), assumes Desdemona's sexual looseness is the cause of the joke. Then the handkerchief is abruptly forgotten.

Farce is never far away, as indeed it isn't in such a thing in life. Iago drives Othello into a trance by inviting him to imagine Cassio lying 'With her, on her; what you will':

> OTHELLO: Pish! Noses, ears and lips. Is it possible? Confess! Handkerchief! – O devil!

– whereupon Cassio rushes in and, like an inconvenient arrival in a Feydeau farce, has to be rushed away again before Othello comes round. In the end Iago, juggling almost too many balls, provokes Roderigo to kill Cassio in the street, but Cassio wounds Roderigo; Iago wounds Cassio, then finishes off Roderigo. Othello drops in for a moment, Iago effortlessly shops Bianca.

It is a spirited mess of course, an adrenaline burst as the action rushes towards its end. All the mechanics will have been familiar staples to the Globe's audience; what they won't have been prepared for is the intensity and finesse of Iago's psychological terrorism and, occasionally, the humbling beauty of Othello's sorrow:

> But yet the pity of it... the pity of it...

The pity, that is, of seeing Desdemona abused by her husband in front of the ducal ambassador – a man who may have been present at Othello's irresistible account of his wooing, observed Desdemona's pride in him, and dined out on it ever since. The pity of Othello visiting his wife as if in a brothel run by Emilia (he even tips her when he leaves): he treats Desdemona like meat on a slab only to find that he can't stop his love and sorrow bucketing out:

> But there where I have garner'd up my heart,
> Where either I must live or bear no life,
> The fountain from the which my current runs
> Or else dries up: to be discarded thence!

The pity that Desdemona should come to feel the self-hatred of the battered wife:

> 'Tis meet I should be us'd so, very meet.
> How have I been behav'd, that he might stick
> The small'st opinion on my least misuse?

Still, her love shines on:

> EMILIA: I would you had never seen him.
>
> DESDEMONA: So would not I; my love doth so approve him
>   That even his stubbornness, his checks and frowns –
>   Prithee, unpin me – have grace and favour in them.

Even on her deathbed she will say the blame lies with

> Nobody, I myself. Farewell!
> Commend me to my kind lord. O, farewell.

The pity that one emotion always lies under another, fury beneath lament, grief beneath foulness. So Othello aches at his wife:

> O thou weed
> Who art so lovely fair and smell'st so sweet
> That the sense aches at thee, would thou hadst ne'er been born.

And pity is hardly the word for the magnificence of the play's last scene, in which Othello throws away the dearest thing he owned:

> My wife! My wife! What wife? I have no wife…

As he finally glimpses a huge loneliness of his own making, his language rises like a tidal wave:

> Where should Othello go?…
> Whip me, ye devils,
> From the possession of this heavenly sight!
> Blow me about in winds, roast me in sulphur,
> Wash me in steep-down gulfs of liquid fire…

– until all he can find for relief are just two alliterative words:

> O Desdemona, Desdemona, dead.

But there is no comfort there, so he collapses further into

> O! O! O!

as if not even Shakespeare can help him any longer.

The play's innocent wives both die at the hands of demented men, for Emilia is also dispatched by her husband for finding him out. Cassio lives, and so does Iago – for a little. Why doesn't Shakespeare kill him off? Does he want to indulge our vindictiveness, letting us imagine the torture he will suffer first? The company turns on him and he is wounded, but

> I bleed, sir, but not killed.

He is promised every kind of physical extremity and he vows to explain nothing, to stay forever silent. His body may be torn apart, but what cannot be killed is the intelligence and the skill of such a man. So the play belongs to an alarming genre which gives no comforting message of good overcoming evil, but rather the fear of evil being for ever. In this way it resembles the Coen brothers' *No Country for Old Men*, at the end of which Javier Bardem's murderous hit man, having taken punishment that would kill a small army, walks calmly away, having outlived all the good guys. Like Iago, he can't be beaten. This is one of the ways in which *Othello* operates – a dread fulfilled that unthinkable insult can be flung in innocent faces, that wickedness may have no limit. That a man can be the victim not of the gods who might kill him for their sport, but of a devil near at hand who knows him all too well.

✦

I was once invited to undertake a Shakespeare teaching project in return for a Fellowship at an academic institution. I didn't have much time and couldn't think of a subject. Eventually I did come up with one and went through the process of peer review, which threw up one enthusiastic endorsement and one memorably scornful rejection. Referring to my phrase 'the actor's point of view' the critic rumbled: 'there is an initial problem here with the word actor: what sort of actor... within what process of making?... This raises the problem of what the nature of this authoritative and singular "actor" entity is.' For all the daft jargon he was right enough: I had chosen to relate the acting – and therefore writing – styles of Shakespeare's plays to the venues they were written for; The Theatre, the Globe, the court and Blackfriars. I had been, as I had suspected I might be, rumbled for my amoral approach to the academic study of Shakespeare. Because of course this was a project in which you can make everything up: there are comments here and there on performances in contemporary accounts, but not much other reading to do. We simply don't have the information. My critic sadly concluded: '...there is no comparator here... the omission of comparator seems very odd.'

In this chapter I've been at it again, but with stronger instincts and in better faith. The matching of plays to their venues is seen by some, like my critical peer, to be self-defeating. Works written for The Theatre and the Globe were in any case revived later for the court and the Blackfriars; and the fact that later plays were premiered at Blackfriars in the winter doesn't mean that they weren't also played at the open-air Globe in the summer.

However, for roughly the first decade of the new century, apart from touring and court appearances, the Globe was Shakespeare's only home. *Julius Caesar*, *As You Like It* and *Henry V* were part of its first season. *Twelfth Night* played at Middle Temple in 1602 and then presumably at the Globe – *Hamlet* had already done so. *Measure for Measure* is known to have played at the court of the new King James I but it wouldn't have had much of a performance life if it wasn't being done at the Globe as well. So the new theatre was the centre of operations, and I think it shows. From the tense dialectic of *Caesar* to the blank cheerlessness of *Othello*, from the lurching, impassioned rhythms of Hamlet's soliloquies to the limpid beauty of Viola stepping out of her amorous mesh and looking for friendly faces in the audience, there is a distinct sense of glory days and confident experiment there, with *Othello* as a kind of climax as James comes to the throne in 1603.

The new King immediately favoured Shakespeare's company and began inviting them to play privately for him. When in November 1604 the dark stories of *Measure for Measure* and *Othello* were revived in front of the King himself at the heart of government, it must have been a remarkable occasion. In one play, the court was watching a pointed parable on leadership being played to a man whose style was very different from his predecessor's; and in the other an account of sexual jealousy to a ruler who was notable among those who knew him for his capacity for that very thing. Back in Elizabeth's reign Shakespeare's company had got into seriously hot water for putting on *Richard II* at a time when the Queen felt she was in danger of deposition. Times seemed to have changed: during the next few years, with some gall, they would take continual risks with her successor. In fact, it was as if Shakespeare had been waiting for him.

7

The Time's Plague

The Wisest Fool in Christendom – Macbeth –
Timon of Athens – King Lear

For all the national mourning for Queen Elizabeth, it was a welcome moment. Despite her longevity and her historic hold on her subjects' affections, after nearly forty-five years on the throne the Virgin Queen was generally seen as the Crotchety Old Maid. She had become remote, wayward, negligent and parsimonious, particularly in the dispensation of knighthoods and other court favours – the lubricants that made Tudor England work. And here, in James, her one-time godchild and the son of her old enemy Mary Stuart Queen of Scots, was a new idea for the public: a fruitful male, with two heirs already born, a writer and intellectual and athlete. Elizabeth had left England still embroiled in an expensive war with Spain and with the two main religions at chronic odds. James would swiftly achieve peace abroad; what was beyond him was religious reconciliation, which, as the son of a Catholic mother executed by his Protestant predecessor, he may well have desired more.

In his own person James was something of an oddball. He always proclaimed that he favoured 'the medium in all things', but he presided over a court of fabulous drunkenness and excess; he was a linguist, a poet and prose writer, but loved hunting more than anything (he once killed all the deer in one of Scotland's royal parks and the English had to restock it). He was neurotic and boorish, paranoid and clever; gay but a father several times over; by turns pasty-faced and bright red from probable porphyria, restless and gawky; once described as the wisest fool in Christendom, with a tongue too big for his mouth, but compared, by himself as well as others, to King Solomon. He would have enjoyed hearing this compliment confirmed at his funeral, when the Bishop of Lincoln based his eulogy on the fact that Solomon had lived for about sixty years, 'and so, you know, did King James' (actually he died at fifty-eight).

The moment of Elizabeth's demise was as significant for Shakespeare as for everyone else. By now the dramatist was a star. His name was being printed on the published versions of the plays – a much higher accolade than it seems now – and he was turning up in celebratory poems by other writers, usually described as 'sweet'. The Globe was flourishing, so he was well-placed to crest the new wave. But if George Bernard Shaw is right to say, as he does in *Maxims for Revolutionists*, that any man over forty is a scoundrel, then he would probably add that the tide begins to turn for Shakespeare a year early, at thirty-nine, as he re-cuts his cloth to serve a new master.

We tend to think of England's national playwright as part of the great display case of Elizabeth's Golden Age – actually a police state with all the instruments of official repression working flat out – but he was to be far more successful under James, partly by reason of his own artistic development and partly through royal benevolence. Only days after his accession the King appointed the Lord Chamberlain's Men as his personal acting troupe and renamed them: from now on they would be the King's Men. It's hard to imagine any subsequent English monarch seeing the theatre as such a priority, but James regarded himself as a philosopher prince and hoped to preside over the kind of cultural renaissance normally attributed to his predecessor; clearly Shakespeare was an asset he could use. Most people would say James's greatest legacy to the world would be his commissioning of a beautiful work of English prose, the King James Bible. I would say that there was another: what his peculiar mixture of generous patronage and a certain moral ambiguity did to deepen and complicate the writing of William Shakespeare.

In one way, the good times were rolling. The King's Men would find themselves playing for James's peripatetic court – at the Banqueting House in Whitehall or at Hampton Court, at Greenwich or at Nonsuch Palace near Cheam in Surrey – on average every three weeks instead of every three months, to an apparently delighted monarch. *The Merchant of Venice* was his favourite, which tells us nothing much, but he also seems to have enjoyed revivals of such earlier Elizabethan pieces as *The Comedy of Errors* as much as the recent *Othello* and *Measure for Measure*; and within six years, the King's Men would be able to overcome all opposition and open their long hoped-for alternative theatre in Blackfriars. Here they could work under cover, in the evenings, by candle light, to a smaller and more controllable audience, and attempt more spectacular scenic effects such as the moment in *Cymbeline* when Jupiter

> *descends in thunder and lightning, sitting upon an eagle: he throws a thunderbolt.*

They could also make quite a bit more money: this was a better-heeled clientele in a more respectable part of town. The spectators surrounding the Blackfriars's thrust stage were all seated, in no danger from the rain. At the Globe the most expensive seats – for those who sat at all – were threepence, and they were in the galleries at some distance from the stage; but for the new privilege of being close and comfortable at the Blackfriars they could be anything up to two shillings. In addition, the company's frequent appearances at court earned them about £10 for a single performance (maybe £2,000 in today's terms), or ten times that for a short season. Within five years or so Shakespeare would be wealthy enough to retire to Stratford, a substantial landowner.

The only obvious thing I can see wrong with the Blackfriars was that, in a sort of quid pro quo with its more glamorous clientele, the latter were allowed to sit on the stage during performances to show off their clothes and to come and go from that conspicuous place throughout the play, if necessary pushing the actors aside if they were in the way. But there was a more significant rub: ceremonial duties came with the company's new status as the King's Men. At the heady moment of accession James had made Shakespeare and his colleagues Grooms of his Chamber: they were each provided with the means to buy four and a half yards of scarlet cloth to fashion themselves new doublets and hose so that they could march in 'royal proceedings' such as James's triumphal entry into London, when they were to act as ushers carrying the canopy. (All such Grooms had to be categorised: for no discernible reason Shakespeare and his colleagues were included under 'Falconers, etc.')

It must have been a strange sight, and a strange feeling for them. This 'Magnificent Entertainment' had been postponed by a year because of plague in 1603, which had carried off nearly 20 per cent of London's population, perhaps including their old colleague Will Kempe, for whom Shakespeare had written the great comedy parts of Dogberry, Bottom and Falstaff. And here is the playwright, dressed up in his obligatory bright red clothes, traipsing through the recently infectious streets, perhaps thinking he would have been better off staying away on tour, the normal recourse from the plague taken by theatre companies. His attitude may have resembled, conversely, that of the great and the good nowadays who, whether or not they care about Shakespeare, find themselves required to process through the streets of Stratford-upon-Avon every April 23rd to celebrate the great man's birthday.

I want to move in at this point and ask him a question. What did he really think of all this – the change of regime, this unknown quantity of a King, his own new status and indeed his bright red clothes? Whether he liked it or not, he was a courtier now, co-opted into the Establishment, never a very good thing for a writer. Was he perhaps feeling just a little bit bought? As we have no idea how Shakespeare dealt with awkward questions in person, we have a sonnet in reply:

> Were't aught to me I bore the canopy,
> With my extern the outward honouring
> Or laid great bases for eternity,
> Which proves more short than waste or ruining?
> Have I not seen dwellers upon form and favour
> Lose all and more by paying too much rent,
> For compound sweet forgoing simple savour,
> Pitiful thrivers in their gazing spent?

This was something of an obsession with Shakespeare: he's always contrasting 'simple savour' with 'compound sweet', truth with pretence, 'faithful friend' with 'flattering foe'. Sincerity and plain dealing seem to have been important to him; but James's court ran on ostentation and hypocrisy, and Shakespeare was being propelled into a queasy relationship with it. The cultural renaissance didn't last long in any case, as events conspired to touch the jumpier nerves in James's personality. He had grown up in violence and instability – his father killed, probably by his doomed mother's next lover, separated from her by a series of dubious protectors, kidnapped as soon as he took power in Scotland (by the Earl of Gowrie, about whom Shakespeare's company daringly presented a now lost play which was quickly banned) – and his insecurity was chronic. So that when two assassination attempts in the first year of his reign were followed by the Gunpowder Plot of 1605, in which he might have lost his life while opening Parliament, the psychological effect was catastrophic.

Much of the melodrama surrounding the Plot – the secret tunnel, the planned explosion from below – was probably worked up politically by the Secretary of State, Robert Cecil, who, like a cynical police chief, may have actively encouraged the conspiracy and then delayed the arrests as long as he dared so as to achieve the maximum impact for himself. Certainly the anti-Catholic backlash, stoked from pulpit as well as parliament, was as indiscriminate and virulent as the Islamophobia that followed the terrorist attacks of 2001 and 2005. It was led by James, whose public pronouncements began to sound a modern, paranoid note: the crafty Cecil had stage-managed events to suggest that it had been the King himself who had saved the day. His Majesty had, this version ran, interpreted an anonymous message of warning about the Plot that nobody else understood and sent his Privy Councillors post haste to explore the cellars of Parliament, where they found Guy Fawkes sitting on his stash. Thus it could be announced, in the statute proclaiming November 5th an occasion of national thanksgiving, that God had directly inspired the King to sense the danger and act quickly to forestall it.

All the same, it was a bad moment for James. Things had been going so well – the economy booming, peace with Spain – but as we now know, the arrival of a new century can be an unpredictable business. James authorised the torture of Fawkes, then instituted a purge against Catholics, the obvious suspects; many of them belonged to old Warwickshire families well known to and probably liked by Shakespeare. (To make matters worse, some of the plotters had rented a house at Clopton, near Stratford, to develop their tactics.) James went on to make Protestant communion compulsory, but Susannah, Shakespeare's daughter, was among many who openly refused to comply: together with a handful of other Stratford-dwellers, she was reported to the ecclesiastical court, though nothing further seems to have come of it.

✦

O, come in, equivocator...

– Macbeth

What did Susannah's discreet father think of all this? Perhaps he was preoccupied with feathering his own nest. With a Scottish King on the throne, he certainly didn't allow himself any more jokes about the Scots, such as he'd given Dromio of Syracuse with his routine about the fat kitchen girl in *The Comedy of Errors*. He even obliged James with a Scottish play, *Macbeth* – a disgraceful piece of royalist temporising as well as a great play – which carefully indulged the King's well-known interest in witchcraft, by which he felt personally threatened since his wife had nearly been killed in a freak storm at sea. More significantly, in writing this account of the sacrilegious murder of a Scottish king, Shakespeare adjusted his source material, in which it was not Lady Macbeth but Banquo who plotted with Macbeth to kill King Duncan. However, Banquo was thought to be the founder of the Stuart dynasty, so James was his descendant. Consequently Banquo, loyal, noble and predicted to be the father of many kings, gets thoroughly whitewashed, and King James, ever nervous about his legitimacy on the throne of his mother's enemy, is soothed by his pet playwright's politic ministrations. Soothed too by Malcolm's endorsement, in the play's dying moments, of James's dream, the union of Scotland and England. And by other things. James had written an anxious treatise on witches, believing that these bearers of diabolical designs on the faithful frequently came in the form of old village women. And he used to tell a story of his mother's death being presaged by a vision in the sky of a dancing, bloody head.

Apart from these obvious echoes (the Witches conjure up the apparition of an armed head to warn Macbeth about the threat of Macduff) the play, written so soon after the national emergency, resounds with loyal denunciations of treachery. There is an extraordinary scene after the murder of Duncan when the Porter at Glamis Castle speculates as to who might be knocking at the gate. Obscure now, it was highly topical:

> Faith, here's an equivocator, that could swear in both the scales
> against either scale; who committed treason enough for God's
> sake, yet could not equivocate to heaven...

The talk of equivocation would have been understood to refer to the trial of the Jesuit priest Father Henry Garnet. Garnet was a devout and peaceful man who had been confessor to some of the Gunpowder Plotters and felt that he was bound by the confessional not to betray their secrets to the Government. So he was swiftly reinterpreted as a Satanic figure, even the Plot's prime mover; the necessary casuistry of the Jesuit – no more than that of a good Catholic trying not to deny his faith – came to be seen as the wiliest equivocation. So in *Macbeth* we see a masterpiece playing in an obsequious key to an increasingly paranoid monarch, and our greatest humanist playwright, possibly a crypto-Catholic himself, endorsing the vicious anti-Catholicism of the time – including the terrible end of Garnet, dragged on a hoop through the streets of London before being hanged and dismembered. His testicles were cut off and burned in front of his face to show he was unworthy to be born or to reproduce, his innards (where he had conceived the plot) likewise, his head (where he had finessed his technique) removed, and his body divided into four to be put out for the birds of the air. How lucky for us that all this prejudice is put by Shakespeare merely into the mouth of a drunken Porter rather than that of the noble Banquo.

Aside from the politics, Shakespeare's ability to haunt and alarm his audience in *Macbeth* is quite insolent: its psychological reach and mastery of suspense comes almost too easily. The first is deeply instinctive by now; and as for the narrative, he is prepared to abandon logic for momentum: he simply can't be troubled with the question of how much the Macbeths have or haven't discussed the murder before, or whether they have or have not had a child. (There is, by normal standards, the sense of a missing scene or two in a very short play.) The headlong action is effortlessly terrifying, as sadistic as in Alfred Hitchcock; stones move and trees speak in a time of blood. It is a caution to actors who tend to speak too slowly or directors who like to over-interpret – I see no reason why a production of the play (or of *The Tempest* or *The Comedy of Errors*) should run for more than two hours. No sooner have the Macbeths committed themselves to the idea of murdering Duncan than night falls, giving them their one predictable opportunity for doing it; no sooner has everyone gone to bed than the deed is done, whereupon there is an immediate hammering at the castle gates from morning guests come to waken the King. The only relief from the onward rush is the somewhat underrated scene in England between Malcolm and Macduff, the first time in the play when the audience can draw any kind of breath.

Perhaps because of this velocity, Shakespeare is able to show how initially incompetent the normally decisive Macbeth is under pressure, making the ridiculous mistake of murdering Duncan's Grooms and so turning everyone's attentions onto himself – a gaffe so serious that Lady Macbeth has to faint to distract attention from it. Banquo immediately takes over as the spokesman of order, provoking Macbeth's paranoia further: in their last conversation before he, as the new king, has him killed, he thoroughly patronises him with many royal we's. Macbeth's real strengths lie elsewhere: finally given the unequivocal part of a tyrant to play, he becomes a masterful one, the role's every murderous impulse within easy reach. Newly empowered, he can even conquer his dependence on his wife. He is a first class operator as long as he feels in charge; better than when he was dictated to by Lady Macbeth, who on the other hand doesn't have the stamina to continue playing her own part. He does not repent like the Thane of Cawdor, nothing in whose life became him like the leaving it; Macbeth's manner to the end is remorseless but highly poetic. However, one of Shakespeare's ironies is that he, and our expectations, are mocked by language of comparable beauty coming from elsewhere:

The west yet glimmers with some streaks of day;
Now spurs the lated traveller apace
To gain the timely inn.

These lovely lines are spoken by a professional murderer 'so weary with disasters' that he will do anything to survive, a poor man whom the successful Macbeth hires to make him feel more secure.

✦

The middle of humanity thou never knewest, but the extremity of both ends.

– Timon of Athens

I have a feeling that *Macbeth* has achieved greatness with time, now that its grovelling to James is less noticeable. A less great play, but a hugely underrated one, somewhat redresses the sycophantic balance. *Timon of Athens* comes very close to describing daily life in James's court – very likely the reason it was never performed in the author's lifetime, and thus a rare example of Shakespeare overplaying his hand a little. James's world was fashion-obsessed, gluttonous, sexually corrupt; cash for official favours was rife, lobbyists were everywhere, and, as if in contrast to the stinginess of the elderly Elizabeth, the Crown habitually made extravagant gifts to its courtiers to purchase their loyalty and create a confining net of obligations. This is exactly and exclusively what happens in the first half of *Timon*, and the play truly comes to life when the hero, suddenly in debt and realising the fraudulence of his friendships, throws his followers out of his house and voluptuously takes on the life of the outcast:

But myself
Who had the world as my confectionary,
The mouths, the tongues, the eyes, the hearts of men
At duty more than I could frame employment,
That numberless upon me stuck as leaves
Do on the oak, have with one winter's brush
Fell from their boughs, and left me open, bare
For every storm that blows.

The play is startlingly modern in theme, and sometimes in utterance: 'confectionary' is a word Shakespeare never used elsewhere, and its meaning is exactly as it is today – a sweetshop. So like James I, Timon seems to have the world as his candy store, but comes to believe that life's only truth is that dog eats dog. He shares this insight with the play's self-appointed moral scourge, Apemantus – described in the cast list as 'a churlish philosopher' – with strict logic and, at the end, a marvellous lurch into fantasy. He switches from 'if thou wert' to the more poetic 'wert thou' to evoke the fabulous unicorn, who arrives as a complete surprise and is, apart from the harmless lamb, the only animal mentioned just once in his speech:

> If thou wert the lion, the fox would beguile thee; if thou wert the lamb, the fox would eat thee; if thou wert the fox, the lion would suspect thee, when peradventure thou wert accused by the ass; if thou wert the ass, thy dullness would torment thee, and still thou lived'st but as a breakfast to the wolf; if thou wert the wolf, thy greediness would afflict thee, and oft thou shouldst hazard thy life for thy dinner; wert thou the unicorn, pride and wrath would confound thee, and make thine own self the conquest of thy fury... What beast couldst thou be that wert not subject to a beast?

Timon of Athens splits into two discrete movements. It opens with a statement of its overall theme not unlike that of the Chorus at the start of *Romeo and Juliet*, but this time cunningly embedded in the dialogue and spoken by the anonymous figure of 'A Poet'. What he says gives the play a sense of sad predetermination – it's to be a parable:

> When Fortune in her shift and change of mood
> Spurns down her late belov'd, all his dependants,
> Which labour'd after him to the mountain's top
> Even on their knees and hands, let him slip down,
> Not one accompanying his declining foot.

The first half duly studies a man compulsively buying friendship to staunch a fearful loneliness: Timon is that rarity among Shakespeare protagonists, a man with no family and no relationships – even the source of his apparently limitless wealth is not explained. He first appears in his courtyard, as a patron of the arts accepting unsolicited tributes – poetry, pictures and jewels – and settling disputes in his fiefdom: he typically offers to sponsor one of his servants who wants to marry a girl of a higher caste. He praises the work of a portrait painter who has caught, as he thinks, the inner truth of his subject; in doing so he unwittingly puts his finger on his own problem and bears out the Poet's melancholy prediction:

> The painting is almost the natural man;
> For since dishonour traffics with man's nature,
> He is but outside...

If this strange ritual is his surgery hour, it is one in which the doctor finds it difficult to concentrate on one patient at a time; if he did, he might be more wary of the ripple of adulation that greets his smallest benevolent gesture. We will soon discover that his lack of attention is constitutional; Timon is forever on the move, unable to settle, a man sorely afraid of something. Freud would call him a narcissist, in the strictest sense of the term: he feels the glow of his kindness even more warmly than do its beneficiaries.

You could also call him a champagne socialist: he seems to think he is at the helm of a philosophical revolution. With a woozy religiosity, he welcomes his guests to one of his regular banquets by insisting that everything in life should be shared:

> there's none
> Can truly say he gives if he receives...

Then, as the evening wears on, he waxes lachrymose:

> We are born to do benefits... O what a precious comfort 'tis to have so many like brothers commanding one another's fortunes... Mine eyes cannot hold out water methinks; to forget their faults, I drink to you...

He is talking to a more than willing audience; no wonder a rich man with such a mindset has attracted such affection. In its muddled idealism, sincere and sometimes soft-headed, this part of the play reminds me very much of the 1960s. Timon of Athens would have understood the kind of party at which anything goes, sexually or pharmaceutically, whose host might be leading the dance or whom you might not even meet because he is upstairs reading Proust; the *Zeitgeist* then being so ambiguous that the murderous Charles Manson was easily mistaken for a hippy. In that sense, Timon starts on Haight Ashbury with flowers in his hair and ends like Hunter S. Thompson, stacking up his dynamite and turning one of his huge collection of shotguns on himself.

Mercilessly as he nails this unusual character, Shakespeare also hates a flatterer; with untypical judgmentalism, Timon's guests are described in the cast list – presumably assembled either by the author or by the scribe responsible for the prompt copy – as 'flattering lords' and 'false friends'. These men – the only women in the play are a couple of whores in the second half – accept Timon's outrageous hospitality with warmth; there are many times in life when it is hard to distinguish tactical bonhomie from friendship, so in a good production they should seem eminently sincere, albeit with a showbiz gloss, or Timon will look too big a fool. Indeed they perhaps think no evil as yet, and would themselves be surprised, if ever their patron should need their help, to find their hands unaccountably paralysed on the way to their pockets.

Timon's big party approaches its end, a bad moment for the host:

FIRST LORD: Where be our men?

SERVANT: Here, my lord, in readiness.

SECOND LORD: Our horses!

TIMON: O my friends,
I have one word to say to you...

Timon's first, unfinished half-line betrays his anxiety – his friends mustn't leave, or if they must, they should, as from some children's party, take a present with them. So everyone gets an extra little item – a jewel here, a cash gift there, even a favourite horse.

Pascal, quoting Tacitus, once commented that there's something annoying about kindness – and of course retribution is afoot. Timon comes to realise that he is not only out of cash but in debt – his creditors start hammering at his door in the early hours. His honest steward Flavius convinces him of the depth of his trouble – Timon's only sign of anger in this half of the play is towards this messenger whom he would shoot for bringing the bad news. He sends requests out to three of his regular guests, on the assumption they will be his Samaritans. Each passes by on the other side: Lucullus claims that it is a bad time to lend without security; Lucius has just made a large purchase and is a trifle short; Sempronius is offended not to have been the first to be asked and refuses in a huff. The scales drop from Timon's eyes, and he throws a viciously jovial final banquet with nothing but stones and tureens of boiling water on the menu. A parody of the Last Supper, it ends with the disciples being driven out as

smiling, smooth, detested parasites,
Courteous destroyers, affable wolves, meek bears;
You fools of fortune, trencher-friends, time's flies...

Timon flees the city: after a final jeremiad outside the walls, he heads, like Lear, for open country and takes up residence in a cave, where he expects to find

The unkindest beast more kinder than mankind.

As the Poet prefaced the first half, an anonymous honest servant of Timon's, with great beauty, now shifts the play's key to its relative minor:

> and his poor self
> A dedicated beggar to the air,
> With his disease of all-shunn'd poverty
> Walks, like contempt, alone...

This is quite a new kind of language, hugely broadening the atmospherics. It is followed by a magnificently sustained aria for the central character – scorching heat alternates in Timon's language with howling wind, the sun with darkness, the desert with the sea. Likewise his temper tilts and bucks between excoriation and lament:

> Common mother, thou
> Whose womb unmeasurable and infinite breast
> Teems and feeds all; whose selfsame mettle
> Whereof thy proud child, arrogant man, is puff'd
> Engenders the black toad and adder blue,
> The gilded newt and eyeless venom'd worm...

By a splendid irony, while digging for roots to eat, he finds a stash of gold, and his old friends seem to smell it from afar: one by one they come and are variously and violently dispatched, sometimes enriched with it, sometimes not. This is where Shakespeare might have ordered things more carefully. The entire second half is a series of instructive interviews with a minimum of narrative: their quality is uneven and the effect a little humpbacked. The impression is of a brilliant draft waiting to be revised, perhaps by Thomas Middleton, Shakespeare's possible collaborator. The best encounter is with Apemantus, who arrives to question Timon's tragic status, pointing out that for all his grand gesture of rejection, Athens has swiftly forgotten about him anyway: nobody knows you when you're down and out. Though he sees himself as a victim, Timon strikes Apemantus as no more than a curmudgeon on a park bench:

> APEMANTUS: Thou art the cap of all the fools alive.
>
> TIMON: Would thou wert clean enough to spit upon...
>
> APEMANTUS: Beast!
>
> TIMON: Slave!
>
> APEMANTUS: Toad!
>
> TIMON: Rogue, rogue, rogue!

This is a soundscape that could have been dreamed up by Samuel Beckett – very like *Waiting for Godot* when Vladimir and Estragon embark on little canters of abuse:

ESTRAGON: That's the idea, let's abuse each other.

VLADIMIR: Moron!

ESTRAGON: Vermin!

VLADIMIR: Abortion!

ESTRAGON: Morpion!

VLADIMIR: Sewer-rat!

ESTRAGON: Curate!

VLADIMIR: Cretin!

ESTRAGON (*with finality*): Critic!

VLADIMIR: Oh! (*He wilts, vanquished, and turns away.*)

There has to be some modulation, and Flavius, who warned Timon of his plight in the first place, turns up:

O you gods!
Is yond despis'd and ruinous man my lord?
Full of decay and failing?

Timon doesn't recognise him at first, treating his claim to be 'an honest poor servant of yours' as a joke, but when he sees Flavius's tears, the mists seem to clear:

Had I a steward
So true, so just, and now so comfortable?

But Flavius may still be an imposter, feigning 'a usuring kindness' for the sake of gold. Finally convinced, Timon rewards him – the only gentle gesture of the Act, but one delivered on his own misanthropic terms:

Go, live rich and happy...
Hate all, curse all, show charity to none;
But let the famish'd flesh slide from the bone
Ere thou relieve the beggar...
be men like blasted woods,
And may diseases lick up their false bloods,
And so, farewell and thrive.

Closure seems near, even a precarious beauty:

My long sickness
Of health and living now begins to mend
And nothing brings me all things...

Then Shakespeare suddenly seems to be back in Stratford. He has planted a mulberry tree, an almost lost species at the time, in his garden

at New Place, and finds himself airlifting Timon out of his wilderness to
Warwickshire:

> I have a tree which grows here in my close
> That mine own use invites me to cut down
> And shortly must I fell it...

However, he cheerfully invites all of Athens to come and hang themselves
from it before he does so. Finally, like Enobarbus in *Antony and
Cleopatra*, he prepares to die of undisclosed causes, writing his own
epitaph in case nobody else does and cancelling language altogether:

> Timon hath made his everlasting mansion
> Upon the beached verge of the salt flood,
> Whom once a day with his embossed froth
> The turbulent surge shall cover...
> Lips, let sour words go by and language end;
> What is amiss, plague and infection mend;
> Graves only be men's works and death their gain;
> Sun, hide thy beams. Timon hath done his reign.

It has been an oddity of a play, fitfully magnificent but strangely unful-
filled. It contains some of Shakespeare's most virulently beautiful writing:
but Timon sometimes seems like a second-rate Lear, an embarrassing
poor relation without Lear's full cause of weeping. His journey from
Camelot to Cardboard City can seem a massive, self-punishing petu-
lance; but this is to ignore the play's peculiar psychology and the wintry
lamentation of its second half. Shakespeare has exposed the vanity of
benevolence: Timon was a man who invariably gave a gift too big for the
friendship, who annoyingly insisted on always paying for dinner, always.
He lent before he was asked and wouldn't accept repayment. Then he
dived headlong into what he most feared, his own company: altruism
turned into comminatory rage, but that was only philanthropy with its
nap reversed. The message is both grim and trite, categorical and without meaning, depressing rather than tragic. *Timon* offers the maledictions
of *King Lear* but little release; nothing is drawn together and the two
extremities of the hero's life remain starkly unresolved.

This irresolution, which has baffled and irritated critics, is perhaps the
point. *Timon* seems to me absolutely of its moment in Shakespeare's life.
With James he has entered a new era – a benediction at first, but rapidly
seen, as Gloucester is about to say in *Lear*, as one of 'machinations, hol-
lowness, treachery and all ruinous disorders'. James was the patron
Shakespeare must have dreamed of, but he charged a high rent; dribbling

embarrassingly from the sides of his mouth when he drank, he was prepared to disembowel good Catholics. Shakespeare has to go trudging
through the London streets all in red, a leader in the theatre but an obe-
dient servant of this King: he is compelled to an 'outward show' while
grieving for his unruly colleague, the anarchic comedian Kempe, who
would perhaps have made a joke of the red costume. Maybe *Timon* could
only have arisen from the emotional hiatus when a man hardly knows what
to feel, pique or outrage. Do I have any cause to feel aggrieved? What con-
stitutes an undeserved hurt? What does ingratitude amount to? What have
we the right to expect from our family, our ruler, our friend? The metaphysics are uncertain. *Timon* and *Lear* will turn out to be two shots at the
same thing. The difference, Shakespeare perceives, is that the family has
to be involved, not a single isolated man. On that basis he now gathers
himself for his most unflinching look into the heart of man's darkness.

✦

We have seen the best of our time...

– King Lear

As King Lear's attendants and family gather to listen to his brainwave of
dividing up the kingdom, the prospect is clear enough. What he proposes
– the splitting of England into three – is an arrangement which will allow
him to look forward to a carefree retirement, its boredom relieved by a
cycle of stopovers with one or other of his three daughters. He plans, at
this time, to 'publish' the scale of allowances their husbands can expect
to receive for their new responsibilities: Albany and Cornwall, already
married to his elder daughters Goneril and Regan, are in attendance,
while two long-standing suitors for his youngest daughter Cordelia's
hand are also awaiting the news.

When people plan to split England up in Shakespeare it always leads
to trouble: Hotspur and the other doomed rebels hope to form a coalition government in this way in *Henry IV Part One* and end up
permanently suspicious of each other. For an entitled king, however, it
is not, on the face of it, such a bad idea, though obviously lacking in tactical caution: even without being a royal, a parent giving away his whole
estate before death to save his children the burden of Inheritance Tax
would do well to have a cautious and undeceived lawyer at his side. Few
benefactors ever accept what every lawyer sadly knows: that much-loved
children have been known to misbehave when a legacy is in hand.

The problem here is that, without knowing it, Lear has lost the bond of intimacy with his daughters; lacking this underpinning, his plan flaps dangerously in the air. His vanity compounds his folly: as well as a despot, he is already 'a very foolish fond old man' – fond in the Shakespearian sense of deluded rather than loving. He requires recognition of his largesse in a more extreme form than Timon does: there is to be a competition among the daughters, out in the open, here, in front of everyone:

> Which of you shall we say doth love us most?

This is a piece of dishonesty: while the daughters compete in eloquence, they are the only ones in the dark about the outcome. From the very opening lines we know that Lear has decided everything in advance and that the court knows it: disasters aside, all three are going to get exactly the same amount of land, though there might be some variation in the cash element. Not for the last time in the play you wish the absent Queen Lear (interestingly, there was reference to one in Shakespeare's source play) would step in to get the old man to stop wasting everybody's time and point out the folly of playing a public practical joke on his children. However, perhaps even the bravest of Shakespeare's women couldn't do that with a Lear; it will be left to a licensed Fool.

The whole arrangement being so reckless and lacking in affection, you find yourself, as so often in Shakespeare, checking on the courtiers' silent reactions. Do they take it all as a sweet and charming ritual or as an embarrassing whim? What is the consensus about Lear's current form as a ruler? Facing up to them all, Goneril, the eldest sister, declares first:

> Sir, I love you more than words can wield the matter;
> Dearer than eyesight, space and liberty;
> Beyond what can be valued, rich or rare;
> No less than life, with grace, health, beauty, honour;
> As much as child e'er lov'd, or father found;
> A love that makes breath poor and speech unable;
> Beyond all manner of so much I love you.

It sounds prepared, and well turned for the occasion – good in a crass way, and perhaps more than he deserves. Not that it stands up to scrutiny: she'd cheerfully go blind, lose her freedom, all the jewellery she might ever receive, her health, her beauty and good report, her power of speech, in fact she'd rather be dead than – what, exactly? Be without her own feeling of love for him. The sense has evaporated in the rhapsody.

In this demented contest it is clearly best to go first: the second sister, Regan, will have a tough job to differentiate her quality of love, as, later in the play, she will her degree of viciousness. Now she can only elaborate a form of 'hear, hear'; only she feels that Goneril

> comes too short; that I profess
> Myself an enemy to all other joys
> Which the most precious square of sense possesses
> And find I am alone felicitate
> In your dear highness' love.

For her too, nothing in life is worth a rap except her love for her father – and these women are both married. Having cleared the fence in only slightly less style, Regan gets

> No less in space, validity and pleasure
> Than that conferr'd on Goneril.

During this performance, Lear's 'last, not least', Cordelia, has forewarned us in asides: she will have nothing to do with any of it. Good, honest Cordelia – but as with many truth-speakers, there is something chilling in her chastity:

> Nothing, my lord...
> Unhappy that I am, I cannot heave
> My heart into my mouth; I love your majesty
> According to my bond; nor more nor less.

'Bond' is ambiguous and well-calculated, its overtones as much legal as spiritual. It's not really true that Cordelia cannot heave her heart into her mouth: the play will prove her capable of a moving description of her mad father picking wildflowers. And what in any case is wrong with speaking, if what is said is the truth? She goes on, drawing a deep breath to fill the rest of her first line:

> Good my lord;
> You have begot me, bred me, lov'd me; I
> Return those duties back as are right fit;
> Obey you, love you, and most honour you.

Why won't Cordelia cooperate in this silly game – he's an old man, could she not manage a little indulgence? Is this her father's stubborn pride, inherited and working in her, or is it a subtle way of competing? Within the integrity of Cordelia is an opportunity for the actress to move from a certain initial priggishness to, eventually, a saving depth of love. She now preaches on the distinction between filial and married loyalty:

> Why have my sisters husbands if they say
> They love you all? Haply when I shall wed,
> The lord whose hand must take my plight shall carry
> Half my love with him, half my care and duty...

No wonder Regan will shortly snap at her:

> Prescribe not us our duties

– and no wonder Lear is repelled by her zeal:

> So young and so untender?

If you haven't seen *King Lear* before, the balance of sympathy here is not so simple, and any production should resist declaring itself too soon. It is depressing to see Goneril and Regan arrive, as they sometimes do, in the red and green clothes of villainy, and Cordelia in the oatmeal of innocence, as if the outcome of the play were already settled. In that case Lear becomes stupider than ever, and there's nothing much interesting to watch. Like Timon's flatterers, each of these parts need to be played from their own point of view, and our judgment suspended as long as possible.

With Cordelia's disclaimer a dam bursts and this enormous play begins to flow. Lear's reaction is hugely disproportionate: he will have nothing more to do with her and all ties are broken now she has deviated from the norm he has invented. He would prefer the company of any 'barbarous Scythian': the sun, the night, the planetary system are his witnesses. The King's fanatical narcissism hints at where the play is heading: he will forever blindly complain of ingratitude, even though his gift to his daughters came from something other than generosity. Cordelia is rapidly paired off and banished: Goneril and Regan can split the third section of England between them. Lear's two sons-in-law become regents to whom, in a burst of furious folly, Lear awards

> my power,
> Pre-eminence and all the large effects,
> That troop with majesty.

There's one small problem for them: in return for giving up the kingdom and presumably his palace, Lear will be visiting each of their households in permanent rotation, with a retinue of a hundred knights – costs to be paid by his hosts, one month at a time with each, presumably until death.

The Earl of Kent, with Cordelia's candour, immediately calls Lear a madman – this is utter folly, politically and parentally inept, and he will shout it from the rooftops. Naturally he is banished for his pains. The question of the impoverished Cordelia's integrity is discussed by two possible suitors – the Duke of Burgundy and the King of France – as if that was what really interested them. Burgundy, who frankly wanted the money, turns her down; France, with perhaps less need of a wealthy wife, accepts her appreciatively.

A dowerless daughter and two more who claim to love their father more than their husbands: not a promising family profile. When Lear leaves, we see the three sisters together for a moment. Is there to be a hint as to why they are so out of kilter? Cordelia's judgment on her siblings is as absolute as her father's was on her:

> ... I know you what you are,
> And like a sister am most loath to call
> Your faults as they are nam'd.

Their plural 'faults'? Is there some deeper grudge here to explain the tension?

Cordelia leaves with her new husband and, still more interestingly, Regan and Goneril are alone. Along with the power, they have inherited a problem – a choleric and sentimental father turning up with a small private army every other month. The elder sister has spotted Lear's real weakness, and it is bitter to her:

> GONERIL: You see how full of changes his age is... he always
> loved our sister most...
>
> REGAN: 'Tis the infirmity of his age; yet he hath ever but
> slenderly known himself.

These two have always lived with the knowledge that they were less favoured, less lovely. Who knows what spitefulness this might have led to in the nursery; their claim on his estate, presented to them on a plate, will be their revenge. Lear has separated them by making them compete with each other: but their collaboration will be all the fiercer, multiplying their resolve by more than two:

> GONERIL: Pray you, let us hit together...
>
> REGAN: We shall further think on't.
>
> GONERIL: We must do something, and in the heat.

Many questions are forming, but only one step is taken at a time. All we know so far is that Lear is a wayward old man who doesn't care to be criticised; that the much-loved Cordelia is oddly unresonant; that the two other sisters, simultaneously enriched and reduced, have looked after themselves, but are not necessarily capable of doing outright harm. By degrees the play will radicalise Goneril; Regan, without the eldest sister's traditional responsibilities, may already be nearer to what she is horribly to become. With so much dysfunction on view, Shakespeare has also ensured that Lear doesn't have to be a king for us to recognise the emotions. The play brings forth a deep and shameful dream known to many: what if my mother or father were to die now and leave me all the money? So far, so normal enough: but we have no inkling of the terrain into which we are headed.

✦

At one point in *King Lear* Edgar, the legitimate son of the Earl of Gloucester, marvels at the 'dark and vicious place' where his bastard brother Edmund was conceived. One might ask Shakespeare the same question about the play. He has taken a recent local story, and crossed it with an old play called *King Leir and his Three Daughters* (which Tolstoy thought superior, but then like Shaw he thought almost anything superior to Shakespeare). Then, with a brief nod to Philip Sidney's *Arcadia* he has invented the ill-starred Gloucester family as a counterpoint to the King's. This is becoming typical enough: in *Hamlet*, two other young men, Fortinbras and Laertes, are alternative versions of Hamlet, and in *Timon*, Apemantus and the avenging warrior Alcibiades suggest other routes the disaffected Timon might have followed. Gloucester is another study in paternal folly shadowing Lear: a mixture of vanity, gullibility and muddled integrity, he moves from clubbish pride in his sexual prowess at having fathered a likely bastard towards death under a tree, his eyes gouged out like an image of Armageddon.

By then he has been the site of the play's cruellest transgression, the onstage blinding which destroys his sight but quickens his sensibility. From where in Shakespeare's imagining did this horrible idea come? What was he drawing on to invent the wickedness of Cornwall and Regan, who, suspecting Gloucester of making common cause with Cordelia against them, capture him in his own house and do such a thing? Worse, it is an off-the-cuff outrage: a few moments before, while Goneril had indeed advised 'pluck out his eyes', Regan had only got as far as 'hang him instantly'. All they've known is that their revenge will be extreme and deviant. Only Cornwall seems to feel the need for a little self-justification: he attributes his revenge to the Earl's 'reprovable badness'. Then, in one of the most chilling moments in Shakespeare, Gloucester, 'tied to the stake', gives them their cue. He explains why he has helped Lear escape to Dover, where he might join the incoming army:

REGAN: Wherefore to Dover?...

GLOUCESTER: Because I would not see thy cruel nails
Pluck out his poor old eyes...

CORNWALL: See't shalt thou never.

Sometimes a knife is used, sometimes bare fingernails; in one recent production, Regan suctioned Gloucester's eyes out with her mouth. The director's choice is as limitless as the characters' depravity: we're unlikely to question the feasibility of the chosen method. Likewise Gloucester's physical trauma, like that of Oedipus, would probably kill him in the instant; but he survives, speaks, and plays an eloquent part in Lear's own descent:

I have no way, and therefore want no eyes;
I stumbled when I saw.

By this time, the play has changed its nature: from the psychodrama of a family it has become a metaphor, a great turning circle. 'I am bound upon a wheel of fire', cries the King; 'Fortune, goodnight, smile once more, turn thy wheel', says Kent in the stocks, where the Fool advises him to

Let go thy hold when a great wheel runs down a hill lest it break
thy neck with following...

Even Edmund admits at his death that 'the wheel is come full circle'. Its velocity is the play's obsession. What is the sudden tipping point between a domestic drama that reminds audiences of their own difficulties with elderly relatives, and the resolve to put a father out in an almost supernatural storm? Within moments of fearfully shrinking from Lear's curse on her sister –

So will you wish on me when the rash fit is on

– Regan is pulling out an honest man's eyes, and eventually the two women, in pursuit of his bastard son, will destroy each other.

Even so quickly may one catch the plague. A minor incident over a garden fence can lead to a man decapitating his neighbour with an electric saw; an imagined slight inflames the mind more than a calculated insult; the very fact of unchecked power makes the idea of genocide quietly entertainable. By the twenty-first century, we have learned how fragile our restraints can be, how we can be sent to hell in a second. On the day that I'm writing, the television news tells of a man who raped both his daughters repeatedly for twenty years, causing them eighteen pregnancies. In the next item, it is reported that aid to Somalia, one of the poorest nations on earth, may have been stolen wholesale by aid workers en route. So what is so strange about *King Lear*?

In sparing us nothing of man's capacity to go to one extreme or another, was Shakespeare simply exploiting his talent to terrify? A little more, I should say: he is also asking what resources a human being can find to survive 'whirlwinds, star-blasting and taking'. In fact a desperate urge for goodness wrangles throughout with the brutal transgressions of Goneril, Regan, Edmund and Cornwall: the play has some of Shakespeare's kindest writing, unexpectedly flowing like clear water. As well as to the obviously 'good' characters – Cordelia, Kent – it is given to those who are struggling within themselves. In between his grievous outbursts, Lear expresses the human capacity to endure in homely terms. Captured in his madness, he protests mildly:

> Why, this would make a man a man of salt
> To use his eyes for garden water-pots,
> Ay, and laying autumn's dust

– and resolves to

> die bravely like a smug bridegroom.

Edgar, the son 'father'd' as Lear is 'childed', advises Gloucester

> Bear free and patient thoughts

then gently releases his breath:

> Men must endure
> Their going hence, even as their coming hither;
> Ripeness is all.

These are sightings of forbearance that, in the forlorn words of Lear, comfort and not burn. The scene in which the King, exhausted by his derangement, awakens and finds his daughter Cordelia with him is profoundly moving even before he stirs, because of the kindness shown to Cordelia by his doctor, played out in front of the simple image of the old man sanely and quietly asleep after all his tribulations. For us too, this is like coming out of a bad dream.

By the same token, when Albany tells his wife Goneril

> You are not worth the dust which the rude wind
> Blows in your face

the audience wants to cheer. Albany is an underrated character. He is so despised by his wife for his embattled benevolence that she compares him to a kitten:

> Marry, your manhood – Mew!

In some way he is the ultimate problem for the director of such a play – a decent, quiet man amidst the mesmerising energies of hatred. 'Whereof comes this?' he cries, horrified by Lear's curse on Goneril. Generally his interjections are mild, occasional, moderate; but whenever he finds his tongue, we regain our moral bearings:

> Tigers, not daughters, what have you perform'd?
> A father and a gracious aged man...
> Most barbarous, most degenerate, have you madded...
> Humanity must perforce prey on itself
> Like monsters of the deep.

'Gracious' is quite a generous description of Lear, but we appreciate Albany's bias; and also that in the end he takes a kind of charge – 'Shut your mouth, dame' – even arresting Edmund, for what good that does. How he and Goneril come to be married is a mystery, but it does allow us to imagine that there was a decent enough woman in her at one time: the same could hardly be said of Regan.

The King, too, keeps glimpsing light in darkness. Apparently mad as a hatter on Dover Beach, he suddenly seems to pull a curtain aside, using Shakespeare's predilection for near-monosyllables to express the plainest truth:

> If thou wilt weep my fortunes, take mine eyes;
> I know thee well enough; thy name is Gloucester;
> Thou must be patient; we came crying hither;
> Thou know'st the first time that we smell the air,
> We waul and cry.

However, such plangent moments in this great role need to be held in check; actors are always drawn to Lear's misery and passion and then, with few exceptions, neglect the 'hideous rashness' of the autocrat that precedes it. An audience comes to pity Lear against mighty odds: they have seen him rampaging around Britain with his private army of hooligans, abusing everyone's hospitality and wanting to hysterectomise his children. In England we owe a great debt to Peter Brook and Paul Scofield (the only actor I know of who has played both Timon and Lear) for showing us this harshness in 1962: but we have followed their example very patchily in the subsequent fifty years.

✦

Watching *King Lear* is like being cast adrift and looking for help. Where wisdom is normally found in Shakespeare – in the old, in the women – it is horribly absent. We turn to the rank outsiders, most of whom profess no wisdom at all. There we find fools of all kinds: fools by nature, blind fools, and one professional, who is then supplanted by a man who pretends to be a lunatic. For the first half of the play the image of the benighted old King with his wise Fool at his side is particularly enduring, like Hamlet with his skull or the two tramps under their tree in *Waiting for Godot*. I recently saw a colleague with dementia being helped along the street by his son and thought of *Lear*; they looked as if they'd been doing it for years. Junius Brutus Booth used his young son Edwin (later to become a yet greater actor) as his dresser, purveyor of brandy in the wings and general saviour: demented after playing Shakespeare, Junius had to be chased around the New England countryside or along the Baltimore waterfront by this old child of his, trying to calm him down and bring him home. It is one of the great Shakespearian ideas – the elderly as a threat to himself and the guardian child old before his time.

Not that Lear's nameless Fool is a kind man exactly. He has a job to do, one done by licensed savants who have kept English kings on the rails from William the Conqueror to Charles I. A fool is a walking paradox. Negligible in the world's eyes, he can reproach the great and lighten their sorrows; always in danger of hanging, he may be their one true friend. This one is Shakespeare's most extreme spokesman of the conscience of a king: the next nearest is Fluellen, reminding Henry V of his Welshness and his common decency.

The Fool impresses at first by his absence: insecure on the first of his parental tours – no one has come out to meet him – Lear keeps asking for his 'pretty knave', whom he hasn't seen for two days, and who, we learn, has 'much pined him away' since Cordelia's departure to France. We also hear that Lear has loyally struck a Gentleman of Goneril's for daring to tick the Fool off: here at last is someone he loves. As things get worse, he will turn to him for his biggest confessions:

> O let me not be mad, not mad, sweet heaven;
> Keep me in temper, I would not be mad...
> O fool, I shall go mad...

– and with his shreds of compassion:

> Poor fool and knave, I have one part in my heart
> That's sorry yet for thee.

Like all entertainers, the Fool calls on various techniques as needed. Sometimes his riffs are diversionary nonsense, topped off with a little vaudevillian tag – 'That's a shelled peascod', 'Whoop, Jug! I love thee'. He makes the unanswerable claim that a man's nose is in the middle of his face in order to keep his eyes on either side of his nose, and that there are seven stars in the sky because there aren't eight. (He'd have liked the joke about how you get four elephants into a Mini – two in the front and two in the back.) He starts jokes he can't finish – about to tell us how an oyster makes his shell, he can't for the moment come up with anything at all. He can be dirty, in the best music-hall tradition:

> She that's a maid now, and laughs at my departure,
> Shall not be a maid long, unless things be cut shorter.

The Fool's most harmless stuff generally precedes some sly dig about men who wear their brains in their heels, Lear's daughters being crab apples, or how a snail carries his house on his back to avoid the danger of giving it away as Lear has done. At other times he takes breathtaking risks, calling Lear a fool for giving away all his other titles and leaving himself with the one he was born with; telling him he has 'pared his wit on both sides, and left nothing in the middle'; saying that the old man is no more than 'Lear's shadow' and that he has done Cordelia a favour by banishing her. He is on a permanent warning –

LEAR: Take heed, sirrah: the whip.

FOOL: Truth's a dog must to kennel

– but he seems to know exactly when the whip might crack, as perhaps one of these days it will. In the meantime, since he can't afford to put a foot wrong, he never does. Roughly tender to the old man, he is truly heartless to everyone else – even to the honest Kent in the stocks, who 'wears cruel garters'. He releases both stability and its opposite into the play, making us doubt the very things we are taking seriously. At one point he stops the action to sing us a little song about how Albion (Britain) 'will come to great confusion' before nonsensically dismissing the warning:

> This prophecy Merlin shall make; for I live before his time.

Soon the Fool's calculated madness is flanked by Lear's real one and on the other side by a further invented one, that of Edgar as Poor Tom. Sheltering in a farmhouse, Lear puts his daughters on trial, sitting on the bench between Tom and his 'yoke-fellow in equity':

> LEAR: Arraign her first; 'tis Goneril. I here take my oath before this honourable assembly, she kicked the poor king her father.
>
> FOOL: Come hither, mistress. Is your name Goneril?
>
> LEAR: She cannot deny it.
>
> FOOL: Cry you mercy, I took you for a joint stool.

A charade like this brings out the best in the Fool: it's the sort of thing he understands. But he also knows he is on the way out. The fascinating arrival of Edgar as a bedlam beggar has transfixed the King, who now turns for comfort not to the Fool but to his new wise nonsense-man:

> You, sir, I entertain for one of my hundred; only I do not like the fashion of your garments; you will say they are Persian; but let them be changed.

Defeated by this 'noble Athenian', the Fool bows out of the play with a most beautiful piece of illogic, as if he and his master had at the last moment found a sweeter way of ordering things:

> LEAR: Make no noise, make no noise; draw the curtains; so, so, so. We'll go to supper i' the morning: so, so, so.
>
> FOOL: And I'll go to bed at noon.

✦

At this point Edgar, Lear's godson and Gloucester's legitimate heir, becomes the nearest the play affords to a narrator. Except that he rarely speaks in his own person: like the Duke in *Measure for Measure*, he is defined not by what he is, which is barely established, but by his manifold disguises. Among other things Shakespeare is saying something here about acting, not only as a self-defence but as an intoxicant.

Edgar bolted from his father's house at the beginning of the play with the household security on his heels, Edmund having convinced their father that Edgar had planned his death. His solution was practical but extreme:

> I will preserve myself, and am bethought
> To take the basest and most poorest shape

That ever penury, in contempt of man,
Brought near to beast; my face I'll grime with filth,
Blanket my loins, elf all my hair in knots,
And with presented nakedness outface
The winds and persecutions of the sky.

Already you sense a zeal beyond the immediate cause. There is some
need for self-abasement in Edgar: taking on the false accusation, he aims
to taste the penitential worst:

LEAR: Did'st thou give all to thy daughters
And art thou come to this?

EDGAR: Who gives anything to poor Tom? Whom the foul fiend
hath led though fire and through flame, through ford and
whirlpool…

Improvising as the naked beggar, he finds an unexpected talent:

LEAR: What hast thou been?

EDGAR: A serving man, proud in heart and mind; that curled
my hair, wore gloves in my cap, served the lust of my
mistress's heart and did the act of darkness with her; swore
as many oaths as I spake words, and broke them in the
sweet face of heaven; one that slept in the contriving of lust
and waked to do it. Wine loved I deeply, dice dearly, and in
women out-paramoured the Turk; false of heart, light of
ear, bloody of hand; hog in sloth, fox in stealth, wolf in
greediness, dog in madness, lion in prey. Let not the
creaking of shoes nor the rustling of silks betray thy poor
heart to woman… still through the hawthorn blows the
cold wind.

Edgar's list has the savagery of Timon, but it is also to the point. The
cast of the play passes through it in a shadowy procession – Oswald the
serving man, Cornwall, bloody of hand, the sexy *arriviste* Edmund and
the incontinent Goneril and Regan, the two women he will perhaps
sleep with. The anxiously repeated sexual imagery, too, reflects the legitimate Edgar's shock at being driven out by a brother got by his father's
'compounding' with his mother 'under the dragon's tail'. The actor's job
is to find pertinence in all these extemporisations: Poor Tom never talks
rubbish, but he does speak in tongues. Even more than the Fool, he is
the Russian *yurodivy* or holy idiot, the man who sees and hears what
nobody else can, reporting his findings in a code nobody mistakes for
nonsense. A moralist outside the moral norm, he is immune. At first,

when he was just Edgar, nobody seemed to know much about him: in fact he was so anonymous that he attracted everyone's random discontents – Regan even preposterously suggesting that he was a companion of Lear's riotous knights. But now that he has started shape-shifting, nobody forgets him, and the King strips off his clothes to follow his example.

Providentially, Edgar meets his father in the storm: Gloucester suddenly appears on the heath to take Lear's party into shelter for food and warmth, having denied the same to his son. Edgar's shock propels him not into a confession but into more extravagant disguise, stinging with pain and blame:

> GLOUCESTER: What are you there? Your names?
>
> EDGAR: Poor Tom, that eats the swimming frog, the toad, the tadpole, the wall-newt and the water... swallows the old rat and the ditch-dog... who is whipped from tithing to tithing, and stock-punished and imprisoned...

Gloucester's response is a thing barely conscious:

> I had a son
> Now outlaw'd from my blood; he sought my life
> But lately, very late; I loved him, friend,
> No father his son dearer; true to tell thee
> The grief hath craz'd my wits.

To save himself from going mad, Edgar dives deeper and deeper: from now on his first reaction is always to become someone else. Even when Gloucester has no eyes with which to recognise him he takes on one vocal disguise after another. Occasionally he turns to us to tell us how bad he is feeling, but it is opaque and unrevealing:

> When we our betters see bearing our woes,
> We scarcely think our miseries our foes...
> How light and portable my pain seems now,
> When that which makes me bend makes the king bow.

The dull language and jingling rhymes, coming so soon after his extravagances, shut us out and frustrate us. Shakespeare has a weakness for these mini-soliloquies: they show an odd lack of self-confidence. There is a moment in *Hamlet* when Claudius informs us in an aside that his conscience is troubling him, a good hour before his great confession in soliloquy; how much better if we, seeing the play for the first time, could have shared Hamlet's doubts about his father's murder for as long as possible. Likewise Edgar's perfunctory revelations are better cut: the near–impossibility of reading his real feelings is part of the point.

Gloucester retains the memory of Poor Tom in the storm, and, once blinded, half-grasps its meaning:

> I' the last night's storm I such a fellow saw
> Which made me think a man a worm; my son
> Came then into my mind.

The story that then begins of the blind old man led by his son to a place of assisted death is the one element Shakespeare took from Philip Sidney's *Arcadia*; significantly, in that story the father knows quite well who the son is. Here it becomes a parable – and an obvious alternative version of Lear and the Fool. Edgar walks his father along flat ground on Dover beach, but manages to persuade him they are climbing steeply and that he can hear the sea below; also that he himself is still Tom, even as he is beginning to shift into something more stable:

> GLOUCESTER: Methinks thy voice is alter'd, and thou speak'st
> In better phrase and matter than thou didst.
>
> EDGAR: Y'are much deceived; in nothing am I chang'd
> But in my garments.

Gloucester is right, but must be told that his brain isn't working. In his new role Edgar is able to paint an imaginary picture of a vertiginous cliff, far above the wheeling birds that seem like beetles, where a tiny man hangs gathering samphire and the fishermen and bobbing boats are small as mice. He watches while, astonishingly, his father throws himself off what he thinks is the cliff edge to fall flat on his face on the open ground. This, even more than Apemantus and Timon abusing each other, resembles the godlessly funny universe of Samuel Beckett: a man forsaken by heaven, his blind eyes flat against the floor in what he thinks is death. Then Edgar miraculously becomes a passer-by on the beach who has witnessed a marvellous survival:

> Hadst thou been aught but gossamer, feathers, air,
> So many fathom down precipitating,
> Thou'dst shivered like an egg; but thou dost breathe…

It is an amazing performance; and true to the play's Manichean swing, Edgar describes his previous character as 'some fiend' whose eyes

> Were two full moons; he had a thousand noses,
> Horns whelk'd and wav'd like the enridged sea.

And so they travel on. On the road, a further Edgar is born. Goneril's steward Oswald turns up to apprehend them, and Edgar – to Gloucester's surprise, presumably – becomes a countryman in order to kill him:

> An chud ha' bin swaggered out of my life, 'twould not ha' bin
> so long as 'tis by a fortnight...

There are times during this odyssey when you long for Edgar to show himself and comfort his father. Indeed he increasingly calls Gloucester 'father' on their travels, but that's an ambiguous title, and his plan is unchanged:

> Why I do trifle thus with his despair
> Is done to cure it.

In retrospect he will describe it as a 'fault' not to have done so. And perhaps this is the grievous centre of the part, that he knows that revealing himself will be the death of the old man. The beautiful idea combines instruction, tough love, but also an element of revenge against the father who has disbelieved in him. In the end he watches Gloucester's

> flaw'd heart...
> 'Twixt two extremes of passion, joy and grief,
> Burst smilingly.

By now Edgar has stood at all the play's compass points, speaking to almost everyone. At the start he was as good a man as Kent, and so a victim of the spreading wickedness; having entered the world of the fools, he ended as the play's main survivor and guarded hope – though in the process, like an overworked actor, he has become a stranger to himself:

> Know, my name is lost...

But then we remember something. His final action was to arrive on the battlefield, chivalric and unappeased, and challenge Edmund, architect of so much misfortune. He killed Edmund: since they have the same father it was a moment of shock as well as satisfaction. So apart from Cornwall's servant avenging Gloucester's blinding by stabbing his master, and apart from Goneril's poisoning of Regan and Regan's stabbing of Goneril, this narrator of ours is the play's major killer, of Oswald and of his own half-brother. The joke is on us, for thinking so simply of heroes and villains: Edgar's actions are what it has taken to restore a degree of sanity. Finally, the play's almost-hero, he summarises this very explicit tragedy in the most enigmatic way. His monosyllables seem to combine an instinct for the truth with a respectful conservatism:

The weight of this sad time we must obey;
Speak what we feel, not what we ought to say;
The oldest hath borne most; we that are young
Shall never see so much, nor live so long.

✦

King Lear brings two fundamental kinds of experience together. It makes perfect sense domestically and sexually – a Stanislavskian model; but it also allows one man to be blinded and yet keep going, and another to invoke Jupiter, Hecate and the sun and to curse his children's reproductive systems. In practice, the part of Lear is obviously a mountain, best attempted when an actor is both old enough (credibility) and young enough (energy). Sentiment is to be avoided. There is a layer of almost ungraspable wickedness beneath the realistic family drama, and much of it originates in Lear. What is it that makes him lash out at his daughters' sexuality and wish them barren – and himself therefore without grandchildren? There is a sickness in him, flaring up when he is thwarted. In his blundering attempt to rid himself of his own neuroses and go unburdened towards death, he inflames those of two of his daughters: his curse on Goneril's fertility wishes away from her the nurturing power that would make her other and better than she is, and liberates her worst instincts. To play Goneril and Regan, and indeed Cordelia, it is helpful for actresses to remember that most of their aberration is Lear's fault – as opposed to that of Edmund, who is his own masterpiece.

As for the later stages of *Lear*, an actor would have to be incompetent for them not to work, and an actor cast in the part is unlikely to be that. But even here the thinking needs to be tough. The best version of Lear's reunion with Cordelia I remember was also the most unexpected; in Richard Eyre's London production of 1997, Ian Holm, rather than being serene in a cleansing white robe – an obvious and very common device – reacted to her with anger and distrust, as if this were yet another trick played on him either by the malevolent gods or his other daughters; the gradual and delayed dropping of the penny was harrowingly beautiful.

Edgar too is a very difficult undertaking – and surprisingly often theatre reviewers, perhaps in bafflement, overlook this very long part (the second biggest in the play) in their assessments. The most successful Edgars are driven by an idiosyncratic passion closer to crazy anger than to grief. The end of the play is a considerable responsibility for him. He and Albany are the only ones left alive, and there is literally nothing left, nothing at all. Even Kent has gone, saying significantly that he has

> a journey, sir, shortly to go;
> My master calls me; I must not say no.

Even by Shakespeare's standards, this must be a mortality record. There is no sense of a people in Lear's kingdom whose future must be considered as at the end of a History play, and therefore no Richmond or even the chilling Fortinbras. There is no hope offered through women and children as the later Shakespeare might have affirmed: Albany is a widower, Edgar an unmarried young man. The old have failed and the women become monstrous; the good (Cordelia) are victims, the weak (the Fool) go to the wall. The wise let you down, and the mad speak a kind of sense. Everything falls in on itself in the end: as in Beckett, hope is a thin gruel. Like Timon, Edgar and Lear have been poor forked animals: Lear was a companion to the wolf and owl, Edgar spoke of the fox and the wild dog as extensions of himself. The penultimate three lines of the play sound soothing, but the fourth declares that the young will never see so much nor live so long. Why? Because the old have ruined the world for them.

However, Edgar said earlier:

> the worst is not,
> So long as we can say 'This is the worst'.

So there is a chance, just a small one. When we need to start again, we take hands. In 1989, two million people made a human chain, one by one by one, for three hundred and fifty miles from Talinn in Estonia through Latvia to Vilnius in Lithuania, to claim Baltic independence from the dark night of Soviet stupidity. Only this week the capital of Bahrain was surrounded by such a chain, in an attempt to oust the Sunni monarchy: at another extreme seventy children in Shrewsbury formed a human SOS to resist the Council's plans to close their school. It seems to be a simple human need, and it starts with just two people. It would be a sentimental thing to see Edgar and Albany take hands at the end of *Lear* – for one thing Edgar's are bloodied – but it could be implied: while they are standing there, and as there are two of them not one, we might be convinced of such an inconceivable act of recovery.

8

Your Actions are My Dreams

The Conscience of the King – The Winter's Tale – Cymbeline

It might seem odd to describe a work of such profound impact as *King Lear* as a political play, much as it would be to praise *War and Peace* for its descriptions of nature. But through its vision of man's capacity for self-induced suffering runs a vein of provocation. I remember seeing *Lear* in 1994, on the day that Prime Minister John Major hit the headlines by condemning London's homeless, sleeping in the streets, as eyesores. It was as if Shakespeare had been listening to the radio that morning and sat himself down for an outraged hour, then sent a new speech over to the Barbican, so that Lear, his bigoted eyes gradually opening, could say that evening:

> Poor naked wretches, wheresoe'er you are,
> That bide the pelting of this pitiless storm,
> How shall your houseless heads and unfed sides,
> Your loop'd and window'd raggedness, defend you
> From seasons such as these?...
> > Take physic, pomp,
> Expose thyself to feel what wretches feel,
> That thou mayst shake the superflux to them
> And show the heavens more just.

Rewind to 1606, when as part of their now regular Christmas season at court, the King's Men performed the play at Whitehall. This may well have been its first performance and in the weeks running up to the occasion there had been much talk of auguries, omens and eclipses, and what they might portend. So King James himself may have been in the first audience to hear Gloucester's grim assessment of the national mood – in the second scene, when things had hardly got started:

> These late eclipses in the sun and moon portend no good to us… Love cools, friendship falls off, brothers divide; in cities, mutinies; in countries, discord; in palaces, treason; and the bond cracked 'twixt son and father.

Shakespeare was leading James into an intellectual trap. Gloucester's speech links cosmic disorder with social unhappiness; James was certainly afraid of the first, but he would have recoiled from any suggestion that he was presiding over the second. But what could he recoil towards? Edmund, Gloucester's illegitimate son, rebuts his father's views in bracingly existential terms:

> This is the excellent foppery of the world, that, when we are sick in fortune – often the surfeit of our own behaviour – we make guilty of our disasters the sun, the moon, and the stars; as if we were villains by necessity, fools by heavenly compulsion, knaves, thieves and treachers by spherical predominance, drunkards, liars and adulterers by an enforced obedience of planetary influence; and all that we are evil in, by a divine thrusting on; an admirable evasion of whoremaster man, to lay his goatish disposition to the charge of a star.

Unable to accept the implicit criticism of the Establishment father, the royal spectator might have found himself warming to his godless son, who is, for lack of a better word, the villain of the piece. To set sympathy spinning from the start like this is a sly manoeuvre typical of the Shakespeare who likes to put his best messages into unwholesome mouths.

King James, intellectual and thug, red in the face as Rufus, is presiding over a court so drunken that the preceding summer his Danish brother-in-law, covered in wine, jelly and cake, had to be 'carried away' from a banquet in a chair while the rest of the company was seen to 'wallow in beastly delights'. A visit by the King's Men may have occasioned more respect than that; if so, on this wintry day, the courtiers, wrapped up in their furs and gowns and nursing their warming wine, can hardly have missed the fictional King's point about the homeless. Especially since he takes up the theme later on. Having learned from Poor Tom the virtue of unaccommodated nakedness, Lear declares:

> Through tatter'd clothes small vices do appear;
> Robes and furr'd gowns hide all.

By this time he is, like Ophelia, in the super-sane world of the mad, and he gleefully turns his attention to the rest of the Establishment:

> See how yond justice rails upon yon simple thief. Hark in thine ear: change places, and handy-dandy, which is the justice, which is the thief?

This to a sightless man who, radicalised by suffering, now dreams of a time when

> distribution should undo excess
> And each man have enough.

These are lines so modern that they can draw an appreciative grunt from an audience; one would like to think that in James's court you could have cut the silence with a knife.

On the other hand, the spectators at Whitehall may not have listened to the play at all, and the playwright could have said what he liked. Perhaps they wished the whole thing was more like the masque they had recently attended when Faith, Hope and Charity were to address the King: in the event, Hope couldn't speak because of terrific drunkenness, Faith staggered away as well and both were found spewing in the Lower Hall. James's usual soirées sound like meetings of the Bullingdon Club. So you do wonder what happened when the King's Men came to the King: were they courteously treated, or like Theseus's attitude to the actors in the *Dream*, were they seen as a way of whiling away the time, good for a bit of after-dinner barracking? Did they have to clear a space on the floor to perform in? Did they get their bag of gold straight away or chase it up later with Jacobean-style invoices? Above all, did the King listen?

If he did, there was plenty for him to reflect on. Next to those he is now offering him, Shakespeare's Elizabethan rulers seem unequivocal and their profiles simple. King John was simply the wrong man for the job. For Richard III the state of kingship was less interesting than the process of acquiring it; once he was on the throne the play faltered a little, since even less could be expected of him than of John. For Henry IV power led to routine worries which he handled with routine resourcefulness – and insomnia, but, since he lacked any kind of charm, *we* were not likely to lose much sleep over *him*. Henry V inherited a job and did it well, just once complaining about his destiny. Henry VI's reign was a vacuum into which more dramatically interesting figures flowed: for Claudius the crown held the same interest as for Richard III. An exception was Richard

II, whose loss of his presumed identity provoked a self-examination more searching than that undertaken by the others, and in that sense he oddly prefigures the Jacobean plays.

A much darker figure by now, Shakespeare is moving through a new and unpredictable world in which things can be seen half in shadow and half in light. Ever more insistently, he is asking: What should a leader expect of himself, and on what nerve does the strain of the office press hardest? James once said that kings were gods on earth and writers shouldn't meddle with them, but his favourite playmaker gambled on catching his conscience as long as he kept reassuring him, as in *Macbeth*, of the legitimacy of his title and the importance of social stability. These are plays about the cost of leadership written by a man who's earned just enough licence to ask questions of his own monarch, who is sitting in the audience in front of him. It's generally done under the cover of brilliant, indirect metaphor: think of Macbeth and you remember the inconvenient imagination that sees daggers in the air and ghosts at the dinner table. King Lear does his penance by standing naked in the weather; he then conducts an insane trial in a hovel with a seeming madman and a loyal courtier obliged to join in; at his side, his Fool is a much smarter individual than he is. In *Measure for Measure*, the 'fantastical duke of dark corners' learns judicial flexibility when he gives up the respect due to his office and sleeps under a prison wall: the picture that comes to mind is of the Doge of Venice slipping through a little door from the Palace over the Bridge of Sighs and into the state penitentiary.

In this play James's own identity is hinted at as well. Duke Vincentio shares very specific character traits with the King, who was known to dislike both crowds and the newly emerging Puritans represented in the play by Angelo. In *Coriolanus* current policies are questioned too: at the beginning the citizens of Rome explode onto the stage reasonably demanding bread, only to be manipulated into line by a particularly cynical politician who clearly despises them; but the original audience would not have forgotten the disastrous famine of a few months earlier, or James's notoriously half-hearted attempts to alleviate it. Not only that, but there had been public protests the previous year, 1607: land enclosures and deforestation in the Midlands were spelling the end of traditional agrarian practice. These disturbances had been put down by James's soldiers with particular brutality, and many of the protesters were hanged, drawn and quartered. The references are startlingly direct: in many ways, in the new reign, the lid is off.

✦

It is required
You do awake your faith.

– The Winter's Tale

Seen from this point of view, *The Winter's Tale*, which played one of its earliest court performances in 1611 on the sixth anniversary of the Gunpowder Plot, is still more audacious. James was exceptionally jealous of his young wife Anne, the daughter of the Queen of Denmark; he had had to wait three months for her to arrive in Scotland and marry him, a delay actually caused by bad sailing weather but one which he attributed to Danish chicanery and perhaps even witchcraft. In the interim he sent her lovelorn poems portraying himself as Leander to her Hero; eventually he ran out of patience and went to Denmark himself to fetch her. Later he threatened to postpone their son's christening because he suspected the child wasn't his. In the play, Leontes has had to wait 'three crabbed months' for Hermione, daughter of the Emperor of Russia, to accept him; his sudden conviction that neither their son nor their imminent second child is his is the mainspring of the action.

Anne seems to have been a more naturally extrovert character than James. As well as possibly suffering from the tongue-loosening condition, easily taken for madness, of George III later, James was described by his personal physician, one Theodore Turquet de Mayerne, as subject to a perversion of his functions from mental disturbance, a victim of 'great fearfulness and dejection... His mind is easily moved suddenly. He is very wrathful, but the fit soon passes off. He has delirium and hallucinations. Sometimes he is melancholy... terrifying insomnia, turbulent nights, laboured breathing, palpitations'. It is hard not to think of the sleepless Leontes, King of Sicily, brooding on imaginary betrayal.

Shakespeare of course figured out such a condition without medical training; and naturally, in relation to James, he operated through suggestive echoes rather than downright satire. And if Leontes, whose frenzied jealousy paralyses his kingdom, were to seem too evident an affront to the King, he could always point innocently to Hermione's statue coming to life at the play's end as proof that all the anguish was only a preparation for a fairytale ending. He could also insist that any resemblance to persons alive or dead was as ever coincidental; and that he was, as a good practitioner, having a second shot (a third if you include *The Merry Wives*) at the theatrical possibilities of flat-out male sexual insecurity. Also that in *The Winter's Tale* he disposes of the whole theme in half the time of *Othello*: by the fourth Act the action has shifted to a sheep-shearing festival in Bohemia, so jealousy is far from the play's only preoccupation.

It opens with Leontes in high and mysterious tension: a misreading of the licence enjoyed by old friends is contaminating his marriage and making him dangerous. He dwells on that three months' delay in securing Hermione's hand all those years ago (he is in his mid-thirties, and their son, Mamillius, sounds about twelve): that reasonable hesitation of hers now seems to him highly significant. He feels it must be payback time, and that his good fortune is beginning to curdle. Although politically powerful, he is a man of perhaps no great personal confidence standing beside a woman much more at ease than he is, the perfect hostess and ambassador. Hermione has been a great stroke of luck in the life of such a self-doubter. She is, by contrast, so self-possessed that even under attack she will remain deeply herself:

> I am not prone to weeping, as our sex
> Commonly are...
> > but I have
> That honourable grief lodg'd here which burns
> Worse than tears drown.

While *Othello*, and later *Cymbeline*, open with their central relationships under circumstantial pressure, in *The Winter's Tale* Shakespeare is careful to make the surface smooth and even, almost idyllic, for everyone except Leontes. Polixenes, King of Bohemia, to whom he has been close since early childhood, means to go home tomorrow after a semi-official visit: we are told that there has always been such affection between the two men that, even though absorbed in running their two countries, they have

> seemed to be together, though absent; shook hands as over a
> vast; and embraced, as it were, from the ends of opposed winds.
> The heavens continue their loves!

Dramatic exposition being what it is, something bad must be in the works. Leontes can't persuade Polixenes to stay another week and calls on Hermione to help. She is much more successful, not least because she spots that Polixenes's main reason for going home is to attend to his duties rather than his family; so he must be gently upbraided by a pregnant wife such as herself on behalf of all women. Prefacing her speech with the plain fact of her feeling for her husband, whom she loves

> not a jar of the clock behind
What lady she her lord

– she goes to work on this family friend with Shakespeare Woman's sexual wit and directness:

> Verily
You shall not go. A lady's 'verily' is
As potent as a lord's. Will you go yet?
Force me to keep you as a prisoner,
Not like a guest... How say you?
My prisoner? Or my guest? By your dread 'verily'
One of them you shall be.

Polixenes capitulates immediately, and in the flush of victory she quizzes him charmingly as to what her husband was like as a little boy. After all, she is a comparatively recent arrival in his life, as is Polixenes's wife in his, and it may be that both women are interrupting a friendship that could have been 'boy eternal'. They humorously agree that this is what women will do, these devils who lead men astray from their infantile path.

Leontes is listening to this harmless wooing of his friend, the repartee and the banter: he should be joining in, but he is not quick-witted enough. Instead he is busy rewriting his and Hermione's story, taking all the humour out of her sentiments. The visible fact of her advanced pregnancy, which should safeguard him against darker thoughts, is having the opposite effect: it seems to increase her provocativeness as she works on Polixenes, her intimate, unavoidable swelling in front of her. Leontes possessively declares her speech her best utterance since the day she finally agreed to marry him – a contrived and anxious comparison coming after her impromptu wit. Unfortunately it has a large consequence, leading Hermione into an unlucky antithesis:

> Why, lo you now, I have spoke to th' purpose twice;
The one for ever earn'd a royal husband;
The other for some while a friend.

There is a problem here for us. In Elizabethan usage the word 'friend' can mean lover, as it often does in Shakespeare's Sonnets; nowadays, conversely, it is usually used between men and women to differentiate between the one and the other. This uncommunicable nuance comes just as the play's critical question rears up: when is it that Leontes's jealousy begins, and what causes it? His reaction comes slamming in, albeit as an aside, exactly on Hermione's use of the ambiguous word:

> Too hot, too hot!
> To mingle friendship far is mingling bloods...

– so it's possible that Shakespeare only intended Leontes to implode on hearing this 'friend'. But from the start his totalitarian imagination has been insisting on its own meanings only. It's easily enough done: I was at a dinner the other night and as parting time approached with talk of early mornings and so on, an attractive wife looked across at her husband and said quite loudly, 'Isn't it time to go to bed?' It momentarily struck me as sexual, though it probably wasn't: Leontes would have heard no other meaning in it.

Leontes has seen that his woman has more influence with Polixenes than he has: why should that be? As for many men, effortless male friendship in adulthood is beyond him; he can't find the companionship which she creates in an instant. His sense of exclusion is sharp; rather than one of the normal paradoxes of love, he perceives a ghastly special intimacy. And so it all starts – the subversion of language, the dream world, the horrible mania. Initially he can acknowledge that the 'liberty' he sees between Hermione and Polixenes could come simply

> From heartiness, from bounty, fertile bosom

– but once his idea takes a deeper root, everything magnetically conforms. The touches on the arm accompanying Hermione's plea are now 'paddling palms and pinching fingers'. His own 'spotted' bed is like 'goads, thorns, nettles, tails of wasps'; and where the evidence doesn't suffice, it can be willed:

> Is whispering nothing?
> Is leaning cheek to cheek? Is meeting noses?
> Kissing with inside lip? Stopping the career
> Of laughter with a sigh?... Horsing foot on foot?
> Skulking in corners? Wishing clocks more swift?
> Hours minutes? Noon midnight?

What is he talking about? He hasn't seen anything of the sort. But all things tend towards his great idea, which contains a high measure of self-regard. He keenly feels his loss of face: he is to play a disgraced part for which 'contempt and clamour' will 'hiss' him to his grave. Listening, you want to slap him. Still, Shakespeare is (crucially) helping the actor to keep the audience, if not on Leontes's side, at least seeing some of his point. After all, who hasn't envied their lover's relationship with an old friend – its ease and its history? And it is true enough that

> Many thousand on us
> Have the disease and feel't not.

With the daring of late Shakespeare, Leontes next turns on his audience, asking the men who it is they think they are sitting beside:

> And many a man there is, even at this present,
> Now, while I speak this, holds his wife by th'arm,
> That little thinks she has been sluic'd in's absence,
> And his pond fish'd by his next neighbour, by
> Sir Smile, his neighbour.

He spatters us with language that would be pornographic if it were not so true to imaginative life; his inner Cabinet – the trusty Camillo and Paulina and Antigonus, and also his son – get the embarrassing benefit of it too. In this overheated situation, anything they say proves Leontes's point: Camillo in particular makes as unfortunate a choice of words as Hermione did, by reporting to him that Polixenes will stay

> To satisfy your highness and the entreaties
> Of our most gracious mistress.
>
> LEONTES: Satisfy?
> Th' entreaties of your mistress? Satisfy?

– and within moments Leontes is hiring him to kill Polixenes.

By the way, some productions have toyed with the alternative: that something really is going on between Polixenes and Hermione. Unlikely: though a muted sexuality is certainly a counter in their negotiation, it is surely of the innocent, duly suppressed kind. Otherwise there seems little point in the play: Shakespeare would hardly put us through *The Winter's Tale* on false pretences.

✦

We watch the progress of Leontes's big mistake with the same dread as when Othello denounced his innocent wife in front of the Duke's ambassadors. His language sparks between fear and assertion:

> There may be in the cup
> A spider steep'd, and one may drink, depart
> And yet partake no venom, for his knowledge
> Is not infected: but if one present
> The abhorr'd ingredient to his eye, make known
> How he hath drunk, he cracks his gorge, his sides,

> With violent hefts. I have drunk, and seen the spider.
> Camillo was his help in this, his pander.
> There is a plot against my life, my crown.
> All's true that is mistrusted.

His vision of his wife as 'slippery... a hobby horse' has got hopelessly caught up with regal paranoia – it is all sexual-political, part of a conspiracy to unseat him. Even his strike against Polixenes has been anticipated, and the result is as much sexual incapacitation as political defeat:

> He has discover'd my design, and I
> Remain a pinch'd thing.

There is another marriage in the play, between Paulina and Antigonus, one of his advisors – a healthy and pragmatic relationship invented by Shakespeare to counterpoint Leontes's psychodrama. Antigonus, comically, cannot control his wife, any more than Leontes, tragically, can control his fantasy of his. Antigonus's refuge is healthy irony: attacked by Leontes for not curbing Paulina's tongue, he admits:

> Hang all the husbands
> That cannot do that feat, you'll leave yourself
> Hardly one subject.

Leontes could learn much from his respectful good humour:

> When she will take the rein, I let her run;
> But she'll not stumble.

Instead he asserts himself by throwing his wife into prison (where she gives birth prematurely) and then exposing her to the shame of a public trial. He is able to do this because he has a secular authority beyond that of Othello or Ford. There's the warning – what if this most intimate pain were supported by temporal power? Shakespeare doesn't write about his kings and queens because he likes them, but because so often their authority intersects with their frailties and lets them indulge malign desires.

The trial is a special madness, a ludicrous thing from Wonderland. Presiding, Leontes's tone is calm and sorrowful, promising fair dealing:

> Let us be clear'd
> Of being tyrannous, since we so openly
> Proceed in justice, which shall have due course
> Either to the guilt or the purgation.

Of course nothing of the sort happens – the matter is beyond argument, no evidence is produced, there is no jury and no appeal. Leontes's reasonable tone measures his derangement: well may Hermione see that

> it shall scarce boot me
> To say Not Guilty: mine integrity
> Being counted falsehood shall, as I express it,
> Be so receiv'd...
> Sir,
> You speak a language that I understand not;
> My life stands in the level of your dreams,
> Which I'll lay down.

Leontes, cowed by her even now, shows an unexpected vulnerability:

> Your actions are my dreams

– before violence overtakes him. Within ten lines he is defying the Delphic Oracle which has declared him mistaken: Hermione collapses, apparently dead, their son Mamillius is also reported dead, Leontes is covered in remorse and embarks on a long repentance. It is all vastly improbable, but Shakespeare is no longer troubled by that kind of logic. What, after all, needs to be achieved? The scales must drop from Leontes's eyes; Paulina must rub his folly in at length, but then be caught short by his manifest sorrow and reinvest him with the qualities he may once have had:

> He is touch'd
> To the noble heart... Take your patience to you,
> And I'll say nothing.

The manner in which *The Winter's Tale* seems to turn itself over into quite another play is one of Shakespeare's greatest surprises, both showy and haunting. Antigonus, charged even before the trial to dispose of Hermione's newborn daughter Perdita, arrives with his precious cargo on the famously non-existent coast of Bohemia, and, caught in a storm, deposits her there:

> Blossom, speed thee well...

Because the play has no further use for him, he is pursued and eaten by a bear. The scene contains something else truly strange. As the storm rumbles, Antigonus reports to us a dream of his supposedly dead mistress Hermione, appearing in his cabin in the pure white robes of holiness:

> ne'er was dream
> So like a waking. To me comes a creature,
> Sometimes her head on one side, some another:
> I never saw a vessel of like sorrow,
> So fill'd and so becoming...
>   thrice bow'd before me,
> And gasping to begin some speech, her eyes
> Became two spouts...

The spectral figure even gives Perdita her name, and that is how, a lost child, she will be known in real life; it also foresees that for doing his duty, Antigonus

>   ne'er shalt see
> Thy wife Paulina more.

So, despite the white robes of a masque, this is not a pretty vision: the apparition struggles to speak, and finally, in a Gothic moment, shrieks and melts into thin air. And in fact Hermione, as we shall discover, is alive. The dream's one narrative purpose is to tell Antigonus, who has been travelling, that she is thought to be dead; but since Antigonus has little time left, it hardly matters. In a play so much concerned with restoration and cure, the whole episode is as disturbing as the actual death of Mamillius.

When Perdita is found by an Old Shepherd, we are on more reassuring Shakespearian ground. Language is reassembled, the stark tones of Leontes's Sicily giving way to the Warwickshire man's natural senses:

> They have scared away two of my best sheep, which I fear the
> wolf will find sooner than the master. If anywhere I have them,
> 'tis by the seaside, browsing of ivy.

Deeper down, we can see Shakespeare the leveller. The baby Perdita, lying there in her bundle, impervious to the din of voices and the storm, is royal, but she strikes the Old Shepherd in quite another light:

> Sure, some scape. Though I am not bookish, yet I can read
> waiting-gentlewoman in this scape: this has been some stair-
> work, some trunk-work, some behind-door work. They were
> warmer that got this than the poor thing is here.

It feels like waking from a bad dream, funny and very mischievous, and it prepares the way, sixteen years later, for the sheep-shearing festival of Bohemia, in which some of the themes of the play's first half are quietly recapitulated. By then Polixenes has become a minor Leontes himself, pursuing his runaway son Florizel still more furiously than Henry IV does Prince Hal. He blocks his engagement to Perdita (now assumed to be the daughter of the Shepherd, even though he is eighty-three) and threatens her first with disfigurement:

> I'll have thy beauty scratched with briars

– and then with

> a death as cruel for thee
> As thou art tender to't.

Perdita meanwhile receives Shakespeare's tenderest attentions. She grows into a source of light, fortitude and grace, harmonising the world around her with her talk of flowers, her acceptance of life, her love for her 'father'. There are few more lovely things in Shakespeare than her – except that the world of which she is the centre is false, a lie created by her elders, to be painfully untangled while the sheep are sheared. That the stranglehold of Sicily is eventually relaxed has everything to do with her, unaware as she is that it is in Sicily she belongs. Meanwhile she responds to the marvellous ritual of renewal with natural sensuality:

> PERDITA: pale primroses,
>   That die unmarried ere they can behold
>   Bright Phoebus in his strength – a malady
>   Most incident to maids... O, these I lack
>   To make you garlands of, and my sweet friend
>   To strew him o'er and o'er!
>
> FLORIZEL: What, like a corse?
>
> PERDITA: No, like a bank for love to lie and play on,
>   Not like a corse; or if, not to be buried,
>   But quick and in mine arms...

The mechanism of sorting out the class problems involves Shakespeare in some familiar stuff – Camillo and Polixenes disguised to observe the sheep shearing, the roguish Autolycus (or in the production I was in, an Irish pedlar called Aut O'Lucas) convincing the Shepherd and his son that they are to be stoned and flayed alive for their deception while affecting not to recognise them. The whole gallimaufry results in most of the cast – Autolycus, Florizel, Perdita, Camillo and Polixenes – processing back to Leontes's court for the play's denouement, where Polixenes will strangely change his character back to the amiable fellow he was before.

Leontes's punishment for his dreadful self-indulgence has been a repentance of enormous length – narratively sixteen years, described in

the theatre with exceptional slowness, step by step, at that most dangerous of Shakespearian moments, the start of Act Five. His rite of passage
is supervised by Paulina, whom he now sees as 'grave and good', and she
is taking no prisoners: while his court entreats him to forget Hermione
and remarry to provide an heir, she reminds him always of her irre-
placeability – for reasons we shall soon learn. Her job is not hard to do:
this man of constant sorrow achingly thinks of his dead wife's eyes as

> Stars, stars
> And all eyes else, dead coals.

Florizel and Perdita arrive, reconnecting Leontes with grief but also hope
– he sees the imprint of his lost Polixenes and Hermione in them, and
also of the son and daughter he might himself have had, had he not
destroyed his own.

In the end all is clarified, though not in view. Perdita's true parent-
age makes her marriage to Florizel acceptable and materially advances
her foster-family. The company is bidden to Paulina's 'private gallery' for
the play's greatly affecting climax, when the statue of Hermione comes to
life and is revealed to be Hermione indeed. The overwhelming emotion
of the scene is prodded through with humour. Leontes comments that

> Hermione was not so much wrinkled, nothing
> So aged as this seems

– and would kiss her, but that, Paulina warns him:

> The ruddiness upon her lip is wet;
> You'll mar it if you kiss it; stain your own
> With oily painting.

Perdita has already been restrained from taking her mother's hand
(Shakespeare always liked to repeat a good joke) by the 'fact' that

> The statue is but newly fix'd, the colour's
> Not dry.

Then Paulina promises to bring it to life, prefacing her miracle with the
play's overriding and beautiful stipulation:

> It is requir'd
> You do awake your faith.

Leontes's inspired response to Hermione's reality:

> O, she's warm

is entirely of a piece with the gorgeous naivety of a fairy tale. The play closes with Leontes, in the spirit of magically happy arrangements, cheerfully marrying Camillo off to Paulina, who, as far as the play shows, has never met him before.

✦

The Winter's Tale is a marvellous bafflement, and not at all easy to do. This is not only because of its many improbabilities, or its extraordinary yoking of one of life's most discordant emotions with an impulse for harmony. Something in the play awakens the fanciful in less confident directors – partly because of its length and partly its wilful variety. The notorious moment of Antigonus's 'Exit pursued by a bear' has led to huge ursine holograms towering over him, or the entire acting company converging on the unfortunate man; I found myself coming on as Leontes with a great bear-glove and striking him down. The fact is we see too much in it. A Mariner has warned Antigonus that there are plenty of wild animals hereabouts, and the original audience – familiar with bears from the bear-baiting sessions that competed for attention on Bankside – must have found it grimly entertaining. Or just entertaining.

At least, when I played Leontes (a little dismayed at how many people said I was perfectly cast), I didn't have to haunt the sheep-shearing scenes as the troubled King to 'unify' the author's wayward work. Or even, as has been done, recognisably double as Autolycus, whatever that would mean (about as much, I'd say, as having Hermione double with Perdita, another occasional device hard to achieve since they appear together at the end). In this play the simple options are usually the best. Many productions, bursting to entertain after the constrictions of the first half, treat the Bohemian sheep-shearing festival as a variant on Glastonbury or Woodstock, a matter of middle-class townies getting back to the land, the pedlar Autolycus as combined drug-pusher and musician. In fact what is being celebrated is harvest, rebirth and sexual regeneration, and Bohemia works simply because of our relief at hearing people talk naturally and saying what they mean after the tense angularities and half-light of Sicily. Cutting does help in the late stages: the play is exceptionally long and Leontes's painfully slow remorse is barely seen till after 10 p.m. Which still leaves one problem I can't solve: where, on a non-Shakespearian proscenium stage, do you put Hermione's statue in the last scene – upstage, so that Leontes plays his discovery of her with his back to the audience, or downstage, where we can't see her face and so appreciate his sense of her wondrous lifelikeness?

However, Hermione is a good part and Leontes a great one, his alternating power and frailty exemplifying a truth in acting: look for the strength in the weak man, the softness in the tyrant. Leontes may be sure of his rectitude, but the more he threatens the smaller he feels, almost shrinking from sight as he rants and raves. I used to kiss a picture of Hermione while condemning her as an adulteress; I crouched on a small chair for the trial while Hermione had the floor of the court; I grabbed the newborn Perdita as if to strangle her, held her at arm's length like an alien object, then hugged her to me to reassure her with my heartbeat while I condemned her to death. I sometimes retreated physically while attacking verbally, and issued denunciations with a tender mournfulness; I spat in Hermione's face then covered my own with my hands. All this was to implicate the audience not only in Leontes's savagery but in the logic of his sorrow.

The Winter's Tale – passionately yearning, technically sophisticated, its narrative almost out of control – invites us to be more honest with ourselves, in matters both shaming and profound. In the process it gets quite uncomfortable; Shakespeare's soliloquy form is more provocative than ever. One night as Leontes I found myself asking the men in the audience to consider the details of their wives' secret lives when among them were two dear friends of mine for whom such secrets were a living, half-acknowledged fact. Then we went on tour with an assistant director who would crouch outside the bedroom of a young actress he favoured but who was otherwise engaged, listening in miserable hopefulness for ecstatic cries. He'd never done such a thing before in his life: the play had created the phenomenon it describes. What its impact was on James I, with his 'delirium and hallucinations', can only be imagined.

✦

Is't enough I am sorry?

– Cymbeline

Significantly there is no 'putter-on' in *The Winter's Tale*, only Leontes's own imagination. But Shakespeare is not done with malign outsiders yet. As if to finish off a sequence, he returns to their influence on jealous husbands with *Cymbeline*, more or less contemporary with *The Winter's Tale*, in which the name of the evil angel, Iachimo, even sounds like a diminutive of Iago. If the new play recalls *Othello* in this way, it resembles *The Winter's Tale* in that even the most murderous jealousy is not its only business. Iachimo himself is not built on the same scale as Iago, but he makes up in showmanship for the improvisational intelligence and fast reflexes of his predecessor. The damage he does to the marriage of Posthumus Leonatus and Imogen – or rather the damage that he authorises Posthumus to do – is obviously central, with the difference that the impact on the wife and the repentance of the husband are more extensively explored.

Dr Johnson complained about the play's 'unresisting imbecility', which shows how silly a clever man can be. The 'imbecility' is actually a highly elaborate system of reassurance for King James, which also, in the matter of the jealousy, applies gentle pressure once again to one of his more sensitive nerves. It is true that to achieve this *Cymbeline* bizarrely mixes together place and time. The Emperor Augustus's invasion of ancient Britain seems here to originate in Renaissance Italy, where courtly gentlemen discuss the activities of Julius Caesar. The Roman troops, hoping to secure their withheld annual tribute from Cymbeline's court, illogically land in Milford Haven in Pembrokeshire – but that is where Henry VII did, to establish the royal line that led to James I. While justifying his choice of period by giving Ovid as bedtime reading to his (English) heroine and making reference to Roman Wars in the Middle East, Shakespeare also feels free to bring in medieval knights, singing eunuchs and turbaned giants. It is as if he hopes to make a great stew from which will arise a Britain unified in time and place to please King James, dreaming as ever of national unification. (Unfortunately he neglects to bring in any Scots or Welsh, which might have made his case more persuasive.) If it was a liberty to venture into sexual jealousy again, Shakespeare's diplomatic *quid pro quo* was this eccentric sop to the King's political vanity.

Nowadays we are less likely to be pleased by the play's confusing range or its political time-serving than by its love story. Imogen's and Posthumus's relationship is based on a remarkable concentration of family misfortune. King Cymbeline is father by an earlier marriage to Imogen, and later to two sons, Guiderius and Arviragus, who were vengefully stolen as babies by an unjustly banished courtier, Belarius, in order to deprive Cymbeline of male heirs. Belarius has brought the boys up in the remote countryside under assumed names. Exactly borrowing an image of Timon's, he feels that in his fall from courtly grace he resembles a tree losing all its leaves in one night, but that still

> This life
> Is nobler than attending for a check,
> Richer than doing nothing for a bauble,
> Prouder than rustling in unpaid-for silk.

(The boys disagree with him, like children complaining about being deprived of television – and therefore the right to make up their own minds – by too right-on parents.)

The King then unwisely married a widow, simply called the Queen – a two-dimensional character hard to distinguish from the Wicked Witch of the West. With her she brings a son of her own, Cloten – a wonderful name for the hooligan he turns out to be – whom she wants to marry Imogen. Imogen has defied both father and stepmother, as Shakespearian daughters will, choosing instead the 'poor but worthy gentleman' Posthumus, so called because his father died during his mother's pregnancy, a death attributed to grief over the loss of Posthumus's two elder brothers. His mother then died in childbirth, so he is a true orphan, and his name will never let him or us forget it. The unlucky young man has been taken up by King Cymbeline and trained at court, where his

> spring became a harvest; liv'd in court,
> Which rare it is to do, most prais'd, most lov'd.

Now he and Imogen (herself virtually orphaned by her father's hostility), finding something of the missing sibling as well as the lover in each other, are to be punished for their marriage with, respectively, banishment and disgrace.

We only see them together for a moment at the start of the play but they are clearly a fine pair, blessed in everything but luck. Posthumus has been introduced as

> a creature such
> As, to seek through the regions of the earth
> For one his like, there would be something failing
> In him that should compare.

But beyond this sweetness of nature Imogen sees a residue of his bereavements in their subdued paradise:

> When he was here
> He did incline to sadness, and oft-times
> Not knowing why.

With her mother dead and her two brothers stolen, she too carries an unusual weight of loss: even the experienced Shakespeare will have his hands full restoring these two to each other. Meanwhile he establishes Imogen as the best kind of heroine. In the play's second scene Pisanio, Posthumus's remarkably eloquent servant (with, confusingly, an Italian name), describes to her how Posthumus, torn from her, has reluctantly sailed away to Italy:

> he did keep
> The deck, with glove, with hat, or handkerchief
> Still waving, as the fits and starts of's mind
> Could best express how slow his soul sail'd on,
> How swift his ship...

Good as this is, Imogen caps it with the mixture of wit, intellect and feeling we associate with Viola, Rosalind or Juliet, albeit in a new kind of disjointed unmetrical verse:

> I would have broke mine eye-strings, crack'd them, but
> To look upon him, till the diminution
> Of space had pointed him sharp as my needle.
> Nay, follow'd him, till he had melted from
> The smallness of a gnat to air, and then
> Have turn'd mine eyes and wept. But good Pisanio...
> I did not take my leave of him, but had
> Most pretty things to say...

As with Desdemona, we dread what further things might be flung at her: and indeed, the melancholy grace of her husband and herself is to be deepened not so much by their parents as by a vicious stranger.

Posthumus makes his way through France to Italy like a pilgrim of love, his homesickness bringing out an odd pugnacity as he champions Imogen, and British womankind in general, wherever he goes. For extolling 'our homegrown dames' and decrying the French he nearly comes to blows with a man in Orleans; in Italy, he finds himself in the company of a Frenchman, a Dutchman, and the Italian Iachimo, and the same thing happens with the direst consequences. Why is Posthumus quite so embattled? Perhaps it is instinctive xenophobia, a miserable symptom of separation, or the orphan's sense of being always at odds with the world.

The conversation between these four different nationalities (Shakespeare liked this ancestor of the music-hall joke – in *Henry V* he introduced a Welshman, a Scotsman and an Irishman in one scene) turns to the relative merits of Italian and English women (oh, these foreigners, Posthumus must think). This time he is a little more circumspect, trying to keep out of trouble. But Iachimo is smart enough to spot insecurity in his monosyllabic visitor. He proposes an extravagant wager (his ten thousand ducats against Posthumus's gold wedding ring) on whether he, Iachimo, can go to England and seduce Imogen: somewhat absurdly, both sides resolve to have 'articles between us' – that is, to have the bet confirmed by lawyers (presumably Italian friends of Iachimo's). This is a recap of Shylock's bond of a pound of flesh with Antonio: it is late in Shakespeare's career now, and some effects are being repeated. Posthumus believes the whole louche affair must be

> but a custom in your tongue

– but Iachimo has smelled him out:

> You are afraid and therein the wiser.

With what the English have always seen as the Italian dedication to sex, Iachimo arranges his trip to England. He fails to interest Imogen directly, not least because of some surprisingly gross language at their first encounter – his idea of a compliment to her being:

> Sluttery to such neat excellence oppos'd
> Should make desire vomit emptiness

– and he even makes to kiss her on the basis that Posthumus has condemned her to lie

> betwixt cold sheets
> Whiles he is vaulting variable ramps.

Then, in the play's most vivid scene, he has himself smuggled into her bedroom in a trunk. While she sleeps (rather deeply), he emerges from it like a demon –

> The crickets sing, and man's o'erlaboured sense
> Repairs itself by rest

– and makes a minute examination of the décor of the room; then, moving in, of a mole on Imogen's breast. The scene begins to fizzle – how far will he go? However, rather than sexuality, he shows a sort of professionalism: he simply steals the bracelet Posthumus has given her (the equivalent of the handkerchief in *Othello*) and returns to Italy with his 'proof', which he effortlessly lays out to Posthumus. Though his account of the room's artwork doesn't prove much, the familiar bracelet coming off Iachimo's Italian wrist before his eyes –

> She stripp'd it from her arm; I see her yet;
>   ...she gave it me,
> And said she priz'd it once

– is the turning point, and the secret mole of course the *coup de grâce*.

Posthumus collapses into the flailings and gasps of Othello or Leontes. But he makes his own contribution to the vocabulary of Shakespearian disgust, a most unpoetic bluntness not unlike Iachimo's with Imogen. As Iachimo begins to enumerate the extent of the bouts he has had with her, Posthumus requests him to

> Spare your arithmetic; never count the turns

– and his threat of revenge, like Lear's 'terrors of the earth', is touchingly feeble:

> I'll do something.

Left alone, his language is jolted out of rhythm by unbearable fantasy:

> perchance he spoke not, but
> Like a full-acorn'd boar, a German one,
> Cried 'O!' and mounted...

Apart from the splendid chauvinism (the boar-like Iachimo is during the course of the play not only German but a 'slight thing of Italy', an 'Italian fiend' and 'some jay of Italy') the orphan's lack of a father opens like a pit beneath him:

> We are all bastards;
> And that most venerable man which I
> Did call my father, was I know not where
> When I was stamp'd.

Like Othello, Posthumus gets a bad press from armchair Shakespearians for believing his tempter's story, but the point is obvious: every man's immune system has a weakness to be found. Othello's vulnerability was age and the pride that helped him succeed in an alien culture; Leontes didn't really believe in himself; the violent haste of Posthumus's and Imogen's separation implies that they are unprepared for life without each other. The consequences of Posthumus's mistake would be as dire as Othello's but that his murderous design on his wife, like that of Leontes, is frustrated by the mechanics of romance.

For the time being, Posthumus goes out of the play, believing that he has arranged for Imogen's extinction by means of Pisanio. During his absence, Imogen stands alone, graduating as a heroine; but unlike *The*

Winter's Tale, the play never allows us to forget what has been done to her. Posthumus's bestial visions of her infidelity – in a sense embodied in the boorish Cloten – hang like a bad smell in the air around her. On the other hand she barely falters in her belief in Posthumus: Iachimo has implied the same things about him to her as he did about her to him, but with absolutely no success. She is taken by Pisanio to Milford Haven – 'O for a horse with wings', cries Shakespeare in affection – allegedly to meet Posthumus, only to learn that Pisanio is under instructions to kill her there. She agrees to the honest man's rescue plan – that she should disguise herself as a boy, assume 'waggish courage' and get hired by the Roman Ambassador, who is about to leave the country after a failed diplomatic mission to Cymbeline; that way she will stand a chance of finding Posthumus in (Renaissance) Italy.

Unlike other Shakespearian cross-dressers, she at first thinks a man's life 'a tedious one', but that doesn't last for long. Finding herself by chance near the cave of Belarius and the two royal sons (now called Polydore and Cadwal), she shelters there; the boys swiftly take to her as a brother (all the more perhaps because she is indeed their sister) and call her Fidele – they specially like her 'neat cookery'. However she makes the mistake of taking a medication for seasickness given, in the belief it was a poison, to Pisanio by the Queen – not, on the face of it, a woman you would want to accept a prescription from. In fact it is a sedative, and Imogen sinks, like Juliet, into narcolepsy. Apparently dead, she provokes from her brothers the lovely lament 'Fear no more the heat of the sun...' (another example – Constance, Romeo – of a specially beautiful speech in Shakespeare based on a mistake the audience is aware of). Imogen recovers, only to find next to her the headless body of Cloten, who has foolishly disguised himself as Posthumus and rushed to Milford Haven to claim her, only to be beheaded by Guiderius/Polydore. Understandably deceived, she cries:

> O, Posthumus, alas
> Where is thy head?

Having negotiated the shock (and the line), she hooks up with the invading Roman army and finds her way back to her husband, alive and in one piece.

Posthumus returns to the action after two Acts of estrangement carrying, as a badge of shame, a handkerchief stained, as he thinks, with Imogen's blood – somewhat inconclusive proof of her death sent him by Pisanio. He is no longer, like Leontes, a feather for each wind that blows

but obdurately firm: stoically mistaken, he is now stoically repentant. Time has done some of its work, like water wearing down a rock: though he still believes Imogen has betrayed him, it now seems a small fault next to his murder of her:

> You married ones,
> If each of you should take this course, how many
> Must murder wives much better than themselves
> For wrying but a little.

It has made him bitterly sorry, but he is, you notice, as deceived as ever: he is like a man dragging a heavy, unnecessary sack around. He has enlisted in the Roman army but now that he's home he will change sides back to Britain; far from patriotism, this is a gamble on the Romans winning, and his real motive is not to gain advantage but to find certain death in the anonymity of war. Suicide is no longer any good to Shakespeare: Posthumus and Leontes have longer debts to pay, and more curious means of doing it.

Posthumus finds it hard to make the world want to destroy him – he keeps encountering good luck – but he goes doggedly on. In the event the Britons are victorious largely due to the heroism of Belarius and the two boys, so Posthumus now re-declares himself a Roman in the hope of being punished by the victors. In the course of this plot-knot, he is given a great reward in a scene (Act Five Scene Four) which, were it not a little overwritten and included the bizarre presence of the Roman god Jupiter dropping in to interest himself in the plight of an individual, would surely be more celebrated than it is. I recommend it heartily to those still looking for precious bits of Shakespeare they don't know. It features quite a funny Jailer –

> O the charity of a penny cord: it sums up thousands in a trice

– and we also hear that beautiful lonely simplicity of the orphan again:

> Is't enough I am sorry?...
> So children temporal fathers do appease...

In a bold variant on Shakespeare's theme of restoration (influenced by the new interest in masques and the technical possibilities of the Blackfriars), Posthumus is about to meet his father for the first time, visited as he sleeps by his ghost and those of his lost brothers and his mother. His father complains to Jupiter

> Hath my poor boy done aught but well,
> Whose face I never saw?

Jupiter, though annoyed by the criticism, judges generously:

> He shall be lord of Lady Imogen
> And happier much by his afflictions made.

The dream evaporates. But Posthumus magically finds a document left behind in his lap, promising that Britain will see better days:

> 'Whenas a lion's whelp shall, to himself unknown, without
> seeking find, and be embraced by a piece of tender air...'

The 'tender air' is later explained as the etymology of the Latin word for woman, 'mulier' ('mollis aer'). This is a bold invention of Shakespeare's – 'mulier' actually comes from 'mollior', simply meaning 'more tender', so the phrase is really just a lovely image of Imogen. Posthumus is content not to understand it yet:

> Be what it is,
> The action of my life is like it, which
> I'll keep, if but for sympathy.

As if all this were not enough, there are, it's been calculated, twenty-four denouements in the last scene, a virtuoso series of reunions to show that Shakespeare can set up impossible odds and still win. In some of his earlier endings someone is left out of the fun – Malvolio, the eponymous merchant of Venice, Don Pedro in *Much Ado*. But in *Cymbeline* no problem ends up without a solution. (King Cymbeline, baffled by yet another marvellous revelation, can only manage 'Doth the world go round?') Though the British have beaten the Romans in battle they offer to pay the tribute to Caesar which was the cause of the contention. The flashiest figure, Iachimo, collapses as a part once his business is done – as does Angelo in *Measure for Measure*, another agent of disruption – and is forgiven. All is restored; Imogen and Posthumus are reunited with the emotional force not only of lovers but something of the twins Viola and Sebastian in *Twelfth Night*. 'Pardon's the word to all', and a battered, happy ending is achieved.

Cymbeline is in many ways unique: it is certainly uniquely odd, and fantastically elaborate, in diction as well as narrative. It should be the most heavily annotated text in the canon: open every page and there are unmetrical passages of such experimental knottiness that it is almost impossible to pull a meaning from them. It's as if Shakespeare were taking a series of hairpin bends at sixty miles an hour. Perhaps for this reason, the occasional simplicity of the language can be profoundly moving. For instance, Belarius's farewell to his custodianship of the King's two sons:

> The benediction of these covering heavens
> Fall on their heads like dew, for they are worthy
> To inlay heaven with stars.

And for all their wild improbability, the final surprises, played with the right mixture of intentness and lightness, are very beautiful.

As for the suffocations of sexual jealousy – and indeed his dance with King James – Shakespeare will not be passing this way again. Imogen is certainly his last great heroine, all the more remarkable for the labyrinthine improbabilities the plot obliges her to survive. She combines the courage of Juliet with the endurance of Desdemona, but is an advance on Desdemona in the anger she feels against Posthumus for his heresy in love. And for all its echoes, there is no character in Shakespeare quite like her husband – his terrible mistake, his long afflicted journey, his steadfast embracing of sorrow. Whether looking steadily for death:

> I, in my own woe charm'd,
> Could not find death where I did hear him groan
> Nor feel him where he struck... Well, I will find him

– or embracing a deprivation which somehow sustains him:

> O Imogen!
> I'll speak to thee in silence

– he is strangely riveting, a most underrated Shakespearian figure, moving towards his embrace with tender air. Finally, he stands raggedly in the court and calls out for his wife as Othello does, too late, for Desdemona:

> O Imogen!
> My queen, my life, my wife! O Imogen!
> Imogen, Imogen!

Of course Imogen, unable to bear it, breaks out of her disguise:

> IMOGEN: Why did you throw your wedded lady from you?
> Think that you are upon a rock, and now
> Throw me again.
>
> POSTHUMUS: Hang there like fruit, my soul,
> Till the tree die.

These lovely lines show Shakespeare abandoning complexity, like an experimental composer now working quietly on the white notes only. In Posthumus, he has allowed a character as destructive as Othello and Leontes to be redeemed, in our eyes as well as his wife's, by the extent of his own regret. A woman writer might not have done it; and for Shakespeare it is time now to close the book on the infinitely guilty and marginally redeemable male. Apart from anything else, King James might start smelling a rat.

9

Love is Merely a Madness

Antony and Cleopatra – Helena – Troilus and Cressida – Coriolanus

Long before Posthumus condemned all women as 'half-workers', Shakespeare's love stories – in the sense of romances wrecked by bad luck rather than character failure – had begun to dry up. Confronted by *Othello* and *The Winter's Tale*, King James increasingly had to look back to revivals of plays of a decade ago for the promise of happy endings and the boys so intriguingly dressed as women who then dressed as boys again. But for Shakespeare the days of love's light wings o'erleaping orchard walls are gone: now the stony limits of competence and character keep it firmly in its place. Shakespeare's apparent pessimism – or new awareness of compromise – may have had something to do with encroaching middle age, as a man's late thirties would then have been seen. Love was at least perishable, as Claudius had predicted in *Hamlet*:

> There lives within the very flame of love
> A kind of wick or snuff that will abate it,
> And nothing is at a like goodness still,
> For goodness, growing to a pleurisy,
> Dies in his own too-much.

It may also be misplaced. From the early 1600s no love relationship sits at the centre of a play unless its basic nature, rather than just its circumstances, is flawed. *Antony and Cleopatra*, a great study of middle-aged folly, is a case in point. The most glorious things are said by the protagonists, but hardly ever to each other: they say them in each other's absence, too late, or provoked by the wrong information. Accused by

Antony of bad faith during their wars with Caesar, Cleopatra decides to frighten him with a rumour of suicide; she has a message sent to that effect, which he receives just as he's arming for the day's battle, attended by his aptly named servant Eros. Like Romeo in Act Five in Mantua, he grasps the awful entirety of the false report and plans with alacrity:

> Unarm, Eros, the long day's task is done,
> And we must sleep... Off, pluck off,
> The seven-fold shield of Ajax cannot keep
> The battery from my heart. O, cleave, my sides,
> Heart, once be stronger than thy continent,
> Crack thy frail case. Apace, Eros, apace...
> I will o'ertake thee, Cleopatra, and there
> Weep for my pardon...
> Eros! I come, my Queen. Eros! Stay for me,
> Where souls do couch on flowers we'll hand in hand
> And with our sprightly port make the ghosts gaze.
> Dido and her Aeneas shall want troops
> And all the haunt be ours.

Having measured his grief by comparison with the immortals, Antony tries to kill himself and fails. He is carried to Cleopatra's monument: however, being together again seems to bring out the competitive instinct in them both, and they have a brief spat, in splendid cadences, as to who should have the last word on the tragedy:

> ANTONY: I am dying, Egypt, dying;
> Give me some wine and let me speak a little.
>
> CLEOPATRA: No, let me speak: and let me rail so high,
> That the false housewife Fortune break her wheel
> Provok'd by my offence.
>
> ANTONY: One word, sweet Queen.

And to rub it in, Shakespeare then dispatches Antony in the middle of one of Cleopatra's speeches, as if to upstage her:

> CLEOPATRA: Hast thou no care of me? Shall I abide
> In this dull world, which in thy absence is
> No better than a sty? O, see, my women
>
> [Antony dies.]
>
> The crown o' the earth doth melt. My lord!
> O, wither'd is the garland of the war,
> The soldier's pole is fallen; young boys and girls
> Are level now with men; the odds is gone,

> And there is nothing left remarkable
> Beneath the visiting moon. [*Swoons.*]

This is a wonderful compound of love, egotism (the loss of the lover causing as much anger as grief), the awkwardness of death and the urge to use language to rob it of meaning. A little later, Cleopatra unforgettably remembers Antony, and almost overcomes death's crassness:

> His face was as the heavens, and therein stuck
> A sun and moon, which kept their course, and lighted
> The little O, the earth...
> His legs bestrid the ocean; his reared arm
> Crested the world; his voice was propertied
> As all the tuned spheres, and that to friends;
> But when he meant to quail and shake the orb,
> He was as rattling thunder. For his bounty,
> There was no winter in't, an autumn 'twas
> That grew the more by reaping; his delights
> Were dolphin-like, they showed his back above
> The element they lived in; in his livery
> Walk'd crowns and crownets, realms and islands were
> As plates dropp'd from his pocket.
> Think you there was, or might be, such a man,
> As this I dreamt of?

To which the soldier Dolabella replies, quite rightly:

> Gentle madam, no.

This is great poetry given to those whose ability to love, as opposed to talking about it, is an open question.

✦

> These lovers cry, O ho, they die,
> Yet that which seems the wound to kill
> Doth turn 'O ho' to 'Ha, ha, he',
> So dying love lives still.

– Troilus and Cressida

Other Shakespeare prototypes are being put into odd moral frames, their ideals looking comic or even a little disreputable. Helena, the nominal heroine of *All's Well That Ends Well* (1604), cures the King of France of a fistula and he gratefully grants her any wish. She requests marriage to the disagreeable Bertram, but he doesn't want her at all and runs away to war. She pursues him around Europe like a stalker, the unstoppable in pursuit of the unlovable; her mission is a debased version of female constancy, the courage of Rosalind or Viola misapplied.

There are two Helenas in Shakespeare, leaving aside Helen of Troy, herself an ideal turned nightmarish. I used to think of the Helena of *A Midsummer Night's Dream* as a figure of pathos, abasing herself before her man and begging love; until a woman friend pointed out that it was the most controlling thing she could do, like running out into traffic in order to be rescued. I have never asked my friend about *All's Well*, whose Helena also makes us wonder what love is; in her the commitment we so admired in Rosalind is a bad joke, no more than a ruthless determination to secure her prize. At one point she enjoys the roguish Parolles's denunciation of virginity, a subject on which she has specifically invited his views – something I think Viola would never have done:

> Virginity breeds mites, much like a cheese... is peevish, proud, idle, made of self-love... the longer kept, the less worth... your virginity, your old virginity, is like one of our French withered pears; it looks ill, it eats drily; marry, 'tis a withered pear; it was formerly better; marry, yet 'tis a withered pear.

Appropriately enough, this play, like *Measure for Measure*, uses the sour device whereby one woman (Helena) is substituted for another in a man's bed to secure her marriage-pledge, a trick which has always seemed to me to require a striking shortsightedness in the victim.

Nothing in love is for sure now: there are Iagos in attendance to poison the tenderness of Othello and Desdemona, and the transgressive, co-dependent Macbeths drown in unholy rapture. And where once Romeo and Juliet, caught in an uncontrollable spasm of unconditional love, were able to change the world but at the cost of their own lives, Troilus and Cressida, victims of themselves, live on, and the world pays absolutely no attention to them.

Shakespeare rarely wrote anything as heartfelt, or as merciless, as this story of the Trojan War seen through the eyes of two Trojan lovers. Troilus is a young warrior, one of King Priam's fifty sons and younger brother of Troy's star warrior Hector; Cressida is the daughter of a priest, Calchas, who's defected to the Greeks, so desertion runs in her family. In the midst of the conflict the couple are manoeuvred into each other's arms by Cressida's racy uncle Pandarus, a far ruder version of the Nurse in *Romeo and Juliet*. The lovers hardly seem to be acquainted, but, on the basis of distant sightings and his titillating reports, have taken a hasty fancy to each other and, sure enough, called it love. However it's a very different thing from Romeo's and Juliet's chance meeting and *coup de foudre* at the Capulets' ball – not only because they are on the same side in the contention but because their feelings are fibrillated by the mortal uncertainty surrounding them.

As a result the lyrical fire stoked by Pandarus gives off a faintly acrid smell:

> TROILUS: O Pandarus...
> I tell thee, I am mad
> In Cressid's love; thou answer'st, 'she is fair'.
> Pour'st in the open ulcer of my heart
> Her eyes, her hair, her cheek, her gait, her voice...
> Thou lay'st in every gash that love hath given me
> The knife that made it.

'Ulcer'? 'Knife'? 'Gash'? Cressida's vocabulary has some of the same rebarbativeness:

> PANDARUS: He will weep you, an 'twere a man born in April.
>
> CRESSIDA: And I'll spring up in his tears, an 'twere a nettle against May.

A nettle nourished by salt tears? Their love has taken on the violence of the time: perhaps it is no more than the urge for survival. Warlike heat from Troilus is about to confront strategy in Cressida. Alone with us, and therefore truthful, she shares her method, her jingling rhymes suggesting a banal *savoir faire*:

> Yet hold I off. Women are angels, wooing;
> Things won are done; joy's soul lies in the doing;
> That she belov'd knows naught that knows not this,
> Men prize the thing ungain'd more than it is.

Meanwhile Troilus's language crackles with military static:

> Why should I war without the walls of Troy
> That find such cruel battle here within?...
> I am weaker than a woman's tear.

His fear is that love may disable him for his main job in life. Waiting in Cressida's orchard to meet her at last, he equates paradise with death: he is

> Like a strange soul upon the Stygian banks
> Staying for waftage

– while his imagination remains on the battlefield:

> and I do fear besides
> That I shall lose distinction in my joys,
> As doth a battle, when they charge on heaps
> The enemy flying.

But then there is a surprise. Cressida, miraculously, turns out to be lovelier at close quarters than at a distance; Troilus is 'bereft of all words' and his anxiety evaporates in lovely cadences. However, even as he capitulates, he shows the preoccupation of all the play's warriors – the judgment of posterity:

> O that I thought it could be in a woman...
> To feed for aye her lamp and flames of love...
> To keep her constancy in plight and youth
> Outliving beauty's outward, with a mind
> That doth renew swifter than blood decays...
> True swains in love shall in the world to come
> Approve their truths by Troilus: when their rhymes,
> Full of protest, of oath, of big compare
> Want similes, truth tir'd with iteration...
> As truth's authentic author to be cited,
> 'As true as Troilus' shall crown up the verse
> And sanctify the numbers.

So love is not enough for him: he must get good reviews in the time to come. His poetry, though gorgeous, is a little condescending, an early sign of trouble. He has lost his violence, but he is inexperienced: his suffocating emphasis that nobody on earth could be as true as he is could make life impossible for a woman. It certainly confronts Cressida with an uncomfortable choice: she either has to match his perfectionism or speak in her own stubbornly practical voice and risk losing him. Remarkably, she splits the difference:

> If I be false, or swerve a hair from truth,
> When time is old and hath forgot itself,
> When waterdrops have worn the stones of Troy,
> And blind oblivion swallow'd cities up
> And mighty states characterless are grated
> To dusty nothing; yet let memory,
> From false to false, among false maids in love
> Upbraid my falsehood...
> Yea, let them say, to stick the heart of falsehood,
> 'As false as Cressid'.

This clatters less; its music is sinuous and natural, matching Troilus's ambition but less full of effort. Significantly, there are seven 'false' or 'falsehoods' in it: Troilus might have preferred the tonic note of affirmation rather than the negative. Still, she has satisfied his need for hyperbole while keeping her own feet on the ground.

Cressida's directness continues to jab into Troilus's narcissism. She acknowledges sexual fantasy in a way that he would shrink from:

> My thoughts were like unbridled children grown
> Too headstrong for their mother – see, we fools,
> Why have I blabb'd?

The primmer commentators – who have gathered round this play with particular zeal – have pounced on this as an early sign of promiscuousness: I would rather call it candour. Feeling she has gone too far for him, she now calls for Troilus to 'stop my mouth'. No sooner has he done so than she reproaches herself:

> 'Twas not my purpose thus to beg a kiss.

This sounds like a traditional feminine reluctance to make the running, but behind it, a certain self-distaste is glowing. She can see 'more dregs than water' in the 'fountain' of their love; she has

> a kind of self resides with you
> But an unkind self, that itself will leave
> To be another's fool.

On this half-promising premise – and before they can talk themselves out of it – Pandarus delightedly whisks them off to bed. There is a feeling of rush, fit-up, neediness and some beauty; the Shakespeare of the Sonnets, a specialist in sexual anticipation and recoil, is preparing us for the inevitable.

He is careful to honour every step of the way. Like Romeo and Juliet hearing the nightingale, the satiated lovers have their moment of rest, as if cool water were washing over them:

> TROILUS: Dear, trouble not yourself; the morn is cold…
>   To bed, to bed; sleep kill those pretty eyes,
>   And give as soft attachment to thy senses
>   As infants' empty of all thought.

This morning-after scene is almost the last time they will be alone, as it was for Romeo and Juliet, though there is a sexual touch Shakespeare didn't chance in the earlier play:

CRESSIDA: My lord, come you again into my chamber;
   You smile and mock me, as if I meant naughtily.
TROILUS: Ha, ha!
CRESSIDA: Come, you are deceiv'd; I think of no such thing.

                                        [*Knocking.*]

That ominous Shakespearian knocking again: war is at the door. Cressida's turncoat father has struck a deal with the Greeks whereby she will become a trophy prisoner on the Greek side in exchange for a Trojan commander they will release. She must leave immediately: the lovers are to be separated by male military bargaining as definitively as Romeo and Juliet were by their parents.

Given how little they have had of each other, the depth of feeling they find at this moment is surprising. As grievously determined as Juliet, Cressida defies kindred and time:

> I have forgot my father;
> I know no touch of consanguinity;
> No kin, no love, no blood, no soul so near me
> As the sweet Troilus – O you gods divine,
> Make Cressid's name the very crown of falsehood,
> If ever she leave Troilus! Time, force and death
> Do to this body what extremes you can;
> But the strong base and building of my love
> Is as the very centre of the earth,
> Drawing all things to it.

But Shakespeare, ever watchful, is continuing to insinuate: 'falsehood' and 'Cressid' in the same line. Troilus's response is extraordinary: musically faultless, typically uncompromising but suddenly adult:

> We two, that with so many thousand sighs
> Did buy each other, must poorly sell ourselves
> With the rude brevity and discharge of one.
> Injurious time now with a robber's haste
> Crams his rich thievery up, he knows not how;
> As many farewells as be stars in heaven,
> With distinct breath and consign'd kisses to them
> He fumbles up into a loose adieu,
> And scants us with a single famish'd kiss
> Distasted with the salt of broken tears.

No more windy approximations, but a Shakespearian tussle between extravagance and detail. Unfortunately he can't sustain it because of his humiliating need for comfort:

TROILUS: Hear me, my love; be thou but true of heart.

CRESSIDA: I true? How now?...

TROILUS: Be thou true
    And I will see thee... But yet be true.

CRESSIDA: O heavens, be true again...
    O heavens, you love me not.

TROILUS: But be not tempted.

CRESSIDA: Do you think I will?

TROILUS: No.

Never did a young man dig his own grave so effectively: Cressida is as hemmed in by his anxiety as she was by his idealism. Further intimidated by the arrival of Cressida's new minder Diomed, a poised and confident man of war, Troilus begins to panic:

TROILUS: I charge thee use her well, even for my charge,
    For by the dreadful Pluto, if thou dost not,
    Though the great bulk Achilles be thy guard,
    I'll cut thy throat.

DIOMED: O be not mov'd, Prince Troilus...

The threat is a mean one, the language of ambush rather than heroism: in the act of standing up for her he seems to Cressida smaller than his rival. She is silent throughout.

Soon she arrives among the Greeks, who treat her with a rough masculinity, kissing her one by one – she is their prisoner, after all; and in due course she gives herself to Diomed. Troilus's insecurity leads him to spy on their crucial meeting, a voyeur at his own disaster – he is accompanied by the very unsympathetic Ulysses, a Greek of absolutely no tenderness to whom Shakespeare has given an extraordinary grasp of political philosophy. Ulysses was the commentator when Cressida arrived among the Greeks:

          Fie, fie upon her!
There's language in her eye, her cheek, her lip,
Nay, her foot speaks...

Now he shares that function with the scatological Thersites, a professional cynic on the skirts of the army whose job is to sustain the fiercest level of denunciation:

Any man may sing her, if he can take her cliff: she's noted...
Lechery, lechery, still wars and lechery; nothing else holds fashion.

With less than no sympathy on every side, Troilus hears Cressida disposing of his precious memories as briefly as she can:

> Troilus, farewell, one eye yet looks on thee;
> But with my heart the other eye doth see.

At this moment she is as opaque to us as to him: never unwilling before to call a spade a spade, she is now speaking not of her body, or even her need for protection, but conventionally of her eye and heart, and Troilus is in neither. She goes out of the play as she entered it, with oddly unrevealing rhymed couplets: we don't know how and in what way she loves Diomed, but to Troilus the treachery is unequivocally carnal. His great speech of sexual betrayal matches Leontes's double vision in *The Winter's Tale*:

> Cressid is mine, tied with the bonds of heaven;
> Instance, O instance, strong as heaven itself;
> The bonds of heaven are slipp'd, dissolv'd and loos'd
> And with another knot, five-finger-tied,
> The fractions of her faith, orts of her love,
> The fragments, scraps, the bits and greasy relics
> Of her o'er-eaten faith, are given to Diomed...

– and it catapults him onto the battlefield with a renewed use for his masculinity. Here, as an unkind fate would have it, his beloved brother Hector is traduced and ambushed by Achilles, slaughtered and dragged around the battlefield like a piece of carrion. Troilus's vicious nihilism is complete:

> ...thou great-siz'd coward,
> No space of earth shall sunder our two hates;
> I'll haunt thee like a wicked conscience still...

This is not the petty cut-throat who fearfully threatened Diomed: actual loss of love has made him a killing machine.

So the tragedy, if that's what it is, is not that Cressida is a faithless hussy (too easy), but that she's a woman on her own who finds herself on the wrong side in a war and sees a not unusual way of surviving her captivity. In the pressure of that painful moment we may agree with Troilus that she is a brute, but in truth a more difficult point is being made, that sexual loyalty may not be able to compete with the flux of war. New love has failed where it could hardly succeed: hatched in a conflict itself caused by a sexual abduction, of Helen by Paris, it couldn't get to the light. No one comes out of the play well: the twin heroes of myth, Hector and

Achilles, have been revealed as, respectively, a moral vacuum and a self-indulgent sulk. The Trojans were louche, the Greeks impossibly pompous: the din has been continuous and intemperate. If Cressida's pragmatism was opportunistic, Troilus's failure was in his intolerant perfectionism: an hysterical suitor, he achieved grace only in the pain of separation, and then closed the play as a fanatic. Throughout, the lovers were accompanied by the insistent third voice of Pandarus, edging Cressida's realism towards pornography and reducing everything to a transaction of the flesh. And in case we were in any doubt, Pandarus behaved with the same lewdness towards Helen of Troy herself in a scene in which her seduction, the whole pretext for the war, was compressed to its barest, least flattering essentials.

✦

I have nightly since
Dreamt of encounters 'twixt thyself and me;
We have been down together in my sleep,
Unbuckling helms, fisting each other's throat,
And wak'd half dead with nothing…

– *Coriolanus*

Coriolanus is pre-eminently a play of politics and war, one of the greatest, but it would be less so if it were not also a story of love – and not entirely of its absence. Troilus and Cressida found their relationship conditioned by conflict and unequal to it; *Coriolanus* proposes a political battle made tenser by the fact that love's particles are misfiring where they should be most reliable – between parent and child. And with blood relations so contaminated, marital love hardly has a chance.

If Troilus is a romantic with a vicious streak, the 'lonely dragon' Coriolanus is a killer with a dash of lyricism. His capacity for affection, though implied by occasional tenderness, is all over the place, astray in the violence and infantilism of his life: it's not that it doesn't exist, but that it is neurotically reserved for his mother. His wife on the other hand he addresses as a 'gracious silence', and hardly bothers to say goodbye to her on leaving Rome for good.

Meanwhile, the alarming little figure of Young Martius, his son, reveals his pathology by chasing a butterfly, toying with it and releasing it several times before administering a *coup de grâce* all the more dreadful for the postponements. Volumnia, his bellicose grandmother, is delighted to hear that

he did so set his teeth and tear it. O I warrant how he
mammocked it!

To her it proves that the boy will be a satisfactory chip off the old block
once he learns to harbour his resources. Troilus, in his extremity, would
approve.

Volumnia is the mother Coriolanus would be very much better off
without. A woman able to declare

> Anger's my meat: I sup upon myself
> And so shall starve with feeding

– she has both fashioned and deformed him. Early on she lists his battle
scars as if she was assembling an album of his sporting achievements:

> O he is wounded, I thank the gods for it… i' the shoulder and
> i' the left arm… he received in the repulse of Tarquin seven
> hurts i' the body… he had before this last expedition twenty-
> five wounds upon him.

There is a physical obsession in this, you might say maternal sexuality.
But what if, his gentle wife Virgilia asks, this trophy son had 'died in the
business'? That would have been fine with Volumnia:

> his good report should have been my son… I had rather had
> eleven die nobly for their country than one voluptuously surfeit
> out of action.

In the end, Coriolanus will be destroyed precisely because Volumnia convinces him to hang up his armour at the wrong moment.

Meanwhile the two of them are rebarbative, but never less than claus-
trophobically close. The intensity of their relationship is unique in
Shakespeare, the only time he investigates a mother and son at play-
length – as opposed to *en passant* in *Hamlet*. Having spent a lifetime
looking at troubled male parents and their children, he has found something new – still more daring from our point of view, since the
imagination stalls at the theatrical practicalities: Volumnia must have
been played by an older boy actor, now grown up, a phenomenon harder
to imagine even than a male Cleopatra or Mistress Quickly.

Coriolanus's delight in violence is genetic; he is a serial killer from
the breast. Far from wanting his mother to leave him at the schoolroom
door, he needs her in the classroom with him, and she seems to be the
only part of his life that causes him to reflect at all. As a result of her
attentions, he is both more and less than a man; a hyperactive hero who
can't take a step without her straightening his clothes. Alert to such

things nowadays, we might think Coriolanus is gay, and in some unacknowledged sense he probably is. His relations with women are certainly troubled. His wife has literally been reduced to silence, while with his comrades-in-arms he speaks like this:

> O let me clip ye
> In arms as sound as when I woo'd; in heart
> As merry as when our nuptial day was done
> And tapers burn'd to bedward.

This is to his military buddy Cominius: with his enemy Aufidius something even more startling emerges. Aufidius, consumed by envy and admiration in equal parts, says that compared to the whole of Rome Coriolanus is

> As is the osprey to the fish, who takes it
> By sovereignty of nature

– while Coriolanus acknowledges him as

> a lion
> That I am proud to hunt.

When they finally meet to make common cause against Rome, Coriolanus presents his throat and Aufidius returns the compliment by admitting:

> Know thou first,
> I lov'd the maid I married; never man
> Sigh'd truer breath. But that I see thee here,
> Thou noble thing, more dances my rapt heart
> Than when I first my wedded mistress saw
> Bestride my threshold.

The character of Aufidius (or indeed the state of his marriage) is not investigated in much depth, but the heat of this is obvious. His old enemy inflames him and is inflamed by him: we are riveted by their attention to each other.

In this skewed world, there is no visible spouse for Volumnia, as there was no wife for Lear or Gloucester or Henry IV; once again, the parental relationships are lopsided. As if to underline this, Shakespeare provides another lodestar in Coriolanus's troubled life, a surrogate father-figure. The articulacy which might have eased the warrior's complicated personality is given to Menenius Agrippa, coruscating spokesman of 'the right hand file'. The language of this man bristles with a contempt for the common people so witty that it is hard to resist, exactly the sort of thing Coriolanus would do if only he would calm down a bit and get some education. In his prejudice he is indeed Menenius's son, making up in assertion for what he lacks in style. Sentimental about his own class, Menenius views the people of Rome as 'beastly plebeians... apron men... garlic-eaters', and sees the best speeches of their Tribunes as not worth 'the wagging of [their] beards' – beards, now he thinks of it, which are in any case not good enough 'to stuff a botcher's cushion'. In his very first scene he develops the conceit of the body, whose every junior part is dependent on the storehouse, the belly – a brilliantly cynical manoeuvre to convince the starving that they have no right to ask the ruling party for food. Almost inevitably, Menenius himself is a bon viveur: he

> loves a cup of hot wine with not a drop of allaying Tiber in't...
> one that converses more with the buttock of the night than with
> the forehead of the morning.

In fact refreshment seems to be integral to his political thinking: as he prepares to plead with his proxy son to spare Rome, he opines that previous overtures have failed because:

> He was not taken well; he had not dined;
> The veins unfill'd, our blood is cold, and then
> We pout upon the morning.

It is as if Falstaff (whose rumbustious prose style he sometimes rivals) were operating in a world where everybody else is starving. Menenius is the hero's missing wit; and the echo of Falstaff and Hal deepens when, to his horror, Coriolanus, who by now has no more mercy 'than there is milk in a male tiger', rejects his plea to spare the Rome on which he has wasted his skills. It causes Coriolanus a sorrow which, like Hal, he can only mildly acknowledge after the event; but it leaves Menenius stunned and helpless. The father has had no influence; the mother, disastrously, too much.

The relationships in *Coriolanus* would themselves provide enough good matter for a play. Instead Shakespeare brilliantly insinuates them into what is above all a political work, his last such and his most far-sighted. The one aspect crucially depends on the other. What has formed this society or been formed by it? Is mother-love contaminated by the play's male violence, or is it that, faced with women like Volumnia, men's relationships inevitably become compensatory and overheated? The genius of the play is that the psychological complexities are sustained without any strain to the headlong narrative.

William Hazlitt said you didn't need to read Burke and Tom Paine to understand the French Revolution, since you got both sides of the argument in *Coriolanus*. So much so that a 1933 Comédie Française production provoked both anti-Fascists and anti-Communists into rioting in the streets, each feeling their position had been attacked. Because of his own manifest doubts, the play has a political density unique in Shakespeare, so much so that it is a shock to hear occasional mention of such old hat as the 'auguries', which in classical terms take over man's responsibility for his fate. In general, although like *Richard III* it features both a big central personality and a complicated argument, the friction between them is no longer distracting. Bringing a set of contradictions on with him, each character is challenged to redefine himself politically and personally; the play approaches tragedy because of a general failure to do so.

✦

The scorn of the military hero Caius Martius for the Roman populace – 'our musty superfluity' – is politely described as pride by his friends, but to us sounds like a psychotic aversion, hysterical and disproportionate. Not only does he not want ordinary people to have political representation; he hardly, in a time of famine, wants them to eat – or live:

> Hang 'em... They say there's grain enough?
> Would the nobility lay aside their ruth
> And let me use my sword, I'd make a quarry
> With thousands of these quarter'd slaves, as high
> As I could pick my lance.

As Rome's pre-eminent warrior, he goes into battle early as, whether he likes it or not, the city's champion and protector (the play is a murderous assignment for the leading actor, who has to fight a battle not at the climax but right at the start, and then build his performance from there). He strikes the city of Corioles 'like a planet', defeating the Volscian army more or less single-handed; in the process he finds his soldiers so lacking in his own recklessness that at one point he threatens, like a demented Henry V, to make war on them instead. He then, in a dazzlingly complicated moment, remembers a poor citizen caught in the crossfire who for some undisclosed reason has given him shelter for the night. He asks that this man be given his freedom and immunity from reprisals; but nothing comes of it because, unfortunately, he can't remember the man's name.

It is at this moment that Caius Martius loses his own name: awarded the title Coriolanus, he too becomes anonymous, his difficult personality forever crouched behind the honorific. This idea becomes poetic as the play moves forward; so much so that towards its end Cominius will report that in his self-imposed banishment the hero seems

> a kind of nothing, titleless,
> Till he had forg'd himself a name a' the fire
> Of burning Rome.

At about the same time Aufidius will have to ask him his name six times in eight lines before getting an answer. And it is the final taunt of being called mere 'Caius Martius', the name his parents gave him, that provokes him to the fury that accelerates his assassination.

Meanwhile he returns to Rome to run for consul, a process that immediately pits him head to head with the electorate. Short of food and repelled both by their right-leaning Senate and their bilious leading soldier, they have acquired a pair of Tribunes to represent them. These men are a nicely observed compound of ideals and careerism, and they suffer from the occupational virus of the left. They detest Coriolanus and deplore his rise: we, repelled by his fascistic instincts, may agree:

> You speak o' the people
> As if you were a god to punish, not
> A man, of their infirmity.

But we can also see the time-serving nature of the two apparatchiks. Intellectually equipped for their job, they are compromised by their envious refusal to acknowledge empirical fact. At one point, they look to discredit Coriolanus by suggesting that his disinclination to become commander-in-chief is so that he may always have someone else to blame if things go wrong:

> giddy censure
> Will then cry out on Martius, 'O, if he
> Had borne the business.'

A respectable enough insight in theory, this completely misses the point of his character, which would be incapable of such a wily thought and is, for better or worse, indifferent to popularity. This pungent moment tells you everything you need to know about the Tribunes' limitations.

As part of the ritual of moving 'from the casque to the cushion', Coriolanus is soon required to listen to his campaign team boasting about him. He finds it physically impossible: since he was unable to take a compliment for his prowess on the battlefield – 'I will go wash' – it is no wonder that now he prefers to sit outside the Senate door. He does little better when he goes to the people to ask for approval, muttering:

> bid them wash their faces
> And keep their teeth clean.

What modesty he summons comes across as arrogance, as perhaps it is; still, he secures the nomination despite some edgy moments. Then the frustrated Tribunes privately persuade the voters to change their minds – and to blame them, the Tribunes, for their initial mistake: in this way they keep themselves on the right side of the argument while using the citizens to cause new trouble for Coriolanus.

Shakespeare's working men and women have thus proved malleable once again. His attitude to them remains a vexing mix of humanity and contempt – no doubt reflecting his horror of anarchy in a pre-constitutional age. In the early plays you seemed to hear from everyone except ordinary people – apart from two agreeable royalist gardeners for a moment in *Richard II*, or a couple of citizens chatting here and there. The aggrieved rebels who followed Jack Cade to London, casually murdering anyone who chanced into their path, seemed an exception; but when they betrayed Cade for the false offer of a King's pardon, they were shown to be equally vulnerable to anyone able to exploit their mix of egalitarianism and venality. Now the voters are centre stage, but no more reliable than before.

Their change of heart of course confirms Coriolanus's views of democracy, and he articulates a definitive conservative argument for firm government, as if resisting calls for a national referendum:

> where gentry, title, wisdom
> Cannot conclude but by the yea and no
> Of general ignorance, it must omit
> Real necessities and give way the while
> To unstable slightness. Purpose so barr'd, it follows
> Nothing is done to purpose.

In an extraordinary central Act which makes Speaker's Question Time seem like a tea party, Coriolanus, having won the people's voices and lost them again, is goaded by the Tribunes to a point where there is virtually a public coup against him: it is a half-hour storm of swirling argument and inflamed temper exemplifying Shakespeare's grasp of the reactive, circular nature of politics. Halfway through the quarrel, Coriolanus looks for his mother's approval – which, knowing her power, she metes out only piecemeal. Thus reproached, he half-comically goes back to the Tribunes determined to eat humble pie; unable to do it, he is banished by public outcry rather than process. As he delivers the most decisive denunciation in the play, flinty, outrageous and overweening, it's not clear who has abandoned whom. The implication that the citizens of Rome are now the audience in the pit of the theatre becomes as unsettling as when Leontes discomforts all complacent husbands:

> You common cry of curs, whose breath I hate
> As reek o' the rotten fens, whose loves I prize
> As the dead carcasses of unburied men,
> That do corrupt my air, I banish you,
> And here remain with your uncertainty…

In Coriolanus's absence, there is a brief Prague Spring. The structures of government, never very clear in the play, have broken. The Tribunes appear to be in charge, boasting that the people are happily singing in their shops and going about their 'functions friendly' – while the Tribunes themselves are, significantly, using the resources of government for their own security:

> Let a guard
> Attend us through the city.

Meanwhile Coriolanus joins up with his Volscian enemy Aufidius, with the express intention of destroying his own city; but at the very moment he is sitting

> in gold, his eye
> Red as 'twould burn Rome

he is re-enlisted by Volumnia, who comes to plead with him, together with Virgilia, young Martius and a family friend, Valeria.

At this point it becomes apparent that Shakespeare is inclining an intricate political debate as close to heroic tragedy as he dares. Typical tropes have already come into play in the immediately preceding scenes, such as the hero's momentary onset of reflectiveness in Act Four, immediately followed by a reversion to type. The banished Coriolanus stood disguised and alone in a street in the 'goodly city' of Antium, home of the hated Volscians: his fury had modulated into the affable stance of a tourist, relieved not to be forever taking sides. But his geniality was short-lived: remembering that he had personally widowed many of the town's citizens and should keep his head down, he nevertheless soon found himself – true to his character – in a roughhouse with Aufidius's servants.

The momentary softening now leads to something more drastic: a quite unexpected lyricism towards his family. It is a sign of anxiety, of course, but nonetheless gorgeous. Volumnia kneels to him, a gesture as mortifying to him as his defection was to her. He is incredulous:

> What is this?
> Your knees to me! To your corrected son!
> Then let the pebbles on the hungry beach
> Fillip the stars; then let the mutinous winds
> Strike the proud cedars 'gainst the fiery sun,
> Murd'ring impossibility, to make
> What cannot be, slight work.

She returns his compliment in the closest possible harmony – the same key, pitch, cadence and rhythm:

> Speak to me, son;
> Thou hast affected the fine strains of honour,
> To imitate the graces of the gods,
> To tear with thunder the wide cheeks of the air
> And yet to charge thy sulphur with a bolt
> That should but rive an oak.

Another object of tenderness is, unexpectedly, Virgilia. Poor Virgilia, hardly better off than Aufidius's wife; Virgilia, whose tears at parting were brushed aside with 'Nay, I prithee, woman'; reproached for her queasiness by her mother-in-law, who once told her she

> should freelier rejoice in that absence wherein he won honour
> than in the embracements of his bed, where he would show
> most love...

Now she is welcomed with

> a kiss,
> Long as my exile, sweet as my revenge!
> Now by the jealous queen of heaven, that kiss
> I carried from thee, dear...

As for the 'poor epitome' their son, whose profession is beyond doubt, his thoughts are to be informed (though the actual violence is skilfully filleted out)

> with nobleness, that thou may'st prove
> To shame invulnerable, and stick i' the wars
> Like a great sea-mark standing every flaw,
> And saving those that eye thee.

Even Valeria, with whom Coriolanus can hardly be on intimate terms, is the object of a sexual compliment:

> chaste as the icicle
> That's curdied by the frost from purest snow
> That hangs on Dian's temple...

They must be quite surprised: their man is becoming a fully fledged Shakespearian hero. But he is dooming himself in the process.

Volumnia's plea when it comes is superbly eloquent, and since she knows her boy, she is not above flat blackmail as well: he will shortly be treading

> on thy mother's womb
> That brought thee to this world:
> ...Thou hast never in thy life
> Show'd thy dear mother any courtesy
> When she (poor hen) fond of no second brood,
> Has cluck'd thee to the wars...
> This fellow had a Volscian to his mother;
> His wife is in Corioles, and his child
> Like him by chance.

Her success is marked by a stage direction absolutely unprecedented in Shakespeare:

> VOLUMNIA: I am hush'd until our city be afire,
>   And then I'll speak a little.
>
> CORIOLANUS (*after holding her by the hand, silent*):
>   O mother, mother!
>   What have you done?...

The play stops, as surely as if an orchestral conductor suddenly lowered his baton in the middle of a bar. Coriolanus's silence is literally the death of him: he turns to Aufidius, whom his change of heart is going to betray:

> CORIOLANUS: Now, good Aufidius,
>   Were you in my stead, would you have heard
>   A mother less? Or granted less, Aufidius?
>
> AUFIDIUS: I was mov'd withal.

Like hell he was. Within a few stage minutes Coriolanus is killed by Aufidius's faction, the price of having left the argument.

In fact his shell was already cracked when Volumnia arrived. His moment of warmth in Antium was followed by his submission to Aufidius – for that is what his offer of alliance was, whatever his gloss on it –

and left him with no more certainty about himself than Richard II or Othello. We have watched him, in his own terms, disintegrate, and his mother has been the last straw. Now, in a final Shakespearian manoeuvre, he goes out in a paradoxical blaze of glory (if glory is what his old self represented) – Caius Martius once more, in crashing major chords:

> Like an eagle in a dove-cote, I
> Flutter'd your Volscians in Corioli:
> Alone I did it. Boy!

He's used up all the play's affirmation: contemplating his dead body, the complicit lords can only say

> Let's make the best of it

– and the play's last line is Aufidius's bleak

> Assist.

It is as perfunctory as a Shakespeare ending gets. In fact Aufidius has provided the true summary several scenes before:

> So our virtues
> Lie in the interpretation of the time.
> And power, unto itself most commendable,
> Hath not a tomb so evident as a chair
> To extol what it hath done.
> One fire drives out one fire; one nail, one nail;
> Rights by rights falter; strengths by strengths do fail.

The skill Shakespeare demonstrates in Act Five in bringing the emotional and political together boils down to the simplest proposition: if Volumnia hadn't come, Rome would have been destroyed, but she did, so her son was instead.

✦

Like all political plays *Coriolanus* attracts impetuous thinking. Once it was regarded as a vehicle for a star glamorous enough to make hot temper, outrageous prejudice and mother-love quite attractive foibles; these days you'll often find the hero down and dirty in East Berlin, or the Gdansk shipyards, in Bucharest or Baghdad – or in any other conflict in which the taking of sides is all too easy. By the late 1980s the feel of Eastern Europe in flux was irresistible, even though it could only ever be a suggestion. Neither Coriolanus nor Menenius is a Hoxha, Ceausescu or a Honecker, though they both have a smack of such men: if the parallel were exact the patricians would have been communists, and Shakespeare's scepticism about democracy would have sat uneasily. A production I was in during the Gulf War of 1990 was, while touring in India, accused of tactlessness, especially in Calcutta, for presenting the Volscians as, it was said, mujaheddin. Margaret Thatcher was overthrown by her own party while we played in England: 'I shall be lov'd when I am lack'd' shouted the arch-Tory Coriolanus to the delight of our alert audiences.

Clearly the play animates latent political prejudices in director and cast. Beware the golden boy Coriolanus in a follow-spot, confronting a crowd of Central Casting citizens with nothing between their ears. On the other hand too much sympathy for the revolutionary cause led Bertolt Brecht, unsettled by the play's impartiality, to rewrite it, idealising the citizenry and painting the protagonist as a despot with nothing personally remarkable about him. (The unfinished work was satirised by Günter Grass in *The Plebeians Rehearse the Uprising*.) Naturally the same problem arises for the actor. When I played the part, I think I was too thuggish, not offering much of his perverse glamour – but then I'd seen a lot of perverse glamour and not quite enough politics in other productions. This was a self-criticism I could only whisper in a radicalised Green Room. One of the Tribunes, a professed Marxist (at least for the time being), spotted during our visit to Tokyo that an extra sound effect had been put into the score at the moment of Coriolanus's death – a discreet phrase on the cello that lent a scintilla of wistfulness to his passing. He declared that if this kind of unsocialist sentimentality was going to creep into our production to mark the death of a hateful class enemy, he for one was withdrawing from the show. The daft oversensitivity of his position – not to mention the fleeting image of him swimming all the way home from Japan – certainly proved the play's ability to polarise.

What everyone faces of course is Shakespeare's confounding tendency to enlist support where we least want to give it. Even in failure, Coriolanus's charisma remains unquestioned, though we also get the sneaking feeling that our response to him is not a thing to be proud of. At the very least there should be some sense of impoverishment at his departure, a guarded sense of loss, if only of a supreme vitality. The man *was* something after all, and if commitment to a single idea is ever a virtue, he was a saint. I have been finishing this chapter at the time of a General Election in Britain, and the Tory grandee Michael Heseltine has just been on a TV panel regretting the difficulties involved in forming coalition governments in a hung parliament. He addressed the studio audience as 'you lords of democracy' – an odd variant on the standard politician's cliché that he is just the public's servant: he didn't actually say 'so-called' before the 'lords', but you could hear the inverted commas forming. The problem was that we, the electorate, had not given the political class a clear mandate – as if the forty million voters were not individuals with differing concerns, but one inconvenient thing, the people, confusing their benevolent rulers who only wanted the best for them. Such a man would have had no difficulty in forming Menenius's parable of the stomach, whereby the citizenry becomes a kind of capillary system feeding the governing engine; on a bad night he might even have described us as a musty superfluity. It was Coriolanus all over, but delivered with the *risqué* charm of Menenius – and made Heseltine, not for the first time, by far the most interesting character on a rather bad-tempered panel.

✦

Coriolanus's failure to remember the name of the man who showed him kindness during the battle made a generous gesture look studied, taught rather than felt. Not that it was exactly insincere: he somehow sensed, in a rarely used part of his brain, that the man deserved well of him, but there was no real warmth in it. But then, warmth is what Coriolanus most fears in himself. His lack of – for want of a better word – feminine sensibility makes his self-regard bombastic; his movement through life is like that of a siege engine. He is really a big, overdeveloped baby. Presumably Volumnia brought him up much as she would like him to do her grandson; certainly his affection for Martius Junior might disappear if the boy wanted to be a chemist. Coriolanus's love for his mother is really fear of her disapproval, or worse; her domineering retaliation is a bedwetter's nightmare. And the instant he speaks kindly to his wife, the momentum that has given him his power is fatally compromised.

The fact is there are men and women whom love is as likely to break as to redeem, and Shakespeare has always noted it. We associate him as time goes on with fairytale mechanisms which reward true contrition: love is a light suddenly seen, and the remaking of the flawed personality a means of salvation. But it's not always so, not yet. When Claudius said of Gertrude, who may have been the strongest motive for his murdering his brother:

> My virtue or my plague, be't either which,
> She's so conjunctive to my life and soul
> That as the star moves not but in his sphere
> I could not but by her

– he was conspicuously losing his grip. As he spoke he was busy plotting Hamlet's death with Laertes: how did he think he could get away with such a plan, how could it possibly work? He could blame Laertes for the naked blade, but how would he explain the poisoned drink he'd blessed himself? In other words he was more rattled even than when Hamlet presented him with a mirror image of his crime in a play; and since the night of Polonius's death, his wife will have nothing to do with him.

The same loss of a woman's validation has a different effect on Troilus, making him, one imagines, very fit for purpose. He will maim and kill and treat women badly, only becoming his grieving self again in the small hours of some mornings. If he questions his new role he will fall into the bitterest sense of self-defeat. He and Coriolanus are awkward cases for whom self-review is dangerous and change fatal: they are also very dependent on female approval. Cressida meanwhile disappears into the crowd: perhaps touched briefly by love, she now narrows her view to the everyday exploitation of her natural resources. The death of Antony, 'triple pillar of the world', is Cleopatra's fault for sure: were it not for the suicide hoax, he would have lived to fight more days, and her rhapsodic lament for him once he's gone implicitly acknowledges that. There seemed no reason – apart from political awkwardness – why she and Antony should not have been together: they were both love-junkies. But they were also like the type of friends who insist to you that, though they live on opposite sides of the world, their relationship will flourish without distracting them from their vocational work. However, in middle age (as Shakespeare is) this seems gloriously silly. Such lovers might better have realised that passionate love might not be the best thing for them: better to decide that recreation is as welcome as desire and a shared joke as good as a poem. Such milder pleasures are, in the words of Perdita:

> flowers
> Of middle summer, and I think they are given
> To men of middle age.

On the other hand, they wouldn't then have been Antony and Cleopatra. Perhaps the only solutions to these tangles will be fantastical, a dream, a great and improbable What If. Marina saves her father Pericles from despair and puts a brothel out of business; Perdita is about to change the world around her. Soon it will be time for the young to suggest not only their passion but the calm of middle age without its folly. So Ferdinand and Miranda in *The Tempest*, in one of Shakespeare's loveliest final images, will wait for their elders to settle their differences by sitting down and patiently playing a game of chess.

IO

Let's Bear Us Like the Time

Ice and Fire – The Tempest – Henry VIII –
The Two Noble Kinsmen – The End of All

For a split second we almost see him. The Thames has frozen over in the midwinter of 1607; people stroll to and fro across the icy platform of tents, improvised barbers' shops, taverns and wrestling booths: so firm does the surface seem that they even start fires on it to keep warm. It's perhaps a little like the South Bank now, with its contortionists' acts and hucksters and hot dog stalls. Shakespeare looks up momentarily, searching for a metaphor for an early speech of Coriolanus, and uses what he can see: the citizens of Rome will be

> no surer, no,
> Than is the coal of fire upon the ice
> Or hailstone in the sun.

That is to say, ice may last longer than a fire, though sun outlives the hail: he never just describes, but always draws an apt and antithetical conclusion. Then, on New Year's Eve, a melancholy bell rings out across the ice. Shakespeare is generally playing at court at Christmas, an important time of year for his company. This time he has broken off because of bad news: his brother Edmund has died. The burial is in Southwark, prefaced by this 'fore-noon knell of the great bell' (a line Shakespeare could have improved); he probably paid the twenty shillings for the bell himself. He was moving crossways through the crowd that day, at that most frustrating right-angle: people would have been going across the frozen river as he followed the little funeral procession along its southern edge to St Saviour's. He might have been alone.

Edmund Shakespeare is one of history's lost figures, but his proximity to another great mystery means that somebody is probably working somewhere on a speculative biography of him. If so, it will be a fine example of making bricks without straw. We know that Edmund was an actor by profession and that he followed William to London, but that's all, so it's tempting to think he may not have made much of a success, but then who knows? What does speak to us about him is that like William he suffered that worst bereavement, the loss of a child: his son, also Edmund, had perished four months before him. The Register describes the boy as 'base born' and no marriage is recorded: no doubt he was begot in the 'lusty stealth of nature' approved by his and his father's namesake, the bastard Edmund in *Lear*, a character who also rails at the epithet 'base' – this is an odd tangled-up half-connection made by a writer looking for names that half-suit his characters. The one death surely expedited the other, and any biographer will no doubt start from that point.

Shakespeare's brushes with mortality have by this time been, in our terms, many; in his, comparatively few. He's lost a seven-year-old sister, Anne, when he was fourteen, his son Hamnet when he was thirty-two, his seventy-year-old father when he was thirty-six, and now a brother; and in the next year his mother is to die, like his father at a ripe-ish old age. But two months after Edmund's death, in February 1608, William becomes a grandfather for the only time during his lifetime when Susannah has a little girl of her own, Elizabeth – to be baptised, like her grandfather, uncles and aunts, in Holy Trinity Church in Stratford. Not so long after this he sets about *The Winter's Tale*, in which Hermione's baby Perdita survives being left on the mountainside: the Old Shepherd sums up the situation to his son, who has just seen the loyal Antigonus perish, with heartfelt Shakespearian simplicity:

Thou met'st with things dying, I with things new born...

Perdita grows up and is reunited with Hermione; Hermione is reconciled to Leontes (though, like Viola and Isabella, she remains silently ambivalent about it). Shakespeare, losing interest in his cat and mouse games with King James and in romantic passion as well, is now, with very few exceptions, allowing uncompromised love only into dispersed families and their impossible reunions. Though Mamillius is truly dead, in other ways this late period of Shakespeare's work is to be one of counterfeit losses and second chances. In *The Tempest* Ariel sings to Ferdinand about his father's death by drowning, even though Ariel knows that he is still alive:

> Full fathom five thy father lies,
> Of his bones are coral made

– and in the co-authored *Pericles*, Shakespeare resoundingly announces his presence when the hero buries his wife at sea soon after she's given birth, not suspecting that she's alive and will survive:

> A terrible childbed hast thou had, my dear;
> No light, no fire; the unfriendly elements
> Forgot thee utterly; nor have I time
> To give thee hallow'd to thy grave, but straight
> Must cast thee, scarcely coffin'd, in the ooze;
> Where, for a monument upon thy bones,
> And aye-remaining lamps, the belching whale
> And humming water must o'erwhelm thy corpse,
> Lying with simple shells…

When loss is experienced so expressively, perhaps what has gone can be restored, and death itself defeated.

Well, if only. Shakespeare will soon be on his way back to Stratford, to face, among other things, the inevitable. His cue to leave London – in one version of events at least – was nothing if not theatrical. If he'd ever written a scene in which a playhouse was burned down, he would perhaps have done it by having Will Kempe run on with his trousers on fire, trying to put out the flames with a bottle of ale. Exactly so: during a 1613 performance of *Henry VIII* (a play you might think rather difficult to ignite), a spark from one of the cannons being used to accompany the elaborate scene in which Henry puts on a masque at Wolsey's house blew onto the theatre's thatched roof and up it all went. The sad event contained a Shakespearian paradox, because the Globe had always been a fire risk: the anxious shareholders, including Shakespeare himself, had countenanced a false economy at the time of its building, and not given its roof the superior-quality thatch they had enjoyed at The Theatre.

According to an onlooker, Sir Henry Wotton (a diplomat with a pleasantly modern turn of phrase), the conflagration didn't at first trouble the audience:

> where being thought at first but an idle smoke, and their eyes
> more attentive to the show, it kindled inwardly, and ran round
> like a train, consuming within less than an hour the whole

house to the very grounds. This was the fatal period of that virtuous fabric wherein yet nothing did perish but wood and straw, and a few forsaken cloaks...

There was only one near-casualty:

one man had his breeches set on fire, that would perhaps have broiled him, if he had not by the benefit of a provident wit put it out with bottle ale.

Providence was also at work in that the company's costume store and scripts all survived – luckily for us. The rebuilt Globe would open in a year, but without Shakespeare as a shareholder. As if on cue, he had sold up and retired to Stratford.

Or had he? You can, as so often in this private life of his, choose your fiction: at the very moment we seem to find him, alternatives arise. Had he already gone? Was he commuting, more or less, and did he personally see the Globe go up in flames? How much time Shakespeare spent in Stratford is forever unclear, though he turns up in the official records there more often from 1609 onwards. During these last few years his family were going over like ninepins: following Edmund and his mother, his brother Gilbert the glover died in 1612 and brother Richard (of whom nothing at all is known and who therefore achieves a sort of Shakespearian ideal) the year after that. However, his sister Joan outlived him by thirty years – the Shakespeare family are a mixture of predictable fragility and, especially among the women, surprising longevity. His daughters made up for Hamnet's premature loss as best they could: Susannah died at sixty-six (in 1649, the year of Charles I's execution); and Judith at seventy-seven, in 1662, having just seen the Restoration in.

The deaths would have been good enough reasons for Shakespeare to be occupied in Stratford. His mother's estate needed settling, and then those of Gilbert and Richard. In 1610 he bought another twenty acres of land. He features in local disputes, discussions about highway repair, and somewhat notoriously in the tangled tale of the Welcombe enclosures, when, after a disastrous fire, landowners such as he sought to enclose arable land, depriving the larger community of its traditional right to cultivate and forcing up the price of grain. In the ensuing row he assiduously sat on the fence, so to speak, and even managed to exact some compensation for giving up his 'right' to enclose his own territory. So the hand that wrote that 'distribution should undo excess' knew how to sign up in its own interests; the half of his brain that sent the citizens in *Coriolanus* after their rations continued to confront the other, which viewed powerless people as fickle and undeserving. Shakespeare is not the only great writer with a cupboard clattering with small skeletons, but he achieves exceptional subtlety in his handling of them: in one speech in *Coriolanus* the First Citizen denounces noblemen who hoard grain that should be feeding hungry mouths – the very thing that Shakespeare had always done, evading the authorities, in Stratford.

As so often, he conspires in the confusion about his whereabouts, as if warning us off – or perhaps exercising the lifelong tendency to duck and weave of the recusant Catholic. He even buys a gatehouse in Blackfriars in 1613, close to the theatre there and across the river from the Globe – an odd thing to do if he was settling back into Stratford life. This was his first investment in London property after a lifetime of lodgings in Shoreditch, Bishopsgate and Southwark. Teasingly enough, the gatehouse – full of back doors, secret passages and escape routes – had previously been used as a bolthole for Catholic priests (men like the despised Garnet referred to in *Macbeth*), and in fact Shakespeare would soon lease some of its rooms to one of the priests' sons.

✦

Now does my project gather to a head,
My charms crack not, my spirits obey, and time
Goes upright with his carriage. How's the day?

– The Tempest

Before the Globe fire Shakespeare had already produced what is generally thought to be his last solo-authored work, *The Tempest* – but surely not for that theatre: with its special effects, it has Blackfriars written all over it. The new facilities would have served the play wonderfully. It opens with a shipwreck more realistic than that of *Twelfth Night*; Ariel, dressed as a harpy, conjures up a banquet from thin air; spirits morph into dogs. There are identifiable pauses for music and candle-trimming: the stage direction that has Ariel and Prospero re-enter to start Act Five immediately after they have closed Act Four is unique in Shakespeare and strongly suggests an interlude in between. There is even, in the new fashion, a masque of goddesses, to our taste something of an embarrassment.

The Tempest can be safely assigned to 1610–11, because for once Shakespeare imports recent news into the play without coding his references. The Virginia Company was attempting to create a colony in the

Americas, complete with four hundred colonists, to be named Jamestown after the King. The ship transporting them had been lost on the 'Isle of Devils' in the Bermudas; but survivors miraculously turned up a year later with their repaired ship and stories of contented occupation – seas replete with fish, skies full of birds and forestfuls of boars. Indeed a handful preferred to stay on in the Bermudas rather than continuing to Virginia, living the Utopian life verbalised by Gonzalo in the play.

So Shakespeare had been reading the papers all right. In fact, where once you could sense him in the library in an inkstained hurry, you now get quite a strong feeling of a man heavier, more corpulent, more respectable, but his eyes bright and alert as ever, shooting the breeze with various court contacts and casting around for a new story with, if anything, a livelier interest now he is not under such pressure to keep producing material for his company. One can imagine him in the Garrick Club at lunchtime today. *The Tempest* is the last of only three plays (after the *Dream* and *Love's Labour's Lost*) without a direct literary source, but, unlike them, with a very evident topical one which he hasn't troubled to disguise.

The play has proved extraordinarily suggestive in ways that may or may not have been in the author's mind. It is about imperialism; such is its sense of confinement that it works superbly when performed by long-term prisoners; it is Shakespeare's farewell to the stage. But whatever else he may have intended, he describes Prospero's island, which many have been eager to take as a symbol, in precise and various natural detail. Prospero's slaves, Caliban and Ariel, so often mused upon as externalisations of his own personality, are, for sure, autonomous, forthright beings – Caliban murderously hauling around his 'burden of wood' in thunder and lightning, Ariel querulous with administrative overwork. Everything fanciful is carefully grounded in the mundane. There is a real sense of hurry and shortness of time: Peter Brook once suggested that Prospero should be acted as if he knew he had a brain tumour and twenty-four hours in which to set his affairs in order. The unities of time and place are observed as closely as they were in *The Comedy of Errors*, a Shakespearian lifetime ago, and these are the two shortest plays in the canon as a result. To make a literal narrative so full of metaphysical implication, its actual tempest reflecting a mental one, demonstrates that Shakespeare is on full song.

What Pericles called 'the rapture of the sea', ever present in the late plays, crashes into this one at its start; with the daring of experience, Shakespeare immediately allows a petty quarrel to break out between the sailors trying to save the ship sinking near Prospero's island and the aristocrats they are preserving, who don't like their language. An uncanny silence follows the storm, with Prospero and his daughter Miranda watching from the shore – you can see the unnatural brightness, the freshened sky, feel the tang in the air and hear the distant subsiding waves. Shakespeare then takes the exceptional risk of having Prospero deliver nearly two hundred lines of explanatory backstory; but he also has the cunning to make Miranda's attention wander a little from time to time, as an ironic comment on his stagecraft as well as on her father's garrulousness.

It seems that as Duke of Milan, Prospero withdrew from office and, intent on self-improvement, lived in a world of books – 'dukedom large enough' for him. He became so rapt in 'secret arts' that he was content to let his brother Antonio – a man he immodestly describes as

> The ivy which had hid my princely trunk
> And suck'd the verdure out on't

– run the state; he was then outraged to find that Antonio wanted recognition for his work. Antonio made a political alliance with the King of Naples – whom Prospero describes as 'an enemy to me inveterate' without explaining why – which gave him the confidence formally to unseat Prospero. Not to kill him, since the people appear to have loved this harmless scholar, but to put him out to sea in 'a rotten carcass of a boat' in the hope that he would drown. Thus has a poor academic been betrayed by wicked politicians, a father cruelly cast to sea with his baby in his arms (no mother, as usual). Rumour doesn't report whether the change of government was an improvement for the Milanese.

Prospero's and Miranda's survival is due to the kindly offices of the one courtier well inclined, the philosophical gasbag Gonzalo, who has smuggled 'stuffs and necessaries' to them; and here they are, installed on the island, where Prospero has perfected his occult arts and singlehandedly created the storm. This will bring his enemies – the shipwrecked Antonio, the King of Naples, his nobles and their servants – into his circle of magical influence, where he has a somewhat obscure design upon them, compounded of mysticism and political advantage:

> I find my zenith doth depend upon
> A most auspicious star, whose influence,
> If now I court not but omit, my fortunes
> Will ever after droop.

The play duly follows the process of exhausting them into submission by magic spells and general debilitation. Ferdinand, the King of Naples's harmless son, is thoroughly punished for falling in love with Miranda by being made to haul logs, thereby mirroring the hard labour imposed on Caliban; Antonio and the King's brother Sebastian develop a plan to murder the King and take power but are foiled; the King's butler Stephano and his jester Trinculo cruelly bribe Caliban – the island's natural owner and the only one in rhythm with its nature – into a plot to murder Prospero, but fail through general ineptitude. Prospero behaves throughout like a vengeful autocrat, often watching from above in what a contemporary property list describes as 'a robe for to go invisible'.

Rather than his own convictions, it is eventually the 'airy spirit' Ariel – who like Caliban has been coerced into serving him – who stops Prospero in his tracks, suggesting that his heart would be moved to pity if he saw the current disarray of the King and his followers:

> PROSPERO: Dost thou think so, spirit?
>
> ARIEL: Mine would, sir, were I human.
>
> PROSPERO: And mine shall.

So, a master taught by his servant, Prospero suddenly decides to forgive:

> Hast thou which art but air, a touch, a feeling
> Of their afflictions, and shall not myself,
> One of their kind, that relish all as sharply
> Passion as they, be kindlier mov'd than thou art?
> Though with their high wrongs I am struck to the quick,
> Yet with my nobler reason 'gainst my fury
> Do I take part. The rarer action is
> In virtue than in vengeance. They being penitent,
> The sole drift of my purpose doth extend
> Not a frown further.

It is the first time in the play he has listened to anything other than his own internal grievance: suddenly he is transformed into an angel of forbearance. Overwhelmed with compassion, he becomes the kind of prophet who comes down from the mountain with a message everyone is already familiar with: obviously it's always better to 'let go', as we would call it now, than to drive yourself mad with *Schadenfreude*. However, his new idea depends for its impact on a contrition from his enemies which is not altogether forthcoming. Pardoned, Antonio retreats into silence, acknowledging Prospero's gesture not at all, perhaps even despising it as he accepts good luck as his due. And so the play returns to the status quo from which it grew in the first place, though we only joined the story, so to speak, in the second: Prospero regains his temporal power, Antonio continues to hate him. Not much has changed.

So as an exemplary tale *The Tempest* lacks force – its virtues really lie elsewhere. The language is effortlessly beautiful, insouciantly delivered, and everything to do with the father and daughter is precisely realised, as are Ariel's lovely songs and curiosity about the mortals (more gentle than was Puck's), and much of Caliban, who, though he would cheerfully rape Miranda, can also spot a jay's nest and knows how to ensnare the nimble marmoset. There is even a little comedy of manners as the aristocratic Ferdinand, newly shipwrecked and encountering Miranda, tries to woo her as if she were a sophisticated court lady, rather than a creature of nature who's never seen a man other than her father before:

> Most sure the goddess
> On whom these airs attend! Vouchsafe my prayer
> May know if you remain upon this island...

On the other hand the lords, both good and bad, are drearily underwritten, and the comedy duo of Trinculo and Stephano, after a promising start, is highly resistible – drunken bullies and knaves. Perhaps as a result the play has a slightly broken-backed effect, and its reputation is strangely neutral: it has always held the stage, yet few people profess profound affection for it. The most distinguished productions have veered away from its ceremonial, masque-like elements into a realistic, hard-driving account of revenge and its relinquishment. And as you may have been noticing, I have a little difficulty with Prospero himself. I have twice been asked to play the part and shied away from it each time, largely out of puzzlement at the play. On both occasions the director suggested that *The Tempest* is a mystery that we would somehow solve together; this is normally a welcome offer to the leading actor, but both times I immediately lost my enthusiasm: with this play I would rather have a director with a firm concept calling the shots.

I am really not sure what we are supposed to feel about Prospero. Is there any moral difference between him and the unseen 'foul witch' Sycorax, who, banished from Algiers with her unborn Caliban, took over the island till Prospero too usurped it? What right does he have to feel wronged and did he perhaps deserve to lose his job in Milan? His folly may not have been as extreme as Lear's in dividing his kingdom, but he has certainly abrogated his privileged office, and Antonio's revenge is less malign than that of Goneril and Regan. Prospero's spiritual journey to all-forgiving mercy (and the resumption of temporal power) has a distinct smack of self-righteousness. On the other hand, for an audience to conclude that he has learned nothing and remains an inefficient leader about to fumble the reins again seems un-Shakespearian (at this end of his career in particular): it leaves us as flat as a production of *Measure for Measure* that sees the Duke as no more than a ruthless manipulator. Compared to Lear's appalled realisation that he has 'ta'en too little care of this' or that the furred gowns of politicians hide all manner of vices, Prospero's journey seems negligible; similarly, where Leontes bitterly repents, Antonio doesn't even begin to.

Still, the play has enough of allegory about it to suggest – at least in the reading – that we should be drawing some conclusions. Perhaps forgiveness is better for you from a purely practical perspective than undying hatred: in Hamlet's words, nothing is either good or bad but thinking makes it so. *The Tempest* is about ways of dealing with the past, and not necessarily from a Christian point of view; historic grudges are not so much come to terms with as put aside. We all feel better about ourselves when the spirit of forgiveness washes over us, even if what it is appeasing remains dormant and unresolved. Prospero's mercy, compromised and secular, is an old man's urge – Shakespeare's too perhaps – for an easier life, a bargain for peace with himself, a way of surviving.

Theatrically, of course, the character is interesting just because of these ambiguities. Sun and shadow play on him by turns. He is a tiresome, self-pitying despot but he does have the range to see that

> we are such stuff
> As dreams are made on, and our little life
> Is rounded with a sleep

– and then, astonishingly, to visualise the invisible, as if he were Oberon, or Mercutio imagining Queen Mab:

> Ye elves of hills, brooks, standing lakes and groves,
> And ye, that on the sands with printless foot
> Do chase the ebbing Neptune and do fly him
> When he comes back; ye demi-puppets that
> By moonshine do the green sour ringlets make
> Whereof the ewe not bites; and you whose pastime
> Is to make midnight mushrooms, that rejoice
> To hear the solemn curfew; by whose aid –
> Weak masters though ye be – I have bedimmed
> The noontide sun, called forth the mutinous winds,
> And 'twixt the green sea and the azured vault
> Set roaring war...

Maybe it's not such a bad part. And fairly clearly there's something in this more than Prospero. Naturally, the speech is often taken as a last message from Shakespeare, he whose words have moved mountains but who has also made the infinite intimate. He has always weaved theatre imagery into the plays – it is the closest he gets to autobiography; he is now so confident that he does it through a disappointed, vindictive recluse. If he is addressing us personally, his alias is very self-mocking.

It is not only Prospero who releases the play from its self-imposed limits. The experience of living through inexplicable events itself draws the characters into a hesitant new community – not so much a late-play harmony as a guarded truce. And human complexity is a Pavlovian instinct in Shakespeare now, even when he is dealing in allegory with the other hand. Caliban can be violent and hateful, but it was Prospero who made him so by tricking and enslaving him; and the most vibrant poetry from the natural world, attuned to climate, topography and the seasons, is left to this slave, who alternates his talk of battering Prospero's skull with an admission that he is so bewitched in his sleep by the island's sounds and sweet airs that on waking he cries to dream again. And perhaps in the end the moral compass rests with the chess-players Ferdinand and Miranda, young people like Romeo and Juliet who teach their elders a new language or one they have forgotten; one which, like Henry V and Katherine, they have had to learn from each other without anybody's help.

✦

> I come no more to make you laugh…
> Be sad, as we would make ye.

– Henry VIII

As it turns out, Prospero's magic staff is only half broken. From the last few years of Shakespeare's life comes not the silence of a country retirement but some intriguing collaborations with the up-and-coming John Fletcher on *Cardenio* and *The Two Noble Kinsmen*, as if he were gracefully ushering in the King's Men's new house dramatist. Fletcher was used to collaborating – he had already brought the company a hit with *Philaster*, a tragi-comedy written with Francis Beaumont; but he also may already have written (alone) *The Woman's Prize or The Tamer Tamed*, a sequel to *The Taming of the Shrew* in which Kate masters

Petruchio. He and Shakespeare probably first worked together on the play that destroyed the Globe, *Henry VIII*, the Prologue to which dolorously warns us:

> Things now
> That bear a weighty and a serious brow,
> Sad, high and working, full of state and woe,
> Such noble scenes as draw the eye to flow,
> We now present.

The spectacle is to be so instructive that the Prologue predicts that if any of it were to raise a smile, why then

> A man may weep upon his wedding day.

It is difficult to consider the ensuing play as being as tragic as all that – in fact it ends on a somewhat forced fanfare to the future – but still this is to be a far cry from the variegated light cast on the nation in Shakespeare's earlier Histories. There's no more effortless mixing of comedy and tragedy, no Falstaff, no Michael Williams, no Jack Cade, no troubled jailers, worried uncles or perceptive citizens, only a few Shakespearian spasms: a limp conversation between three Gentlemen about French fashions, a rough and tumble description of London's citizens overwhelming the police at the baby Elizabeth's christening:

> Bless me, what a fry of fornication is at door... this one christening will beget a thousand

– and a rather saucy exchange between the innocent Anne Boleyn and an Old Lady in which the racier critics have spotted a unique Shakespearian reference to *fellatio*. Such are the set pieces Shakespeare was perhaps called in to provide; another being his well-known Queen in the Dock Speech – here that of Queen Katherine, similar to but more pugnacious than that of Hermione in *The Winter's Tale*.

But how one wishes, tackling this clotted account of Henry's divorce of Katherine of Aragon in favour of Anne Boleyn and the decline and fall of Cardinal Wolsey, that the vitality and vernacular of the *Henry IV*s or even the *Henry VI*s had been directed into this more recent stretch of history – recent enough, it must be said, for warning posts to be staked out around it for the unwary dramatist. The issue of Henry VIII's relations with Rome and with his wives was still sensitive; and in any case, for good political reasons, Shakespeare had never seemed entirely at ease referring unambiguously to contemporary events. Our problem when he does so, as here, is that often we half-get the point only to find it slipping away because of references to unfamiliar people we never meet, but who would have been well remembered at the time.

This is especially a pity since the themes are so promising: the figure of Wolsey, the overweening spin doctor who begins to take over the kingdom; the rights and wrongs of high taxation (17 per cent on the cloth trade); the sense that in divorcing Katherine Henry is simultaneously swayed by superstitious fear (all their sons have died), tormented by married love for her *and* infatuated with Boleyn. It is all matter for a passionate political drama: ten years earlier and left to himself Shakespeare would certainly have made something of it. The play does develop force towards the end, and a kind of transcendentalism as it approaches the death of the rejected Queen Katherine, who has a vision of figures in white with garlands, and the birth of the future Queen Elizabeth. At this point the writing becomes beautiful without exactly being moving, glistening and precious but without the deep urge for reconciliation to be found in other late Shakespeares. Like *King John*, *Henry VIII* has a sentimental smack that made it extremely popular in the nineteenth century: passages from Beerbohm Tree's productions of both plays were filmed, though only *John* survives. The technological opportunities offered by *Henry VIII* would also have appealed to the Victorian public (Charles Kean's production featured spotlights for the first time), and Henry Irving's Lyceum audiences would specially have liked the many processions and ceremonies described in fatiguing detail in the text. This is like a storyboard for a movie rather than the rich hint of theatrical improvisation that animates *Henry V* (among the first Globe plays as *Henry VIII* is the last), in which

> A crooked figure may
> Attest in little place a million.

As for the offending cannon that burned down the theatre in 1613, it is not clear whether it was situated backstage for a sound effect (perhaps perilously close to the eaves) or was physically brought on; if, as seems likely, it was the latter, this was a thing Shakespeare, who used to conjure whole battles with words alone, would hardly have done at one time, so he was well hoist with his own petard.

The play is certainly quite dependent on its visual display. Its emotions – even those of Wolsey and Katherine – are elegantly protested rather than convincingly felt. There is one unexpectedly touching role, that of Griffith, a gentleman usher who persuades the dying Katherine to moderate her vindictiveness towards Wolsey, but he is fairminded rather than stirring. His is the play's one positive judgment on the hated Cardinal; it is highly revisionist and a bit hopeful:

> His overthrow heap'd happiness upon him;
> For then and not till then he felt himself
> And found the blessedness of being little.

Wolsey is redeemed only by this late report; we have seen him in his pomp, trying to inflict high taxes but defeated in his aim by Queen Katherine and negotiating Henry's divorce from her – he succeeds in this but loses his place with the King in the process by leaking the news of the royal affair with Anne Boleyn. He is criticised remorselessly as a 'butcher's cur... this Ipswich fellow... holy fox... king cardinal... scarlet sin... bold bad man... of an unbounded stomach'. At the moment of his fall, Shakespeare allows a much more extended taunting of him by the other courtiers than he would have done in earlier days. Wolsey's repentance is then long drawn-out and hard to believe – though the facile elegiac cadences of his farewell to greatness made a great impression on me when I was thirteen, so much so that I won a verse-speaking prize for performing it and even dressed up, I forget how, as the Cardinal, with an appropriate sad face to be photographed doing so.

In a play in which the Shakespearian energies have become reflective and studied, what comes off best, after Katherine's defence, is the Archbishop of Canterbury's speech over the infant Elizabeth I, in which her glorious future is predicted for those in the audience able to remember it. (Fortunately no one still living could have witnessed the fate of her mother Boleyn, swiftly executed by Henry, and his four further kingly marriages.) To achieve this, Shakespeare charmingly allows his Archbishop a godly prescience as he predicts that the child will live long, die a virgin and be succeeded by a yet more wonderful monarch – James I, who at a court performance would be sitting there watching the play. It may not be quite what the audience (at least its younger section who recalled Elizabeth from her decline) remembered from their own experience, but that's show business. Her birth – her gender such a cause of vexation to her father that the Old Lady at first pretends to him that she is a boy – completes a panegyric circle connecting the monarch under whom Shakespeare grew up with his current royal audience.

This is where the play's real urge – energetic propaganda – becomes evident once and for all. *Henry VIII* is subtitled *All is True*, which has to be a joke. There is one moment of literal authenticity: the actual trial of Katherine took place in Blackfriars Hall in 1529, and is now recapitulated in situ, as the Hall enclosed the new Blackfriars Playhouse. Nobody alive would remember this, though a grandparent might have told them about it; still, it would have had the same general frisson as watching Shakespeare's Richard II deposed in Westminster Hall would have done. Elsewhere his adherence to historical fact is no more evident than it was in the earlier Histories. In those too, internal truths were sometimes skewed by expediency – as in the account of Richard III and Henry Tudor – but now expediency seems the writer's main motive. The play's music is that of reassurance, and its main purpose a morale booster, asserting Protestant values. This is Shakespeare as master-opportunist, the political trimmer who condemned the Jesuits in *Macbeth*; *Henry VIII* is the late gesture of a worldly and highly accommodating genius.

✦

The fact is that air is definitely going out of the balloon. These late collaborations offer the wistful pleasure of seeing a great sportsman beyond his glory days or a star reduced by age to bit parts: the quality is still there but over a shorter distance. *Cardenio* disappeared, though it continues to be peered around for (a reconstruction of it was produced at the RSC in 2011). *The Two Noble Kinsmen*, first performed in 1613 at the Blackfriars as the Globe burned down, is another co-authorship with Fletcher in which Shakespeare's voice is heard at some distance. This business of collaborating, unusual in a copyright-conscious age, is intriguing: how did they do it? Were the partners in the same room? Probably not. Who started an idea running? If Fletcher, how did he broach the matter ('Sweet Will, I prithee…'); or if Shakespeare, whose opinion of his own work we know nothing about but whom we like to think of as a dear and modest fellow, did he quietly offer ('Although it ill beseemeth me…')?

The least credible possibility is that Fletcher would dismantle and rewrite what Shakespeare had already done, so we probably have all that intact. But then, Shakespeare may sometimes have started a theme off, then left its development to his colleague, as Rembrandt could to a pupil: this might explain the text's lumpiness, half shining and half opaque. Except that Fletcher was rather more than a pupil, and certainly an apter collaborator than Wilkins, whose lurid imagination dominated much of *Pericles* in such an extreme contrast to the beautiful parts. Or, if part of Shakespeare's job was to go over Fletcher's work and streamline it, he was remarkably tolerant of the new man's prolixity, because there much of it still is, albeit looking as if Fletcher was on good form that day.

Perhaps Shakespeare was routinely respectful, in an old master's way, to a new celebrity. Or perhaps the final result was of little concern to him.

Much of the eccentric pleasure of reading *Henry VIII* and *The Two Noble Kinsmen* is to compare very good writing with that of genius, as if in the middle of a Salieri piece Mozart were to burst through for a few bars. Scholars, armed with sophisticated variants of spell-searches, cherry-pick on the basis of image clusters to identify the passages they will like best to attribute to Shakespeare. Most theatre practitioners don't really need such aids. If you're used to swallowing Shakespeare whole and, in Old Hamlet's words, letting him course through every gate and alley of the body, you're likely to know that the Gentleman's description in *Henry VIII* of the hysteria in the crowd gathering for Anne's Coronation is his:

> Such joy
> I never saw before. Great-bellied women,
> That had not half a week to go, like rams
> In the old time of war, would shake the press,
> And make 'em reel before 'em. No man living
> Could say 'This is my wife' there, all were woven
> So strangely in one piece.

Rhythmically, this is a little like *Cymbeline*. I would also put money on the line and a half from the King as he exits 'frowning upon Wolsey', his nobles smugly murmuring around him:

> Read o'er this... and then to breakfast with
> What appetite you have.

But I would have doubts about Buckingham's comment on Wolsey:

> No man's pie is freed
> From his ambitious finger

– and about the King's choice of Blackfriars as a venue to discuss his divorce as 'the most convenient place that I can think of'.

✦

> If the tale we have told
> (For 'tis no other) any way content ye
> (For to that honest purpose was it meant ye),
> We have our end; and ye shall have ere long
> I dare say many a better, to prolong

Your old loves to us. We and all our might
Rest at your service. Gentlemen, goodnight.

— Epilogue, *The Two Noble Kinsmen*

If, in *Henry VIII*, Shakespeare was mainly summoned for his specialities – wronged wives, vigorous low-life, a bad man's repentance – then in *The Two Noble Kinsmen* the authorial contrasts are not quite so steep. In one way, the play has some Shakespearian continuity. Theseus's and Hippolyta's nuptials, inherited from Chaucer's *Knight's Tale* (to which the whole play is indebted – Chaucer was tremendously popular at the opening of the new century), have already been wryly investigated in *A Midsummer Night's Dream*. Now, in the new play's first scene, they meet the ancient story line of *Antigone*: the wives of three of the victims of King Creon of Thebes appeal to Theseus to force Creon to allow them to bury their dead husbands. And Hippolyta's part is much developed as a source of independent wisdom from the hints of it in the *Dream*.

For most of the new play Theseus has his hands full with a more time-consuming arbitration than that between Egeus and Hermia. He has to deal with the tragic-silly story of Palamon and Arcite, two nephews of Creon who have become his prisoners and who declare to each other:

PALAMON: Is there record of any two that lov'd
Better than we do, Arcite?

ARCITE: Sure there cannot.

They then glimpse the same girl (Emilia, Hippolyta's sister) from their prison window, are immediately smitten with her, and, on the instant, become furious rivals to the death. However, their duel is enchantingly gallant: released and out in the woods, Palamon brings Arcite wine and a venison dinner to strengthen him for their battle, whereupon they fall to reminiscing about their shared past, drinking toasts to each other and

To the wenches we have known in our days.

After this they considerately arm each other for the fight ('Do I pinch you? Is't not too heavy?') and lend each other pieces of their fighting equipment, oiling the whole mortal process with loving attentions. This is not some bizarre psychological displacement or a way of putting off the crucial moment: they devotedly feel such things must be done with love between two men separated by arbitrary sexual passion. The duel is daft, because neither lover can conceivably be thought to have wronged the other; their jealousy is not explored because it's not really felt, or perhaps is buried too deep beneath noble thoughts. In a somewhat abstract way this conceit further ventilates the same-sex friendship of *The Two Gentlemen of Verona*, and also the relationships in the *Dream* between Titania and the votaress who was mother to her little changeling boy and between Hermia and Helena – without the tension of the first play or the comedy of the second.

I've never been in *The Two Noble Kinsmen* but I assume it must be difficult to play; and its very sketchy stage history suggests uncertainty as to whether this central friendship should be taken as a Shakespearian tragedy *manqué* or a big joke. In writing about it I find my own facetiousness creeping in; in the playing that would be a soft comic option, a postmodernist cheat. The whole business was more likely seriously meant – except perhaps the fine moment when the two men discuss their beloved and Palamon breaks stately convention to say bluntly:

> I saw her first.

Why are Palamon and Arcite so very fond of each other? They're not brothers, they're cousins; and they don't half go on about it, finding in their affection strength enough to survive as prisoners of war – to survive everything, in fact, except sexual rivalry. Perhaps some new style is being felt for, in which the Chaucerian grace of two 'parfit gentle knights' is to combine with whimsicality, somewhat in the manner of Don Quixote. The idea that there is nothing more intelligent to be done about their situation than a big fight certainly tilts the play into the definition of comedy famously made by Henri Bergson – that it generally depends on human beings being reduced to behaving like automata. But it is also difficult not to like two friends who remain remorselessly cheerful while duelling each other to the death. In the end, the play makes an eccentric bid for tragic status – there's a death, and a conclusion both beautiful and sombre, albeit prefaced by much masque-like ritual. For a last play it does not even attempt the rather shaky appeasements of *The Tempest*: it is more uncomfortable, less surefooted in the delivery but in its way more original.

The story of the two friends is not the only tragi-comic mélange in the play. It is thought that Shakespeare rather than Fletcher is responsible for developing a theme minutely hinted at in *The Knight's Tale*: the, to us, more accessible story of the Jailer's Daughter. Hers is a big part that surely deserved a name: but then so did the Duke in *Measure for Measure* and the King in *Hamlet*. Her narrative potential is never quite followed through, but arises from her having placed her father in mortal jeopardy by helping Palamon escape from prison. On the basis of one kiss from Palamon, she has become crazed with love for him:

> Lord, the difference of men!...
>   To marry him is hopeless,
> To be his whore is witless. Out upon't!...
> I love him beyond love and beyond reason...
> I care not. I am desperate... Let him do
> What he will with me, so he use me kindly,
> For use me so he shall, or I'll proclaim him.

In a series of soliloquies she becomes madder and madder along Ophelia's lines, overwhelmed by fantasies:

> O for a prick now like a nightingale
> To lay my breast against. I shall sleep like a top else.

Some of the derangement is beautifully done, even if it somewhat outstays its welcome – Jacobean audiences never tired of seeing Bedlam imitated on the stage. She ends with a tenderly lubricious scene in which she accepts another anonymous figure, a 'Wooer', because he is disguised as Palamon; in an odd inversion of the bed-trick, they indeed go off together, she as anxious as when she first met Palamon to be used kindly:

> JAILER'S DAUGHTER: But you shall not hurt me.
>
> WOOER: I will not, sweet.
>
> JAILER'S DAUGHTER: If you do, love, I'll cry.

– and thence into their somewhat unusual marriage. You even feel she might be quite happy, since she knew little of the actual reality of Palamon in the first place.

Back in the main plot, meanwhile, lurks a treat still better than the prison scene in *Cymbeline*. Anyone who has longed for a brand new Shakespeare play in which every line is a surprise should give themselves the pleasure of reading Act Five of *The Two Noble Kinsmen*. In preparation for their struggle – a mortal outcome from a pin's head of plot – Arcite prays to Mars:

> Thou, mighty one, that with thy power hast turn'd
> Green Neptune into purple;
> Whose havoc in vast field comets prewarn,
> Unearthed skulls proclaim, whose breath blows down
> The teeming Ceres' foison, who dost pluck
> With hand armipotent from forth blue clouds
> The mason'd turrets, that both mak'st and break'st

> The stony girths of cities; me thy pupil,
> Youngest follower of thy drum, instruct this day
> With military skill, that to thy laud
> I may advance my streamer, and by thee
> Be styl'd the lord o' th' day.

Palamon then addresses Venus:

> Our stars must glister with new fire or be
> Today extinct...
> Hail, sovereign queen of secrets, who hast power
> To call the fiercest tyrant from his rage
> And weep unto a girl, that hast the might,
> Even with an eye-glance, to choke Mars's drum
> And turn th' alarm to whispers, that canst make
> A cripple flourish with his crutch and cure him
> Before Apollo, that mayst force the king
> To be his subjects' vassal, and induce
> Stale gravity to dance. The poll'd bachelor,
> Whose youth like wanton boys through bonfires
> Have skipped thy flame, at seventy thou canst catch
> And make him to the scorn of his hoarse throat
> Abuse young lays of love...

How do we know so surely that these speeches were written by Shakespeare? Or almost all of them: there's a little strangeness in Palamon's fifth and sixth lines, as if he were tolerantly leaving something unimproved. But there are echoes here of Prospero and Pericles and even Perdita: throughout you catch that inimitable timbre, the accumulating force, the glittering light. The same trick of making emotionally connected characters – Petruchio and Kate, Volumnia and Coriolanus – echo each other's rhythm and diction; the repeated conditional clauses of Arcite, Palamon's overhanging 'induce' with its swing into 'stale gravity to dance' (a dactyl surrounded by monosyllables), the operatic union of form and content: this is no weakening hand, no o'erthrown charms.

Emilia, object of Palamon's and Arcite's affections, then places a silver hind on an altar full of spices and sets it alight: it vanishes and a rose tree appears in its place, bearing one rose which then falls – all of it extending the mystery Emilia is seeking an answer to. She follows this masque magic with an account of the differences between the two men which is, suddenly, Shakespeare at his most observant – even if they are presented in ways which, it must be said, we've not really seen for ourselves:

Arcite is gently visag'd, yet his eye
Is like an engine bent, or a sharp weapon
In a soft sheath; mercy and manly courage
Are bedfellows in his visage. Palamon
Has a most menacing aspect; his brow
Is graved, and seems to bury what it frowns on;
Yet sometime 'tis not so, but alters to
The quality of his thoughts. Long time his eye
Will dwell upon his object. Melancholy
Becomes him nobly; so does Arcite's mirth.
But Palamon's sadness is a kind of mirth,
So mingled as if mirth did make him sad
And sadness merry.

Not only is Shakespeare improving on what we've seen, but I can hear *Troilus and Cressida* in the first, physical description, and *Twelfth Night* in the second, interior one. It is as good as anything he has done in this line.

The narrative suspense of the play's denouement – a mix of Jacobean masque, an unflinching view of death and an unexpectedly horrible reversal – gives way to a remarkable final summary from Theseus:

Never Fortune
Did play a subtler game; the conquer'd triumphs,
The victor has the loss... O you heavenly charmers,
What things you make of us! For what we lack
We laugh, for what we have are sorry, still
Are children in some kind. Let us be thankful
For that which is, and with you leave dispute
That is above our question. Let's go off
And bear us like the time.

This, which would have graced any late play, is a hymn not just to the gods above but to the god of dramatic plots; good advice not only to the human race, afflicted by heaven, but to an audience left to puzzle over Shakespeare's lifelong hold on them. Easy as it is to believe that he was taking leave when Prospero broke his staff and drowned his book 'deeper than did ever plummet sound', it is here, in this oddity of a play, like a piano piece for two pairs of hands, that I really see him laying down his pen.

✦

> We must all part
> Into this sea of air.

> *– Timon of Athens*

Imagination plays around the sketchy facts of Shakespeare's approaching end, joining them up and blending them with fantasy. I vote, uncontroversially, that he's back in Stratford, living a quieter life, among his ain folk, people he's probably known all his life – far more celebrated among them as a local dignitary and a courtier of King James than for his plays. And rich – by now he's been earning something like £250 a year, five times the annual wage of a schoolmaster such as his own Thomas Jenkins and twenty times that of the workmen who helped him build the Globe. Whether or not he's been back much since he left Anne and the children here in the 1580s, he's immortalised Warwickshire from a distance, continuing to use old Warwickshire spellings such as 'scilens' for 'silence', and giving Puck's magic flower in *A Midsummer Night's Dream*, which is a pansy, its Warwickshire name, love-in-idleness. In *As You Like It*, he reimagined the real Forest of Arden – a thick swathe of woodland that, when he was growing up, stretched right across the Midlands north of Stratford, but which was now much deforested for building – as a newly mysterious place where you might meet not only a serpent but a good-natured lioness, sit under palm trees, have a drastic change of personality, see 'books in the running brooks' and 'good in everything'. He's even celebrated the wildflowers of Warwickshire:

> rank fumitory and furrow weeds,
> … hardocks, hemlock, nettles, cuckoo-flowers,
> Darnel, and all the idle weeds that grow
> In our sustaining corn.

But presumably he's tired, with his own restless argument. I wonder if he ever, sitting in the pub with Stratford friends talking Stratford business, achieved the stoicism of Shallow and Silence in their Gloucestershire orchard in *Henry IV Part Two*. This is a scene that, in the faltering rhythms of the elderly, its shying away from the unknown into quotidian comforts and in its vivid invisible characters, once and for all proves that Shakespeare was not so much a literary man as someone who sat and earwigged other people's conversations in alehouses:

> SHALLOW: I was once of Clement's Inn, where I think they will
> talk of mad Shallow yet.

> SILENCE: You were called lusty Shallow then, cousin.

SHALLOW: By the mass, I was called anything; and I would have done anything too, and roundly too. There was I, and little John Doit of Staffordshire, and Black George Barnes, and Francis Pickbone, and Will Squele, a Cotswold man: you had not four such swinge-bucklers in all the Inns of Court again… and I may say we knew where the bona-robas were, and had the best of them all at commandment… Jesu! Jesu! The mad days that I have spent! And to see how many of mine old acquaintance are dead!

SILENCE: We shall all follow, cousin.

SHALLOW: Certain, 'tis certain; very sure, very sure; death, as the Psalmist says, is certain to all; all shall die. How a good yoke of bullocks at Stamford Fair?

SILENCE: Truly, cousin, I was not there.

SHALLOW: Death is certain. Is old Double of your town living yet?

SILENCE: Dead, sir.

SHALLOW: Jesu! Jesu! Dead! A' drew a good bow; and dead! A' shot a fine shoot: John of Gaunt loved him well, and betted much money on his head. Dead!… How a score of ewes now?

SILENCE: Thereafter as they be; a score of good ewes may be worth ten pounds.

SHALLOW: And is old Double dead?

And by tradition it's after just one such night of drinking with fellow Warwickshire poet Michael Drayton and Ben Jonson (to one of whose children Shakespeare may have been godfather) that he got lost on his way home, contracted a fever, and slipped away from us, in his self-effacing way.

Or, again, did he? Alcohol doesn't normally cause mortal fever – unless Shakespeare, reliving his memories of *King Lear*, threw off all his lendings on the road to become a naked wretch in the dead of night. The improbable theory was in fact put about by a vicar of Stratford in the 1660s – a man of God so unfamiliar with Shakespeare's works, by the way, that he once made a note in his diary to peruse them in order not to seem ignorant to his parishioners. It was taken up much later by the playwright Edward Bond in *Bingo*, as a matter of dramatic opportunism: Shakespeare becomes ill in the Warwickshire snow (in April?), retires to bed muttering 'Was anything done?' and eventually takes poison supplied by Ben Jonson.

It is not the most startling of the Shakespeare death theories. Syphilis, about which he'd made so many jokes, has also been suggested, combined with writer's cramp – a paralysis of the hand known at the time as 'scrivener's palsy' that can indeed afflict an overworked scribbler. The night-out story has in turn generated the idea that Shakespeare was a heavy drinker, which seems most unlikely, even if the wilder feats of his imagination (*A Midsummer Night's Dream*) might suggest to us, in our imaginative poverty, some pharmacological influence.

What is certain is that 1616 was a bad year for fevers in Stratford. It had been a warm, stormy winter, and next to Shakespeare's house, New Place, ran a murky little stream perfect for the breeding of typhus. In the event, his funeral would follow hotfoot on his death, and he was buried unusually deep in the ground, both things suggesting a fear of infection. He may have reverted to the old faith on his deathbed and received extreme Catholic unction; together with the grace note about the Black-friars priest's hole, it's an attractive idea, but no more reliable than any other.

His quiet departure from life – attended by whom? His doctor son-in-law John Hall presumably, among others – came only a month after, following various false starts, he'd signed off his will in the shakiest of hands. He left money to his sister Joan; his wife famously got the 'second best bed'. That may not have been such a slight – Anne would have received a third of the estate by law anyway, and the second best bed was probably the matrimonial one, the best being kept for visitors. However, there is, to be sure, a certain frostiness in the phrasing. Susannah got almost everything else, significantly more than Judith. Shakespeare allowed nothing into this document – no revealing talk of who should have manuscripts or papers – that identifies him as a writer or casts any light at all on his work: this may have been characteristic or just customary, since small bequests were generally registered elsewhere. The only reference to his London life is a gift of money to Richard Burbage to buy a gold ring, for old times' sake, and also to Heminges and Condell, with whom he may have started assembling the texts they would finally publish in the 1623 First Folio. Much as we would like to find a random comment that *Macbeth* was hell to write or that he never liked Will Kempe, there's nothing anywhere by Shakespeare on Shakespeare – which of course is the void from which the authorship controversy starts.

Altogether it sounds like a humdrum, disagreeable few months coming after a less than soothing retirement, and Shakespeare will have needed all of Shallow's and Silence's stoicism. In 1613 his beloved

Susannah, wife of Dr Hall and a pillar of the community, had had to defend herself (successfully, but these things stick) against a libel that she'd had an affair with a local haberdasher and contracted gonorrhoea. Only three months before Shakespeare's death his other daughter Judith married Thomas Quiney, a young man from a family well known to the Shakespeares, but she did so during Lent without the special licence required to do so, with the result that both of them were excommunicated. Worse, a month before the marriage a girl who had been impregnated elsewhere by Quiney died, together with her baby. Quiney was brought to court and fined for fornication, and the scandal was out there for all to see. Shakespeare, who may have married Anne Hathaway all those years ago under duress, struck Quiney out of his will, and his bequest to Judith is staked out with cautious provisos. When the moment came, he would have been laid out to be viewed, embalmed and 'wound' with herbs and flowers. There was no great fuss about his funeral: strictly family and friends. I imagine a quiet procession, following part of the same route as for his baptism service, down Chapel Lane from his house and then right along the fields by the river to Holy Trinity Church. It was a dignified enough event – he was heading for a distinguished resting place in the chancel, where he would later be joined by Anne and Susannah. But for some reason I get the feeling of an overcast sky above the smallish procession; and in the churchyard, traversed countless times since by visitors and as a short cut to the theatre by actors living on the old, south side of town, a few daffodils coming before the swallow dares. I was once married in this church, you might say over Shakespeare's dead body.

And it was happening in Stratford, not Westminster Abbey in the company of Chaucer and Spenser and later Ben Jonson, attended by all the West End crowd. A genius who minded his own business was returning to the silence he obviously preferred, leaving behind him the clamour of voices he'd given breath to like some great ventriloquist. Above his tomb in Stratford church stands a singularly unrevealing bust, stolid and humourless, which only suggests that you wouldn't have wanted to cross him if you were a tenant farmer on his land. Carved by a Dutch neighbour in Southwark and presumably approved by the family, this is where you see the patrician Shakespeare, bald and self-satisfied, with the hint of a not very fair round belly: unlike the earlier earringed, slightly Semitic figure in the so-called Chandos portrait, or the dreary Droeshout engraving, which makes his head very big, as if a kid was drawing a picture of a brainy man. There's precious little else to find. No image that has come down of Shakespeare is particularly helpful, but it hardly matters: his life was a prolonged act of self-effacement that has nevertheless left the world more vibrant.

Sweet William Shakespeare may of course have been a haughty and prickly man, silent out of pride not modesty. But the sneaking feeling won't quite go away that all this would have made him laugh; that he was blessed with a real indifference, a belief that you owe nothing to the future. Compared to the flamboyance of Ben Jonson and the rock 'n' roll manners of Christopher Marlowe, Shakespeare's seems a wilfully obscure personality. And just as he once warned us not to interpret him through his works because his nature was

> subdued
> To what it works in, like the dyer's hand

he took the time at the end of his life to write his own epitaph. It has a somewhat admonitory tone, as if from the pen of Timon of Athens:

> Good friend, for Jesu's sake forbear
> To dig the dust enclosed here;
> Blessed be the man who spares these stones
> And cursed be he that moves my bones.

That's what he was afraid of: he knew that coffins were sometimes dug up if their tenant was felt to be a waste of space and the bodies thrown into the charnel house. The grave could then be used for someone more important. And even William Shakespeare of Stratford thought this could happen to him.

Conclusion

The State We're In (Part Two)

November 2011

The Royal Shakespeare Company has pulled down its Jam Factory in Stratford and replaced it with a spanking new auditorium which backs onto the ever-popular Swan, and could be mistaken for it. Some of us had briefly railed against the old theatre's destruction, though it was fairly clear that something had to be done about it, if only for safety's sake. The redevelopment of the site has cost £112 million, and includes, as well as better working conditions for all, new foyers and restaurants, a big new merchandising outlet with tube maps whose stations are named after Shakespearian characters, and a somewhat forbidding 118-foot tower, to the top of which, at a cost of £2.50, visitors can travel by lift and get a good view of Stratford-upon-Avon. The tower also houses the theatre's public stairways, which can thus be maintained at the tourists' cost.

It was ever thus: in one way and another, merchandising and art in Stratford have rubbed gently against each other since the aptly named Thomas Sharpe started selling 'genuine' bits of Shakespeare's mulberry tree to visitors in the 1750s. David Garrick, wearing a pair of gloves supposedly owned by the great man, presented his Jubilee for a rain-sodden weekend in 1769, establishing the town's tourist credentials and reciting an Ode of his own devising about Shakespeare: however, not a word by the playwright himself was spoken. In 1773 the eccentric bibliophile and editor George Steevens was recalling (somehow) that Shakespeare loved a certain earthen half-pint mug from which he took draughts of ale on Saturday afternoons. The only surprise about this is that nobody seems to be claiming ownership of it now.

Echoing the Globe and the Blackfriars of long ago, the new theatre has a thrust stage with audience on three sides. The side seats run back to meet the surviving stone proscenium of the old theatre; there are some metres of depth behind this arch, but that area will be difficult to use since it is at a right angle to the view of most people at the sides. The space is impressive, not very flexible, potent and just like the Swan. No, it's bigger, with 1,040 seats where the Swan has 430 and the old theatre had about 1,300: the most distant of them is 15 metres away from the stage, a fraction of what it was before. The philosophy is clear: only thrust stages such as this or the Swan will do for Shakespeare – or indeed anything else the RSC choose to do for the next few generations, from Restoration comedy to Lucy Prebble, that is thought too big for the Other Place up the road. Some see this as right and proper, some as a pity. I don't know how it will feel to play on the new stage – early reports are mixed – but it is certainly impossible for an actor to step out of the wings of the Swan without getting a warm blast of history, a sure and sudden knowledge of what it would have been like to start a performance on a Jacobean stage.

At the unveiling ceremony for the new theatre everyone was thinking their own thoughts; sponsors loudly reassuring themselves (especially about the acoustics, though they hadn't yet been tried); actors and directors sniffing at it like cats entering a new room and wondering, wondering; set designers thinking they might be out of a job; instinctive rebels finding it not funky enough or sufficiently like Peter Brook's Bouffes du Nord in Paris. Or whatever. The best moment was when Antony Sher stood alone on the stage and did Prospero's speech of farewell from *The Tempest*, with simplicity, passion and grace. It might have seemed an odd choice, a farewell speech to open a theatre, but it's a piece that gets done at Shakespeare celebrations. It dissolved all the arguments, proving that in the end all that matters is that an actor unencumbered by anything but the text and able to command attention with eyes and voice will always bring Shakespeare to life. No, 'bring' implies effort: Shakespeare leaps out of such an actor like a salmon. And of course it would have been the same wherever he was, in a football stadium or in your sitting room.

So the new theatre bears assertive witness to the current passion for thrust stages, which certainly bring the audience into closer contact with the players – some of them, some of the time. It will serve very well for plays which open with some Chorus figure striding on and inviting us to use our imagination, but it will be tricky to do a scene – in a gentlemen's club say, or an old folks' home – in which people are randomly sitting around and don't feel much like moving. For almost anywhere you stand on such a platform, some spectators cannot see your face; if a proscenium presents traditional visibility problems, then the thrust multiplies them by three. Staging has to be extremely careful, indeed pedantic: where you stand in relation to your colleague is critical, since the two of you must ideally be in line with one of the diagonal downstage exit corridors, and any variation in your position or theirs obstructs some member of the public's view. The rule when you're not on such a diagonal is to keep moving, keep changing the angle, even if the play doesn't need or benefit from it: stillness has to be very selective. There is a science to all this, but since it is determined by the architecture not the play, it is not a very creative one. But then you could say that was ever the case; and certainly the added intimacy justifies a lot.

The argument also runs that you can hear the actors better. Not so: thrust stages take far more vocal energy than is generally imagined. If the actor has his back to the audience, as indeed he always partly has, he has to send his lines over his head, somewhat in the manner of a soccer player doing an overhead kick. This has led some senior members of the profession to fret about whether young performers, minimally trained in the classics and mistaking the audience's proximity for intimacy, will be able to speak strongly and clearly enough. Leaving aside the Oedipal snobbery of this – patronage of one end of the profession by the other is only a way of reminding them that we're still here – it's not so much of a problem. What's to fear? Today's young actors, who, whatever you may have been told, have an aspiration for classical work identical with ours, are an inspiring group – passionately engaged, resourceful, extremely talented and hard-working – in whose hands the future can confidently be left. Those of them who go to Stratford will overcome any difficulties they find because they have no choice: £112 million is unlikely to be spent more than once in a lifetime, so this is, for the moment, emphatically it. Not even the baby born today will see a Shakespeare play in Stratford except on a thrust stage or, once it reopens, the small room of The Other Place.

✦

At the National Theatre in London Rory Kinnear has been having a deserved triumph as Hamlet. Every phrase that comes out of his mouth has been considered; he speaks as if Shakespearian verse is his natural means; his control of the house is complete. There is no actorly flourish, no vibrato. And he's been doing it in a theatre they said such a thing couldn't be done in: the Olivier, our own 1,160-seat indoor Epidaurus without its magic acoustic.

Much of Kinnear's career has been closely associated with the National, in which he has played each auditorium; no doubt he will now go into the Cottesloe again and concentrate the energy necessary for the Olivier into a whisper. This is a really important interchange for a modern stage actor. When an experienced player works in a small space, behind the performance, available but used sparingly, is the banked-up knowledge and power learned in the big ones. You know it's there, withheld till it's needed. Likewise, some of the credit for the current good health of our theatre is due to the fact that many of its actors have by now done a lot of film work: this is very good for a classical performer, concentrating the attention and taking the wind out of any rhetorical habit. If you spend months in front of a camera which ruthlessly picks up every half-truth or unclear emotion, you will certainly return to the theatre stronger in artistic authority – not to mention prestige and credibility with a non-theatre audience.

At the same time Shakespeare has himself become feasible for cinema investment and – even in its current philistine phase – for television. This has much to do with Baz Luhrmann's brilliant *William Shakespeare's Romeo + Juliet* and the Shakespeare films of Kenneth Branagh, Olivier's successor in this field. The RSC's recent *Hamlet* with David Tennant transferred without effort from stage to television and achieved high viewing figures. Its modernism was a relief: the presence of CCTV cameras all over the Court of Elsinore neatly obviated the necessity for Claudius and Polonius to be forever hunching behind curtains to eavesdrop, and, obeying a hoary old tradition, inadvertently wiggling the curtain at a certain moment so that Hamlet might see he is being observed as he talks to Ophelia. Trevor Nunn's filmed *Macbeth* from 1978 has been followed by Rupert Goold's of 2010 – also a brilliant treatment, but significantly different, in that whereas the first removed literal context and drew you deep into the characters' minds, the latter set the play in a field hospital and resolved its second half into an impermeable image of totalitarian rule – Stalin, Pol Pot, Mugabe. There will be a big audience for such a version, intrigued and attracted to the play as never before. There will also be those who believe that the treatment closes it down, neutralising Shakespeare's diabolical trick of giving the devil more than his due – in this case making you feel sympathy for the Macbeths even in their brutal decline. For one audience the sight of Lady

Macbeth dead on a hospital trolley and Macbeth throwing the sheet back over her face in 'Tomorrow and tomorrow and tomorrow' connects them potently with the Shakespeare who creates contemporary images: another will always remember Ian McKellen saying to Judi Dench after the banquet 'We are yet but young in deed' and the peculiarly sympathetic jolt it gave to the heart.

✦

So obviously, if Shakespeare believed, like Juliet's Nurse, that 'death's the end of all', he couldn't have been more wrong. Like stubborn roots, the plays have survived, despite the sense of conspiracy between the man, apparently in permanent flight from being known, and fate, many times almost granting him his wish. Mortality was first defied when the 1613 fire at the Globe failed to spread to where all the playscripts were kept, thus depriving Shakespeare of lasting anonymity. Then the far-sighted Heminges and Condell denied him it again: incensed by the 'injurious imposters' who had published bootleg versions of the plays, they presented them all, in the Folio of 1623, 'cured and perfect in their limbs'. Around half the canon would not have survived if they hadn't, including *Macbeth*, *Twelfth Night* and *The Tempest*, since they hadn't been published separately. We may marvel at the pitifully abbreviated forms in which the plays then leaked out for the best part of a century – *The Gravemakers* (*Hamlet* Act Five Scene One only), *The Bouncing Knight* (a bit of *Henry IV Part One*) and *The Merry Conceited Humours of Bottom the Weaver* – but they kept the engine ticking over. The fact that David Garrick too was a wicked editor of the texts – Romeo and Juliet get a touching brief reunion and Laertes and Horatio survive to run Denmark – is less important than the gesture of respect symbolised by his Jubilee. William Macready and Samuel Phelps as actor-managers restored the primacy of the full texts in the Victorian period, though they were themselves upstaged as actors by the clearly extraordinary Edmund Kean, who made you feel, according to Coleridge, that you were reading Shakespeare by flashes of lightning.

All these actors worked in big, demonstrative proscenium theatres. If it wasn't for the radical William Poel in England in the late 1890s and Ben Iden Payne in the US doing fluent, text-faithful versions of the plays on replicas of the Globe stage (an idea more showily developed by Harley Granville Barker in his Savoy season just before the first War), we might have gone on assuming that the bombast and pictorialism we associate with Henry Irving's Lyceum or Beerbohm Tree's Her Majesty's was

Shakespeare's natural manner. Then there was Lilian Baylis's Old Vic, John Gielgud, Olivier's wartime seasons at the New Theatre, the founding of the RSC, and all that followed. 2012 will see London's strangely named Cultural Olympiad (it sounds like a trial of physical strength) featuring live Shakespeare all over the place: he is the man we still turn to when celebrating ourselves. Already you can see him in every shape and size: making money in the West End of London in the hands of commercial stars who started their careers in the classics; in arenas and rooms, conceptualised to within an inch of his life; or simplicity itself in the open air in Regent's Park or in recreations of the Globe in Tokyo, the gardens of the Villa Borghese in Rome, or on its original site in Southwark. The latter theatre promises all thirty-seven plays in thirty-seven different languages for next year, and the RSC a World Shakespeare Festival along similar lines.

So whether he likes it or not, we continue to do Shakespeare proud. We drag him into our world – or in my case cart him around in a suitcase – wondering what he would think of the global recession, the Arab Spring, the London riots, of Fukushima, of the internet: he'd have had plenty to say about them, but it would all be concealed in a play set in Illyria. Shakespeare books keep bucketing out each year, their focus increasingly biographical and human, as if well-researched minutiae – a signature on a document here, a brush with the law there – were a better way of getting close than the texts and his contemporaries' adulation. Gratifyingly, practice rather than literary criticism is regarded as the norm, pretty much. I doubt if it would have been possible, when I began working, for me to write books about Shakespeare and expect them to be read by scholars; but now the academics have come over, and the old intellectual suspicion of spit and sawdust has almost completely evaporated. In academe, an actor is more likely to be quizzed about a certain gesture done in a production twenty years ago than lectured about feminine endings or the ur-Hamlet. One professor admitted to me that he devoutly touched an RSC poster hanging framed on the wall on his way into work each morning. I was particularly glad to hear which one it was that he chose.

✦

Such are the consolations and the cues for hope as we, and more essential services, struggle financially with the kind of violent pruning you wouldn't do to the sturdiest rose tree. At the time of writing, arts organisations in the UK are attempting to recover from a savage round of cuts forced on the Arts Council by a government who sometimes give the impression of moving though an alphabetical list of national enterprises to hack them down in turn – C for Culture, E for Education, H for Health, P for Pensions. The language applied is in my memory uniquely cynical: the word 'progressive' is often used in a sense exactly opposite to its meaning, and the catchphrase 'We're all in it together' is likewise diametrically opposed to the obvious truth. The worst thing we can do in the arts is to bleat or even remotely to suggest that we are a special case or comparable in importance to the Health Service or Education: it takes very little to turn the British public against 'whingeing luvvies'. There are many ways of falling on your sword, and one is for high-profile practitioners to denounce the government as fools and philistines. They may be knaves but they are not fools and perhaps not philistines: they are conducting an ideological battle with a high degree of cunning and mendacity. They know the argument about the arts as an investment but it doesn't mean enough to them; they also have a sneaking regard for arts campaigning at its best since we tend to use language well, to see an argument in the round, and we are plausible – so we're in with half a chance. By far the most intelligent responses so far have been those that ask (tongue moving to cheek) for confirmation that the money we sacrifice now will be restored to us when the government has successfully balanced its books.

By the time this book is published, this will be old news, but it is safe to assume that many smaller organisations will be going to the wall, while the Royal Opera House, with its unique ability to raise private funding, will be continuing to pay its executive vast salaries partly out of the public purse. When Menenius proposed the allegory of the body in *Coriolanus*, whereby the stomach (the body politic) is kept healthy by its capillary system (the people), he was trying to pull a conservative fast one. However, even he would have blanched at the current Prime Minister's direct attack on the Civil Service, his own most immediate capillary system. Perhaps the idea, with a slight adjustment, could be interpreted more genially: there are all sorts of stomachs and many feeds. Certainly our artistic health will rapidly decline if it ceases to be fed by the many small companies that nourish the talent that will one day run the National Theatre. Good old Shakespeare: a simple metaphor with many uses.

✦

In his beautiful memoir of his family *My Father's Fortune*, Michael Frayn talks about the half-lovable, half-embarrassing locutions of his father. 'Hotchamachacha,' he'd cry, to hint at a mysterious secret, to his family's bafflement. Well, my father used to call Shakespeare Wobbledagger, and did so as a matter of paternal joshing with the same relish as he wilfully mispronounced rock 'n' roll as if there were one apostrophe only, after the letter 'n', and it was thus pronounced rocknerroll rather than rockuhnroll. It drove me crazy. But like Frayn Senior he was only exercising the privilege of translation into his own language, just as the Russians used to render Shakespeare's name by yoking together the Russian words for 'shake' and 'spear'.

Fathers are cunning creatures, and mine was a lawyer to boot. I assumed he was also trying to annoy me when he said that he detested *Twelfth Night* above all plays. Actually it was a love-test: he was making me defend a pro-Shakespeare position I had embraced somewhat hysterically. And even then I understood his feeling about *Twelfth Night* quite well: if you've a mind to, you can find as many chronic irritations in it as in most of the plays. For one thing, the fact that once found, a good joke is sure to be repeated. In Act Three Andrew Aguecheek has a very funny coward's duel with Viola/Cesario. Then he mistakenly pursues Viola's twin Sebastian, challenges him as well, and gets beaten up. The only purpose of this second duel is so that Olivia shall hear the disturbance, enter and come face to face with Sebastian and fall in love with him. Also, it's not funny – Sebastian is highly capable of looking after himself, the mechanism is obvious and the harmless Aguecheek ends up with a broken head.

I have to admit that the fun people have in Shakespeare is usually at someone else's expense. This same Act Four of *Twelfth Night* was enough to provoke my then nine-year-old granddaughter, already incensed by the cruelty of Malvolio's being eavesdropped on as he finds Olivia's supposed letter, to distress at Aguecheek's misfortune; then to outrage that Olivia should so easily switch her affections from Cesario, whom she now sees is Viola, to the twin brother Sebastian. According to her, Olivia was guided only by how the twins looked, not the kind of people they were inside. It was the sort of response that makes one hopeful not only for the theatre but for the future of the world.

And apart from *Twelfth Night*, what about Shakespeare's interminable Act Fours in general, when the accelerating action stops either for plot conveniences or for a series of parleys before the battle? Or the dirty jokes, so often about that great comedy in life, the Sexually Transmitted

Disease? Here, Shakespeare approaches the infantile humour of Mozart, wandering off into innuendo (a word he would have made a good innuendo from) at the slightest provocation. Even when the joke is clean, he will over-explain. The Gravedigger, apparently not knowing who he's speaking to, refers to Hamlet as being

> mad, and sent into England.
>
> HAMLET: Ay, marry, why was he sent into England?
>
> GRAVEDIGGER: Why, because he was mad; he shall recover his
>   wits there; or if he do not, 'tis no great matter there.

A good laugh, with a classic build to the punchline. But then Hamlet has an uncharacteristic fit of obtuseness, so the whole thing has to be explained:

> HAMLET: Why?
>
> GRAVEDIGGER: 'Twill not be seen in him there; there the men
>   are as mad as he

– and there goes the laugh, rolling gently away like tumbleweed, Hamlet reduced to a feed and the audience treated like idiots. Other good sources of comedy are race, national stereotypes and gender. The heroine of *The Merchant of Venice* shudders at the thought of being married to a black man; much of the fun for Katherine in *Henry V* is that she pronounces English words so that they sound dirty. Mercutio's stream of filth directed at the Nurse is meant to be funny but is quite offensive.

And more seriously, what about Hamlet's madness, the central fraud in a great play? All the characters talk about it; he himself promises a performance of it after meeting the Ghost; but, apart from a handful of grotesqueries, he talks nothing but searing good sense at all times. The court is intelligent: do they think Hamlet's snidery about them is a form of insanity? I think not: Claudius, Polonius, Gertrude and the rest speak in the same way as Hamlet, only less well and guided by different priorities. And this is in a play in which Shakespeare got to the truth of real madness with Ophelia, who is moving exactly to the degree that her confusion is punctured by moments of clear, heartbroken vision.

And what about that question that won't quite go away – the Macbeths' children? The lack of them is crucial to the matter of succession in the play: but Lady Macbeth says she has been a mother and would have refused to suckle her baby if she had known the father would go back on his word as Macbeth has done. There's no further information, but whoever is playing Macbeth is surely going to have to react to this in one way or another. Perhaps it's a surprise – a child before she knew him or a painful memory of a dead one of their own – but he can't just do nothing, and a few lines later he admiringly urges her to 'bring forth men-children only'. It all sounds like a Shakespearian slip to me.

The plays' openings are very variable in quality. Why make conventional use of an introductory Chorus in *Romeo and Juliet* to tell you, for some reason, the story's outcome? Or, in *The Taming of the Shrew*, to do a tiresome two-scene Induction in which a drunken tinker is persuaded he is really a Lord and settles down to watch the play – a framing device suggesting the show itself might not be interesting enough? And there are a handful of stinkers: it's almost impossible to get your bearings at the start of *Cymbeline*, where the sixty-five lines of confusing backstory –

> Howsoe'er 'tis strange...
> Yet it is true, sir

– are as labyrinthine as the play's denouements at the other end.

The same with the endings. Every beautiful modulation such as *Love's Labour's Lost* or *A Midsummer Night's Dream* is balanced by a *Merry Wives* or a *Coriolanus*, when you feel Shakespeare hurriedly donning his overcoat:

> AUFIDIUS: Though in this city he
> Hath widow'd and unchilded many a one,
> Yet he shall have a noble memory.
> Assist.

Others close with remorse or threats of punishment quickly pronounced, whereupon everyone is bidden inside for more talk of this and that, since at that time they had to get off a stage lit by daylight without technical help. The unseemly haste sometimes starts ten minutes or so before the end, as if a warning bell were ringing. The wicked Duke Frederick's conversion in *As You Like It* is ridiculous; and so is *Much Ado*'s limp coda in which it's announced that the wicked Don John has been captured in flight and Benedick promises to 'devise... brave punishments' for him – the only result of which is to remind us of a character we'd happily forgotten. Throughout Shakespeare there are bits of plot forever overlooked, contradictory information, blithe authorial incompleteness.

My rallies with my provocateur father certainly left me with a healthy dash of scepticism about sweet William to go with all the other feelings. On the other hand, I tell him (rising to my feet in defence), don't talk to me about *Hamlet*. For one thing, it has one of the greatest opening scenes ever written (though it's not often played very well). Shakespeare has a real gift for this when he tries – the caught breath, the panicky interruptions, the terror of any movement in the surrounding dark. Elsewhere, he will thrust you into the action in mid-dialogue as one character tries to shut another up –

> Cease to persuade, my loving Proteus

– says one gentleman of Verona, intent on travelling, to the other;

> Sir Hugh, persuade me not

– says Shallow, determined to prosecute Falstaff at the start of *The Merry Wives*;

> Tush, never tell me

– says the offended Roderigo, determined to have no more of Iago's blandishments. In each case you are in the action in a moment, in the middle of an argument, finding out about the characters on the hoof.

And then there are all the great moments. His madness may be a bit of a problem, but Shakespeare also sensed that Hamlet would be infinitely moving if, suspecting that the climactic duel is rigged, his main thought would be to shelter his friend Horatio from the possibility rather than to cancel the entertainment:

> If it be now, 'tis not to come; if it be not to come, it will be now;
> if it be not now, yet it will come... Let be.

And what about Beatrice running 'like a lapwing' close to the ground to eavesdrop, or Rosalind's irresistible blend of passion and humour:

> O coz coz coz, my pretty little coz, that thou didst know how
> many fathom deep I am in love! But it cannot be sounded; my
> affection hath an unknown bottom, like the Bay of Portugal...

Or Shakespeare's sense with Ulysses in *Troilus* that a skilled politician can be a master of beautiful metaphor as well. Or his knowledge that Richard II would surely need to call for a mirror during his deposition – not to admire himself but to check his identity now that he is neither king nor commoner, halfway between God and the assassin's knife. How did he see beyond the racial stereotype for Shylock (and, I admit, then shorten his vision again for the standard stage Jew, Tubal, in the same play)? When Charmian kills herself in *Antony and Cleopatra*, moments after Cleopatra, she says just as she dies:

> Ah, soldier!

What does she mean? It's a brilliant mystery. Perhaps she sees the blurred figure of the soldier in attendance, and it suddenly reminds her of Antony, whose death has led to hers and her mistress's? What special knowledge lies behind Edgar's last speech in *Lear*? What about the dramatic effrontery of a Gravedigger joking about a skull with a Prince in disguise and the skull turning out to be the Prince's old friend's and the grave his lover's? Or a man falling forward from his knees to the ground thinking he's plunged headlong onto Dover Beach? Or another wearing yellow stockings and cross-garters instead of butler's livery? And haven't you sometimes felt a line of verse, from almost any character, arching away like a great elegant bridge over your half-achieved ideas and unexpressed feelings: a bridge that, now you see it, you always knew was there, simple and complete?

Then what about the buoyancy and good humour, the sheer neighbourliness of some of the jokes? What kind of inspired flourish, in *Henry IV Part Two*, not only brings the figure of Rumour onto the stage, but has him 'painted with tongues'? How is Shakespeare able to think so symphonically that he can construct hypnotic set pieces the length of a scene, its subject turning and turning in the light, theme growing out of theme? Take Act Two Scene Four of *Twelfth Night*, when Feste's singing creates a confrontation between Orsino and Viola/Cesario that almost blows the play's main secret (disguise), and set it beside Act Two Scene Seven of *As You Like It*, in the course of which Jaques does the Seven Ages of Man, another bitter song is sung and Orlando is shown unexpected kindness by the Banished Duke. In both, you see breathtaking stratifications of character and mood, their waves folding and tumbling over each other. And why, to sum up personally, whenever I've been offered a Shakespeare part that's been on my wishlist, have I walked the floor all night talking to myself, suddenly alive with ideas about an old play strangely eloquent in the twenty-first century? Or why, in playing it, does my head buzz throughout with memories, comparisons, parallels, random emotions and thoughts, none of which I can remember when I'm through? The other day someone suggested a certain line of poetry might be by Shakespeare but I knew it wasn't because I'd have recognised something about it if it was, something to do with its swoop and surge, its simultaneous abandon and intellectual aptness.

Also, you use Wobbledagger every day, for one thing when you criticise someone: quite useful for a barrister. Shakespeare saw that the best kind of invective is onomatopoeic as much as accurate – so Kent in *King Lear* calls Oswald:

A knave, a rascal, an eater of broken meats, a base, proud, shallow, beggarly three-suited, hundred-pound, filthy, worsted stocking knave, a lily-livered, action-taking knave, a whoreson glass-gazing, super-serviceable, finical rogue, one trunk-inherited slave, one that would be a bawd in way of good service, and art nothing but the composition of a knave, beggar, coward, pandar and the son and heir of a mongrel bitch.

This is Shakespeare as Lewis Carroll: he would surely have loved the Jabberwocky. In fact most of his best comedy lies not in the situations, which amount to a small handful (mistaken identity leading the field), but in this rolling thunder of language itself, its fantastic twists and foibles. Together with Chaucer, he invented much of it himself. Why? Because English wasn't good enough for him yet, simply wouldn't go as far as he could. Mining esoteric words was not enough – he made a lot up, to our continuing amazement. If I said to an acting colleague:

O Lord, it's horrid, I've slept not one wink. It's all Greek to me. The naked truth is that I always get short shrift from that lonely well-read critic, knitting his brows with green-eyed jealousy, that stony-hearted villain, that bloody-minded blinking idiot; he sets my teeth on edge. I wish he was as dead as a doornail: I'm a laughing stock. The game is up, vanished into thin air, at one fell swoop. I want fair play, that's the long and the short of it.

– and they answered:

What the dickens? If the truth were known, he laughed himself into stitches. You're more sinned against than sinning; but to give the devil his due he's writing more in sorrow than in anger, and we're all flesh and blood. He's not the devil incarnate; tut tut, don't get in a pickle.

– whereupon I signed off:

By Jove, cold comfort. I suspect foul play. But be that as it may, it's all one to me.

– we'd have been using, apart from the little links, only words and phrases invented by Shakespeare.

He might be surprised by this but I doubt if he'd be impressed. He seems to have been so uninterested in posterity that he didn't hesitate to incorporate the day's news into a scene if he thought he could get a laugh from it. And then, presumably, take it out again. In the trade we view such moments with a mixture of interest and dismay. Though he retreated into classical alibis on big matters, Shakespeare's references to small current events are unabashed. When in *Twelfth Night*, Fabian warns Andrew Aguecheek that unless he takes care he will

> hang like an icicle on a Dutchman's beard

– the reference is to the recently reported hardships of William Barents's expedition to the Arctic: we don't understand it but its exuberance is such that we wouldn't want to cut it. Barely concealed too is the sour comment, boldly put into the mouth of Hamlet, on the boy players ('little eyases') who were occupying the Blackfriars Theatre when Shakespeare's company should have been there; also the Danish Gravedigger in the same play sending his mate to get him a drink at the pub near to the Globe Theatre ('get thee to Yaughan'). It's an odd effect. If, as happened in the last World Cup, a goalkeeper's error cost England victory against the USA, there it would be, in a story set in Ancient Rome perhaps:

> Thou art as fickle, sure
> As are the nerveless hands of England's guard.

Sure enough, in 2410 some future Professor Stanley Wells will feel the penny drop – wasn't there a big football tournament that year...? And not only that, but wasn't the name of the erring goalie, Robert Green, the same as that of the man who attacked the 'upstart crow' Shakespeare when he first arrived in London in 1592?

✦

Brian Friel once wrote a play, *Afterplay*, in which two Chekhov characters, Andrei from *Three Sisters* and Sonia from *Uncle Vanya*, meet twenty years later in a Moscow café. Then again, an eminent Shakespearian of my acquaintance used to play a game on honeymoon with his new bride, also a distinguished expert in the field. They would say, perhaps at any hour of the day or night: What would happen if, say, Mercutio met Cleopatra? What would they talk about? Or if Juliet bumped into Launcelot Gobbo? Or Falstaff had to spend the evening with Titus Andronicus?

The Chekhov characters of course would have a good deal in common: since the author died, the large fact of the Russian Revolution had formed a portal for any number of people, fictional or real, to go jostling through together. The equivalent doorway in Shakespeare is not an historical event but the peculiar nature of the writer himself, the kinship which, for all his fabulous range, he allows his characters to share. If the Helena of *All's Well* met her namesake from the *Dream* the talk would surely be of stalking tactics; Hamlet would declare that 'the readiness' and Edgar that 'ripeness' was 'all'. I once idly sketched out a scene, all in Shakespeare's lines, in which three of his great braggarts – Parolles in *All's Well*, Pistol in *Henry IV* and *Henry V* and Lucio in *Measure for Measure* – met in a bar. There would be an immediate and skilful battle to avoid standing the drinks ('base is the slave that pays'); Pistol would chase a passing strumpet ('I will discharge upon her with two bullets'), then pick a fight with Parolles and fall downstairs while Parolles and Lucio agreed on his epitaph:

> LUCIO: A very superficial, ignorant, unweighing fellow.
>
> PAROLLES: In his sleep he does little harm, save to his bedclothes about him; but they know his conditions and lay him in straw.

Though it has a high element of silliness, there was something instructive in this. None of my three braggarts – Shakespearian virtuosi washed in sourer currents – are in the sources Shakespeare used for their plays; and interestingly, all three operate in stories in which the authority figures are hard to like. In the end they no doubt deserve their various fates, but you feel a little sorry for them. Lucio is made to marry a whore, largely for being impertinent to the disguised Duke. Parolles is captured by his fellow soldiers, infuriated by his boastfulness; pretending to be Russian enemies they extract crucial military secrets from him with no trouble at all, and he ends the play seeing he doesn't add up to much as a man. Pistol too overplays his hand by making fun of a Welshman on St David's Day; Fluellen beats him into eating a raw leek. See how Shakespeare takes leave of two of them:

> PAROLLES: Yet am I thankful; if my heart were great,
> 'Twould burst at this. Captain I'll be no more;
> But I will eat and drink, and sleep as soft
> As captain shall; simply the thing I am
> Shall make me live...
> Rust, sword! Cool, blushes! and Parolles, live
> Safest in shame! Being fool'd, by foolery thrive!
> There's place and means for every man alive.
>
> PISTOL: Doth Fortune play the huswife with me now?
> News have I that my Nell is dead i' the spital
> Of malady of France;

> And there my rendezvous is quite cut off.
> Old I do wax, and from my weary limbs
> Honour is cudgell'd. Well, bawd I'll turn,
> And something lean to cutpurse of quick hand.
> To England will I steal, and there I'll steal;
> And patches will I get unto these scars
> And swear I got them in the Gallia wars.

The same rhythms, the same defiance, the same lack of self-pity: they sound like cousins. But then so in a way do all Shakespeare's people, whether they operate in the pub, the blasted heath or the exotic East. Diverse as he was, all his characters share his gifts and his blood group; either all or none of them speak for him.

✦

The idea of meeting Shakespeare seems something like meeting God, but more humorous. Meanwhile, we remain tantalised, infernally curious about him – as if anything new we learned about its author could leave us any the wiser about *Antony and Cleopatra*. It is certainly quite hard to understand a writer so self-effacing, to whom the autobiographical assumptions we generally make about artists are so inapplicable. We end up poking around in his back yard, like the man who plundered Bob Dylan's garbage in the hope of finding clues to *Highway 61 Revisited*. The occasional, probably apocryphal story of Shakespeare in his daily world is welcome and endearing: his quiet refusal to join a group, but also the trick he supposedly pulled on Richard Burbage by intercepting a billet-doux from a female admirer of Burbage's Richard III one afternoon. He took advantage of it himself, afterwards calling from the lady's window to the late-arriving Burbage that, after all, William the Conqueror preceded Richard III. I like to think he did a good imitation of Burbage's Hunchback to pull this trick, and so wasn't such a bad actor.

Anyway, I do know what he was like. Last year I worked on a performed version of the Sonnets with Peter Brook. Forgiven for playing fast and loose with the plays, you can still be ticked off by biographers for reading too much into these poems, for thinking they are any more than another Shakespearian fiction. But they're written in the first person and nobody else speaks; a rival who turns up at one point is established as another professional writer; the running cast list of three remains unchanged throughout a cycle perhaps written across twenty years – curious. The poet must surely have been some version of Shakespeare:

dark and obsessive, awkwardly intelligent even when he'd prefer not to be, and a bit sorry for himself; begging for ordinary love, feeling denied of it, finding it wasn't what he expected, wanting to be free of it, being momentarily reassured, separated from himself as well as more himself because of it, resigned to its helplessness. And life being short, he will sometimes have gazed in dismay from his bed like Philip Larkin in *Aubade* –

> Waking at four to soundless dark, I stare

– and heard a single blackbird begin the dawn chorus with the same relief as Marcellus feels on hearing the cock crow in *Hamlet*. I fancy Shakespeare then jumps out of bed, straps on his sword, steps out onto Bankside and goes to work. Moving through the crowd, I can hear the timbre of his voice and note his body language: how fast he tends to walk, his turns of phrase and characteristic moues, and I can sense whether his smile is sudden or slow, what sort of thing makes him laugh and in what way.

That's my fiction, telling you more about me than Shakespeare perhaps. What we do know is that everyone was shorter then, with bad teeth, in constant danger of plague, and you might not always recognise the spoken language as English. Shakespeare had grown up in a market town where everyone knew their neighbour's business, where you could be placed in the stocks for being disrespectful about an official, where you couldn't have guests from elsewhere without the Mayor agreeing, where woolly caps had to be worn on a Sunday. Now he is a Londoner, and invisible if he wants to be, in the third largest city in Europe and perhaps the most hectic; where everyone kisses on greeting and on taking leave, as we are now learning to do again. Half of the population are under twenty. If a beggar returns to the city after being expelled he can be executed. The severed heads, tongues and hands that Shakespeare initially put into his plays (until he found he could do it better in words) were no surprise to crowds used to watching public mutilations and executions. It was all like the London of *Shakespeare in Love* but filthier, smelly, degraded and verminous; however, to judge from the Rose Theatre discoveries and still more from the sensational Cheapside Hoard unearthed in 1912, the jewellery and ornaments, watches and scent bottles that emerged from this swamp were, like the poetry of Shakespeare, of an unparalleled delicacy and beauty.

✦

The difficulty of writing a concluding chapter to a book about Shake-speare is that the book refuses to close: you make your report and hope not to change your mind before publication. The subject is so especially volatile that all sorts of new ideas continually arise; in the practice too, you quite regularly change your opinion about how to handle the verse, about modern or traditional dress, and have routine periods of doubt as to whether he really was that good. For instance, I've changed my mind about Hamlet. I used to think that anyone of sufficient expertise could play it, that it adapted to the individual actor as Gielgud said it did; but now I believe it needs a particular kind of performer, one who justifies Ophelia's description of him, one with the rare gift for being simultane-ously one of us and an archetype. Such an actor can readily combine the two kinds of twenty-first-century Hamlet – the sardonic ironist you can appreciate from a distance, cleverer and sharper and more impossibly fluent than ourselves; and the highly approachable one, whose character you can define only by saying that it's not unlike your own and yes, you would do and say much as he does.

It's also in the nature of the theatre that the beliefs you have held for years can be blown away in a couple of hours. Marianne Elliott's brilliant production set in Cuba at last reconciled me completely to *Much Ado*. Earlier in this book I wrote about *The Tempest*, and I stand by what I said, certainly: it is indeed what I think you encounter as you face up to the play. But Declan Donnellan's recent production was done with the Russian actors he has been working with from time to time for some years. It is riotously and dexterously funny (who would have thought you'd look forward to Stephano's and Trinculo's next appearance?); much of its comedy is, as befits the play, very wet; Prospero is a bitter fellow with nothing of the magus about him, though when he finally dons his double-breasted suit to return to Milan (Moscow) he suddenly looks the most impressive mafioso on the stage. There are a number of Ariels, including one who plays each of the logs carried around by Ferdinand. The whole enterprise is suffused with a palpable affection between director and cast; Russian inventiveness (which can be infinite) is given the gentlest Western discipline. And best of all perhaps, when the company finally leave the island, Miranda briefly races back and embraces Caliban, the creature who wanted to rape her; for in the end she has more in common with him than with the suits she is leaving with, who will neutralise her natural impulses as quickly as the Christians absorb the Jewish Jessica in *The Merchant of Venice*. I never once thought about Shakespeare's farewell to the stage, the Bermudas, all the symbolism and masque: the play, a free-standing act of the imagination, reinvented itself in front of me. I haven't changed my chapter: for one thing the Russians, working easily in Boris Pasternak's translation, don't have to worry about how to speak the sometimes archaic verse. But I might write differently about it next time.

In ways like this, Shakespeare just keeps on rolling, as he will long after us. He brings us together, with each other and ourselves. I used to think this about him. Now I think that. Soon I will think otherwise. Then I die. That's the state I'm in. Renault and Levi have used him to advertise new cars and 501 jeans. Billboard images of Juliet are constantly asking wherefore Romeo art, perhaps thinking they're referring to his whereabouts. Guests on *Desert Island Discs* are given the complete works to take with them whether they like it or not. His words have been co-opted by politicians of every complexion – a desperate measure, since he never expresses an opinion of his own. The M40 motorway announces Warwickshire as Shakespeare's County: television and the newspapers quote from him, knowingly or not, most days.

He also remains, despite the financial plight of Eastern Europe, an attractive sponsorship option, so Hungary has a thriving international Shakespeare Festival, as does Craiova in Romania, while the British Council in Bucharest found it worth their while last year to bring me to a remote town in the north of the country to do a week of workshops on *Hamlet*. I don't know if this says something wonderful about the world or something stupid. Next month *Sweet William* goes to Stockholm, and I wonder what surprises that will bring. I shan't need the surtitles in Sweden though, and I think the billboards will be right, unlike the ones at another European venue which announced the show as *Noble Shakespeare* with William Pennington.

I've heard this noble Shakespeare described as not a writer but a landscape, part of most people's lives. Not so: to most people his words must seem as irrelevant as those of some visiting statesman. We say he's universal, but really that's a figure of speech: to a large part of the world he is as unlikely as a square meal. We say he is the great humanist, but he isn't really that either: injustice is rampant in the plays and dozens of characters go to undeserved deaths for theatrical effect without a trace of authorial regret. But in any community with the leisure or determination to clear a space in its midst for storytelling, Shakespeare, an ordinary man and not really an intellectual, reminds us of what matters and what doesn't. We still don't know a single one of his opinions, but we often quote from him without realising we're doing it, to make our own more persuasive. And he makes us all talented – there are moments when we can feel ourselves on the brink, just the brink, of seeing what he saw as he pounded the fields to Charlecote, weaved his way along Bankside or looked up from his desk in Stratford to see the mulberry tree he had planted in his garden at New Place. It seems that wherever you are, Shakespeare is very good for the health, and not just the individual health. To read him to yourself or think about him alone is certainly one of life's enrichments. But ideally, it's only a preparation for an increasingly unlikely civic act. You have to go out if you can, arrive somewhere at a certain time, negotiate a little with your fellow citizens, and become part of the process whereby a hundred, five hundred, a thousand people of completely different sensibilities, experiences of life and senses of humour become that singular organism, an audience, all held on the same breath as Hamlet approaches the praying Claudius with his sword upraised or as young Flute as Thisbe finds his form. On a good night you leave the high music and astonishing simplicities, the insinuation, protest and reconciliation, in an exhilarated state – alive, hugely entertained, ready for more healthy argument, more tolerant, less easily deceived: and maybe ready to go home and, like me all those years ago, pull out a copy of *Macbeth* and try out a couple of speeches. And as for me, you know what I feel by now: this is a man who's got in everywhere in my life. Which is perhaps what Victor Hugo meant when he said:

> He strides over proprieties, he overthrows Aristotle... He does not keep Lent. He overflows like vegetation, like germination, like light, like flame.

Or as the great movie producer Sam Goldwyn once put it, no less eloquently:

> Fantastic! And it was all written with a feather!

Index